# The Verbless Clause in Biblical Hebrew

## Linguistic Approaches

# Linguistic Studies in Ancient West Semitic

*edited by*

M. O'Connor and Cynthia L. Miller

The series Linguistic Studies in Ancient West Semitic is devoted to the ancient West Semitic languages, including Hebrew, Aramaic, Ugaritic, and their near congeners. It includes monographs, collections of essays, and text editions informed by the approaches of linguistic science. The material studied will span from the earliest texts to the rise of Islam.

# The Verbless Clause in Biblical Hebrew

## Linguistic Approaches

*edited by*

CYNTHIA L. MILLER

EISENBRAUNS
Winona Lake, Indiana
1999

Image on front cover: a portion of Deuteronomy 6, including Deut 6:4, from the Leningrad Codex. Acknowledgment:

Digital Image of a Photograph by Bruce and Kenneth Zuckerman, West Semitic Research in collaboration with the Ancient Biblical Manuscript Center. Courtesy Russian National Library (Saltykov-Shchedrin).

Cataloging in Publication Data

The verbless clause in Biblical Hebrew : linguistic approaches / edited by Cynthia L. Miller.
     p.   cm. — (Linguistic studies in ancient West Semitic ; 1)
     Includes bibliographical references and index.
     ISBN 1-57506-036-1 (cloth : alk. paper)
     1. Hebrew language—Clauses.  2. Bible. O.T.—Language, style.
I. Miller, Cynthia L. (Cynthia Lynn), 1957–  .  II. Series.
PJ4711.V47   1999
492.4′5—dc21                                                      98-45884
                                                                          CIP

# Contents

## SEMANTIC AND PRAGMATIC APPROACHES

## INDEXES

# Abbreviations of Terms and Phrases

| | |
|---|---|
| Adj | adjective (cf. detAdj, indetAdj) |
| AdjP | adjective phrase |
| App | apposition |
| attribRC | attributive relative clause (cf. RC) |
| BH | Biblical Hebrew |
| CC | contextualizing constituent |
| CMod | clause modifier |
| CNC | compound nominal clause |
| Conj | conjunction |
| ConjP | conjunction phrase |
| Cop | copula |
| defNP | definite noun phrase (cf. NP, detNP, indetNP, indefNP) |
| demPro | demonstrative pronoun (cf. Pro) |
| detAdj | determinate adjective phrase |
| detNP | determinate noun phrase (cf. NP, defNP, indetNP, indefNP) |
| DetP | determiner phrase |
| detPP | determined prepositional phrase |
| Ex | particle of existence (cf. negEx) |
| f. | feminine |
| GB | government-binding theory |
| gP | grammatical predicate (cf. P) |
| gS | grammatical subject (cf. S) |
| indefNP | indefinite noun phrase (cf. NP, indetNP, defNP, detNP) |
| indetAdj | indeterminate adjective phrase |
| indetNP | indeterminate noun phrase (cf. NP, indefNP, defNP, detNP) |
| indetPP | indetermined prepositional phrase |
| Inf | infinitive |
| interr | interrogative word (cf. Q) |
| interrPro | interrogative pronoun |
| Loc | locative; locative interrogative |
| m. | masculine |
| M | mood |
| MP | mood phrase |
| NC | nominal clause (cf. CNC) |
| negEx | particle of negative existence (cf. Ex) |
| NP | noun phrase (cf. defNP, detNP, indefNP, indetNP) |
| Obj | object |

| | |
|---|---|
| P | predicate; syntactical predicate (Niccacci) (cf. gP); preposition (DeCaen) (cf. PP) |
| PC | predicate clause |
| PComp | predicate complement |
| Pd | *casus pendens* |
| persPro | personal pronoun |
| pl. | plural |
| pleoPro | pleonastic pronoun |
| PN | personal name |
| pos1 | position 1 (i.e., initial position) |
| pos2 | position 2 (i.e., non-initial position) |
| Poss | possessive relation |
| PP | prepositional phrase |
| PPro1 | preposition with suffixed pronoun in first position in clause |
| PPro2 | preposition with suffixed pronoun in second position in clause |
| Pro | pronoun (cf. demPro, interrPro, persPro, pleoPro) |
| Pro1 | pronoun in first position in clause |
| Pro2 | pronoun in second position in clause |
| P–S | predicate–subject order (cf. S–P) |
| Ptc | participle |
| PtcP | participial phrase |
| Q | interrogative (DeCaen) (cf. interr) |
| RC | relative clause (cf. attribRC) |
| S | subject; syntactical subject (Niccacci) (cf. gS) |
| s. | singular |
| sc | supplementary constituent |
| S–P | subject–predicate order (cf. P–S) |
| spec | specification |
| spec-MP | specifier of mood phrase |
| spec-NP | specifier of noun phrase |
| spec-TP | specifier of tense phrase |
| spec-VP | specifier of verb phrase |
| SVO | subject–verb–object |
| suf | suffix |
| T | tense |
| t | trace |
| Ti | time |
| TP | tense phrase |
| V | verb |
| V1 | verb is in initial position |
| V2 | verb is in second position |
| VComp | verbal complement |
| VO | verb–object |
| Voc | vocative |

| | |
|---|---|
| VP | verb phrase |
| VSO | verb–subject–object |
| v(v). | verse(s) |
| X | any clausal constituent; any syntactic head (DeCaen) |
| Y-movement | Yiddish-movement |
| ק | Qere reading |

# Abbreviations of Journals and Series

| | |
|---|---|
| ATSAT | Arbeiten zu Text und Sprache im Alten Testament |
| *CTA* | *Corpus des tablettes en cunéiformes alphabétiques* |
| *ETL* | *Ephemerides Theologicae Lovanienses* |
| *HALAT* | L. Koehler and W. Baumgartner, *Hebräisches und Aramäisches Lexikon zum Alten Testament* |
| *HUCA* | *Hebrew Union College Annual* |
| ICC | International Critical Commentary |
| *Int* | *Interpretation* |
| *IOS* | *Israel Oriental Studies* |
| *JANES* | *Journal of the Ancient Near Eastern Society (of Columbia University)* |
| *JAOS* | *Journal of the American Oriental Society* |
| *JBL* | *Journal of Biblical Literature* |
| *JEOL* | *Jaarbericht . . . Ex Oriente Lux* |
| *JNES* | *Journal of Near Eastern Studies* |
| *JNSL* | *Journal of Northwest Semitic Languages* |
| JSOTSup | Journal for the Study of the Old Testament Supplement Series |
| *JSS* | *Journal of Semitic Studies* |
| *KAI* | H. Donner and W. Röllig, *Kanaanäische und Aramäische Inschriften* |
| SBLSS | Society of Biblical Literature Semeia Studies |
| *UF* | *Ugarit-Forschungen* |
| *VT* | *Vetus Testamentum* |
| WBC | Word Biblical Commentary |
| *ZAH* | *Zeitschrift für Althebraistik* |
| *ZAW* | *Zeitschrift für die Alttestamentliche Wissenschaft* |
| *ZDMG* | *Zeitschrift der Deutschen Morgenländischen Gesellschaft* |

# Preface

Most of the essays included in this volume were originally presented in 1996 at the "Linguistics and Biblical Hebrew Section" of the Society of Biblical Literature annual meeting. Additional essays by Janet Dyk and Eep Talstra, Walter Groß, Takamitsu Muraoka, Alviero Niccacci, and Lénart J. de Regt have been included to provide additional vantage points. Francis I. Andersen and Jacob Hoftijzer, who engaged in a lively discussion on the verbless clause nearly thirty years ago, had also hoped to contribute to the volume, but each found himself unable to do so. The continuing discussion in this volume is, hopefully, both a tribute to and an extension of their earlier scholarship on this important syntactic construction.

Linguistic discussions necessarily involve an appropriate metalinguistic vocabulary. The writers have taken care to explain the terminology they employ; the subject index provides readers with the location of definitions as well as additional discussions of linguistic terms and concepts. In addition, the use of abbreviations and logical symbolism has been minimized. When abbreviations are used, they have, as much as possible, been brought into uniformity across essays in accordance with standard linguistic practice. The only minor disadvantage of uniform abbreviations is that the customary abbreviations employed by a particular author in other publications may not be the same as those found here.

Grateful thanks are due to Jim Eisenbraun and his staff, especially Beverly Butrin Fields, for their care in copyediting and typesetting the volume, to Lynn MacLeod Hand for preparation of the subject index, and to Joseph Cotner for assistance with proofreading the Hebrew. Special thanks also to the Wisconsin Society of Jewish Learning for their financial assistance in the preparation of the volume.

# Basic Issues

✦ ✦ ✦

# Pivotal Issues in Analyzing
# the Verbless Clause

CYNTHIA L. MILLER

*University of Wisconsin–Madison*

## 1. Introduction

The constructions analyzed in this volume may well be considered syntactically marginal. Unlike ordinary clauses in which predication is obtained by means of a finite verb, verbless (or, nominal) clauses represent a predication by means of the collocation of nominal elements apart from a fully inflected verbal form. Verbless predications, then, are liminal constructions occupying a gray area between verbal clauses and nominal phrases. Like verbal clauses, they express a predication (though verbless predications differ from verbal ones in not indicating tense, aspect, or mood); like nominal phrases, they are composed of nominal elements.

Although verbless clauses are syntactically marginal, they should not be considered statistically marginal cross-linguistically; they are commonly represented among the world's languages, even though they are absent in most Indo-European languages.[1] Most importantly for our purposes, verbless clauses are an important syntactic feature of Biblical Hebrew, occurring nearly two thousand times in the Pentateuch alone.[2] Nonetheless, the position of syntactic marginality occupied by verbless predications in Biblical Hebrew

*Author's note*: I am grateful to William Adler and Patrick R. Bennett for their comments and suggestions.

1. Émile Benveniste, *Problems in General Linguistics* (trans. Mary Elizabeth Meek; Miami Linguistic Series 8; Coral Gables, Fla.: University of Miami Press, 1971) 131–32. Verbless predications occur in the Slavic languages and in Greek; traces of verbless predications appear in Latin.

2. Francis I. Andersen, *The Hebrew Verbless Clause in the Pentateuch* (Journal of Biblical Literature Monograph Series 14; New York and Nashville: Abingdon, 1970) 17.

(as in other languages) does pose difficulties for syntactic analysis, difficulties that are sometimes directly related to questions of interpretation.

The most striking example of a verbless predication in the Hebrew Bible, and one that resists any simple resolution, involves the central theological affirmation of the *Shema*ʿ: יְהוָה אֱלֹהֵינוּ יְהוָה אֶחָד. As is well known, there are four nominal elements: a divine personal name occurring twice, a common noun with possessive pronominal suffix, and a numeral. Although indisputably a predication is expressed, it is not clear how the four elements comprise one or more predications. A brief survey of five possible parsings of this verse will highlight the problems.[3]

If understood as two predications, both in the order S (Subject)–P (Predicate), then the verse reads: 'The LORD is our God. The LORD is one'.[4] Although this parsing seems to be supported by the Masoretic accents, it remains problematic for two reasons. First, verbless predications of the order S–P usually express a predication whose central concern is to identify the subject, an interpretation that is theologically problematic within the context.[5] Furthermore, the phrase יְהוָה אֱלֹהֵינוּ in Deuteronomy is elsewhere always used to mean 'the LORD our God'; that is, the second word is appositional to the first.[6]

A second parsing understands the first three words to be a complex subject with the final word אֶחָד as the predicate. Translations of this parsing include 'the LORD our God, the LORD is one'[7] and (with the first two words as a *casus pendens*) 'As for the LORD our God, the LORD is one'.[8] This parsing understands the order of clausal constituents to be S–P; the predicate is a numeral that classifies (that is, it gives information about) the subject. But such a parsing is problematic, because a numeral that functions as a predicate usually precedes rather than follows its subject.[9]

---

3. See also the discussion of possible parsings in B. K. Waltke and M. O'Connor, *Introduction to Biblical Hebrew Syntax* (Winona Lake, Ind.: Eisenbrauns, 1990) 135.

4. Cyrus H. Gordon, "His Name is 'One'," *JNES* 29 (1970) 198–99. Based on the similar wording in Zech 14:9 בַּיּוֹם הַהוּא יִהְיֶה יְהוָה אֶחָד וּשְׁמוֹ אֶחָד 'on that day the LORD will be one and his name 'One'), Gordon argues that אֶחָד is the official name of God at the end of days. Thus, in his view, the clause יְהוָה אֶחָד is a clause of identification, not classification.

5. Andersen, *The Hebrew Verbless Clause in the Pentateuch*, 47.

6. Jeffrey H. Tigay, *Deuteronomy* (JPS Torah Commentary; Philadelphia: Jewish Publication Society, 1996) 439; see also Moshe Weinfeld, *Deuteronomy 1–11* (AB 5; New York: Doubleday, 1991) 337.

7. Wolfgang Schneider, *Grammatik des biblischen Hebräisch: Ein Lehrbuch* (Munich: Claudius, 1974) 192.

8. Hoftijzer suggests that the first two words may be a *casus pendens* but does not provide a translation (J. Hoftijzer, "The Nominal Clause Reconsidered," *VT* 23 [1973] 446–510, esp. 484).

9. Andersen, *The Hebrew Verbless Clause in the Pentateuch*, 47. For the order P–S where the predicate is a numeral, see, for example, Gen 6:15: שְׁלֹשׁ מֵאוֹת אַמָּה אֹרֶךְ הַתֵּבָה

A third parsing understands יהוה אֱלֹהֵינוּ as the subject and יהוה אֶחָד as the predicate with אֶחָד modifying יהוה. The sentence is translated: 'the LORD our God is one LORD'.[10] But a proper name (here the divine name יהוה) is not a count noun, and thus it would be highly anomalous for it to be modified by a numeral.

A fourth parsing, accepted by Rashi and Ibn Ezra as well as many moderns, understands the final word as though it is equal to לְבַדּוֹ, translating 'the LORD is our God, the LORD alone'.[11] In this interpretation there is a single predication identical to the first option above (with order S–P); here, however, the subject is repeated and the final word is understood as an adverbial. But this parsing is unlikely, because it imparts a grammatical function and lexical interpretation to אֶחָד that is otherwise unparalleled in the Bible.[12]

A final parsing understands both the subject and the predicate to be discontinuous. The subject is אֶחָד . . . אֱלֹהֵינוּ 'our one God', and the predicate is יהוה . . . . יהוה 'the LORD . . . the LORD'. The sentence should thus be translated: 'Our one God is the LORD, the LORD'.[13] This parsing has two advantages. It preserves P-S order in a classifying clause by understanding יהוה as predicate and אֱלֹהֵינוּ as subject. It also understands the numeral as modifying the common noun אֱלֹהִים rather than the proper noun יהוה. However, discontinuity of both subject and predicate seems to be unparalleled both in the biblical text and from a cross-linguistic point of view. As a result, this interpretation has not met with wide acceptance.

As we have seen, the difficulties in interpreting the affirmation of the *Shemaʿ* hinge partly upon difficulties in determining a correct syntactic parsing of predications that are nonverbal and thus syntactically marginal. More importantly, the unusual features of the verbless predication(s) of the *Shemaʿ* are highlighted by placing them within the broader context of the syntax of

---

'three hundred cubits is the height of the ark' (cited in Andersen, p. 63, #117). Weinfeld notes that the Nash Papyrus reads [א]יהוה אחד הו *(Deuteronomy 1–11,* 332). In that reading, יהוה is a *casus pendens* and the predicate is אחד; the clause then has the order P–S that is expected when the predicate is a numeral.

10. S. R. Driver, *Deuteronomy* (ICC; 3d ed.; Edinburgh: T. & T. Clark, 1969) 89. Weinfeld (*Deuteronomy 1–11,* 337–38) accepts this translation but argues that the connotation of *oneness* here also includes the concept of *aloneness.*

11. Tigay, *Deuteronomy,* 76, 438–40; Duane L. Christensen, *Deuteronomy 1–11* (WBC 6A; Dallas: Word, 1991) 142. A variation of this position is held by McBride, who translates 'Our God is Yahweh, Yahweh alone' (S. Dean McBride, "The Yoke of the Kingdom: An Exposition of Deut. 6:4–5," *Int* 27 [1973] 273–306, esp. 274).

12. Driver, *Deuteronomy,* 89–90. For theological reasons for rejecting this interpretation, see J. Gerald Janzen, "On the Most Important Word in the Shema (Deuteronomy VI 4–5)," *VT* 37 (1987) 280–300.

13. Andersen, *The Hebrew Verbless Clause in the Pentateuch,* 47.

verbless predications generally. An informed linguistic analysis of the syntax of verbless clauses is thus critical for biblical interpretation.

Undoubtedly, the syntactic marginality of verbless clauses and the challenges in interpreting them have proven both problematic and intriguing for Hebraists. Although much progress has been made in describing and understanding verbless clauses,[14] uncertainty remains about their internal syntactic structure, their integration along with verbal clauses into an account of Biblical Hebrew syntax, and their distribution and rhetorical function on a text-linguistic level. This introduction explores the basic issues involved in the analysis and interpretation of the verbless clause, issues examined in greater detail in the following essays.

## 2. Terminology and Delimitation

Among Hebraists and linguists, there is little agreement about what to call predications lacking a finite verb. Some Hebraists prefer *nominal clause*, others *verbless clause*. Some linguists use the term *small clause*; others reject the category entirely. These disagreements stem from differences concerning three matters: the essential or most salient feature of this clausal category, the constructions that comprise the category, and the correct analysis of the syntactic structure of the category. As we will observe, choices concerning nomenclature have important ramifications for linguistic analysis: a *nominal clause* is not necessarily a *verbless clause*.

### 2.1. Nominal Clause

The term *nominal clause* is derived from medieval Arab grammarians. They divided all predications into two categories: verbal sentences, in which the verb is initial in the sentence, and nominal sentences, in which a nominal element is initial. The distinction between nominal and verbal sentences is reflected in the terminology used to describe their parts. In nominal sentences, the subject was referred to as the *mubtada'* (lit., 'that with which a beginning is made') and the predicate as the *ḫabar* (lit., 'the announcement' or 'information'). The use of these two terms is similar to the recognition by linguists in this century that the information in predications may be divided into two parts: the topic (given information) and the comment (new information).[15]

---

14. For historical overviews of the scholarship on the topic, see especially Dyk and Talstra (in this volume, pp. 133–85) §2.1, Groß (pp. 19–49) §1, Muraoka (pp. 187–213) §1, Niccacci (pp. 215–48) §1.2.

15. For an early formulation of topic and comment (using the terms *theme* and *rheme*), see especially Jan Firbas, "On Defining the Theme in Functional Sentence Analysis," *Travaux linguistiques de Prague* 1 (1964) 267–80; idem, "On the Thematic and the Non-thematic

Verbal sentences, however, were divided by the medieval grammarians into two different parts: the *fiʿl* (lit., 'action' or verb') followed by the *fāʿil* (lit., 'agent').[16] Within the category of the nominal sentences, the grammarians also included sentences that contained verbs when the verb was not in initial position in the sentence. Thus, in sentences with the order subject–verb, the constituent that we think of as the subject was called by the grammarians the *mubtadaʾ*, and the verb was called the *ḫabar*.

The distinction between nominal and verbal sentences was based on the grammarians' observations of various kinds of sentences. In the first, illustrated by *qāma Zaydun* ('Zaydun got up'), the verb is initial in the sentence and the agent follows. In the second, illustrated by *Zaydun ʾaḫūka* ('Zaydun is your brother'), a predication is formed without a verb; *Zaydun* is the *mubtadaʾ* and *ʾaḫūka* is the *ḫabar*.[17] A third type, illustrated by *Zaydun qāma*, patterns like the second with respect to word order. More importantly, the first and third types differ with respect to verbal agreement with the number of the subject.[18] In the first, if the subject is plural, this fact is not indexed in the

Section of the Sentence," in *Style and Text: Studies Presented to Nils Erik Enkvist* (ed. Håkan Ringbom; Stockholm: Språkförlaget Skriptor AB, 1975) 317–34. For a connection of the terms *topic* and *comment* with *mubtadaʾ* and *ḫabar*, respectively, see Diethelm Michel, "Probleme des Nominalsatzes im biblischen Hebräisch," *ZAH* 7 (1994) 215–24. For a somewhat different understanding, see Georgine Ayoub and Georges Bohas, "Les grammairiens arabes, la phrase nominale et le bon sens," in *The History of Linguistics in the Near East* (ed. Cornelis H. M. Versteegh, Konrad Koerner, and Hans-J. Niederehe; Amsterdam Studies in the Theory and History of Linguistic Science 28; Amsterdam: Benjamins, 1983) 31–48.

16. In addition to these specific terms for subject and predicate in nominal and verbal sentences, respectively, the grammarians from the 10th century onward used general terms to denote subject (*al-musnad ʾilayhi*) and predicate (*al-musnad*) in both kinds of clauses (Aryeh Levin, "The Grammatical Terms *al-musnad, al-musnad ʾilayhi* and *al-ʾisnād*," *JAOS* 101 [1981] 145–65).

17. In Arabic, the nominative case is also the citation form of the noun; both nouns in a verbless predication are in the nominative case, except that a locational predicate is in the accusative case. From a comparative point of view, it is interesting to note languages in which the citation form is not nominative and a nominal predicate is in the citation form. Examples are attested in Cushitic (Dick Hayward, *The Arbore Language: A First Investigation* [Kuschitische Sprachstudien / Cushitic Language Studies; Hamburg: Buske, 1984] 114–15, 135–46), in Nilotic (A. N. Tucker and M. A. Bryan, *Linguistic Analyses: The Non-Bantu Languages of North-Eastern Africa* [London: Oxford University Press, 1966] 431–34, 483–85), and in Bantu languages (Patrick Bennett, personal communication; see also Bernard Comrie, "The Typology of Predicate Case Marking," *Essays on Language Function and Language Type Dedicated to T. Givón* [ed. Joan Bybee, John Haiman, and Sandra A. Thompson; Amsterdam/Philadelphia: Benjamins, 1977] 39–50).

18. Agreement of person and gender is indexed on the verb regardless of whether the sentence is verbal or nominal: (a) verbal *qāmat Hindu(n)* ('Hind got up [f.]'), (b) nominal *Hindu qāmat*. The Arab grammarians interpreted the verbal affixes indexing number and

verbal morphology: *qāma al-mudarrisūna* ('the teachers [pl.] got up [s.]').[19]
On the basis of this observation, the grammarians concluded that the verb
does not index the agent, and thus *al-mudarrisūna* is the agent (*fāʿil*) of the
verb. But in the third type of sentence, verbal morphology indexes the plural
subject: *al-mudarrisūna qāmū* ('the teachers [pl.] got up [pl.]'). Since the verbal morphology indicates that the agent is indexed in the verb, and each verb,
they believed, can have only one agent, the grammarians concluded that *al-
mudarrisūna* is not the agent of the verb but is rather the *mubtada'* of a nominal sentence. Thus, the asymmetry in verbal morphology when the verb is not
initial in the sentence led them to the conclusion that the third type of sentence
is nominal, not verbal, in spite of the presence of an inflected verbal form.[20]

The terminology of the Arab grammarians was applied to Biblical Hebrew
and has been maintained by some writers in this volume.[21] Some writers, such
as Niccacci (pp. 215–48; see §3.2), use the term *nominal clause* broadly to include verbal clauses of SV [subject–verb] order within the rubric of nominal
clauses, thus maintaining the syntactic analysis of the Arab grammarians as
well as their terminology. For him, the phrase *simple nominal clause* serves to
differentiate nominal clauses without verbs from *compound nominal clauses*
with verbs. Other writers included herein, most notably Groß (pp. 19–49), reject the syntactic analysis that includes verbal clauses within the category of
nominal clause, while maintaining the term *nominal clause* as narrowly construed to refer exclusively to clauses without verbs. Because an examination
of nominal clauses as broadly construed by the Arab grammarians would involve a much wider array of syntactic questions, the focus of the volume is
upon nominal clauses in the narrow sense.

### 2.2. Verbless Clause

The term *verbless clause* (or nonverbal clause) designates the category on
the basis of a syntactic feature that is *not* present; that is, predication is

---

gender in (a) as particles (*ḥuruf*) denoting number and gender but not indexing the agent
(since the personal name following was the agent). In (b), they considered the verb to index
the agent. Their understanding of the syntax of the clauses thus influenced their interpretation of the verbal morphology. See Aryeh Levin, "The Distinction between Nominal and
Verbal Sentences according to the Arab Grammarians," *Zeitschrift für arabische Linguistik*
15 (1985) 118–27, esp. 120–21; and Gideon Goldenberg, "Subject and Predicate in Arab
Grammatical Tradition," *ZDMG* 138 (1988) 39–73, esp. 64–65.

19. Gender, however, is still indexed; cf. *qāmat al-mudarrisātu* 'the teachers (f. pl.) got
up (f. s.)'. The verb ignores number but indexes gender.

20. For the arguments of the grammarians and further examples, see Levin, "The Distinction between Nominal and Verbal Sentences according to the Arab Grammarians"; and
Goldenberg, "Subject and Predicate in Arab Grammatical Tradition," 64–67.

21. For the history of the term as applied to Biblical Hebrew phenomena, see Groß (in
this volume, pp. 19–49) §1.

achieved without a verb. Although the term implicitly assumes the primacy of clauses predicated by means of a verbal form, not all writers make that assumption. Rather, they use the term to describe the surface structure of the construction. Positing a category of verbless clauses does not, however, simplify the syntactic analysis; two major problems remain (see also §3 below).

First, the limits of the category are still open to dispute. For example, participles lack the morphological indications both of person and of tense/aspect that are found in finite verbs; clauses containing participles could be considered verbless clauses since the verbal form is not fully inflected. But such clauses on another analysis could be considered verbal clauses since the predications represented by participles necessarily include the semantic information inherent in the lexeme of the verbal root—unlike copular constructions, participles may represent predications that are not simply equational (that is, predicating the identification or classification of the subject). Some writers herein include participles in their analysis of verbless clauses (Buth §3, pp. 87–94; Dyk and Talstra §3.3.1, pp. 164–66; Lowery §5.7, p. 270; Niccacci, pp. 215–48; and Revell §6.1, pp. 311–13); others omit them (Groß, pp. 19–49; de Regt, pp. 273–96).

Second, to what extent are verbless clauses lacking a verb? Verbless clauses have sometimes been understood as having an underlying form of the verb היה that has been deleted. By this analysis, verbless clauses are a subset of the general category of verbal clauses; verbless clauses and verbal clauses share clausal features such as order of subject and predicate and types of complements and adjuncts (see especially DeCaen, pp. 109–31; and Sinclair, pp. 51–75). An alternate perspective, however, considers verbless clauses and verbal clauses to be two primary, opposing categories. In studies espousing that view, there is no attempt to correlate clausal features across the two categories of clauses.

## 2.3. Small Clause

Within generative linguistics, the term *small clause* (as opposed to *full clause*) has been used to refer to a set of constructions that expresses a subject–predicate relation without a fully inflected verbal form such as that found in full clauses. The term *small clause* is thus based on the observation that such clauses are "morphologically less complex than full clauses."[22]

The predicate in a small clause may be a noun, adjective, preposition, or noninflected verbal form (e.g., infinitive, gerund, participle). Examples of full clauses and their small clause counterparts in English are the following (italic

---

22. Anna Cardinaletti and Maria Teresa Guasti, "Small Clauses: Some Controversies and Issues of Acquisition," *Small Clauses* (ed. Anna Cardinaletti and Maria Teresa Guasti; Syntax and Semantics 28; New York: Academic, 1995) 2.

type indicates both full clauses and small clauses that are embedded as the complement of a larger sentence):

(1)  Full clause:
         We consider that *Mary is intelligent.*
(1a) Small clause: predication with an adjective
         We consider *Mary intelligent.*
(1b) Small clause: predication with an infinitival clause
         We consider *Mary to be intelligent.*

(2)  Full clauses with fully inflected verbal forms:
         We saw that *John ran.*
         We saw that *John was running.*
(2a) Small clauses without fully inflected verbal forms:
         We saw *John run.*
         We saw *John running.*

Although Hebraists will not be inclined to include most infinitival constructions along with verbless constructions in a single clausal category, many of the syntactic issues raised by linguists in their study of small clauses will be relevant to the discussion in §3 below.

**2.4.** Summary

Problems of delimitation and classification of verbless clauses involve the following issues: Should clauses containing a finite verb ever be included? Should clauses containing nonfinite verbal forms (especially participles) be included? Are verbless/nominal/small clauses a subset of fully formed clauses with a finite verb, or are they a completely separate category? Another problem of delimitation involves clauses that structurally meet the definition of verbless clauses as a result of the ellipsis of a finite verb other than היה (see Dyk and Talstra §1.2, pp. 134–35).

As we have seen, choices of terminology often reflect the authors' syntactic analyses and may also reflect their decisions concerning the delimitation of the category described. For other writers, the terms *verbless clause* and *nominal clause* are simply interchangeable. However, the differences attested among Hebraists concerning both terminology and delimitation of the category point to broader syntactic issues, to which we now turn.

**3.** Syntactic Issues

From the viewpoint of a strict grammatical hierarchy, syntactic issues surrounding verbless clauses in Biblical Hebrew may be identified at three levels:

(1) issues relating to the internal syntax of verbless clauses (for example, identification of subject and predicate, linear order of constituents, the syntax of tripartite verbless clauses), (2) issues concerning the external syntax of the verbless clause, that is, the relationship of verbless clauses to other clause types (for example, verbal clauses and copular clauses with היה, יֵשׁ, and אֵין) and the integration of verbless clauses into larger syntactic structures (for example, through coordination or subordination), and (3) issues concerning verbless clauses at the level of text or discourse. Since all of these issues are relevant to more than one hierarchical level, I consider them here topically. As we shall see, the syntactic problems are not merely theoretical but impinge upon questions of interpretation and exegesis.

### 3.1. Identification of Subject and Predicate

In a verbless clause, predication is achieved without an inflected verb; identification of the constituent that functions as predicate is thus crucial to a correct reading of the sentence. But because verbless predications (apart from participles) are copular constructions, the semantic content of the predication mirrors that of the English verb *to be*; that is, the semantics of the predication relate to stative notions of existence or equation, rather than to actions or events. As a result, determination of subject and predicate may be difficult:

(3)　Exod 9:27　יהוה הַצַּדִּיק

Taken in isolation, it is difficult to determine whether the divine name is the subject or the predicate. The NJPSV understands it to be the subject and translates 'The LORD is in the right'; Andersen, however, insists that it is the predicate and translates 'the one in the right is YHWH'.[23] Such difficulties in determining subject and predicate led Hoftijzer to reject the use of the terms altogether and analyze verbless clauses on the basis of strictly formal features rather than functional ones.[24]

Three strategies for identifying the subject and predicate are explored in this volume: formal grammatical features of the constituents, semantic and pragmatic features of constituents, and the linear order of constituents. Some authors employ multiple strategies for identifying subject and predicate, and rank the strategies in importance.

The first strategy relates to the identification of lexical categories or morphological features that correlate with subjects and predicates. For example,

---

23. Andersen, *The Hebrew Verbless Clause in the Pentateuch*, 63 (#109). See also the discussion in Buth (pp. 79–108) §2.5, example (9).

24. Hoftijzer, "The Nominal Clause Reconsidered," 477, 487–88, 510. For other examples in which the identification of S and P is difficult, see pp. 470–72.

prepositional phrases and undetermined adjectival phrases are to be identified
as predicates, proper nouns (usually) as subjects. The lexical and morphological forms are then ranked with respect to their suitability as subjects or predicates. I noted above (§2.2) the particular problem that participles pose.

The second strategy relates to semantic and/or pragmatic features of the
constituents. Most frequently, the relative definiteness of a constituent is considered. For example, when a noun phrase that is determined with the definite
article appears juxtaposed with a noun phrase without the definite article, the
former is considered more definite and thus the subject, while the latter is
taken to be the predicate:

(4)  Gen 46:32

וְהָאֲנָשִׁים רֹעֵי צֹאן      and the men are sheep-herders (lit.,
                                    herders of sheep)

The first noun phrase (וְהָאֲנָשִׁים) is definite and thus the subject; the second
(רֹעֵי צֹאן) is indefinite and thus the predicate.

As is readily apparent, the strategy of identifying the semantic definiteness
of a constituent has strong correlations to the strategy of identifying formal
morphological features (see especially Lowery, pp. 251–72). Other kinds of
semantic and pragmatic features that do not rely on formal morphological features may, however, be invoked. Referentiality, the degree to which a constituent refers to an item already mentioned in the context, may be used as a test
of subjecthood; the subject is then the constituent that has co-referential links
to a constituent in a previous clause (see Revell, pp. 297–319). Or the ways in
which subject and predicate differ with respect to the flow of information may
be described as given or presupposed information (the subject) and new or
focused information (the predicate) (see van Wolde §2.2, pp. 323–28; §3.2,
pp. 330–32). Attention to the semantic and pragmatic features of the larger
context may be particularly useful when the formal features of constituents
(or their levels of definiteness) do not differentiate subject and predicate, as in
the following:

(5)  1 Kgs 22:4

כָּמוֹנִי כָמוֹךָ כְּעַמִּי כְעַמֶּךָ      lit., like me like you, like my people
כְּסוּסַי כְּסוּסֶיךָ                     like your people, like my horses
                                              like your horses

Here there are three verbless clauses, each consisting of two constituents; both
constituents are prepositional phrases. Differentiation of subject and predicate
is not possible on the basis of the morphological category of the constituents.

The third strategy relates to the linear order of constituents, that is, a determination of the order of subject and predicate. Although linear order is rarely
employed as a primary means of determining subject and predicate, it is often

used in conjunction with other strategies and especially to differentiate cases of formal ambiguity. Some writers, however, reject linear order entirely as a means of determining subject and predicate (see Dyk and Talstra §2.2, pp. 149–56; §3.7, pp. 182–84).

### 3.2. Word Order

We have already seen that word order is sometimes used to determine subject and predicate in verbless clauses. But word order also relates to verbless clauses with respect to two other interrelated syntactic questions.

First, is there a basic, default order of subject and predicate in verbless clauses? This is a question that cannot ultimately be solved merely by a statistical analysis of the most frequent word order, since it relates to theoretical issues of language typology and pragmatics. Nonetheless, how one answers this question is important, for the answer determines whether a particular order of constituents should be considered pragmatically neutral as opposed to other orders which are pragmatically marked (for a definition of the concept, see van Wolde §2.1, pp. 321–23). In addition, if a basic order is posited, then one must determine whether the order of subject and predicate is the same as, or different from, the order in verbal clauses.

Second, given the fact that both arrangements of subject and predicate are attested in Hebrew verbless clauses, what conditions the variation? That is, why is the order subject–predicate found alongside the order predicate–subject? Essentially, two answers are possible. The linear order can be correlated narrowly to formal morphological features of constituents or more broadly to macrostructural concerns or features of informational structuring; both possibilities relate to issues described in §3.1.[25]

### 3.3. Tripartite Verbless Clauses

A distinct class of verbless clauses is composed, at least on the surface, of three core constitutents—subject, predicate, and independent third-person pronoun (see especially Muraoka, pp. 187–213).[26] Two orders of constituents are attested, one in which the pronoun is medial in the clause and one in which

---

25. For example, Revell (§4.4, pp. 307–8) connects the order of constituents to two related concerns of informational structuring: (1) an item with high referentiality to what precedes is placed in initial position in order to maintain topic continuity; (2) the topic of the verbless clause is usually placed before the comment. Often the topic is also the item with the highest referentiality.

26. Additional discussions appear in Buth (§5, pp. 100–106), Dyk and Talstra (§3.5.1, pp. 173–76), Niccacci (§3.3, pp. 245–48), and Revell (§3, pp. 302–5). Niccacci (§1.2, pp. 221–26) objects to the designation of this construction as a "three-member nominal clause." In his analysis, the nominal clause has only two constituents; a third constituent may be added either at the beginning (as a *casus pendens*) or at the end (as an apposition).

it is final. As an example of the two orders, compare the following: (a) with
the pronoun in medial position, and (b) with the pronoun in final position:

(6a) 1 Sam 17:14

וְדָוִד הוּא הַקָּטָן    and David is the youngest

(6b) Jer 31:9

וְאֶפְרַיִם בְּכֹרִי הוּא    and Ephraim is my firstborn

A syntactic analysis of such clauses is, however, fraught with difficulties.
The pronoun has sometimes been considered simply a copula; others suggest
that it provides emphasis or prominence. More importantly, the syntactic relationships among the three constituents is in question. Should the initial constituent be considered a *casus pendens* (in traditional terms) and thus as
standing outside of the nominal clause proper? Or is the initial element best
considered an instance of transformations described by linguists as extraposition, topicalization, or Y(iddish)-movement? In addition, should the final element ever be considered an instance of right-dislocation or apposition?

### 3.4. Integration into a Syntactic Account

In integrating verbless clauses into a syntactic account of Biblical Hebrew,
three kinds of issues are involved.

First, how are verbless clauses similar (or dissimilar) to verbal clauses? Although some writers maintain a rigid distinction between verbal and verbless
clauses, others argue that the two kinds of clauses share any of a variety of
features—the basic order of constituents (see DeCaen, pp. 109–31), the basic
distinction of being either nominal or verbal depending upon the order of constituents (see Niccacci, pp. 215–48), and the same kinds of complements and
adjuncts as verbal clauses with היה (see Sinclair, pp. 51–75). Especially important to this question is the relation of verbless clauses to verbal clauses
with היה. Are verbless clauses simply clauses in which היה has been deleted?
If so, then verbless clauses and verbal clauses can be analyzed in a unified
way, but new questions are raised. What, for example, is the difference text-
linguistically between a backgrounding clause in narrative that uses היה and
one that uses a verbless clause?

Second, how do verbless clauses relate to clauses with the existential elements יֵשׁ and אַיִן? Is the underlying syntactic structure different for these
clauses? And how do they differ text-linguistically?

Third, many writers investigate the ways in which verbless clauses are integrated into larger syntactic structures—through coordination, subordination
(especially with כי), or apposition. Attention to the broader syntactic context
outside of the verbless clause may provide insight into the linear arrangement
of constituents within the clause.

**3.5.** Text-Linguistic Considerations

A final area of inquiry involves the distribution and function of verbless clauses on a text-linguistic level, especially with respect to narrative, direct speech, and macrostructural divisions.

In narrative, verbless clauses may provide backgrounded information, that is, information that is not a part of the linear order of events making up the storyline (see van Wolde §3.2, pp. 330–32). Synchronous events and circumstantial information may be represented with verbless clauses. Characterization of participants in narrative may be understood more fully by recognizing the use of verbless clauses to introduce new participants and to provide important information concerning central participants (see especially de Regt, pp. 273–96). Direct speech may similarly show particular distributions of verbless clauses.[27] In addition, direct speech allows for reduced verbless clauses in which either subject or predicate is elided.

Verbless clauses also function on a macrostructural level at the boundaries of paragraphs or sections and at the beginnings and ends of narratives, genealogies, and lists. The distributional facts concerning verbless clauses thus point to their important discourse-pragmatic functions.

**4.** Conclusions

The essays included in this volume examine the specific issues described above, thus continuing the scholarly debate concerning the description and analysis of verbless clauses that was begun by medieval grammarians and furthered in this century, especially by Andersen and Hoftijzer. And since interpretation first depends upon a parsing and understanding of syntactic components, the questions posed here are critical to biblical exegesis.

In the decades since Andersen and Hoftijzer wrote on verbless predications, the science of linguistics has experienced extraordinary advances. As a result, the options available to Hebraists for syntactic analysis are no longer limited to the binary choice of either a structural analysis or a functional analysis, a choice at the center of the debate between Andersen and Hoftijzer. With the rise of generative syntax, cognitive linguistics, and informational structuring, Hebraists are confronted with far greater choices for analyzing Biblical Hebrew syntax. A representative selection of these new theoretical

---

27. For example, Revell notes that in a verbless clause with one constituent as a pronoun, the pronoun is often in second position at the beginning of direct speech (§2.3, example [9], p. 300). When an asyndetic verbless clause begins a speech, usually the comment (rather than the topic) is initial (Revell §6.1, pp. 311–13). See also the discussion throughout de Regt's essay (pp. 273–96).

approaches is presented among the essays, including generative syntax (and Government-Binding theory, a specific variety of generative syntax), functional grammar, generative-functional syntax, informational structuring, and Praguian discourse-pragmatics. The last decades have also seen an increased interest in the analysis of macrostructural features of language and linguistic theories for understanding those features. Since a macrostructural analysis is particularly important to the interpretation of the biblical text, the rise of discourse analysis and text-linguistics provides important theoretical tools for Hebraists. These theoretical stances also feature prominently in the essays included here.

The essays, then, approach the problems of verbless predications from a variety of theoretical linguistic positions and presuppositions. Although the authors often do not agree—concerning either the specific linguistic approach to be taken or the syntactic analysis of a specific verse—the essays demonstrate the ramifications of theory for both syntactic interpretation and for questions of discourse comprehension by providing comparative models for the application of linguistics to Biblical Hebrew syntax. Where the results of the various approaches converge, we have multiple lines of evidence that an analysis is correct.

Finally, the application of modern linguistic theory to questions of Biblical Hebrew syntax is important for the linguistic community as well. Most linguistic studies of small clauses have heretofore exclusively used Modern Hebrew examples.[28] In some respects, however, Biblical Hebrew exhibits different syntactic facts about verbless predications than those in Modern Hebrew. Although a comparison of these two varieties of Hebrew is outside of the scope of the present volume, three important syntactic differences are mentioned here briefly. Most significantly, the word order in Modern Hebrew is S–P.[29] In verbless predications, this fact means that a sentence with S–P word order such as (7a) sounds natural in Modern Hebrew, whereas a sentence such as (7b) with P–S word order does not:

(7a) Zeph 3:5

יהוה צַדִּיק בְּקִרְבָּהּ     The LORD in her midst is righteous.

---

28. For studies examining similar constructions in Modern Hebrew, see, for example, Edit Doron, *Verbless Predicates in Hebrew* (Ph.D. dissertation, University of Texas, 1983); and Susan Rothstein, "Small Clauses and Copular Constructions," in *Small Clauses* (ed. Anna Cardinaletti and Maria Teresa Guasti; Syntax and Semantics 28; New York: Academic, 1995) 27–48.

29. Of interest is MacDonald's observation that P–S order in verbless clauses occurs prominently in direct discourse in the Bible (J. MacDonald, "Some Distinctive Characteristics of Israelite Spoken Hebrew," *BiOr* 32 [1975] 162–75, esp. 163–64).

(7b) 2 Chr 12:6

צַדִּיק יְהוָה     The LORD is righteous.

The situation is similar when there is a "pleonastic" pronoun in the verbless predication (as discussed above in §3.3). A sentence such as (8a) with S–P order would be acceptable in Modern Hebrew; (8b) with P–S order is not:

(8a)

יהוה הוא צדיק     The LORD (he) is righteous.

(8b) Lam 1:18

צַדִּיק הוּא יְהוָה     The LORD (he) is righteous.

Second, it is significant that predications in which the pleonastic pronoun appears as the final element in a verbless predication (as in [6b] above) are completely unacceptable in Modern Hebrew, though commonly attested in Biblical Hebrew.

Finally, some linguists have argued that verbless predications in Modern Hebrew may be divided into two categories with different underlying structures.[30] The different underlying structures are reflected in a variation in surface syntax—in one variety, the pleonastic pronoun is optionally inserted between subject and predicate (as in [9a]); in another variety, the pleonastic pronoun is obligatory (as in [9b]):

(9a)

דני על־הגג

דני הוא על־הגג     Dani is on the roof.

(9b)

דני הוא הרפא     Dani is the doctor.
(cf. the unacceptable sentence דני הרפא)

Sentences such as (9b) differ from those in (9a) in asserting the identity of the subject. Of note, then, is the occurrence in Biblical Hebrew of predications analogous to those in (9b) in which the identity of the subject is predicated both with the pronoun (as in [9c]) and without the pronoun (as in [9d]):

(9c) 1 Kgs 8:60

יְהוָה הוּא הָאֱלֹהִים     The LORD (he) is God.

(9d) Josh 22:34

יְהוָה הָאֱלֹהִים     The LORD is God.

Clearly, the syntactic facts of Biblical Hebrew differ from those of Modern Hebrew. The essays included here will thus provide a body of data for further linguistic inquiry into diachronic developments in Hebrew syntax.

---

30. See Rothstein, "Small Clauses and Copular Constructions," 33–42.

# Is There Really a Compound Nominal Clause in Biblical Hebrew?

WALTER GROSS

*University of Tübingen*

In the following study I examine the Compound Nominal Clause (= CNC), specifically in clauses with a finite verb that does not occupy the first position. Its occurrence in such instances has been a steady source of misunderstanding among Hebraists. The CNC blurs the boundaries of the clausal field as well as the basic categories of nominal and verbal clauses; it unreflectedly jumbles the syntactic elements of form and the pragmatic aspects of clauses; it promotes the ambivalent or contradictory use of syntactic terms such as *subject*. In fact, the CNC ultimately proves unsuitable for a syntactic analysis of ancient Hebrew. The point has little to do with just another arbitrary detail of grammatical nomenclature. Rather, inasmuch as the CNC is a concept that not merely describes (heuristic) but also interprets (for example, pragmatic function), the structure of Hebrew clausal syntax is itself at stake.

The favor the CNC has found among some grammarians to this day as well as the problematic consequences of its use with regard both to the other syntactic terminology and to the internal system of the syntactic sections of Hebrew grammars are understandable only in reference to the history of scholarship and to the intensive (despite, in the last two centuries, shrinking) contact between Hebrew and Arabic studies. The history of Hebrew scholarship, unfortunately, has not yet been written. Thus I must limit myself to the main lines of its development relevant to my subject. Accordingly, the following essay consists of two main sections. In the first, I delineate the introduction of the concept CNC in terms of its evolution among select, but representative, grammars and grammarians. In the second, I systematically present the arguments

*Author's note*: I wish to thank John Frymire for translating my originally-German essay into English.

against its use. Therein I discuss in more detail a type of Hebrew clause that, it seems to me, is especially and patently incompatible with the concept of the CNC. Last, I return to several of the observations that will have arisen during the discussion of this term and attempt to suggest how they can be more precisely formulated.

## 1. Observations on the Historical Development of the Concept of the CNC

### 1.1. The Discovery of the Nominal Clause and the Debate about the CNC in the Nineteenth Century

#### 1.1.1. Before E. Kautzsch

In his first revision of what by then was the 22d edition of W. Gesenius's Hebrew grammar[1] (the most influential of the 19th century), E. Kautzsch made an observation that, given decades of flourishing Hebrew studies, was shocking but right on target nonetheless: "Scarcely a word has been written about the difference between the nominal and the verbal clause, a difference which, strictly speaking, is fundamental to the issue of syntax."[2] How is that possible?

Gesenius had properly assembled all of the pertinent syntactic data: clauses without finite verbs and the varying succession of the constituents of the clause; comparably structured clauses with היה; and *pendens* constructions. But Gesenius could not consider the nominal clause as an independent

---

1. In 1813 Gesenius published his short elementary *Hebräische Grammatik* (part 1 of his *Hebräisches Elementarbuch* [Halle: Renger, 1813]). Next came his longer and more detailed *Ausführliches grammatisch-kritisches Lehrgebäude der hebräischen Sprache mit Vergleichung der verwandten Dialekte* (Leipzig: Vogel, 1817). His later editions of the *Hebräische Grammatik* averaged somewhere between these two works in length. Altogether Gesenius personally published 13 significantly revised editions. After 1845, E. Rödiger completed the 14th–21st editions, and after 1878, E. Kautzsch the 22d–28th (1909), both substantially revising the previous works. Kautzsch's 28th (1909) edition has become authoritative in German and in English as well, through the translation of A. E. Cowley (*Gesenius' Hebrew Grammar as Edited and Enlarged by the Late E. Kautzsch: Second English Edition Revised in Accordance with the Twenty-Eighth German Edition (1909)* [2d ed.; Oxford: Clarendon, 1910; reprint Oxford, 1983]). G. Bergsträßer's 29th edition was issued in two parts: *Hebräische Grammatik mit Benutzung der von E. Kautzsch bearbeiteten 28. Auflage von Wilhelm Gesenius' hebräischer Grammatik verfaßt, I. Teil: Einleitung, Schrift- und Lautlehre* (Leipzig: Vogel, 1918); and *II. Teil: Verbum* (Leipzig: Hinrichs, 1929). But as he himself stated, what he had produced was "in Wahrheit eine neue hebräische Grammatik" (1.i). He was unable to complete the projected third part, which was to cover syntax. For Gesenius's character and influence, see R. Smend, *Deutsche Alttestamentler in drei Jahrhunderten* (Göttingen: Vandenhoeck & Ruprecht, 1989).
2. E. Kautzsch, *Wilhelm Gesenius' hebräische Grammatik nach E. Rödiger völlig umgearbeitet und herausgegeben* (22d ed.; Leipzig: Vogel, 1878) vi.

syntactic category, because from the beginning he adhered to the theory that verbless clauses would result from the omission of the *verbum substantivum* היה. In short, fundamental to his concept of grammatical propriety was the idea that a finite form of this verb belonged in every clause that appeared, on the surface, to be verbless. For example, "if an adjective constitutes the *predicate* of a clause in which the *verbum substantivum* is omitted, it then normally occurs *before* the substantive."[3] It is true that in his *Thesaurus* he conceded that the *verbum substantivum* was missing in the majority of cases, but he retained the verb "to omit": *in plerisque huius generis exemplis verbum substantivum omitti poterat et saepius omittitur quam ponitur.*[4] Further, he polemicized against his main scholarly and personal opponent, H. Ewald, whose description of the use of the *verbum substantivum* was far too limited in Gesenius's opinion. Later he at least avoided the use of that ominous verb "to omit," formulating instead the position that the subject and nominal predicate were "most commonly arranged without any copula."[5]

E. Rödiger, Gesenius's student, successor, and reviser, lacked the confidence to deviate decidedly from his master. Although he failed to introduce the term "nominal clause," he still suggested a divergent position from Gesenius when he asserted that through the addition of the *verbum substantivum* as a copula, "the clause becomes a verbal clause."[6] Beginning with the first edition of his Hebrew grammar, H. Ewald had rightfully demonstrated that subject and predicate were "simply placed next to one another without the copula of a 'to be' verb."[7] He even explained the rise of the copula היה as a late development in the history of the Hebrew language. Nevertheless, lacking a systematic idea of how to group these different constructions, he too merely lumped the varying constructions with verbal and nominal predicates together. In his numerous and significant later revisions of the work, Ewald never went beyond this earlier explanation.[8]

---

3. Gesenius, *Ausführliches Lehrgebäude*, 706, §183a: "Verbindung des Substantivs mit dem Adjectiv," which one finds within the larger section III: "Syntax des Nomen," followed by the following chapters: "Syntax des Pronomen," "Syntax des Verbi," "Syntax der Partikeln," and "Vermischte Idiotismen des hebräischen Styls." There is, however, no separate chapter on the clause.

4. Idem, *Thesaurus philologicus criticus linguae hebraeae et chaldaeae Veteris Testamenti: Tomi primi fasciculus posterior* (Leipzig: Vogel, 1835) 374.

5. Idem, *Hebräische Grammatik* (12th ed.; Leipzig: Renger, 1839) 248, §141.

6. E. Rödiger, *Wilhelm Gesenius' hebräische Grammatik: Neu bearbeitet und herausgegeben. 19. verbesserte und vermehrte Auflage* (Leipzig: Seemann, 1862) 270, §144.

7. H. Ewald, *Grammatik der hebräischen Sprache ausführlich bearbeitet* (Leipzig: Hahn, 1827) 632, §347.

8. See, for example, idem, *Ausführliches Lehrbuch der hebräischen Sprache des Alten Bundes* (8th ed.; Göttingen: Dieterich, 1870) 759ff., §§296–97. This is all the more puzzling given the exceptional merit of Ewald's studies of Hebrew syntax. On Ewald, see J. Wellhausen, *Grundrisse zum Alten Testament* (ed. R. Smend; Theologische Bücherei 27; Munich:

### 1.1.2. E. Kautzsch

Thus it was E. Kautzsch who became the first scholar to introduce the familiar native Arabic grammatical distinction (first made in Sîbawaihi's *al-Kitāb*, 8th century) between the nominal clause and the verbal clause as a structuring principle in Hebrew syntax. He successfully established this distinction when he inserted the following section into the 22d edition of Gesenius's grammar at §144a: "The Distinction between Nominal and Verbal Clauses."[9] It is true that he first did so by imposing the definitions of the native Arabic grammarians onto Hebrew syntax (that is, a clause beginning with a finite verb is a "verbal clause"; every clause beginning with a noun is a "nominal clause"; when this noun is followed by a finite verb, the clause is termed a "compound nominal clause"). For the Arabic terms (*mubtada'* and *ḫabar*) he then substituted the language of the Greco-Roman grammatical tradition (subject and predicate), a practice then common among many European authors of Arabic grammars,[10] and a practice that, for both terms, gave rise to great confusion.

European philology, oriented toward linguistic history and comparative Semitic languages, thus encountered the native Arabic grammarians, all of whom had lacked concepts of linguistic development; who had investigated the language only through a few of its literary manifestations such as the Qur'ān, classical poetry, and the so-called Bedouin language; who had paid homage to a peculiar concept of analogy; and whose notions of grammar had been influenced by theological and juridical modes of thought.[11] To this day, both the interpretation of Arabic grammatical terms and their bearing on syntactic data (with regard to their Greco-Roman grammatical counterparts), remain hotly debated. This much, however, is clear: supposing that Arabic terms actually do refer to syntactic information that is comparable to their supposed Greco-Roman counterparts, the correspondence of the one to the

---

Christian Kaiser, 1965), who writes: "Die hebräische Syntax ist von Ewald beinahe erst begründet und seitdem wenig gefördert worden, am wenigsten durch die Versuche, das Schema der arabischen Schulgrammatiker auf sie zu übertragen" (p. 123).

9. E. Kautzsch, *Wilhelm Gesenius' hebräische Grammatik* (22d ed., 1878) 308.

10. Cf. the then oft-cited presentation of E. Trumpp, *Über den arabischen Satzbau nach der Anschauung der arabischen Grammatiker* (Sitzungsberichte der philosophisch-philologischen und historischen Classe der k.b. Akademie der Wissenschaften zu München, 1879, Bd. 2; Munich: Straub, 1879) 353. See further A. Müller, *Dr. C. P. Caspari's Arabische Grammatik bearbeitet, 5. Auflage* (Halle, 1887), translated and revised by W. Wright, *A Grammar of the Arabic Language: Translated from the German of Caspari and edited with numerous additions and corrections; 3d Edition, Revised by W. Robertson Smith and M. J. de Goeje. Vol. II: Syntax* (Cambridge: Cambridge University Press, 1898) 250, §112.

11. Cf. C. H. M. Versteegh, "The Arabic Terminology of Syntactic Position," *Arabica* 25 (1978) 261–81.

other is, at best, only partial.[12] As the following discussion demonstrates, the imposing of these grammatical concepts onto Hebrew gave rise to unresolvable problems. First, it offered no means to distinguish *pendens* constructions

---

12. Here a few relevant comments must suffice. In reference to the classical European grammatical tradition, U. Mosel impressively discusses the incompatibility of the two linguistic systems in her unpublished dissertation, *Die syntaktische Terminologie bei Sîbawaih* (Munich, 1975): "Nicht ein einziger Terminus bei Sîbawaih [entspricht] einem lateinischen" (p. 5); "Die Begriffe Subjekt und Objekt sind Sîbawaih gar nicht bekannt" (p. 7). From there she notes that "eine Übersetzung von Sîbawaihs Termini mit in der heutigen Arabistik gebräuchlichen Termini abzulehnen ist" (p. 9). G. Ayoub and G. Bohas seek an approach on the part of generative grammar based on Chomsky's *Extended Revised Standard Version* in "Les grammairiens arabes, la phrase nominale et le bon sens," *Historiographia Linguistica* 8/2 (= *The History of Linguistics in the Near East* [Robert Henry Robins festschrift; 1981] 267–84). In a monograph rich in materials, J. Owens (*The Foundations of Grammar: An Introduction to Medieval Arabic Grammatical Theory* [Amsterdam Studies in the Theory and History of Linguistic Science, Series 3: Studies in the History of the Language Sciences 45; Amsterdam: Benjamins, 1988]) undertakes to demonstrate that at least the implicit principles of the Arabic grammarians have their counterparts in modern linguistics and that one can speak, for example, of the structural or possibly even of the deep structural considerations of the Arabic grammarians. He renders *mubtada'–ḫabar* with topic–comment (p. 32). See the remark made by Versteegh in another context: "It is, therefore irrelevant and unnecessary to seek for parallels in modern syntactic theory. The only legitimate reason for choosing such terms as translations of Arabic terms—although it is a rather risky one—could be the wish to smooth the harshness or strangeness of a literal translation" ("Arabic Terminology," 265). For Sîbawaih, see the very concise remarks of Versteegh in "Sibawayhi, Abû Bišr ʿAmr ibn ʿUtmān," in *Lexicon Grammaticorum: Who's Who in the History of World Linguistics* (ed. H. Stammerjohann; Tübingen: Max Niemeyer, 1996) 856–59. He renders the pair *mubtada'/ḫabar* 'topic/predicate' and with good reason denies their structural comparability with the pair subject/predicate. For a brief overview of the hardly quiet debate over this issue among the different schools of Arabic grammarians since the 19th century, see H. Fleisch, *Traité de philologie Arabe, I: Préliminaires, phonétique, morphologie nominale* (Beirut: Imprimerie Catholique, 1961). There is, consequently, a danger of mystification when D. Michel uses the Arabic terms *mubtada'* (understood as 'Insbildsetzung') and *ḫabar* (understood as 'Aussage') instead of *subject* and *predicate* for the analysis of Hebrew nominal clauses but otherwise ignores the internal system of Arabic ("Probleme des Nominalsatzes im biblischen Hebräisch," *ZAH* 7 [1994] 215–24). In fact, H. Ewald had already warned against the "irrthum," in 1870, "daß das Arabische wie wir es kennen die älteste und beste gestalt des Semitischen so bewahrt habe daß man es auch bei allem anderen Semitischen als das urbild zu grunde legen müsse" (*Ausführliches Lehrbuch der hebräischen Sprache* [8th ed., 1870] xii). Ewald could make such a judgment as an expert: already in 1831 he had published his own Arabic grammar (*Grammatica critica linguae Arabicae cum brevi metrorum doctrina* [2 vols.; Leipzig: Hahniana, 1831–33]), wherein he rejected the idea of simply adopting the system of the native Arabic grammarians. Cf. the judgment of Wellhausen: "Gegen Ewald als Arabist wandte sich namentlich G. W. Freytag in Bonn, weil er sich erdreisten wollte, über die von de Sacy wiederbelebte Tradition der alten einheimischen Schulen von Kufa und Basra hinauszugehen" (Smend [ed.], *Julius Wellhausen*, 125).

from other clauses with, for example, direct objects preceding the finite verb
but without pronominal resumption of the direct object after the verb. Nor can
it do justice to the fact that, in Hebrew sentences with topicalization of a dependent part of the clause other than the grammatical subject, the topicalized
element (that is, the constituent preceding the verb) is often introduced by את
or a preposition, whereas it should be realized in the "nominative" according
to the Arabic grammatical theory of the CNC.[13]

In 1878, E. Kautzsch introduced the following definition:

> Every clause that begins with an independent subject (noun or separate pro-
> noun) is called a *nominal clause*; namely, (a) a *simple nominal clause* if the
> predicate is a noun (substantive, adjective, or participle); (b) a *compound nomi-
> nal clause* if the predicate is a finite verb. . . . Every clause which begins with a
> finite verb is called a *verbal clause*.[14]

Kautzsch corroborated these assertions both morphologically and, in terms of
the clause, functionally: (1) Every verb morphologically conveys its subject
within itself. In this respect the verb is an independent verbal clause unto itself. However, if a substantive which is co-referential with the subject that is
indexed in the verb occurs after the verb, the substantive is not itself the subject of the clause, but rather "epexegese," apposition to the subject contained
in, and conveyed by, the verb.[15] The phrase אָמַר הַמֶּלֶךְ means 'he spoke,
namely the king'. From this, one understands the following: because apposi-
tions must follow the words to which they refer, the reverse order of clausal
members (that is, noun before the verb) indicates a CNC. In the 25th edition,
Kautzsch departed from the position that the finite verb was an independent
clause unto itself, favoring instead the following equally problematic assertion, based on his idea of Hebrew's historical development: the finite verb
may indeed be initially an independent nominal clause unto itself in the first
and second persons (קטלת 'killer you' or 'you killing'), but in the third person, the finite verb is only a noun (קטל 'killer') and hence not a complete
clause. The formation of a complete clause is contingent upon the addition of
a subject.[16] (2) Nominal clauses refer to "something *fixed, a state* or in short,

---

13. For the time being, *pendens* constructions are not under consideration.

14. Kautzsch, *Wilhelm Gesenius' hebräische Grammatik* (22d ed., 1878) 308–9, §144a.

15. Already suggested by H. Ewald, *Grammatik der hebräischen Sprache*, 634, §348.
This thesis has survived into our newest Hebrew grammars.

16. Kautzsch, *Wilhelm Gesenius' hebräische Grammatik völlig umgearbeitet: 25. vielfach verbesserte und vermehrte Auflage mit einer neuen Bearbeitung der Syntax* (Leipzig:
Vogel, 1889) 435, §140. In the 28th edition in 1909, however, he returned to his original position: "Aber auch die 3. *Sing. Perf.*, die keinerlei Hinweis auf das Subjekt enthält, muß als
ein selbständiger Verbalsatz betrachtet werden" (*Wilhelm Gesenius' hebräische Grammatik
völlig umgearbeitet: 28. vielfach verbesserte und vermehrte Auflage* [Leipzig: Vogel, 1909]
471, §140c). Contrary to this resurrected position of 1909, C. Brockelmann followed

*a being* so and so," whereas verbal clauses signify "something *moveable* and *in progress*, an *event* or *action*." He likewise reckoned nominal clauses with independent personal pronouns or הָיָה (as a copula) to be among the compound nominal clauses.[17]

In §145 (1878), "The Position of the Parts of Speech in the Clause: The So-Called *Casus Absoluti*," Kautzsch readily offered pertinent observations that were taken from older editions of Gesenius's grammar but completely resisted integration into his new definitions. For example, in order to highlight specific elements in the clause, the "natural word order" is changed, and the emphasized unit of the clause is placed in the first position—and this without changing the clause type. Thus, in contrast to his definition, the Hebrew often moves the adjectival predicate in the nominal clause in front of the subject.[18] In verbal clauses (*sic*) he reconciled the word order "object–verb–subject" as well as "subject–object–verb."[19] Above all, indicators of time often precede the verb. Kautzsch noted as much but without comment about how he determined the clause-type of such utterances.

*Pendens* constructions prove to be especially unwieldy, their characterization and syntactic arrangement being subject to much deviation within the Hebrew grammars.[20] Kautzsch assigned them collectively to the CNC. In the

---

P. Lagarde and adopted Kautzsch's position of 1909 but avoided their erstwhile consequences, arguing again on the basis of ideas of the language's historical development: "wie wir, sicher in Übereinstimmung mit dem arab. Sprachgefühl selbst, das dem Verb nachfolgende Subjekt nicht mehr als Apposition zu dem im Verbum liegenden Pron. auffassen" (*Grundriß der vergleichenden Grammatik der semitischen Sprachen, II: Syntax* [Berlin: Reuther & Reichard, 1913] 171, §93).

17. Cf. Kautzsch, *Wilhelm Gesenius' hebräische Grammatik* (22d ed., 1878) 267, §121; 310, §144b.

18. Ibid., 309, §144a; 311, §145.

19. Ibid., 311, §145.

20. Gesenius spoke of the "nominativus absolutus" and of "absoluter Construction . . . bey anderen Casibus" (*Ausführliches Lehrgebäude*, 723ff., §189). In 1839, he abandoned the term *nominativus absolutus* and used instead *casus absoluti* and the "absolute" position at the beginning of the clause (*Hebräische Grammatik*, 249–50, §142). Ewald stayed closer to the Arabic mode of expression: "Das Hauptnomen . . . steht oft abgerissen im Anfange des Satzes" (*Ausführliches Lehrbuch der hebräischen Sprache* [5th ed., 1844] 573–74, §301). In his *Wilhelm Gesenius' hebräische Grammatik*, Kautzsch first suggested the "sogen[nannte] *Casus absoluti* " ([22d ed., 1878] 311, §145) but later preferred the designation "zusammengesetzter Satz" ([25th ed., 1889] 443–44, §143). Following the psycholinguistic tradition of W. Wundt, C. Brockelmann chose the term "dominierende Vorstellung" (*Grundriß der vergleichenden Grammatik*, 439–40, §271), whereas H. Reckendorf spoke of the "Isolirung des natürlichen Subjekts" (*Die syntaktischen Verhältnisse des Arabischen* [Leiden: Brill, 1898] 782, §257). The older grammars give just a few examples. I have gathered all of the types of *pendens* constructions found in the Hebrew Bible in *Die Pendenskonstruktion im biblischen Hebräisch: Studien zum althebräischen Satz I* (ATSAT 27; St. Ottilien: EOS, 1987).

case of Ps 74:17 (קַיִץ וָחֹרֶף אַתָּה יְצַרְתָּם 'winter and summer—you have made them'), he argues, "*Winter and summer* are not to be construed as an object, but rather as the subject of a compound nominal clause (CNC)."[21] The reason is likely that the *pendentia* do not have אֵת attached to them as indicators that they function in the sentence as objects, though in the case of undetermined substantives and poetry, אֵת would not be expected. The opposite situation arises in Gen 47:21 (וְאֶת הָעָם הֶעֱבִיר אֹתוֹ 'the people—he carries them across'), where אֵת occurs before the *pendens*. Kautzsch observed that in this case the *pendens* should not be taken as the subject of the CNC but as "the object preceding absolutely."[22] As to how the entire utterance should be syntactically classified, Kautzsch betrayed not a word. Similarly, he failed to comment on the case of Ps 74:17, where a clause assimilates a *pendens* and begins with the independent personal pronoun as its subject—and consequently (following his terminology) already is a CNC without the *pendens*.

This model is manifestly inconsistent. No wonder, then, that Kautzsch radically altered it in the 25th edition of 1889.[23] One year previously, in 1888, C. Albrecht had published an influential article on Hebrew nominal clauses in which he diverged from native Arabic grammar. Therein he established a plausible principle. The type of clause, he argued, should not be determined by the type of the word that occurs first in the clause, but rather by its predicate:

> All languages distinguish between verbal and nominal clauses on the basis of the various types of words which can form a predicate. Verbal clauses are those in which the subject is a (virtual) noun, and the predicate a finite verb. Nominal clauses are those in which both the subject and the predicate are (virtual) nouns. When such virtual nouns functioning as subjects or predicates are realized by an independent clause, what we have is a compound sentence. Accordingly, the difference between the types of clause is determined by the difference of the types of words in the predicate.[24]

In 1889 Kautzsch adopted all three definitions:[25]

---

21. Kautzsch, *Wilhelm Gesenius' hebräische Grammatik* (22d ed., 1878) 312, §145.

22. Ibid., 312, §145.

23. Ibid. (25th ed., 1889). Because the relevant paragraphs remained identical in subsequent editions, I cite the more accessible 28th edition of 1909, also translated by A. E. Cowley (2d ed.; Oxford: Clarendon, 1910; reprint, Oxford, 1983).

24. C. Albrecht, "Die Wortstellung im hebräischen Nominalsatze," *ZAW* 7 (1887) 218–24 (here p. 218). In a sequel to his article a year later, Albrecht, borrowing from H. Nöldeke's *Kurzgefasste Syrische Grammatik* (Leipzig: Weigel, 1880), argued expressly against Kautzsch and his thesis that a nominal clause with an independent personal pronoun as "copula" should be a CNC ("Die Wortstellung im hebräischen Nominalsatze, Teil II," *ZAW* 8 [1888] 249–63 [here p. 251]).

25. F. I. Andersen called attention to this point in *The Hebrew Verbless Clause in the Pentateuch* (Journal of Biblical Literature Monograph Series 14; Nashville and New York: Abingdon, 1970) 17.

Every clause in which the subject and predicate consist of a noun or its equivalent, is called a *nominal clause*. . . . Every clause in which the subject consists of
a noun (or pronoun included in a verbal form), and in which the predicate consists of a finite verb, is called a *verbal clause*. . . . Every clause in which the subject or predicate itself consists of a full clause, is called a *compound sentence*.[26]

Here he breaks away *expressis verbis* from his earlier position, from the native
Arabic grammarians, and from the concept of the CNC. The position of the
clausal members no longer plays a role in the determination of the type of
clause; and what remains debated are minor issues. In his assessment of
clauses with a copula he oscillates. Clauses with the copula היה are simple
nominal clauses.[27] Those with independent personal pronouns as the copula
he classifies, conforming to Albrecht's system, as simple nominal clauses,[28]
contrary to later, where he prefers CNC.[29] Harmless from the perspective of
the syntactic system but ultimately impractical, Kautzsch wound up placing
*pendens* constructions[30]—and only these—under the rubric *compound sentences* (as opposed to CNC). Both H. Reckendorf and C. Brockelmann[31] had
handled the issue more plausibly, placing under this rubric syndetic and asyndetic complex sentences (as opposed to simple clauses). Kautzsch, on the
other hand, placed these under the syntactically vague heading "Special Kinds
of Sentences."[32]

Although Kautzsch now determined the type of clause from the types of
words in the predicate alone, he still sought, with regard to the different performative functions of clauses, to make distinctions within the group of verbal
clauses. He also attempted to integrate into his system those aspects of the
clause that formerly, following the Arabic grammarians, he had designated
with the term CNC. His chosen formulation, with expressions such as "proper"
and "naturally," was indebted to a romantic view of language and well suited

---

26. Kautzsch, *Wilhelm Gesenius' hebräische Grammatik* (25th ed., 1889) 434–35 (=
28th ed., 1909, p. 470, §140). The parenthetical modification was first added in the 1909
(28th) edition. The English translation is slightly different from Cowley, *Gesenius' Hebrew
Grammar*, 450, §140a–d.

27. Kautzsch, *Wilhelm Gesenius' hebräische Grammatik* (25th ed., 1889) 439, §141;
441, §142 (= 28th ed., 1909; pp. 475, §141; 477, §142). In §142 he makes a rather unclear
attempt to distinguish היה as a full verb (resulting in a verbal clause) and as a copula (resulting in a nominal clause).

28. Ibid. (25th ed., 1889) 438, §141.

29. Ibid. (28th ed., 1909) 474, §141.

30. In §143 he speaks of *casus pendens*.

31. Reckendorf, *Die syntaktischen Verhältnisse des Arabischen*; Brockelmann, *Grundriß der vergleichenden Grammatik*.

32. Kautzsch, *Wilhelm Gesenius' hebräische Grammatik* (28th ed., 1909) 493ff. Here
he was followed by P. Joüon, who spoke of "propositions particulières," in his *Grammaire
de l'Hébreu biblique* (Rome: Pontifical Biblical Institute, 1923) 478ff.

both to promote confusion and to pave the way for those who, since the middle of this century, have sought to bring the CNC back into Hebrew studies—all this because he did not distinguish clearly enough the aspects of grammatical form from pragmatic and narrative function.

Kautzsch argues that the "proper" verbal clause accentuates the action of the subject and accordingly precedes the subject "naturally," even when unnecessary (necessary only in the verb forms *wa=yiqtol* and *w=qatal*). In most other instances,

> the position of the subject at the beginning of the verbal clause is to be explained from the fact that the clause is not intended to introduce a new fact carrying on the narrative, but rather to describe a *state*. Verbal clauses of this kind approximate closely in character to nominal clauses, and not infrequently (viz., when the verbal form might just as well be read as a participle) it is doubtful whether the writer did not in fact intend a noun clause.[33]

### 1.1.3. Contemporaries of E. Kautzsch

Thus Kautzsch achieved a formal, internally consistent concept of Hebrew syntax in 1889. On the basis of his own corrective, the CNC, after an eleven-year reign, fell out of favor once again in Hebrew studies. The work of prominent Semitists in the following decades, at least in German-speaking scholarship, suggests that the rejection of the CNC would continue. In his syntax of 1897, E. König upheld the judgment that clause-types should be defined solely on the basis of the part of speech contained in the predicate.[34] In this context he avoided the term "CNC" and in reference to H. Reckendorf and T. Nöldeke, among others, argued explicitly against the conception of the Arabic grammarians.[35] He emphasized that "nominal clauses," through the addition of היה, formally go over to the category of the "verbal clauses." In individual cases, however, it remains difficult to decide whether היה only acts as a copula, in which case then the function of this sentence comes at least close to that of the nominal clause.[36]

In his Arabic syntax of 1898, H. Reckendorf followed the same methodological line and even rejected the concept of the CNC within Arabic: "The

---

33. Kautzsch, *Wilhelm Gesenius' hebräische Grammatik* (25th ed., 1889) 440, §142 (= 28th ed., 1909, p. 476, §142); trans. Cowley, p. 455, §142; his italics.

34. E. König, *Historisch-kritisches Lehrgebäude der hebräischen Sprache mit comparativer Berücksichtigung des Semitischen überhaupt, Zweite Hälfte 2. (Schluss-)Theil: Syntax* (Leipzig: Hinrichs, 1897) 363, §326c.

35. Ibid., 363–64, §326d.

36. Ibid., 428, §338s. For the handling of this problem in the Hebrew grammars of the 20th century and for a critique of the idea of the *copula*, see R. Bartelmus, *HYH: Bedeutung und Funktion eines hebräischen "Allerweltswortes"—zugleich ein Beitrag zur Frage des hebräischen Tempussystems* (ATSAT 17; St. Ottilien: EOS, 1982) 1–3, 92ff. Insofar as there is a danger that the difference (familiar in the Indo-Germanic languages) between 'becoming'

entire precept raises up an essential sign out of a secondary one. It forces a kind of sophistry upon Arabic, in which it still appears somewhat viable, whereas in the other Semitic languages it simply has no use."[37] He classified sentences of the order "subject–finite verb" as verbal clauses with "inversion." For the syntactic analysis and the determination of clause-types, he used the categories "grammatical subject–grammatical object." And yet to the contrary, in order to describe the semantic and pragmatic function of certain orders of elements within the clause, he set up the terms "natural subject–natural predicate";[38] the "natural subject" being "the one compelling itself with singular energy," the "part of the clause which constitutes the starting point of the sentence . . . regardless in which grammatical category it belongs."[39] He discussed *pendens* constructions in great detail under the heading "The Isolation of the Natural Subject," a section appearing after subjunctive clauses under the larger rubric "Compound Sentences."

Invoking the authority of Nöldeke and Reckendorf in the introduction to his comparative syntax, C. Brockelmann stated: "Here, the theories of the native Arabic grammarians must remain completely out of the question."[40] For him, the CNC thus failed to exist. In accordance with W. Wundt, he gave *pendens* constructions the psycholinguistic designation "dominating idea" and placed them (contrary to Reckendorf) among the "simple expanded sentences,"[41] as opposed to compound sentences. On the basis of speculation

---

(*werden*) and 'being' (*sein*) leads to semantic prejudices within the debate among Hebraists, the remarks of E. Jenni are noteworthy:

> Das Hebräische unterscheidet bei allen Verben, die als eine der Bedeutungskomponenten einen zeitlich bestimmten Zustand enthalten, nicht zwischen dem andauernden Zustand und dem Eintreten des Zustandes, während wir in sehr vielen Fällen den Unterschied lexikalisieren und ausdrücken müssen. Nicht der Hebräer, aber das hebräische Lexikon ist weitgehend blind für den Unterschied zwischen Inchoativ/Ingressiv einerseits und Durativ oder besser Nicht-Ingressiv andererseits.

Cf. Jenni, "Lexikalisch-semantische Strukturunterschiede: Hebräisch ḤDL-deutsch 'aufhören/unterlassen,'" *ZAH* 7 (1994) 124–32 (here p. 127).

37. Reckendorf, *Die syntaktischen Verhältnisse des Arabischen*, 2. Reckendorf maintained the essentials of this position in his *Arabische Syntax* (Heidelberg: Carl Winter's Universitätsbuchhandlung, 1921).

38. Cf. Reckendorf, *Die syntaktischen Verhältnisse des Arabischen*, 3, §3 and, for example, 782, §257. In reference to the contemporary discussion among the so-called "Junggrammatiker," he rejected the use of terms such as the "logical" and "psychological" subject.

39. Ibid., 782, §257.

40. Brockelmann, *Grundriß der vergleichenden Grammatik*, 4.

41. Brockelmann's term is "einfache bekleidete Sätze," that is, clauses that include additional elements beyond the subject and predicate. He handles *pendentia* to complex sentences or to a partial clause of a complex sentence exclusively under compound sentences.

about the history of the language, he suggested that *pendens* constructions
originally would not have possessed inflectional endings, inasmuch as they
would have stood outside of the clausal context.[42] Nominal clauses in which
an independent personal pronoun is joined to the subject and predicate "properly" belonged to these *pendens* constructions. But according to Brockelmann, this construction had already so much diminished to a "copula" that he
classified it not as a *pendens* construction (which meant for him "simple expanded sentences") but as having its own category, the "three-member nominal clauses."[43] Here he also classified the clauses with היה as copula.[44]

**1.1.4.** Intermediate Results

By the beginning of this century, then, the following convictions had been
worked out within Hebrew studies: The observations of the native Arab grammarians were certainly worth consideration but not their complex system itself or the category of the CNC within it, especially since the placement of
clausal members was much more free in Hebrew than in Arabic.[45] As elements of syntactic form, the types of clauses (nominal clause and verbal
clause) were to be formally determined solely on the basis of the part of
speech of the predicate. The semantic, pragmatic, narrative, and stylistic functions of concrete nominal and verbal clauses were in need of subsequent clarification. To that end, however, no single, common terminology acquired
general acceptance.

This consensus seemed well established and was followed, for example, by
Joüon in his grammar of 1923.[46] To this day, it has also proved useful to the

---

42. Ibid., 440, §271.

43. Ibid., 102ff., §52, 53. In so doing, he contradicts S. R. Driver (*A Treatise on the Use
of the Tenses in Hebrew and Some Other Syntactical Questions* [3d ed.; Oxford: Clarendon,
1892] 267–74, §198–210), who denied completely any copular function to the independent
personal pronoun: together with the predicate, it forms a "complete sentence" and simultaneously recapitulates the preceding lexemic subject. Most recently, A. Niccacci agrees with
Driver, in "Simple Nominal Clause (SNC) or Verbless Clause in Biblical Hebrew Prose,"
*ZAH* 6 (1993) 216–27: There is no copula in Hebrew; neither היה nor the independent personal pronoun fulfills this function.

44. Brockelmann, *Grundriß der vergleichenden Grammatik*, 107ff., §55.

45. See above all the careful examination of this issue by A. Bloch, *Vers und Sprache
im Altarabischen: Metrische und syntaktische Untersuchungen* (Acta Tropica Supplementa
5; Basel: Recht und Gesellschaft, 1946).

46. Joüon, *Grammaire de l'Hébreu biblique*, 474, §155k. What is more, he even maintained against all others (and rightly so; cf. below, §2) that in verbal clauses the order
should occur "normalement" subject–verb. T. Muraoka, in reference to his own monograph (*Emphatic Words and Structures in Biblical Hebrew* [Leiden: Brill, 1985]), incor-
rectly "corrected" Joüon in his revision and translation of the 1923 French grammar; cf.
P. Joüon, *A Grammar of Biblical Hebrew* (trans. and rev. by T. Muraoka; Subsidia Biblica 14;
2 vols.; Rome: Pontifical Biblical Institute, 1991) 578, §155k: "The statistically dominant

Hebrew grammars in which the structural methods of contemporary linguistics have been utilized and the methodological and terminological separation of the various levels of description and meaning advocated. One need only compare the grammars of W. Richter, B. K. Waltke and M. O'Connor, and T. Muraoka.[47]

But in Arabic studies, Reckendorf and Brockelmann could in no way establish their decisive, methodological dismissal of native Arabic grammar.[48] The result has been that, since the middle of this century, a few authors of Hebrew grammars, without explicitly giving reasons for re-implementing the concept, have returned again to the theory of the CNC. In doing so they have either reproduced, ignored, or intensified the internal contradictions of this grammatical appropriation of Arabic, contradictions which, in the debates of the late 19th century, had been made manifestly evident.

**1.2.** The Renewal of the Concept CNC since the Middle of This Century

**1.2.1.** Moderate Advocates

Authors whom I term "moderate advocates" have essentially resurrected Kautzsch's original position of 1878.

In his 1955 revision of G. Beer's Hebrew grammar, R. Meyer proposed a combination derivative of Kautzsch (1889 = 1909) and Brockelmann: three-member nominal clauses, verbal clauses with a stressed subject in the first position, and the "compound sentence" as a designation only of *pendens* constructions (at least in the heading title of the relevant paragraph, as opposed to the text body, where he used the term CNC).[49] In his third, revised edition of

---

and unmarked *word-order* in the verbal clause is: Verb–Subject." He discusses *pendens* constructions under the heading *Casus pendens*.

47. Richter, *Grundlagen einer althebräischen Grammatik, B. Die Beschreibungsebenen, III: Der Satz (Satztheorie)* (ATSAT 13; St. Ottilien: EOS, 1980); B. K. Waltke and M. O'Connor, *An Introduction to Biblical Hebrew Syntax* (Winona Lake, Ind.: Eisenbrauns, 1990); Muraoka, *A Grammar of Biblical Hebrew*, esp. for the CNC, pp. 562–63. Muraoka's assertion (p. 587) that I advocate this hypothesis of the CNC is erroneous. The above concept of the verbal clause is also supported by W. R. Garr, *Dialect Geography of Syria–Palestine, 1000–586 B.C.E.* (Philadelphia: University of Pennsylvania Press, 1985) 189ff.

48. The numerous reprints of the Arabic grammar of W. Wright (*A Grammar of the Arabic Language, Translated from the German of Caspari and edited with numerous editions and corrections, II: Syntax* [3d ed.; rev. W. Robertson Smith and M. J. de Goeje; Cambridge: Cambridge University Press, 1898]), which is closely based on the concepts of the Arabic grammarians, provide a clear indication of this up to the present day. Indeed, the influence of this branch of Arabic scholarship is to be noted for the revival of the CNC by H. S. Nyberg, *Hebreisk Grammatik* (Stockholm: Geber, 1952) §85.

49. R. Meyer, *Hebräische Grammatik von D. Dr. Georg Beer*, vol. 2: *Formenlehre II, Syntax und Flexionstabelle* (2d ed.; Sammlung Göschen 764/764a; Berlin: de Gruyter, 1955) 96, §90; 97ff., §92.

1972 that appeared for the first time solely under his name, Meyer retained the
concept at one point, only to reject it at another: in reference to D. Michel (see
below, under "extreme advocates"), Meyer began §92.4b with the observation
that "a verbal clause with a subject in the first position can already be spoken
of as a CNC with a verbal predicate."[50] As a result, one may take the same
sentence, הַנָּחָשׁ הִשִּׁיאַנִי (Gen 3:13b), translate it 'the snake has lead me astray',
and use it as an example for the word order "subject–verb" in a verbal clause
(§91); or translate it 'the snake—it has led me astray' and thus find an
example of a CNC with a verbal predicate (§92). Given the fact that the nominal clause / verbal clause is a fundamental syntactic dichotomy, one can only
characterize this as terminological degeneration.[51]

The 1974 grammar of W. Schneider, which superseded O. Grether's,
proved very influential in the academic teaching of Hebrew. Here one finds
scenes replayed from Kautzsch (1878), including his adaptation of native
Arabic grammar.[52] He determines the type of clause, nominal or verbal, on the
basis of the type of word with which the clause begins (§44.1.2). Because the
finite verb already contains its subject in itself through the personal morpheme, a following lexemic subject relates to this morphemic subject as an
apposition (§44.5.2). In the nominal clause, the following identifications are
valid: subject = the given = theme; predicate = the new = *rhēma* (§44.3).
Where a substantive precedes a finite verb, there is a CNC (§44.1.2.3).

Nevertheless, Schneider appears uncertain in the case of the CNC. His first
example turns out to be, of all things, Gen 1:2a with היה! He hesitated to include clauses of the order "temporal modifier–verb–subject"[53] or clauses in
which a nominal (but not the subject) member of the clause precedes the verb
(for example, Gen 1:5b: וְלַחֹשֶׁךְ קָרָא לָיְלָה 'but the darkness he named night')
among the CNCs. This was not, however, because they challenge the definition he had supplied above but because of their semantic performance: "because here no state is described" (§44.1.2.4). Indeed, the clause in Ps 11:4c
(עֵינָיו יֶחֱזוּ) also fails to describe a state, but in this case the native Arabic

---

50. Idem, *Hebräische Grammatik*, vol. 3: *Satzlehre* (3d ed.; Sammlung Göschen 5765;
Berlin: de Gruyter, 1972) 14.

51. It does not get any better in the same section when he expounds on the verbal clause
in 1 Kgs 6:29 with a preceding direct object, which he falsely construes as a *pendens* construction: "Darüber hinaus kann ein Obj. synt[aktisch] als Subjekt gelten" (ibid., 14). Such
formulations lead *all* syntactic terminology *ad absurdum*.

52. W. Schneider, *Grammatik des biblischen Hebräisch: Völlig neue Bearbeitung der*
*"Hebräischen Grammatik für den akademischen Unterricht" von Oskar Grether* (Munich:
Claudius, 1974) 159–67, §44.

53. For just this case, O. Grether had expressly contested an impairment of the "Wesen"
of the "reiner Verbalsatz" (*Hebräische Grammatik für den akademischen Unterricht* [Mu-
nich: Evangelischer Presseverband für Bayern, 1951] §94k).

grammar was pressed into service; thus the clause must be a CNC, and he translated, 'His eyes: they are looking' (§44.4). Moreover, his inflexible combination of the type of word (substantive), position (first in the clause), and pragmatic function (theme) proved a hindrance in his attempt to realize a consistent theme–rhēma analysis. The Spirit of God is not aforementioned in Gen 1:2c, but because of its position in the clause, it must be "something known" (§43.3.1.1). He simply fails to ask whether an alternate ordering of parts within the clause might have been possible. In short, incomplete designations of form, a failure to discuss the possibility of alternative ordering, and a priori assignments of function combine to form an inextricably subjective hodgepodge.

Replacing W. Hollenberg's (and K. Budde's and W. Baumgartner's) Hebrew school "textbook," which had enjoyed some 120 years of continued use, E. Jenni was much more discriminating in his grammar of 1978.[54] But in this attempt to update long-held textbook generalizations with the fruits of modern research, he too was unable to provide any kind of terminological or systematic clarification of these issues. Furthermore, he also jumbled the attributions of form and function. "The simple narrative or determinative statement, which gives prominence to no other clausal member except the verb, has the following basic scheme: verb–subject–predicate complements." The nominal subject occurring after the verb is an apposition to the pronominal subject contained in the verb form itself.[55] Verbal clauses in which the verb occurs after the first position are termed "inverted verbal clauses."[56] In the case of chiasm, one has two verbal clauses. Nevertheless Jenni translates יְהֹוָה נָתַן by way of the theory of the CNC: 'It is YHWH who has given'.[57] With sudden nonchalance, he adds "the possibility that the predicate of a nominal clause consists of an entire clause (nominal or verbal)," that is, the classic definition of the CNC, even though the term is not yet used here. As examples he names not only *pendens* constructions but also Ps 103:19, in which the subject and the locative precede the verb. And yet he translates as though it were a normal verbal clause: 'YHWH has built his throne in heaven'.[58] Ultimately he explains that it should be exclusively "a question of terminology, whether one wants to classify a sentence like Gen 18:17 (וַיהֹוָה אָמָר 'but YHWH thought . . .') as a CNC or rather as an inverted verbal clause, if only one distinguishes

---

54. W. Hollenberg, *Hebräisches Schulbuch* (24th ed.; Basel and Stuttgart: Helbing & Lichtenhahn, 1963); E. Jenni, *Lehrbuch der hebräischen Sprache des Alten Testaments: Neubearbeitung des "Hebräischen Schulbuchs" von Hollenberg-Budde* (Basel and Stuttgart: Helbing & Lichtenhahn, 1978).

55. Ibid., 60, §5.3.1.

56. Ibid., 71, §6.3.1.6.

57. Ibid., 72, §6.3.1.7.

58. Ibid., 108, §9.3.5.

them from common verbal clauses (Gen 18:20: וַיֹּאמֶר יְהוָה) in terms of their meaning."[59] In the end, then, it is just a matter of function. For more than a third of all Hebrew sentences with finite verbs, classifying them as nominal or verbal clauses amounts to mere terminological *quisquiliae*. If this is the case, must one not also ask if the distinction between the nominal and the verbal clause is, after all, as crucial a matter as is generally contended?

### 1.2.2. Extreme Advocates

In his dissertation of 1960, D. Michel primarily investigated the order of clausal members in the Psalms.[60] He expressly referred to the native Arabic grammarians, distinguishing between the verbal and nominal clause and the CNC accordingly. Discussing the verbal clause, he asserted that "the finite verb always occurs at the beginning of the clause; exclusively adverbial modifiers can occur before the finite verb. Should the actor (*Handlungsträger*) be explicitly signified, it then follows the verb in the attributive position."[61] He also includes prepositional objects among the "adverbial modifiers," next to temporal modifiers (Ps 22:5a: בְּךָ בָּטְחוּ אֲבֹתֵינוּ 'in you our fathers placed trust'). At first it seems as though this thesis extends further than its formulation suggests: all nonsubjects may precede the verb in a verbal clause. Put another way, as if the thesis is much tighter than it at first seems, this means: whether or not an order of clausal elements occurs as a verbal clause is decided only by the position of the subject. Michel did not attempt to establish this isolation of the subject. From the perspective of a valency grammar, that is, a grammar in which the verb is the dominating sentence core, such a thesis seems downright absurd.

"We call a CNC a sentence whose predicate consists of a full clause, nominal or verbal."[62] Along with Nyberg, Michel terms the preceding subject of the CNC the '*supra*-subject' (*Übersubjekt*), and it can (but need not) be identical with the subject of the verbal clause = predicate of the CNC. Attempting to establish this, Michel refers to the ostensible function of all such sentences: "The clauses, namely those in which the predicate is a finite verb preceded by the subject, relate not to a course of action; rather, they want to tell something about the subject by referring to an action."[63] Consequently Michel maintains in all seriousness: the verbal clause בְּךָ בָּטְחוּ אֲבֹתֵינוּ 'in you our fathers placed trust' relates the execution of an action, for the subject follows the verb, which

---

59. Ibid., 112, §9.4.9.

60. D. Michel, *Tempora und Satzstellung in den Psalmen* (Abhandlungen zur Evangelischen Theologie 1; Bonn: Bouvier, 1960).

61. Ibid., 177.

62. Ibid., 179.

63. Ibid. ("Die Sätze nämlich . . . berichten keinen Handlungsablauf, sondern führen eine Handlung zur Prädizierung des Subjekts an").

is preceded only by the prepositional object. To the contrary, the clause Ps 37:13a (אֲדֹנָי יִשְׂחַק־לוֹ 'the Lord derides him') is a CNC. It relates no action but instead predicates something about YHWH because, in this case, the subject occurs first. In Ps 74:17 (קַיִץ וָחֹרֶף אַתָּה יְצַרְתָּם 'summer and winter: You are the one, who has fashioned them'),[64] the *pendens* (here: direct object) is actually the *supra*-subject of the CNC. Admittedly, its predicate is a CNC as well.[65] Whether or not the Hebrew language supports this meaning through some indication of the syntactic surface structure is simply not asked: it is an aprioristic statement.

This a priori, circular argument becomes especially apparent at Ps 29:10ab (יְהוָה לַמַּבּוּל יָשָׁב וַיֵּשֶׁב יְהוָה מֶלֶךְ לְעוֹלָם). A partial chiasm of the two clauses allows two verbs to meet in the middle of the verse; both are different forms of the same root: יָשָׁב וַיֵּשֶׁב. Verse 10a, as a CNC, must express a state, whereas 10b must express an action, because it is a verbal clause. Michel distinctly points to the sequence of the CNC and verbal clause, claiming that "a state continues prior to, or at the entrance or realization of, the action." Without using a subordinate clause (which, however, is not indicated by the Hebrew), Michel cannot even express this with his translation: 'Since YHWH reigns over the original flood, so reigns YHWH as king eternally'.[66]

A. Niccacci's discussion of the issue is more discriminating, closer to the texts, and enhanced by a number of linguistic tools. But ultimately he has proposed, in a peculiar way, the most extreme position, one made all the more conspicuous by his use of prose texts.[67] On the one hand, he takes over the concept of the CNC, but in a more generalized form wherein the subject plays a less determinative role: "A verbal clause begins with a verb, a noun clause begins with a noun. A verbal clause tells us *what the subject does*, in other words, what the action is; a noun clause tells us *who the subject is*. If a noun is followed by a verb the noun clause is complex."[68] In his opinion, however (following German adaptations of H. Weinrich's grammatical theories in Hebrew), the sequence x-*qatal* (where x = any substantival constituent, frequently a noun phrase in the grammatical role of subject) is, on the other hand, typical for the type of utterance termed "report" in "discourse" (contrary to *wa=yiqtol* for the utterance of the type "narrative"); and further it would be inappropriate to maintain that in reports only subjects matter but never actions.

---

64. Cf. above, §1.1.2 on Kautzsch.
65. Michel, *Tempora und Satzstellung*, 181.
66. Ibid., 184.
67. A. Niccacci, *The Syntax of the Verb in Classical Hebrew Prose* (trans. W. G. E. Watson; JSOTSup 86; Sheffield: JSOT Press, 1990). Here I can only discuss the directly relevant sections of his hypothesis.
68. Ibid., 23. See on this point pp. 27–28 and 166–67: the nominal element that opens the CNC can be subject, object, or adverbial.

Thus he concedes that indeed Gen 3:13b, הַנָּחָשׁ הִשִּׁיאַנִי, could be held to be a verbal clause (answering the question: what is going on?), though, according to his own definition, it would probably be a CNC (answering the question: who is it, who has led you astray?).[69] In his summary he then returns to this point, only to name two groups of examples that have nominal elements before the verb and that, nevertheless, are not CNCs but rather verbal clauses: "the x-jussive YIQTOL construction . . . and the x-QATAL report construction."[70]

Thus it initially appears that for Niccacci the determination of clause-type lies in the grammatical, formal features of the constituent in clause-initial position. But a systematic, syntactic consideration reveals that formal features provide dubious assistance for Niccacci in the identification of clause-types; in fact, the pragmatic function of the clause is his decisive criterion. According to Niccacci, the noun that begins the CNC (which here should be strictly distinguished from *pendens* constructions) is always "emphasized"; and it plays the part of the predicate of the clause.[71] In so doing, he has taken what, since Kautzsch, has been the conventional syntactic interpretation of the category of the CNC and turned it on its head. He can now reformulate his definition of the types of clauses. And yet he means something entirely different by these words than, for example, what has been meant by them in the grammatical discussions of Richter or Waltke-O'Connor: "A clause is verbal when the predicate is a finite verb and nominal when the predicate is a noun."[72]

For Niccacci the predicate designates not the verb or the noun respectively (insofar as it agrees in number, gender, and person with only one other noun) but rather, what is new or important in the statement. Hence he can assert: "In Hebrew a finite verbal form is a predicate when it comes first in the clause. When, instead, it is preceded by an element of any kind (other than *waw*) the verbal form is not the predicate and therefore the clause is nominal (CNC)."[73] Three years later (and by simply postulating this thesis as opposed to proving it) he formulated his basic principle as follows: "The first position of the sentence belongs to the predicate in Biblical Hebrew."[74] Yet because elsewhere he acknowledges nominal clauses of the sequence "subject–predicate" (for

---

69. Ibid., 23–24. This consideration was still missing in the previously published Italian original, Niccacci, *Sintassi del verbo ebraico nella prosa biblica classica* (Studium Biblicum Franciscanum Analecta 23; Jerusalem: Franciscan, 1986) 17.

70. Niccacci, *The Syntax of the Verb*, 174–75.

71. Ibid., 28. Regarding the strict distinction of the *pendens* construction, see p. 148: "'Casus pendens' . . . does not really occupy the first position of the clause but is placed outside it ('extra-position') and reference to it is usually made by an anaphoric or resumptive pronoun." In principle I agree with this point.

72. Ibid.

73. Ibid.

74. Idem, "Simple Nominal Clause or Verbless Clause," 217.

example, circumstantial sentences), he must distinguish the predicate between "class and function." When and how he does so, however, is not clear in that he uses the same word (that is, *predicate*) for both. Thus one also fails to understand how he determines subject and predicate in individual cases without avoiding the circular argument inherent to his a priori assertion.[75]

He devotes the better part of his book to a detailed and penetrating study of verbal word order and verbal functions, of the types of texts such as narrative, report, and discourse, and of textual grammatical phenomena such as foreground–background. I must confess, however, that I have never understood how he combines these analyses in his argument with his definition of the types of clauses.[76] In 1991 Niccacci affirmed his system once again and carried this enduring terminological position to its conclusion: because the preceding noun in the CNC is the predicate, the finite verb is its subject![77] In discourse he further accepts that x-*qatal* and x-*yiqtol*, in the jussive as well as the indicative function, are not CNCs but verbal clauses. In so doing he changes the definition of the verbal clause: a clause is verbal if it contains a finite verb in the first position, *or* ("oppure") if it indicates the zero-grade (the first level) of communication.[78]

As such, his definition is unattractive because both of its halves depend upon completely different sets of rules. It is clear, however, that for Niccacci the performative functions of clauses are so fundamental in the configuration of larger segments of text that those functions determine the sentences as nominal or verbal clauses by the arrangement of otherwise formally identical sequences of clausal constituents. In the end, then, verbal clause and nominal clause are not form-designating but rather function-interpreting terms!

---

75. He concedes that this assessment of the initial or noninitial position of the finite verb does not apply in the case of Hebrew poetics, in idem, *Lettura sintattica della prosa ebraico-biblica: Principi e applicazioni* (Studium Biblicum Franciscanum Analecta 31; Jerusalem: Franciscan, 1991) v.

76. The examination of the relation of verbal form, verbal position, and verbal function, tied to the symbolization x-*qatal*, *yiqtol*-x, etc., rightly takes into account only the opposition initial and noninitial position in the clause and refers to the finite verb *as a word*. For these regularities, *wayyiqtol* (short form) // x-*qatal* and *w=qatal*-x // x-*yiqtol* (long form), it is uninteresting whether the "x" entering before the verb is a conjunction, interrogative particle, negation, *infinitivus absolutus*, or consists of one or more clausal members. To the contrary, the question of the relation between word order within the clause and clause-type is concerned with the finite verb *as a verbal predicate*, that is, *as a clausal constituent*. In this sense, however, a (for example) directly preceding negation or a directly preceding *infinitivus absolutus* belongs to the verbal predicate.

77. Niccacci, *Lettura sintattica della prosa*, 6. Cf. also p. 20: "Nella proposizione nominale complessa l'elemento 'x' reca enfasi ed è il predicato, mentre il verbo finito è declassato al rango di 'soggetto.'"

78. Ibid., 29.

## 2. Arguments against the Concept of the CNC

On the basis of grammatical theory, the most integral argument against the CNC would indeed emphasize that it is important to distinguish between linguistic levels technically and terminologically, even though they act together in concrete sentences. On the level of grammar, clauses are to be grammatically distinguished *not* according to the fortuitously encountered word at the beginning of an utterance but according to the type of word in the predicate. The predicate grammatically demonstrates its formal relationship to a noun in the clause, and its formal relationship with that noun is proved through the rules of grammatical agreement and independent from the respective speaker's specific intention. So defined, such nominal or verbal clauses, either individually in their changing realizations or acting together in a larger segment of text, may accomplish pragmatic functions that refer partly to the single clause and partly to the context. To that end, the concept of the CNC is misleading, because it unreflectively and inextricably mixes elements of the concrete utterance with the linguistic structure of the utterance itself, on the one hand, and it combines elements of the grammatical-syntactic linguistic levels with pragmatic ones, on the other. Many applicable observations about language enumerated by the Arabic grammarians all the way up to Niccacci could be noted, described, and interpreted, not on the grammatical level, where clauses distinguish themselves as nominal or verbal, but on the pragmatic level, which is likewise clearly structured upon rules. Such noting, describing, and interpreting could thus be done on the basis of (admittedly not yet clearly distinguished) criteria such as topicalization, topic-comment, theme-rhēma, given-new, focus-background, aboutness, functional sentence perspective, and so on.

However, by describing an analysis on the basis of these criteria, one could well get the false impression that the problem is merely one of terminology. This is not true for the following two reasons: (1) The concept of the CNC—especially one that is fixed on the position of the subject—is not fully applicable to Hebrew, where variation in the order of clausal constituents is characterized by a relatively high degree of freedom. As such, the CNC misjudges the syntactic structure of Hebrew clauses. (2) The concept of the CNC sets its sights almost exclusively on the first position in the clause (without precisely defining what that means) and frequently on the aspect of focus or emphasis. Neither of these is suited to the language. First, the initial position of the clause also serves other pragmatic functions. Second, the Hebrew language possesses the means to direct the focus on parts of the clause other than the first position. Neither the variety of linguistic phenomena nor their regularities can be suitably grasped within the limits of the CNC theory. In the following section, I attempt to demonstrate this through concrete examples.

**2.1.** Clauses with a Nominal/Pronominal Constituent
    before the Finite Verb

In a way that remains methodologically unacceptable, the advocates of the CNC mix the *syntactic* fact that a nominal or pronominal[79] constituent occurs before the finite verb with the *semantic* assertion that such clauses speak not of actions but rather of states of being (especially when it is the subject that precedes the verb); mixing both with the *pragmatic* thesis that such preceding constituents convey "emphasis." The semantic and the pragmatic theses in this generalization fail to hold true, as is demonstrated by both general considerations and concrete examples.[80]

*General Considerations.* Out of regard for the rules of syntax, one must distinguish between the obligatory and free positioning of the clausal constituents. Although obligatory positioning can also convey pragmatic effects, it is only in the free positioning of constituents that pragmatic functions are demonstrable and then only by attempts at exchanging the location of the constituents.[81] Research on living languages has demonstrated that the number of various sequences of clausal constituents that highlight a single point of focus is small. It has shown, too, that depending on the context, most sequences of clausal constituents varyingly allow for an extensive focal range. To this add the fact that there are neutral sequences of constituents that signal absolutely no point of emphasis. Contrasting pairs of clauses reveal that a clause can contain numerous points of contrast, the second or third of which generally follow after the verb. Clauses with *wa=yiqtol* or *w=qatal*-x can (necessarily after the verb) contain emphasized clausal constituents in which the emphasis is signaled (for example, through particles like גם).[82] In short, the search for points of emphasis may by no means be restricted to the first position of the clause.

One of the peculiarities of the Hebrew verbal system is seen in the following: there are no simple coordinating syndetic clausal sequences with the verb

---

79. In the following, I will speak only of nominal constituents. It should be understood that they may be pronominally realized.

80. The following examples are based on a more thorough examination of Deuteronomy, Judges, and 2 Kings, in my *Die Satzteilfolge im Verbalsatz alttestamentlicher Prosa* (Forschungen zum Alten Testament 17; Tübingen: Mohr, Siebeck, 1996).

81. The assertion that the verb in the initial position of the clause (for example, in *wa=yiqtol* or *w=qatal*-x clauses) carries emphasis is irrelevant because these verb formations require a clause-initial position of the verb out of grammatical and syntactic necessity; no clausal members fully integrated into the clause may precede these verbal forms but solely *pendentia*. To suggest otherwise would result in the questionable thesis that Hebrew *must* accentuate the verb in 'and- then' sequences.

82. Cf. C. H. J. van der Merwe, *The Old Hebrew Particle* gam: *A Syntactic-Semantic Description of* gam *in Gn–2Kg* (ATSAT 34; St. Ottilien: EOS, 1990).

in the first position; as a rule these occur only in the form of *wa=yiqtol* and *w=qatal* chains, but they also semantically indicate a progression ('and-then' sequence). Should the progression be interrupted and instead formulated as either an 'on the one hand–on the other' or a 'neither-nor' relationship of two circumstances, then the speaker of ancient Hebrew must break this chain by placing a constituent before the verb. In such cases, whoever explains that the preverbal constituent is necessarily emphasized indirectly makes the implausible assertion that Hebrew can only arrange clausal constituents—and *not* facts or actions (that is, complete sentences)—in such a way that they are either parallel to, or in contrast with, one another.

Undoubtedly, the strongest and most typical point of focus in the Hebrew clause is the position before the finite verb.[83] But this is just as true for all other clausal constituents as it is for the subject. In this regard, the Hebrew language offers no grounds for privileging the subject as such (and so doing amounts to the thesis of the CNC in its rigorous form). But above all else: the position before the finite verb does not signal focusing in every case,[84] for just as it does in living languages, this position also commands other functions in Hebrew. This fact should be verified in the following *select, concrete examples*.[85] It will then follow that the theory of the CNC is not applicable to the structure of the Hebrew verbal clause and that even the correct observations of the theory are interpreted from a narrow and distorted point of view.

(1) Whereas *ceteris paribus* a nominal constituent that is neither subject nor temporal modifier carries focus in nearly all cases, when a subject or temporal modifier precedes the verb this general rule does not apply.[86] The following cases demonstrate nonfocused subjects occurring before the verb:

(a) In asyndetic narrating or reporting clauses at the beginning of discourse:

---

83. This is the applicable observation that underlies CNC theory and that surely is not properly explained by it.

84. Cf. also J. Myhill, "Non-emphatic Fronting in Biblical Hebrew," *Theoretical Linguistics* 21 (1995) 93–144.

85. The citations are from W. Richter, *Biblia Hebraica transcripta: BHt; das ist das ganze Alte Testament transkribiert, mit Satzeinteilungen versehen und durch die Version tiberisch-masoretischer Autoritäten bereichert, auf der sie gründet. Genesis–2 Chronik + Sirach* (ATSAT 33/1–16; St. Ottilien: EOS, 1991–93).

86. Since the position before the verb is typically one of focus, these constituents are also focused in this position in the preponderant number of examples—but not strictly as a rule. For them, the clause-initial position is the neutral one. Because Hebrew verbal clauses dominantly have only one position for nominal constituents before the verb, the subject and temporal modifier occur in concurrence. If neither carries focus, then the temporal modifier precedes the verb and the subject follows the verb. I do not address examples with temporal modifiers because grammarians do not doubt that they can be unfocused before the verb.

(1)  1 Kgs 20:17d

אֲנָשִׁים יָצְאוּ מִשֹּׁמְרוֹן  Men have been coming out of
Samaria.

(2)  2 Kgs 1:6b

אִישׁ עָלָה לִקְרָאתֵנוּ  A man came climbing up toward us.

In discourse-initial clauses through which a brief narrative is begun, all members of the clause are rhēma, new information. They do not seek to convey a
descriptive statement about "a man" but to report a first action. Thus they answer the question "What happened?" In 2 Kgs 1:6b, this is especially clear,
because the messengers answer a directly preceding question of the king
("How is it that you're already back?").

(b) In asyndetic clauses that depict the answer to a request at the beginning
of discourse:

(3)  Judg 6:18a + e

אַל־נָא תָמֻשׁ מִזֶּה עַד־בֹּאִי אֵלֶיךָ  Please don't remove yourself from
... אָנֹכִי אֵשֵׁב עַד שׁוּבֶךָ  here, until I come to you. . . . I will
remain sitting here, until you return.

Because the preceding request is directed to the person who answers, the subject of the answering clause contains no new information. Rather, as theme it
is manifestly not emphasized although it is fashioned as an independent personal pronoun. Also, the context fails to correspond to the idea of reproduc-
tion evoked by the CNC thesis ("of me it is to be said: I will do it"). The
request does not suggest that the person asked should do something in contrast
to others who do not but that the person should complete a specified action instead of forbearing it.

(c) In causal כִּי-clauses that follow the clause they explain:[87]

(4)  Gen 43:5c

כִּי־הָאִישׁ אָמַר אֵלֵינוּ  For the man said to us.

(5)  1 Chr 5:9b

כִּי מִקְנֵיהֶם רָבוּ בְּאֶרֶץ גִּלְעָד  For their herds were numerous in
the land of Gilead.

(d) In syndetic clauses beginning a part of a narrative or a scene in which
the narrative function is determined as either background description[88] or as a

---

87. For these clauses, see also B. L. Bandstra, *The Syntax of Particle "KY" in Biblical
Hebrew and Ugaritic* (Ph.D. dissertation, Yale University, 1982).

88. Cf. here my "Syntaktische Erscheinungen am Anfang althebräischer Erzählungen:
Hintergrund und Vordergrund," in *Congress Volume: Vienna, 1980* (ed. J. A. Emerton;
VTSup 32; Leiden: Brill, 1981) 131–45. This is perhaps true for 2 Kgs 4:38a, for in 38b–c

relative narrative opening:[89]

> (6)  2 Kgs 4:1a
>
> וְאִשָּׁה אַחַת מִנְּשֵׁי בְנֵי־הַנְּבִיאִים     A woman from the women of the
> צָעֲקָה אֶל־אֱלִישָׁע לֵאמֹר          prophet-followers called out to Elisha.
>
> (7)  2 Kgs 4:38a
>
> וֶאֱלִישָׁע שָׁב הַגִּלְגָּלָה     Elisha returned to Gilgal.
>
> (8)  2 Kgs 4:42a
>
> וְאִישׁ בָּא מִבַּעַל שָׁלִשָׁה     A man came from Baal-Shalisha.

(e) In authoral commentaries that occur within the narrative itself and that are fashioned as syndetic verbal clauses:

> (9)  2 Kgs 10:19
>
> וְיֵהוּא עָשָׂה בְעָקְבָּה לְמַעַן     But Jehu acted in deceit in order to
> הַאֲבִיד אֶת־עֹבְדֵי הַבָּעַל       annihilate the servants of Baal.

Here, too, it is not to be paraphrased 'of Jehu it is to be said, that he acts deceitfully' but rather 'to this proceeding or to this command of Jehu it is to be said: Jehu acts deceitfully'.

(f) In syndetic clauses of the form *w*=subject–*qatal* that act as narrative recourse or supplement information:

> (10)  Josh 2:6a
>
> וְהִיא הֶעֱלָתַם הַגָּגָה     But she had allowed them to climb
>                              up to the roof.

Since Rahab has been referred to since v. 3 as either acting or herself speaking, she is not stressed as the subject in v. 6a. Instead of focusing attention on Rahab, the clause mentions an action that occurred previously in the narrative.

> (11)  1 Sam 4:18g
>
> וְהוּא שָׁפַט אֶת־יִשְׂרָאֵל     He had judged Israel for
> אַרְבָּעִים שָׁנָה            forty years.[90]

---

two clauses, one nominal and one participial, follow with a clear background function. These cannot be considered circumstantial clauses, for these must follow their referent clause; and 38c, on semantic grounds, cannot simultaneously be a circumstantial clause to 38a.

89. Since it is the beginning of an episode as opposed to the absolute beginning of a book; cf. H.-J. Stipp, *Elischa–Propheten–Gottesmänner: Die Kompositionsgeschichte des Elischazyklus und verwandter Texte, rekonstruiert auf der Basis von Text- und Literarkritik zu 1 Kön 20.22 und 2 Kön 2–7* (ATSAT 24; St. Ottilien: EOS, 1987) 361ff. This function is especially clear in 2 Kgs 4:1a (*w*=subject–*qatal*), because it explicitly introduces the first unit of discourse in the ensuing dialogue.

90. Rather often, I select examples with independent personal pronouns as the subject because, in such cases, it is semantically registered that this subject is mentioned in the

(2) As the selected examples demonstrate, the Hebrew language could form types of verbal clauses that, without focusing, placed the subject (and only the subject) in front out of syntactic necessity. The reason is that the subject, differing in this regard from all of the other verb-dependent constituents, can occur before the finite verb, not only when it is the point of focus, but frequently when it is used neutrally and without emphasis.

(a) To this group belong, for example, temporal clauses and the accompanying main clause in asyndetic temporal complex sentences of the type subject–*qatal*–*w*=subject–*qatal*.[91] Naturally, in such cases, the preceding subjects of the temporal antecedent clause and of the main clause can stand in opposition to one another and thus carry contrasting points of focus. But this clausal formation principally serves to place two actions in two clauses in a temporal relationship to one another. Of the following examples, it can at least be said that the preceding subject of the temporal antecedent clause is not focused:

(12) Gen 19:23

| | |
|---|---|
| הַשֶּׁמֶשׁ יָצָא עַל־הָאָרֶץ וְלוֹט | Barely had the sun gone down over |
| בָּא צֹעֲרָה | the land when Lot had arrived in Zoar. |

(13) 1 Sam 9:5ab

| | |
|---|---|
| הֵמָּה בָּאוּ בְּאֶרֶץ צוּף וְשָׁאוּל | Hardly had they come into the land |
| אָמַר לְנַעֲרוֹ | of Zuph, when Saul said to his servant. |

Here also the subject of the main clause does not carry emphasis, and it has no contrast, since the subjects of both clauses are partially identical.

(b) Here one should also mention circumstantial clauses with a finite predicate:[92]

---

preceding context. Futhermore, although a subject of this kind can also carry contrastive focus, personal pronouns demonstrate more clearly than personal names that the subject is not emphasized.

91. Cf. E. Kuhr, *Die Ausdrucksmittel der konjunktionslosen Hypotaxe in der ältesten hebräischen Prosa: Ein Beitrag zur historischen Syntax des Hebräischen* (Beiträge zur semitischen Philologie und Linguistik 7; Leipzig: Hinrichs, 1929) 33ff.

92. In contrast to the preceding century, when Hebrew grammars referred to such clauses as a sentence expressing a state (*Zustandssatz*) in the sense of the native Arabic grammarians and the CNC theory, since the late 19th century the term 'circumstantial sentence' (*Umstandssatz*) has come into general acceptance. Such "circumstances" could be "states" but are usually accompanying actions. In Hebrew, circumstantial clauses with a finite predicate seldom occur because, insofar as they designate simultaneous actions, they are almost always realized as participial clauses. This and the fact that the Hebrews also answered the question "What are you doing there?" with a participial clause (whereas the interrogative clause can also be formulated with x-*yiqtol* in the long form; cf. Gen 37:15–16) demonstrate that the participial clause should not be analyzed as a subgroup of nominal clauses. To my mind, the participial clause, in accordance with its form and function, forms its own category next to the nominal and verbal clause. Whether and to what extent a

(14) Josh 8:14ef

וְהוּא לֹא יָדַע כִּי־אֹרֵב לוֹ          But he did not know that an ambush
מֵאַחֲרֵי הָעִיר                         lurked for him behind the city.

(3) The position before the finite verb serves not only to focus but also, for instance, to connect (without regard to whether the preceding constituent refers to a subject or another part of the clause). This is especially clear where a constituent placed before the verb is identical with a constituent of the immediately preceding clause. In this case the constituent preceding the verb is not rhēma but theme—not new but old information.

(15) Exod 23:8ab

וְשֹׁחַד לֹא תִקָּח כִּי הַשֹּׁחַד יְעַוֵּר          And a bribe you should not accept,
פִּקְחִים                                 for a bribe makes the seeing blind.[93]

(16) 1 Kgs 12:1ab

וַיֵּלֶךְ רְחַבְעָם שְׁכֶם כִּי שְׁכֶם בָּא          And Rehoboam went to Shechem,
כָל־יִשְׂרָאֵל לְהַמְלִיךְ אֹתוֹ          for to Shechem had come all Israel
                                           in order to make him king.

(4) When actions are not represented as directly following one another but enumerated in relationships of "on the one hand–on the other" or "neither-nor," a nominal element of the clause appears before the finite verb. Should the clause consist only of a verb and of a nominal constituent that is not the subject, then even a nonsubject can appear before the verb without itself carrying emphasis.[94]

---

*syntactic* difference exists between the supplementing of information or authorial commentary and a circumstantial clause is a complex question that, given the few relevant formal characteristics, cannot be addressed adequately here.

93. See also the undetermined first occurrence and the determined resumption.

94. For the formal variants of enumerations, see my *Satzteilfolge im Verbalsatz*, 98–99, 199–200. Should the enumerating clauses contain more than one nominal constituent, then there is more than one possibility for realization; in such cases the clausal member around which the enumeration is organized precedes the verb. In 2 Kgs 23:12a and 13a both the verbs and the objects alternate next to a constant subject; from there the objects precede the verb. In 2 Kgs 25:10a, 11a, 12, 13a, and 15a, instead of the objects, it is in part the subjects and verbs that alternate; the different subjects refer in large part to the "new Babylonian conquerer," and their differentiation arouses no interest; from there the objects once again precede the verb. In 2 Kgs 17:30a, b, c, 31a, the verbs are identical, whereas the subjects alternate like the objects. Here the enumeration is organized around the subjects, which in each case occur before the verb. It thus seems questionable to me, whether or not it makes sense also to discuss such phenomena under the rubric of emphasis or focusing. In any case, nominal clause characteristics completely deviate from these types of sentences.

(17) Deut 7:5b–e

מִזְבְּחֹתֵיהֶם תִּתֹּצוּ וּמַצֵּבֹתָם     Their altars you should tear down
תְּשַׁבֵּרוּ וַאֲשֵׁירֵהֶם תְּגַדֵּעוּן     and their pillars break in pieces and
וּפְסִילֵיהֶם תִּשְׂרְפוּן בָּאֵשׁ     their Asherim fell and their graven
                                             images burn in fire.

(18) Deut 9:9bc

לֶחֶם לֹא אָכַלְתִּי וּמַיִם     Neither bread have I eaten nor
לֹא שָׁתִיתִי     water have I drunk.

**2.2.** Clauses with Two or Three Different Nominal Constituents
before the Finite Verb

Although this type of clause occurs very rarely in prose,[95] it is so frequent
in poetry[96] that without hesitation we may consider it viable for the syntactic
system of rules for Hebrew. In terms of syntactic and pragmatic considerations, this type of clause is of much interest. In §2.1 above, there arose a fact
familiar from other languages, though confusing: if a constituent is placed before the finite verb not out of grammatical obligation (for example, topicalized
כֹה or interrogative) but freely chosen, it may be used in a variety of pragmatic
ways, primarily for focus, but also, for example, to connect without focus.[97]
But in the clauses considered here, there could be additional factors at work.
There is, on the one hand, the first position of the clause, which is allocated for
topicalization; and on the other, the position directly before the verb, which is
allocated for a nontopicalized initial constituent. In his *Theory of Functional*

---

95. Without having undertaken a systematic search, I am familiar with the following
prose examples: Clauses with two different nominal constituents before the verb: Gen 5:1b;
7:8–9; 8:19; 14:10d; 17:6c; 23:6d; 31:29b, 42b; 35:11f; 41:11b; Exod 12:4c, 10b; 16:18d;
18:23d; Lev 17:11d; Num 22:33d; 30:9a; 36:7b, 9b; Deut 2:10; 2:28a, 28c; 12:22c; 18:14a;
24:16c; Judg 17:6b; 21:25b; 2 Kgs 5:13d; 8:12g; 14:6d; 16:15c; 25:10a, 30; Jer 31:30a;
34:5c; Ezek 1:9b, 12a, 17a; 3:18e, 19c, 19d, 20g, 21e; 4:11a, 16d; 5:2a, 4a, 12a, 12c, 12d;
6:6a, 10b, 12a, 12b, 12c; 9:10c; 10:11a, 22b; 11:21b; 12:6a, 18a, 18b, 19c, 19d; 14:14b,
20d; 16:43c, 51a; 17:21b; 18:7d, 11a, 16d, 19c, 30a; 20:7b, 8c, 39a, 11b, 11c; 22:31c;
33:26c; Ezra 4:3c; Neh 2:3b; 2 Chr 25:4e. Clauses with three different nominal constituents
before the verb: Lev 7:17; Num 28:15; 1 Sam 9:9; 1 Kgs 10:29, 20:40; Jer 48:36.

96. Cf. Bloch, *Vers und Sprache im Altarabischen*, 39; T. Collins, *Line-Forms in
Hebrew Poetry: A Grammatical Approach to the Stylistic Study of the Hebrew Prophets*
(Studia Pohl: Series Maior 7; Rome: Pontifical Biblical Institute, 1978) passim and tables
203–6; M. O'Connor, *Hebrew Verse Structure* (rev. ed.; Winona Lake, Ind.: Eisenbrauns,
1997) 342–44.

97. S. C. Dik (*The Theory of Functional Grammar, Part I: The Structure of the Clause*
[Functional Grammar Series 9; Dordrecht: Foris, 1989] 349) formulates this as a universal
norm for language as follows (P1 = "a universally relevant clause-initial position"): "If P1
is not occupied by some P1–constituent, it may be used for constituents with (Given) Topic
or Focus function."

*Grammar*, S. C. Dik has demonstrated that several languages have a further "special position" before the finite verb that is nonetheless outside the point of focus:

> The most common "extra position" is the position immediately before the Verb. Languages which have this position typically use it for Focus constituents, while using P1 [= clause-initial position] for Topic placement. Such languages have two special positions in the Prefield; constituents without special pragmatic function end up in the Postfield.[98]

It is true that nothing from Dik's models completely fits the Hebrew. However, it has aspects that do offer themselves for an analysis of pertinent Hebrew clauses. In what follows, Dik's claims will be examined solely for their incompatibility with the theory of the CNC. To this end I employ the 173 relevant instances in the book of Isaiah.[99]

At any rate, since verbal clauses in poetry predominantly have no more than two constituents besides the verb, 90% of these instances (even when not out of syntactic necessity) are de facto clauses wherein the finite verb occupies the last position. Tie this circumstance to the fact that none of the constituents occurring before the verb is pronominally resumed after the verb.[100] Add to this the fact that the syntactic dependence of a nonsubject constituent upon a following verb is most often indicated by means of a preposition or את. Taken together, these three facts make it extremely unlikely that the CNC theory can precisely analyze such a clause and accordingly unlikely that this theory is suitable for a language such as Hebrew, which counts such clauses among the constituents of its syntactic system.

For my argument I do not adduce instances in which the subject occurs at the beginning of the clause, since such constructions remain debatable. However, let us briefly examine two such instances—Isa 11:6b and 32:16b.

---

98. Ibid., 365.

99. Isa 1:15d, 27a; 2:18; 3:9b, 14a, 17b, 25a; 5:8b, 17b, 24a, 24c, 28c; 8:19c; 9:18c, 19e; 10:7a, 7b, 14b, 18a, 34b; 11:1b, 6b, 7c, 8b, 10b; 13:8d, 14b, 14c, 18a; 14:16a, 25c, 30b, 31d; 15:2b, 3b, 5a, 5d; 16:9c, 10d, 11a; 17:5b, 7b, 13a; 18:6c; 24:16a, 16h, 18d; 26:19f; 28:7a, 27b, 29a; 29:4e, 16b, 18b, 19b, 22c; 30:4b, 24a, 33b; 31:3h, 9a; 32:1b, 6a, 6c, 7b, 8a, 8b, 16b; 33:7b, 12b, 16a, 17a; 34:7c, 14b, 16d; 37:22d, 24c; 38:19b; 40:10a, 11a, 12b, 15c, 19b, 24f, 26e, 26f, 27d, 29b; 41:1e, 3c, 6a, 15d, 17c, 27c; 42:1d, 4d, 8b, 12b, 13a; 44:17a, 19h; 45:2a, 14b; 46:2d, 4b, 6b; 47:9b, 15c; 48:3a, 11c, 16c, 21c; 49:1c, 4c, 12a, 18f, 22e, 25d, 25e, 26b; 50:9c; 51:4c, 5c, 5d, 6c, 6d, 6e; 52:4c; 53:4a, 6a, 6b, 10f, 11d, 12e; 54:3b, 10c; 55:5b; 56:7d, 11e; 57:16c; 58:2a, 8b; 59:3d, 7a, 14b, 18c; 60:1d, 2d, 4e, 4f, 6b, 9a, 13a, 19b, 22c; 61:6a, 7c, 11b; 62:1d, 6b; 63:9c, 19f; 64:1b, 2b, 5d; 65:12b, 20b, 20c, 25b; 66:2a, 3f, 14c, 15a. In my "Ein verdrängter bibelhebräischer Satztyp: Sätze mit zwei oder mehr unterschiedlichen Konstituenten vor dem Verbum finitum," *JNSL* 23 (1997) 15–41, I have analyzed these clauses from a different perspective.

100. In this case there would be a *pendens* construction, but these will not be considered here.

(19) Isa 11:6ab

וְגָר זְאֵב עִם־כֶּבֶשׂ        And the wolf shall be a guest of the
                                        lamb,

וְנָמֵר עִם־גְּדִי יִרְבָּץ        and the leopard with the kid shall graze.

(20) Isa 32:16ab

וְשָׁכַן בַּמִּדְבָּר מִשְׁפָּט        And law shall dwell in the desert,

וּצְדָקָה בַּכַּרְמֶל תֵּשֵׁב        and justice in the orchard shall
                                        linger.

The advocates of the CNC theory interpret these sequences as follows: the subject functions as a *pendens* before a clause that is understood, for its part, as either (in the stricter theory) a verbal clause with a focused, preceding member[101] or as (in the expanded theory) a CNC.[102] To my mind nothing supports

---

101. The stricter theory does not consider this a CNC, because the subject does not follow the verb.

102. Muraoka (*Emphatic Words and Structures*, 40–41) has already objected to the attempt by Driver (*Treatise on the Use of the Tenses*, 280, §208.3) to construe the sequence "subject–object–verb" as a *pendens* construction—a subject in *pendens* position that is placed in a verbal clause with an object before the verb. In cases of clauses with the subject in the first position and then an additional constituent before verb, the translations of Isaiah commentators show that they certainly and frequently follow Driver's analysis. It is indeed important (in terms of the interpretation supported here that these examples are verbal clauses with several nominal constituents before the finite verb) that the examples call on a thesis proved for clauses with only one constituent before the verb. The subject can also occur unfocused before the verb:

Isa 1:15d        יְדֵיכֶם דָּמִים מָלֵאוּ        Your hands are full of blood.

Even when the text perhaps plays with nuances of meaning of כַּף and יד, ידיכם accomodates the object כפיכם from 15a. Moreover, מידכם occurs already in 12b. Thus 15d serves as a good example for the thesis that (at least in some clauses) the initial position serves to connect or resume (Given Topic) and that only the position directly before the verb serves to focus. The clause can be paraphrased (here without intending a syntactic interpretation of the clause as a *pendens* construction) 'of your hands it is to say: they are full of blood'. Only 'are full of blood' is focused.

Isa 8:19c        הֲלוֹא־עַם אֶל־אֱלֹהָיו יִדְרֹשׁ        Does not a people consult its
                                                        (ancestral) gods?

The clause is quite varyingly interpreted. But independent of whether אלהיו refers to YHWH, deified ancestors, or the gods of unknown peoples, or whether the following segment ('for the living the dead') runs parallel to it or stands in opposition to it, only the prepositional object carries the focus—not the undetermined subject.

Isa 56:7d        כִּי בֵיתִי בֵּית־תְּפִלָּה יִקָּרֵא        For my house will be called a house of
                        לְכָל־הָעַמִּים        prayer for all peoples.

The name of the house is YHWH's house of prayer (mentioned in 56:5a), which we know from 56:7b. Here, in 7d, it is asserted that it should serve as a house of prayer 'for all peoples'—this prepositional attribute alone serves as the second component of the doubled

such a view. But this is not to deny it completely, because a subject in *pendens* position must not be pronominally resumed—it is enough that there is congruence of the finite verb.

On the contrary, this way out is blocked in cases where another constituent inaugurates a clause in which the subject stands directly before the verb. Compare Isa 10:14b and 40:27d.[103]

(21) Isa 10:14b

| וְכֶאֱסֹף בֵּיצִים עֲזֻבוֹת | And like one gathers forsaken eggs, |
| כָּל־הָאָרֶץ אֲנִי אָסָפְתִּי | so the entire earth I have gathered. |

(22) Isa 40:27cd

| נִסְתְּרָה דַרְכִּי מֵיהוָה | Hidden is my way from YHWH, |
| וּמֵאֱלֹהַי מִשְׁפָּטִי יַעֲבוֹר | and my right eludes my God. |

In clauses of this sequence of members, the subject occurring before the verb does not have to be the point of focus:

(23) Isa 29:4e

| וּמֵעָפָר אִמְרָתֵךְ תְּצַפְצֵף | And out of the dust your speech shall (merely) peep. |

---

subject: 'house of prayer' (maybe) together with its word of reference is focused. This is reinforced by its separation from its word of reference and its sole position in the primary field (that is, after the verb), together with the exacting modifier 'all peoples'. But a constituent that follows the subject and precedes the verb can also be unfocused in this position:

| Isa 18:6bc | וְקָץ עָלָיו הָעַיִט וְכָל־בֶּהֱמַת | The birds of prey shall summer upon |
| | הָאָרֶץ עָלָיו תֶּחֱרָף | them, and all the beasts of the earth shall winter upon them. |

The two clauses in 6bc form a complete chiastic pair. If one observes the respective, clause-internal focus–background structure, the result is that both the subject and the verb are focused via contrast: the birds of prey summer—the beasts of the earth winter; the locative עליו remains the same but, unlike the subject, stands in the background. In spite of the difference in number, it is referentially identical to the subject in 6a, which cannot be focused there because it is not named but only indicated morphologically by the verb. The word order after the finite verb corresponds to these focused relationships, which have arisen out of the content of clause 6b: the separation of the subject from the verb by a pronominalized clausal unit signals the preferred position of a subject when it is focused, at least in prose; and a pronominalized nonsubject standing next to the verb is never focused when it is followed by the subject (Groß, *Die Satzteilfolge im Verbalsatz*, 290–91). The positioning of עליו before the finite verb in 6c is to be explained above all by the fully accomplished chiasm at 6bc. Whether this positioning of a pronominalized nonsubject follows general rules of word order in cases where *two* constituents precede the verb would require an investigation with a larger statistical basis than the book of Isaiah.

103. Further examples at Isa 11:8b, 10b; 15:2b; 16:9c; 24:16h; 29:18b, 22c; 31:3h; 40:26f; 42:4d; 46:4b; 49:25d, 25e; 51:5d; 53:4a, 11d; 60:9a; 64:1b, 2b; 66:2a, 3f.

Already in 29:4b and in 4c, both the locative modifiers 'out of the earth/under-world' and 'out of the dust' stand focused as the only constituents before the verb. In 29:4de both are taken up again in focus. Nothing suggests focusing in the case of 'your speech' in 29:4e.

Taken together with examples from the previous footnote, this strengthens the judgment that one-sided (even exclusive) concentration on the aspect of focus/emphasis obstructs a view of the manifold functions of the language and of the different rules governing it.

. Finally, there are clauses without a lexemically expressed subject in which two other constituents precede the finite verb. Compare Isa 15:5d and 42:8b.[104]

(24) Isa 15:5d

כִּי דֶּרֶךְ חוֹרֹנַיִם זַעֲקַת־שֶׁבֶר        Yea, on the road to Horonaim cries
יְעֹעֵרוּ        of ruination one lifts up.

(25) Isa 42:8b

וּכְבוֹדִי לְאַחֵר לֹא־אֶתֵּן        And my honor to no other shall
I give.

Both clauses demonstrate once again that, in its strict sense, the theory of the CNC errs when it isolates the subject in its alleged function from utterances with a finite verb in order to determine clause type.

The results of this second section may be summarized as follows: Largely independent of whether or not the occupying element is the subject, the positions before the verb will be filled according to pragmatic, stylistic (especially in poetry), and (less often) grammatical criteria. The question of whether a nominal constituent occurs before the verb (and if so, which constituent and on what grounds) has nothing to do with the question of whether the clause-type of the utterance is to be termed a nominal clause, verbal clause, or specifically a CNC. In short, because it contributes nothing toward our understanding of the structure and function of Hebrew sentences, the category of the CNC should be dismissed from Hebrew studies completely.

---

104. Further examples at Isa 10:18a; 24:16a; 32:6c; 40:11a, 12b, 15c, 26e; 41:1e, 3c, 15d, 27c; 42:1d, 12b; 44:19h; 46:6b; 48:3a, 16c; 49:4c, 18f, 26b; 58:2a; 61:7c.

# Are Nominal Clauses a Distinct
# Clausal Type?

CAMERON SINCLAIR

*Chapman University*

## 1. Introduction

It has been traditional in the study of Biblical Hebrew to recognize a basic distinction in clause-types between nominal and verbal clauses. Thus the classic traditional grammar of Biblical Hebrew, *Gesenius' Hebrew Grammar*, in the initial discussion of the syntax of the sentence divides the treatment of sentence grammar into three major parts: Noun clauses, Verbal clauses, and Compound Sentences.[1] Similarly, in Joüon and Muraoka, *Part Three: Syntax* of *A Grammar of Biblical Hebrew*, the initial discussion of clauses is divided into the same basic categories.[2] This distinction is often made in widely used introductory Hebrew grammars as well. Thus in C. L. Seow's introduction to Hebrew, nominal sentences are treated as a distinct type of clause, distinguished even from verbless clauses with predicate adjectives.[3] Bruce K. Waltke and M. O'Connor, in their recent study, *An Introduction to Biblical Hebrew Syntax*, also refer to the traditional distinction: "In a *verbal clause* the predicate is a verb" and "in a *verbless* (or nominal) *clause* there is no verbal marker of predication." They go on to point out, however, that

> Hebrew, like many other languages, including Latin and Classical Greek, may predicate a noun or adjective directly without a *copula* (that is, some form of

---

1. GKC 450–58, §§140–42.

2. P. Joüon, *A Grammar of Biblical Hebrew* (trans. and rev. by T. Muraoka; 2 vols.; Subsidia Biblica 14/1–2; Rome: Pontifical Biblical Institute, 1991 [hereafter, Joüon and Muraoka]) 561–86, §§153–55.

3. C. L. Seow, *A Grammar for Biblical Hebrew* (Nashville: Abingdon, 1987) 41. Seow uses verbless sentences for excellent pedagogical reasons in the early part of the grammar, however. Students read texts from the Hebrew Scriptures early in the course, while learning basic grammar, without having to master the more complex verbal paradigms until later.

היה, which corresponds to English 'to be'). In languages where the copula may be optional, it is usually required if the comment is set in past or future time in contrast to present time (or in some mood other than indicative), or if the situation is highlighted. The surface function of the copula is thus to mark the surface structure tense, mood or aspect.[4]

The discussion here clearly implies a different approach to the traditional classification. It is this perspective that I intend to develop at greater length in this paper, exploring the rationale behind it and supplementing the account of Waltke and O'Connor in certain ways.

## 2. Preliminaries

It is important to note that the traditional account does not misrepresent the facts descriptively. Most clauses occur with a verbal constituent, but clauses that occur without one are by no means infrequent, and they do take the kinds of nonverbal predicates generally listed in such descriptions. The question I want to raise, however, is the rationale behind the omission of a copula. What is omitted and how should this be represented in the grammar of Hebrew? In fact, I will argue that the simplest and most insightful way to describe nominal clauses is to regard them as essentially identical with a *subclass* of the clauses in which the verb היה can occur but has been omitted, thus creating the so-called nominal clauses. A single, unified description of the syntax of clauses employing the copula היה and of nominal clauses is clearly preferable, since it will enable us to account for all of the syntactic phenomena they each exhibit together, rather than treating them as if they were completely unrelated grammatical phenomena.

It should also be clear that the subclass of uses of the verb היה, to which I am referring, is its use as a *copula*. The English verb *to be* can be used just like Hebrew היה with meanings different from those associated with their uses as copulas. English examples occur in such expressions as *I think, therefore **I am***; ***To be** or not **to be***; *God **is***; *If it's going **to be**, it's got to be me*; and so on.[5] The situation is quite similar in Hebrew, where the most appropriate glosses for translation into English, for example, are expressions such as the following:

(1)  Isa 7:7

לֹא תִהְיֶה     it will not *happen*

(2)  Amos 3:6

אִם־תִּהְיֶה רָעָה בְּעִיר     when a disaster *occurs* in a city

---

4. B. K. Waltke and M. O'Connor, *An Introduction to Biblical Hebrew Syntax* (Winona Lake, Ind.: Eisenbrauns, 1990) 72.

5. The final example comes from the title of a recent publication.

(3) Gen 9:2

וּמוֹרַאֲכֶם וְחִתְּכֶם יִהְיֶה עַל
כָּל־חַיַּת הָאָרֶץ

And the fear and dread of you shall *fall* upon every beast of the earth

(4) Gen 1:5

וַיְהִי־עֶרֶב וַיְהִי־בֹקֶר

evening *came*, then morning *came*

(5) Isa 2:2

וְהָיָה בְּאַחֲרִית הַיָּמִים

it will *come to pass* in the last days

(6) Jer 1:11

וַיְהִי דְבַר־יְהוָה אֵלַי

the word of the LORD *came* to me[6]

The most important observation to make in all of these cases is that the absence of an overt predicate complement appears to evoke some sense of the *being* or *occurrence* of the subject in certain situations that partly overlap in English and Hebrew. The appropriateness of the glosses suggested in the standard lexicons, therefore, depends on the meaning and character of the subject. For this reason, it does not seem appropriate to refer to the expressions that occur for these uses of היה as definitions—more precisely, they are simply translation glosses, expressions of *existence, occurrence,* or *being,* determined by their congruence with the semantics of the subject and the use of idiomatic English. In addition, it appears that Hebrew idiom allows us to speak of the *existence, occurrence,* or *being* of an even broader range of phenomena than English does—periods of time, events, emotions, disasters, or the word of the LORD (to a prophet), and so on. This explains the need for a broader variety of appropriate glosses in idiomatic English to represent uses of היה in Hebrew that have no exact English parallel.

It should be noted, however, that even in such cases the meaning of the verb is substantially the same as in the Hebrew cases more closely parallel to English. The underlying meaning is that of *being, existence,* or *occurrence,* depending on the semantics and nature of the subject. Thus, when the subject is conceived as an *event*, the gloss 'occur' would be most appropriate in English. When it is conceived as a *state,* some expression of *existence* would be more appropriate in English.

When the subject of היה is a proposition, normally in the form of a clause, the verb is represented as the *impersonal* use in *The Dictionary of Classical Hebrew.*[7] For example:

---

6. Ludwig Koehler and Walter Baumgartner, *The Hebrew and Aramaic Lexicon to the Old Testament* (3 vols.; Leiden: Brill, 1994–96) 243.

7. David A. J. Clines (ed.), *The Dictionary of Classical Hebrew* (Sheffield: Sheffield Academic Press, 1995) 2.513–14.

(7) Gen 4:14

וְהָיָה כָל־מֹצְאִי יַהַרְגֵנִי:   It will be that anyone finding me
will kill me.

But again the basic meaning is the *occurrence, existence,* or *being* of the notion expressed in the proposition. Indeed, in such cases the content of the
proposition is really the underlying subject of the verb היה. It should be apparent that this analysis of היה accounts for the similarity between *be* and היה in
English and Hebrew. It also explains the underlying similarity of היה as a copula to its noncopular uses in Hebrew.

I am assuming in this discussion that verbless clauses are in fact complete
clauses with both subjects and predicates, just like any other clause with an
overt verb. It is not at all obvious what alternative analyses might be available
for these structures, given their autonomy and their ability to occur with adverbials of various kinds. Nevertheless, this view, which I assume will not be
controversial here, is requisite to the position I am arguing. A few examples,
will suffice to suggest one kind of evidence that supports this assumption:

(8) 2 Sam 23:14

וְדָוִד אָז בַּמְּצוּדָה וּמַצַּב     And David was *then* in the
פְּלִשְׁתִּים אָז בֵּית לָחֶם:   stronghold; and the garrison of the
Philistines was *then* in Bethlehem.

(9) 1 Kgs 19:9

וַיֹּאמֶר לוֹ מַה־לְּךָ פֹה אֵלִיָּהוּ:   And he said to him, "What are you
doing *here*, Elijah?"

(10) Deut 29:14

כִּי אֶת־אֲשֶׁר יֶשְׁנוֹ פֹּה עִמָּנוּ     (I am making this covenant) . . .
עֹמֵד הַיּוֹם לִפְנֵי יְהוָה אֱלֹהֵינוּ   with him that is standing *here* with
וְאֵת אֲשֶׁר אֵינֶנּוּ פֹּה עִמָּנוּ הַיּוֹם :   us *today* before the Lord our God,
and also with him that is not *here*
with us *today*.

The adverbials אָז in (8) and פֹה in (9) as well as פֹה and הַיּוֹם in (10) all show
that these are normal, complete predications.

## 3. Empty Forms

As already noted above, Waltke and O'Connor discuss nominal clauses
briefly in their study of the syntax of Biblical Hebrew. Like Andersen, they
refer to these clauses as *verbless* instead of *nominal* and point out that such

clauses occur in "many other languages including Greek and Latin."[8] They also quote the distinguished British linguist, John Lyons, to the effect that a verb in any language equivalent to *to be* "is not itself a constituent of deep structure, but a semantically empty 'dummy verb' " used "for the specification of certain distinctions" that are normally attached to the verb when no other word is available for this purpose. Since "sentences that are temporally, modally and aspectually 'unmarked' . . . do not need the 'dummy' carrier," it is generally omitted in such cases.[9]

Many other languages as diverse as Russian and Chinese also permit the copula to be omitted.[10] Such "dummy" forms, so-called because they are devoid of normal semantic meaning, exist both for morphological and syntactic reasons. In morphology they generally provide a base to which other morphemes can be attached, as Lyons observes. For example, in English the first verb in the auxiliary provides for a range of morphological and syntactic phenomena. Thus tense, agreement, negation, and sentence reassertion are all expressed by means of this verb. But if there is no auxiliary in deep structure, then the semantically empty auxiliary verb *do* is introduced as a base "support" to which tense, agreement, negation, or sentence reassertion can be attached, as in *He **did** go*, *He **didn't** go*. Similarly, the syntactic device that changes a declarative sentence into a so-called yes/no question—often requesting confirmation of some assumed state of affairs—is also expressed by the movement of the first auxiliary verb into initial position before the subject as in, ***Did** he go?* or ***Didn't** he go?*

The pronouns *it* and *there* also serve as empty forms in English in certain expressions such as *It's hot*, *It's too late*, *There's a man at the door*, and so on. These pronouns appear to convey no semantic content, merely fulfilling the requirement that English, unlike Hebrew, must always have a surface (overt) subject. As is well known, Hebrew permits its pronoun subjects to be omitted unless they are emphasized for some reason. Hebrew differs from English, however, in that it has a richer morphology than the latter, so that the person, gender, and number of the unexpressed pronoun can normally be inferred from agreement morphemes.

Finally, of special relevance to the discussion of nominal clauses is the fact that the formal study of logic by mathematicians and logicians, much of

---

8. Waltke and O'Connor, *Introduction to Biblical Hebrew Syntax*, 72; and Francis I. Andersen, *The Hebrew Verbless Clause in the Pentateuch* (Journal of Biblical Literature Monograph Series 14: New York and Nashville: Abingdon, 1970) 17–30.

9. John Lyons, *Introduction to Theoretical Linguistics* (Cambridge: Cambridge University Press, 1968) 322–23.

10. Personal communication with native speakers of these languages.

whose work has now been appropriated in the study of truth conditional semantics within contemporary linguistics, has long taken a quite similar view
of the verb *to be*.[11] In such works, nouns, adjectives, or prepositions, along
with the complements they require, serve as predicates of the propositions in
which they occur, while the verb *to be* seems merely to adjoin them to their
subjects. If these nouns, adjectives, and prepositions serve as predicates, the
role of *to be* appears to provide no meaning at all.

## 4. The ∅ Variant of היה

It is not clear, however, that היה and English *to be* even in their function as
copulas are merely dummy morphemes in the sense that they contain no information at all and are thus without representation in deep structure, as Waltke
and O'Connor, following Lyons, indicate. The English verb *to be*, though
lacking meaning similar to meanings in most other verbs, does play a role in
linking the subject to its class membership, to its identity, its location, and
various other functions expressed in the predicate, just as Andersen observes
in his study of verbless clauses.[12] Logicians refer to the *class-inclusion* property of the copula, for example, as its *isa* use, as in *A man **is a** mammal*. The
same property, of course, is present in the Hebrew copula היה, as well as in its
∅ representation in the so-called verbless clauses.

But a second analysis both of *be* and היה is possible. The analysis sketched
in Waltke and O'Connor, based on the observations of Lyons, assumes that the
copula is a dummy element devoid of any meaning and thus not a *constituent*
in the deep structure. But it is also possible to take היה as a constituent in the
deep structure that is *understood* though unexpressed in the surface structure.
Notice that two structures that occur in the same syntactic environment and
exhibit the same function and meaning may be treated as variants of the same
grammatical category even when one is empty (with no overt representation
whatever). This is most obvious at the morphological level. For example, the
plural morpheme in nouns is represented by a range of diverse forms in English: /-s/, /-z/, and /-əz/ for regular nouns, in addition to alternating vowels in
irregular forms such as *man, men, goose, geese*, and so on. But in addition to
these, we also have examples of singular nouns such as *sheep, fish*, and *deer*
that occur in identical forms with plural verbs, as in *The sheep **are** in the fold*,

---

11. See, for example, James D. McCawley, *Everything That Linguists Have Always
Wanted to Know about Logic but Were Ashamed to Ask* (2d ed.; Chicago: University of Chi-
cago Press, 1993); Gennaro Chierchia and Sally McConnell-Ginet, *Meaning and Grammar:
An Introduction to Semantics* (Cambridge, Mass.: MIT Press, 1990); James R. Hurford,
*Semantics: A Coursebook* (Cambridge: Cambridge University Press, 1983).

12. Andersen, *The Hebrew Verbless Clause in the Pentateuch*.

*The fish **are** in the pond*, or *The deer **are** everywhere*. In such cases we recognize that *sheep, fish,* and *deer* are plural despite the absence of any overt marker and use a ∅ morpheme to mark this reality in meaning and use.

Exactly the same use of a ∅ morpheme occurs in Hebrew grammar. We already noted that subject pronouns can be omitted in Hebrew because they are implied by the verb's morphology. In addition many nouns are unmarked for feminine gender, for example, ארץ, עיר, גמל, נהר. But though unmarked, these have to be treated as feminine because of gender agreement. In addition, many nouns are singular in form, for example, קהל, חיל, בקר, צאן, but are often treated as plural.[13] It is common to attribute such presumed "anomalies" to the collective meaning of these nouns and this does occur, for example, in some expressions such as English *The faculty is/are* . . . depending on whether they are acting as a unit or as individuals, but in many languages these differences are simply arbitrary. Contrast the difference between American and British collectives. American: *The team is winning, The government is planning.* But British: *The team are winning, The government are planning.* No *individual* or *unit* intent is expressible in such cases without using a different locution. Observations such as the ones in this paragraph suggest that the similarity between the function and/or meaning of היה and the ∅ copula in verbless sentences might well be treated comparably.

A similar phenomenon also operates at the syntactic level. This is clearest in cases of ellipsis, of various kinds. The ellipsis of the object of a transitive verb where it is obvious from the context is common in Hebrew, though the reality of its presence in meaning is no less real. Several examples of this phenomenon can be found in the following passage:

(11) 2 Kgs 4:39–41      (A companion of the prophet Elisha found some wild gourds in the field . . .)

וַיְפַלַּח אֶל־סִיר הַנָּזִיד . . .    and he cut [*them*] up into the pot of stew. . . .

וַיִּצְקוּ לַאֲנָשִׁים לֶאֱכוֹל . . .    Then they poured [*it*] out for the men to eat . . .

וְלֹא יָכְלוּ לֶאֱכֹל:    but they were not able to eat [*it*].

וַיֹּאמֶר וּקְחוּ־קֶמַח וַיַּשְׁלֵךְ אֶל־הַסִּיר    So he said, "Take some flour and throw [*it*] into the pot."

וַיֹּאמֶר צַק לָעָם וְיֹאכֵלוּ    Then he said, "Pour [*it*] out for the people so they can eat[*it*]."

וְלֹא הָיָה דָּבָר רָע בַּסִּיר:    And there was nothing harmful in the pot.

The brackets show five examples of transitive verbs with their objects ellipted in this brief passage.[14] The only way to make sense of such phenomena is to

---

13. For קהל and חיל used in agreement with plural verbs, see Exod 12:6 and 1 Sam 17:20, respectively.

14. I have discussed this and related phenomena in "The Valence of the Hebrew Verb," *JANES* 20 (1991) 63–81.

assume the presence of meaning that is inferred pragmatically though it is not overtly represented.

Another kind of ellipsis where meaning is readily observable though not overtly represented occurs in the grammatical process called gapping.[15] The following is an example in English: *Ed teaches a class in Hebrew grammar at the university in the fall and Bill in the spring.* The VP constituent of the second clause, *teaches a class in Hebrew grammar at the university,* is clearly present in the *meaning* of that clause even though it has been ellipsed in accord with the principles of English grammar.

Examples in Hebrew also occur, especially in poetry, where parallelism provides opportunities for its occurrence. Examples will illustrate this kind of ellipsis.

(12) Ps 146:3

אַל־תִּבְטְחוּ בִנְדִיבִים בְּבֶן־אָדָם    Don't put your trust in the powerful,
שֶׁאֵין לוֹ תְשׁוּעָה    in mortal man, who cannot save.

Notice that the admonition אַל־תִּבְטְחוּ 'Don't put your trust (in) . . .' is *understood* in the second clause, in which only the second prepositional phrase is overtly expressed.

(13) Ps 19:10–11

יִרְאַת יְהוָה טְהוֹרָה עוֹמֶדֶת    The fear of the Lord is pure, enduring
לָעַד מִשְׁפְּטֵי־יְהוָה אֱמֶת    forever; the judgments of the Lord
צָדְקוּ יַחְדָּו:    are true, altogether righteous;
הַנֶּחֱמָדִים מִזָּהָב וּמִפַּז רָב    more desirable than gold, than much
וּמְתוּקִים מִדְּבַשׁ וְנֹפֶת צוּפִים:    pure gold, sweeter than honey, than
                              that strained from the comb.

In these verses, יִרְאַת יְהוָה 'the fear of the Lord' is to be *understood* with עוֹמֶדֶת לָעַד 'enduring forever', and מִשְׁפְּטֵי־יְהוָה 'the judgments of the Lord' is to be *understood* with צָדְקוּ יַחְדָּו 'altogether righteous'. In the second line, the two topics יִרְאַת יְהוָה 'the fear of the Lord' and מִשְׁפְּטֵי־יְהוָה 'the judgments of the Lord' are *understood* with הַנֶּחֱמָדִים מִזָּהָב 'more desirable than gold' and the words מְתוּקִים מִדְּבַשׁ 'sweeter than honey', which are themselves *understood* with וּמִפַּז רָב 'than much pure gold' and וְנֹפֶת צוּפִים 'than that strained from the comb', respectively. In examples of gapping, ellipsis is defined in terms of the immediate context, while in cases of the ellipsis of היה, it is defined generally as a property of the sentence-type and its verb. Yet the two situations are alike in that a principle of grammar is available in both cases that allows for such ellipsis. Many other kinds of ellipsis exist, but these are

---

15. This is discussed with many examples in M. O'Connor, *Hebrew Verse Structure* (Winona Lake, Ind: Eisenbrauns, 1980) 401–7.

sufficient to illustrate the phenomenon as well as to show the plausibility of treating verbless clauses as a case of the simple ellipsis of the copula when it is not needed to provide morphological information that would have to be attached to the overt verb היה, were it present.

## 5. Complements as Syntactic Properties

Finally, it is important to note that just as a given verb may have more than one meaning, it may take a number of different types of syntactic complements. Where a verb subcategorizes for more than one type of complement, and ellipsis is not involved, the verb often exhibits a difference in meaning, though at times it may be subtle.[16] Thus there is often a correlation between the complements a verb takes and its meanings. This can be illustrated using two well-attested verbs, נתן 'to give' (something) to a person, 'to put/ place' (something) in a location, 'to allow' (someone) to do something; and ידע 'to know' a proposition, a person, or how to do (something). Consider the following prototypical examples of the syntax of נתן:

(14) Gen 28:4

וְיִתֶּן־לְךָ אֶת־בִּרְכַּת אַבְרָהָם    May he give to you the blessing of Abraham.

In its most common meaning, 'to give', illustrated here, the verb נתן takes a direct object, marked here by אֶת־; as well as an indirect object, normally introduced by the preposition ל (sometimes אֶל). But when נתן means 'to set' or 'to place', it takes a direct object and a prepositional phrase indicating a *location*, as in example (15):

(15) Gen 1:17

וַיִּתֵּן אֹתָם אֱלֹהִים בִּרְקִיעַ    Then God placed them in the dome
הַשָּׁמָיִם    of the heavens.

And נתן is also used with direct object and infinitive complements to express *permission*, as in the following example:

---

16. An example from English is the verb *to grow*, which occurs as an intransitive verb in *Fruit grows well in Florida*, but as a transitive verb with **causative** meaning in *Ed grows fruit in his yard* and with a still different meaning when it takes an adjective, as in *Ed grew angry*, where the verb means roughly *became*. The verb *to turn* has syntactic properties and meanings that are strikingly parallel to *to grow*. There is a set of English verbs—*give, lend, send*, and others—that take both direct and indirect object complements; another group—*put, set, place*, and others—take a direct object and location complements; a group—*think, believe, hope*, and others—that take clause objects; and a set—*want, expect, like*—that takes an infinitive complement; to name only a few of the syntactic subcategories of verbs that must be recognized in English, and in many other languages.

(16) Job 9:18

לֹא־יִתְּנֵנִי הָשֵׁב רוּחִי    He will not allow me to catch my
breath.

While these comments do not exhaust what can be said about the syntactic
structure of נתן, they do define its major syntactic properties.

The verb ידע also exhibits distinctive syntactic properties, as the following
show:

(17) Ezek 30:8

וְיָדְעוּ כִּי־אֲנִי יְהוָה    Then they will know that I am the
LORD.

(18) Gen 29:5

וַיֹּאמֶר לָהֶם הַיְדַעְתֶּם אֶת־לָבָן    Then he said to them, "Do you
בֶּן־נָחוֹר    know Laban the son of Nahor?"

(19) Jer 4:22

חֲכָמִים הֵמָּה לְהָרַע וּלְהֵיטִיב    They are clever doing evil but how
לֹא יָדָעוּ    to do good, they do not know.

The most basic syntactic distinction in the use of ידע is its ability to take both
a clausal object, as in (17), and a noun object, as in (18), where knowing
someone means to be acquainted with that person. Infinitives are also nouns,
but they allow for clausal structure in ways that simple nouns do not, so they
should probably be distinguished, as in example (19). These two verbs illustrate how verbs subcategorize for the different kinds of complements they can
take, often with quite different meanings.

Just as in the above examples, the set of complements a given verb can take
is for the most part fairly clear for well-attested verbs. The range of complements that the verb היה can take is especially significant because it is so well
attested and takes such a broad array of complement types. The fact that the
predicates of verbless clauses are at least equally well attested and just as
broad in type as the predicates of היה and the fact that they can occur with essentially the same array of complement types as היה are, therefore, compelling
evidence that היה in its use as a copula and the predicate of verbless sentences
are in fact identical—the result of the omission of the former in the creation of
the latter.

If, as I have argued, the set of complement types permitted with היה is
identical to the types that occur in nonverbal sentences, it makes a great deal
more sense to think of such verbless clauses in Hebrew as the result of the
omission of the underlying copula היה, a phenomenon common to many languages for essentially the same reason, rather than to assume that Hebrew
clauses in general are to be classified into two general types, one with verbs
and the other without them at all. In other words, it makes more sense to see

verbless clauses as a phenomenon of the verb היה rather than as implying a basic dichotomy in the clause-types of the language as a whole, as the traditional description implies.

## 6. Types of Complements of היה and Their Reflexes in Verbless Clauses

Among these sets of complements of היה are: noun phrases, adjective phrases, adverbial phrases, numeral quantifiers, prepositional phrases, and participles. All of these complement constituents occur with their own potential complements and adjuncts. In the following examples, I provide a substantial number of examples exhibiting the virtual identity of the complement types taken by היה and the types that occur in the predicates of nonverbal sentences. Since there are no other verbs with such a broad array of complements, let alone identical syntactic complement types, this evidence is compelling.

In the presentation of the examples below I will first provide a set of examples exhibiting clauses or sentences with the verb היה overtly present and in construction with a number of examples from one of the types of complements it takes. I will then present a second set of examples—this time of verbless sentences, exhibiting complements to the ∅ copula that I claim serves as a variant to היה. It is important to note that the *verbal identity* of complements with and without היה can never be achieved, since we cannot today assess the knowledge of native speakers of BH, which do not exist. But it is also important to note that it is identity of complement-types that is required, not verbal identity.

The status of the ∅ predicate as complement will be obvious since a predicate can only occur in verbless sentences if a complement of some kind is present. Without such complements, there would be no predicate and thus no verbless clause at all. As already noted, the predicate complement of ∅ may take additional complements of its own as well. When these additional complements occur, I will often identify their status as such—normally, by providing some evidence that they are required either by the complement that forms the predicate of the verbless clause or by one of the predicate's own complements, if any occur. Adjuncts also occur with some frequency in these predicates, but they cannot form the predicate alone. If they did, they would be complements by definition.[17] Their optional status disallows their service as

---

17. The fundamental distinction between *complements* and *adjuncts* is the fact that complements are required to *complete* their heads while *adjuncts* are always optional and can occur in any order except between the complement and its head—at least in deep structure. Since one cannot have a nominal sentence without a predicate, some part of the predicate is always a complement within the verbless clause.

complements.[18] When adjuncts do occur, they frequently assume the form of prepositional phrases.[19] Prepositional phrases qualify noun phrases or verb phrases. When they modify verb phrases, they are always adverbial in function. I will identify many adjuncts among the following examples, though it will not always be possible to ascertain whether a constituent is a complement or an adjunct with complete certainty. This is because the available data may be too limited and new data cannot be created to help decide these cases conclusively.

## 7. Evidence of Complement Types

### 7.1a. Noun Phrases as Predicate Complements of היה

Since these are among the most familiar and frequent complements of היה, just a few examples are provided. These complements are typically used to express identity, class membership, relationships, descriptions, status, and a host of other identifying or characterizing phenomena. They also appear in a few idiomatic expressions.

(20) Josh 17:1

כִּי הוּא הָיָה אִישׁ מִלְחָמָה    because he was a man of war

מִלְחָמָה is clearly a complement of אִישׁ within the predicate complement, giving אִישׁ its distinctive meaning.

(21) 1 Sam 17:42

כִּי־הָיָה נַעַר    for he was a youth

(22) 2 Sam 4:4

בֶּן־חָמֵשׁ שָׁנִים הָיָה    He was five years old.

חָמֵשׁ שָׁנִים is a complement within the predicate idiom.

(23) Judg 11:1

וְיִפְתָּח הַגִּלְעָדִי הָיָה גִּבּוֹר חַיִל    Now Jephthah the Gileadite was a mighty warrior.

This is an obvious example of a descriptive complement.

(24) 2 Sam 8:10

כִּי־אִישׁ מִלְחָמוֹת תֹּעִי הָיָה    For Hadadezer was a man of wars
הֲדַדְעָזֶר    with Toi.

---

18. Adjuncts are *optional* in the sense that they are not required by the syntax of the predicate or any of its constituent members, though they may be required for the writer to communicate what s/he has in mind.

19. I will use the expression *prepositional phrase* to apply to both separable and inseparable prepositions and their complements in Hebrew.

The complement NP appears to function as an adverbial in this example: 'had been at war with Toi'. It is probably an idiomatic expression.

(25)  1 Sam 6:9

מִקְרֶה הוּא הָיָה לָנוּ   it was a chance happening to us

The predicate NP מִקְרֶה is the complement of the verb, but לָנוּ does not appear to be a complement to it.

(26)  Gen 35:10

כִּי אִם־יִשְׂרָאֵל יִהְיֶה שְׁמֶךָ   but Israel will be your name

When the predicate is a personal name, an inalienable possession, the verb היה is frequently omitted. This example shows that it can be included if needed.

(27)  Exod 1:5

וַיְהִי כָּל־נֶפֶשׁ יֹצְאֵי יֶרֶךְ־יַעֲקֹב   And all the people born to Jacob
שִׁבְעִים נָפֶשׁ   were seventy persons.

I assume that the clause following וַיְהִי is its subject. It also contains a construct participle with its complement in the genitive relation. The participial phrase qualifies כָּל־נֶפֶשׁ in this example but as an identifying adjunct. The predicate complement of the main clause is a numerically quantified NP.

**7.1b.** Noun Phrases as Predicate Complements in Verbless Clauses

These are also very common and appear to express the full range of possible complements.

(28)  1 Sam 9:2a

וּשְׁמוֹ שָׁאוּל   and his name was Saul

The complement שָׁאוּל serves to provide simple identity here.

(29)  2 Sam 13:20

אָחִיךְ הוּא   he is your brother

Similarly this complement, אָחִיךְ, provides identity in terms of this relationship.

(30)  Gen 42:32

שְׁנֵים־עָשָׂר אֲנַחְנוּ אַחִים   We are twelve brothers.

Here אַחִים serves as the identifying complement head of the NP, of which שְׁנֵים־עָשָׂר is a numeral qualifier, though it is separated from its head, probably to provide focus.

(31)  Gen 46:27

וּבְנֵי יוֹסֵף אֲשֶׁר־יֻלַּד־לוֹ בְמִצְרַיִם   and the sons of Joseph, who were born
נֶפֶשׁ שְׁנָיִם   to him in Egypt, were two persons

The predicate complement provides new numerical information.

(32) Deut 4:6

עַם־חָכָם וְנָבוֹן הַגּוֹי    This great nation is a people of
הַגָּדוֹל הַזֶּה    wisdom and understanding.

The predicate is a compound complement NP. The use of such constructions is often said to be due to the poverty of adjectives in Hebrew. Predicate adjectives do occur in Hebrew, as the following examples show, but they are less common than in many other languages.

(33) Josh 17:1

כִּי־הוּא בְּכוֹר יוֹסֵף    for he was the firstborn of Joseph

This note of identity is in all probability an indicator of status. The predicate is obviously a complement. Relational nouns like בְּכוֹר often imply some complement, just as *He was **the son/father/child of*** expects some complement.

(34) Judg 11:1

וְהוּא בֶּן־אִשָּׁה זוֹנָה    and he was the son of a prostitute

This note of identity is also a clear case of a complement with its own complement, used here as an indicator of (low) status.

(35) Gen 5:1

זֶה סֵפֶר תּוֹלְדֹת אָדָם    This is the book of the generations
of Adam.

A word in the construct requires a (genitive) complement by definition. זֶה is very frequently used without היה but may be used with it if needed, as in Exod 10:7.

(36) Num 4:15

אֵלֶּה מַשָּׂא בְנֵי־קְהָת    These are the things in the tent of
בְּאֹהֶל מוֹעֵד    meeting to be carried by the
Kohathites.

The construct here apparently takes the subjective genitive as its complement. The בְנֵי־קְהָת will be doing the carrying to which מַשָּׂא clearly alludes. The genitive status of בְנֵי־קְהָת requires that it be recognized as a complement.

(37) Gen 6:4

הֵמָּה הַגִּבֹּרִים אֲשֶׁר מֵעוֹלָם    these are the mighty men that were
אַנְשֵׁי הַשֵּׁם    of old, men of renown

The use of the definite article in this context suggests that the predicate is a referring expression—that is to say, these are the heroic figures everyone has heard about.

(38) Exod 16:16

זֶה הַדָּבָר אֲשֶׁר צִוָּה יְהֹוָה     This is the thing which the LORD has commanded.

The subject is deictic; the predicate is a referring expression with a relative clause.

(39) Exod 15:3

יְהֹוָה אִישׁ מִלְחָמָה     The LORD is a man of war.

The predicate complement is a characterizing metaphor consisting of a head noun with its genitive complement. Compare the same construction in (20) above with היה.

(40) Deut 33:22

דָּן גּוּר אַרְיֵה     Dan is a lion's cub.

Like the previous example, this is a metaphorical characterization whose complement is a genitive phrase.

**7.2a.** Adjective Phrases as Predicate Complements of היה

(41) Gen 3:1

וְהַנָּחָשׁ הָיָה עָרוּם מִכֹּל     Now the serpent was more crafty
חַיַּת הַשָּׂדֶה     than any other wild animal.

The comparative meaning of the adjective is indicated by its integration with the following prepositional phrase as its complement.

(42) Josh 19:9

כִּי־הָיָה חֵלֶק בְּנֵי־יְהוּדָה     because the portion of the sons of
רַב מֵהֶם     Judah was too large for them

The comparison expressed by רַב מֵהֶם is a complement to the verb.

(43) 1 Sam 3:1

וּדְבַר־יְהֹוָה הָיָה יָקָר בַּיָּמִים     And the word of the LORD was rare
הָהֵם     in those days.

The adjectival status of יָקָר is clear, but the prepositional phrase בַּיָּמִים הָהֵם is an adjunct to the verb rather than a complement like יָקָר.

**7.2b.** Adjective Phrases as Predicate Complements in Verbless Clauses

(44) Gen 2:18

לֹא־טוֹב הֱיוֹת הָאָדָם לְבַדּוֹ     It is not good for the man to be alone.

The subject here is an infinitive clause using היה in its infinitive form with an adverb complement. The infinitive clause subject has a negative adjective complement as predicate.

(45) Gen 29:19

טוֹב תִּתִּי אֹתָהּ לָךְ מִתִּתִּי אֹתָהּ    It is better that I give her to you than
לְאִישׁ אַחֵר    that I should give her to any other man.

The predicate adjective טוֹב occurs here in the comparison between the propositions expressed in the two clauses. The first clause is its subject and the second its comparative complement.

(46) Num 9:13

וְהָאִישׁ אֲשֶׁר־הוּא טָהוֹר    but the man who is clean . . .

The adjective here occurs as the predicate complement of a verbless relative clause.

(47) 1 Sam 9:2a

וְאֵין אִישׁ מִבְּנֵי יִשְׂרָאֵל    And there was not a man among the
טוֹב מִמֶּנּוּ    Israelites more handsome than he . . .

The comparative adjective complement occurs here in the predicate of a negative verbless clause. On the other hand, the prepositional phrase מִבְּנֵי יִשְׂרָאֵל qualifying אִישׁ is not its complement, though it is similar in form to the complement following the predicate adjective טוֹב.

(48) 1 Sam 9:2b

[וְאֵין אִישׁ מִבְּנֵי יִשְׂרָאֵל טוֹב    from his shoulders and above he
מִמֶּנּוּ] מִשִּׁכְמוֹ וָמַעְלָה גָּבֹהַּ    was taller than any of the people
מִכָּל־הָעָם

The adjective complement in the second half of this text also takes a comparative complement, מִכָּל־הָעָם. The subject of the predicate גָּבֹהַּ is in the previous clause.

(49) Ezek 9:9

עֲוֹן בֵּית־יִשְׂרָאֵל וִיהוּדָה    The guilt of the house of Israel and
גָּדוֹל בִּמְאֹד    Judah is exceedingly great.

This is a straightforward example of a modified predicate adjective complement. The two genitive expressions following the construct עֲוֹן in the subject of the nominal clause are also complements of its head, עֲוֹן.

(50) Gen 33:13

אֲדֹנִי יֹדֵעַ כִּי־הַיְלָדִים רַכִּים    My Lord knows that the children
are frail.

A simple predicate adjective complement in an embedded object clause.

**7.3a.** Prepositional Phrases as Predicate Complements of היה

(51) Exod 1:5

וְיוֹסֵף הָיָה בְמִצְרָיִם     And Joseph was in Egypt.

The prepositional phrase is the predicate complement expressing the thematic role, location.

(52) Exod 10:23

וּלְכָל־בְּנֵי יִשְׂרָאֵל הָיָה אוֹר     But for all the Israelites there was

בְּמוֹשְׁבֹתָם     light in their dwellings.

אוֹר is the subject of היה here, and בְּמוֹשְׁבֹתָם is its predicate complement.

(53) Isa 5:1

כֶּרֶם הָיָה לִידִידִי בְּקֶרֶן     My beloved had a vineyard on a

בֶּן־שָׁמֶן     very fertile hill.

The prepositional phrase used to express possession, לִידִידִי, serves also as the complement to the verb היה in this sentence, but the prepositional phrase, בְּקֶרֶן בֶּן־שָׁמֶן, is clearly an adjunct.

(54) Num 32:1

וּמִקְנֶה רַב הָיָה לִבְנֵי רְאוּבֵן     Now to the Reubenites and the

וְלִבְנֵי־גָד עָצוּם מְאֹד     Gadites belonged innumerable cattle.

The common means of expressing possession by means of the prepositional phrase introduced by ל occurs here. This clearly shows these two prepositional phrases to be conjoined complements of the same verb.

(55) Josh 5:1

וְלֹא־הָיָה בָם עוֹד רוּחַ מִפְּנֵי     And there was no longer any spirit

בְּנֵי־יִשְׂרָאֵל     in them, because of the Israelites.

The subject רוּחַ follows the copula and the prepositional phrase בָם, which is clearly a complement. The following prepositional phrase, מִפְּנֵי בְּנֵי־יִשְׂרָאֵל, is only an adjunct.

(56) Josh 10:14

וְלֹא הָיָה כַּיּוֹם הַהוּא לְפָנָיו     There has not been a day like that

וְאַחֲרָיו     day before or after.

The ellipted subject יוֹם is anticipated from the object of the prepositional phrase כַּיּוֹם הַהוּא. Though the prepositional phrase כַּיּוֹם הַהוּא itself must be a complement, the adverbials associated with it are not.

(57) Josh 22:20

וְעַל־כָּל־עֲדַת יִשְׂרָאֵל הָיָה קָצֶף    and wrath was upon all the
congregation of Israel

The subject of the clause follows the verb, and the prepositional phrase predicate, which is a complement, precedes it.

(58) Judg 6:40

וְעַל־כָּל־הָאָרֶץ הָיָה טָל    and there was dew on all the ground

The subject follows the verb, and the prepositional phrase predicate complement precedes it, just as in the previous example.

(59) 1 Sam 9:2

וְלוֹ־הָיָה בֵן    He had a son.

The same order as in the two previous examples. The prepositional phrase is the predicate complement to the verb.

(60) 1 Sam 18:12

כִּי־הָיָה יְהוָה עִמּוֹ    because the Lord was with him

The predicate prepositional phrase again serves as the complement to the verb.

(61) 1 Sam 20:13

וִיהִי יְהוָה עִמָּךְ כַּאֲשֶׁר הָיָה    May the Lord be with you, as he
עִם־אָבִי    has been with my father.

Two illustrations occur in this brief two-clause example. Both prepositional phrases are complements of their respective verbs.

(62) 2 Sam 6:23

וּלְמִיכַל בַּת־שָׁאוּל לֹא־הָיָה    And Michal the daughter of Saul
לָהּ יָלֶד עַד יוֹם מוֹתָהּ    had no child to the day of her death.

The subject of the verb is יָלֶד, and the predicate complement is בַּת־ וּלְמִיכַל שָׁאוּל, recapitulated in a resumptive prepositional phrase לָהּ. Another prepositional phrase, עַד יוֹם מוֹתָהּ, is an adjunct serving as an adverbial of duration and modifying the negated verb of the clause.

(63) 2 Sam 13:20

הַאֲמִינוֹן אָחִיךְ הָיָה עִמָּךְ    Has Amnon your brother been with
you?

The prepositional phrase עִמָּךְ serves as the predicate and complement to the verb of the clause.

(64) 2 Sam 14:25

מִכַּף רַגְלוֹ וְעַד קָדְקֳדוֹ
לֹא־הָיָה בוֹ מוּם

from the sole of his foot to the
crown of his head there was no
blemish in him

The predicate prepositional phrase בוֹ is a complement to the verb of the
clause, but the two initial prepositional phrases are adjuncts.

(65) Num 9:13

וּבְדֶרֶךְ לֹא־הָיָה    and he was not on a journey

The subject is inferred from the number and gender agreement of the verb.
The prepositional phrase בְדֶרֶךְ is the predicate complement.

### 7.3b. Prepositional Phrases as Predicate Complements in Verbless Clauses

(66) Deut 29:28

הַנִּסְתָּרֹת לַיהוָה אֱלֹהֵינוּ
וְהַנִּגְלֹת לָנוּ וּלְבָנֵינוּ עַד־עוֹלָם

The secret things belong to the
LORD our God, but the revealed
things belong to us and to our
children forever.

This sentence consists of two predicate prepositional phrase complements
of the Ø copulas expressing possession of the two subjects. The second predicate is actually a compound composed of two conjoint prepositional phrases.
The two predications are conceptually united by their contrasting roles. A
third prepositional phrase עַד־עוֹלָם acts as an adverbial of duration apparently
modifying both predications and serving as an adjunct, not a complement of
these predications.

(67) Num 5:8

אִם־אֵין לָאִישׁ גֹּאֵל לְהָשִׁיב
הָאָשָׁם אֵלָיו הָאָשָׁם הַמּוּשָׁב
לַיהוָה לַכֹּהֵן

If the injured party has no next of
kin to whom restitution may be
made for the wrong, the restitution
for wrong belongs to the LORD for
the priest . . .

This sentence consists of two verbless clauses in a conditional sentence exhibiting somewhat complex syntax. In the protasis, a possible situation is explored, namely, one in which there might be no גֹּאֵל (a next of kin who could
act to secure "damages" on behalf of the aggrieved relative). The subject of the
protasis is גֹּאֵל, with an infinitive phrase complement לְהָשִׁיב הָאָשָׁם אֵלָיו having a prepositional phrase complement of its own, אֵלָיו. Its predicate is לָאִישׁ,
a prepositional phrase expressing "possession" and serving as a complement
to the Ø copula in the negative clause. The apodosis (or proposed resolution)

is that in such cases any "damages to be paid back" go to the L<small>ORD</small> for the priests. The subject of the apodosis is הָאָשָׁם הַמּוּשָׁב 'the damages to be paid back', and the predicate complement of the ∅ copula in this clause is the prepositional phrase לַיהוָה, also expressing "possession." But this clause concludes with an additional prepositional phrase לַכֹּהֵן, which is an adjunct of the predication in the apodosis.

(68) Gen 25:23

שְׁנֵי גֹיִים בְּבִטְנֵךְ          Two nations are in your womb.

The predicate complement here is also a prepositional phrase בְּבִטְנֵךְ to the ∅ copula.

(69) Gen 27:27

רֵיחַ בְּנִי כְּרֵיחַ שָׂדֶה          the smell of my son is like the smell of a field

The prepositional phrase predicate כְּרֵיחַ שָׂדֶה is the complement of a ∅ copula. כְּרֵיחַ takes the genitive שָׂדֶה as its own complement.

(70) Deut 33:3

כָּל־קְדֹשָׁיו בְּיָדֶךָ          all his holy ones were in your charge

The prepositional phrase is the complement to the ∅ predicate of the clause.

(71) 2 Sam 4:4

וְלִיהוֹנָתָן בֶּן־שָׁאוּל בֵּן          And Jonathan, the son of Saul, had
נְכֵה רַגְלָיִם                          a son who was lame.

The prepositional phrase וְלִיהוֹנָתָן is the predicate complement of the ∅ copula in this verbless sentence, but the phrase נְכֵה רַגְלָיִם is an appositive adjunct.

**7.4a.  Numeral Quantifiers as Predicate Complements of** היה

(72) 1 Kgs 6:17

וְאַרְבָּעִים בָּאַמָּה הָיָה הַבָּיִת          And the house, that is, the temple in
הוּא הַהֵיכָל לְפָנָי                        front, was forty cubits long.

As frequently happens, the predicate complement precedes the verb. In addition, the prepositional phrase designating the unit of measurement בָּאַמָּה is singular. Together they constitute the predicate complement of הָיָה in this sentence.

**7.4b.** Numeral Quantifiers as Predicate Complements
 in Verbless Clauses

(73) Gen 46:27

כָּל־הַנֶּפֶשׁ לְבֵית־יַעֲקֹב הַבָּאָה
מִצְרַיְמָה שִׁבְעִים

All the persons of the house of Jacob, that came into Egypt, were seventy.

The predicate numeral here is a complement of the ∅ copula.

(74) Num 2:9

כָּל־הַפְּקֻדִים לְמַחֲנֵה יְהוּדָה
מְאַת אֶלֶף וּשְׁמֹנִים אֶלֶף
וְשֵׁשֶׁת־אֲלָפִים וְאַרְבַּע־מֵאוֹת

All that were counted of the camp of Judah were one hundred and eighty-six thousand and four hundred.

The predicate numeral is a complement to the ∅ copula.

(75) Num 3:22

פְּקֻדֵיהֶם בְּמִסְפַּר כָּל־זָכָר
מִבֶּן־חֹדֶשׁ וָמַעְלָה פְּקֻדֵיהֶם
שִׁבְעַת אֲלָפִים וַחֲמֵשׁ מֵאוֹת

Their number by count, all the males from a month old and upward, their number was seven thousand five hundred.

The predicate numeral is a complement.

(76) Num 3:39

כָּל־פְּקוּדֵי הַלְוִיִּם . . . כָּל־זָכָר
מִבֶּן־חֹדֶשׁ וָמַעְלָה שְׁנַיִם
וְעֶשְׂרִים אָלֶף

Those counted of the Levites . . . all the males from a month old and upward, were twenty-two thousand.

The last three examples are very clear instances of numerical predicates in verbless clauses. All are predicates and thus complements of their ∅ copulas.

**7.5a.** Participles as Predicate Complements of היה

(77) 1 Sam 2:11

וְהַנַּעַר הָיָה מְשָׁרֵת אֶת־יְהוָה
אֶת־פְּנֵי עֵלִי הַכֹּהֵן

And the boy was ministering to the LORD, in the presence of Eli the priest.

The object of the participle אֶת־יְהוָה is the complement of the predicate participle, exactly like the corresponding finite verb.

(78) Gen 4:2

וַיְהִי־הֶבֶל רֹעֵה צֹאן
וְקַיִן הָיָה עֹבֵד אֲדָמָה

Now Abel was a keeper of sheep, and Cain was a tiller of the ground.

As verbal adjectives, the participles רֹעֶה and עֹבֵד take complements exactly as their corresponding transitive verbs do, and thus their "direct objects" here are their complements as well.

(79) 1 Sam 17:34

רֹעֶה הָיָה עַבְדְּךָ לְאָבִיו בַּצֹּאן    Your servant was watching the sheep for his father.

The two prepositional phrases לְאָבִיו 'for his father' and בַּצֹּאן 'among the sheep' are both adjuncts, though the participle רֹעֶה as the predicate is a complement.

(80) 2 Sam 3:6

וְאַבְנֵר הָיָה מִתְחַזֵּק בְּבֵית    Abner was strengthening himself in
שָׁאוּל    the house of Saul.

The predicate participle is certainly a complement of the verb הָיָה, and the prepositional phrase בְּבֵית שָׁאוּל appears to be a complement of the participle.

(81) 1 Kgs 5:1

וּשְׁלֹמֹה הָיָה מוֹשֵׁל בְּכָל־    And Solomon was ruling over all
הַמַּמְלָכוֹת מִן־הַנָּהָר אֶרֶץ    the kingdoms from the River unto
פְּלִשְׁתִּים    the land of the Philistines.

The verb משׁל 'to rule over' with the prepositional phrase introduced by ב suggests that the phrase בְּכָל־הַמַּמְלָכוֹת is a complement of the participle מוֹשֵׁל, but that the phrases following are adjuncts, not complements.

**7.5b.** Participles as Predicate Complements in Verbless Clauses

(82) 1 Sam 3:1

וְהַנַּעַר שְׁמוּאֵל מְשָׁרֵת אֶת־    Now the boy Samuel was
יְהוָה לִפְנֵי עֵלִי    ministering to the LORD in the presence of Eli.

The words אֶת־יְהוָה are identified by אֶת־ as the object of the participle מְשָׁרֵת and thus are complements of the participle, but the prepositional phrase following, לִפְנֵי עֵלִי, is an adjunct. Compare (77), with nearly identical wording and the copula הָיָה.

(83) Gen 4:10

דְּמֵי אָחִיךָ צֹעֲקִים אֵלַי    your brother's blood is crying out to
מִן־הָאֲדָמָה    me from the ground!

The prepositional phrase אֵלַי may be a complement of the participle, but the following prepositional phrase מִן־הָאֲדָמָה appears to be an adjunct.

(84) Deut 4:3

עֵינֵיכֶם הָרֹאֹת אֵת אֲשֶׁר־עָשָׂה
יְהוָה בְּבַעַל פְּעוֹר

Your eyes are those that have seen what the LORD did regarding Baal Peor.

The particle אֵת identifies the following embedded clause as the complement of the participle הָרֹאֹת, but the prepositional phrase בְּבַעַל פְּעוֹר appears to be an adjunct.

(85) Gen 33:13

אֲדֹנִי יֹדֵעַ כִּי־הַיְלָדִים רַכִּים

My lord knows that the children are frail.

The object clause following יֹדֵעַ is clearly the complement of the verb יֹדֵעַ, and the predicate adjective of this clause, רַכִּים, is clearly a complement as its predicate.

**7.6a.** Adverbs as Predicate Complements of היה

(86) Num 33:14

וְלֹא־הָיָה שָׁם מַיִם לָעָם
לִשְׁתּוֹת

And there was no water there for the people to drink.

The predicate adverb שָׁם is the complement of היה here, but the infinitive construction appears to be an adjunct of the clause.

(87) Gen 2:18

לֹא־טוֹב הֱיוֹת הָאָדָם לְבַדּוֹ

It is not good for the man to be alone.

The subject here is an infinitive clause using היה in its infinitive form, with an adverb לְבַדּוֹ as complement.

(88) Judg 7:1

וּמַחֲנֵה מִדְיָן הָיָה־לוֹ מִצָּפוֹן
מִגִּבְעַת הַמּוֹרֶה בָּעֵמֶק

and the camp of Midian was north of him, below the hill of Moreh, in the valley

The prepositional phrases לוֹ מִצָּפוֹן appear to be complements to the verb היה.

(89) 1 Sam 21:7

כִּי לֹא־הָיָה שָׁם לֶחֶם

for there was no bread there

The word שָׁם is the complement of the verb היה here.

(90) 2 Sam 10:9

כִּי־הָיְתָה אֵלָיו פְּנֵי הַמִּלְחָמָה
מִפָּנִים וּמֵאָחוֹר

that the line of battle against him was in front and in the rear

Only אֵלָיו appears to be a possible complement to the verb here.

(91) 2 Sam 24:16

וּמַלְאַךְ יְהוָה הָיָה עִם־גֹּרֶן    The angel of the LORD was by the
הָאֲרַוְנָה [ק] הַיְבֻסִי    threshing floor of Araunah the
   Jebusite.

The prepositional phrase following הָיָה serves as its complement and the genitive הָאֲרַוְנָה is the complement of גֹּרֶן.

**7.6b.** Adverbs as Predicate Complements in Verbless Clauses

(92) Gen 42:1

כִּי יֶשׁ־שֶׁבֶר בְּמִצְרָיִם    that there was grain in Egypt

The prepositional phrase בְּמִצְרָיִם is the predicate complement of the verbless clause.

(93) Exod 32:17

קוֹל מִלְחָמָה בַּמַּחֲנֶה    The sound of war is in the camp.

The prepositional phrase בַּמַּחֲנֶה is the predicate complement here as well.

(94) Deut 32:49

הַר־נְבוֹ אֲשֶׁר בְּאֶרֶץ מוֹאָב אֲשֶׁר    Mount Nebo, which is in the land of
עַל־פְּנֵי יְרֵחוֹ    Moab, across from Jericho.

מוֹאָב serves as the genitive complement of בְּאֶרֶץ and יְרֵחוֹ as the complement of its compound preposition עַל־פְּנֵי.

(95) 1 Sam 9:11

הֲיֵשׁ בָּזֶה הָרֹאֶה    Is the seer here?

The prepositional phrase בָּזֶה serves as an adverbial complement here.

(96) 1 Sam 21:9

וְאַיִן יֶשׁ־פֹּה תַחַת־יָדְךָ חֲנִית    Is there not here with you a spear or
אוֹ־חָרֶב    a sword?

The adverb פֹּה serves as a predicate complement in this verbless clause.

(97) 1 Kgs 17:3

אֲשֶׁר עַל־פְּנֵי הַיַּרְדֵּן    which is east of the Jordan

The predicate complement here is the prepositional phrase עַל־פְּנֵי הַיַּרְדֵּן.

## 8. Conclusion

The constituent types identified and illustrated above as complements both in clauses with היה and in verbless clauses are a small selection of those that actually occur in the Hebrew scriptures, but they support the claim made in this paper that nominal or verbless sentences exhibit the same range of complement types as sentences that appear with the verb היה when it functions as a copula.

It is well known that verbs tend to exhibit a rather limited range of complements. Some occur merely as intransitives without any complement at all. Others occur with one or even two objects, often in one of the derived stems, where the underlying subject of its noncausative counterpart turns up as a first or second object in its derived stem.[20] Certain verbs occur with prepositional phrases as their complements or take full clauses as their subjects or objects. But it is highly unlikely that one could find another Hebrew verb exhibiting the full range of complements that occur with היה. Yet it is exactly that set of complements that can co-occur with the Ø verb, as the examples above show. This correspondence between the complements of these two clause-types is compelling evidence that they are not really two clause-types at all but, rather, variants of a single type in which the verb occurs when it is needed to support various clausal morpheme markers but is otherwise simply omitted.

In its use as a copula, the verb היה exists primarily, therefore, because it is often needed to support morphemes that mark aspect and/or tense, as well as agreement and mood. Morphemes expressing these meanings are commonly attached to the verbal constituent in the sentences of most languages, because they exhibit meanings related to the propositions expressed in sentences as a whole. When the need to express such meanings is absent, there is no compelling reason to retain the verb and it is merely dropped. The so-called nominal sentence is the effect of this process.

---

20. For a full discussion of such changes in verbal complements, see my paper, "The Valence of the Hebrew Verb."

# Syntactic Approaches

✦  ✦  ✦

# Word Order in the Verbless Clause: A Generative-Functional Approach

RANDALL BUTH

*Jerusalem University College*

✧ ✧ ✧

## 1. Introduction

The basic premise of this paper is as follows: a generative-functional approach to the Biblical Hebrew (BH) nominal (or verbless) clause provides a simple, adequate, linguistic framework. It explains the discontinuities in the data and is able to unite and explain the lists and ad hoc rules of many theories.

We will find that the neutral core of both a verbless clause and a participial clause is Subject–Predicate in order and that material in front of the Subject is specially marked. Naturally, this will aid any Hebrew reader in interpreting a text. Of course, we will find that the fronted material has been placed there for more than one reason, or in other words, by more than one function.

These results are so promising and valuable for resolving the theoretical contrasts among various Hebrew grammarians that they justify a brief introduction to some general linguistic concepts and terminology.

## 2. Linguistic Terms and Categories

**2.1.** By *generative* I refer to a process of producing a clause from an abstract predication. For example, in an abstract predication (example [1] below) one could join an argument/term such as 'horse' to a predicate 'being beautiful' and produce, or generate, the following two specific clauses (2a) and (2b):

(1) Predicate: יפה (approximately 'beautiful' in English)
Argument: הסוס (approximately 'the horse' in English)

(2a) יפה הסוס

(Semantically[1] approximate to 'the horse is beautiful')

(2b) הסוס יפה

(Semantically approximate to 'the horse is beautiful')

**2.2.** The abstraction of generative grammar is forty years old within the field of linguistics and comes in many flavors.[2] Within biblical studies it is often treated as irrelevant or just another conceptual framework to be used or not, according to personal taste. We will see, however, that asking how any one clause in the Hebrew Bible was "generated" forces us to recognize similar patterns within the multiple lists of some theories and sometimes even helps us recognize when one or more constituents of a clause are being moved in out-of-the-ordinary ways.

**2.3.** *Functional* refers to communicative goals and contextual reference. Functional rules are within the description of rules of generating clauses from predications (that is, from the structure of abstract thought or propositions). Thus, a grammar that potentially generates both (2a) and (2b) is incomplete unless it provides a framework for generating one or the other in a specific communication situation.

**2.4.** I also work within a Praguian-generative-functional framework that distinguishes syntax from semantics from pragmatics.[3]

**2.4.1.** *Syntax* with BH clauses refers to a grammatical relationship of Subject to Predicate. The Subject is the grammatical point of reference for what is talked about in a clause; the Predicate is the semantic communication about the Subject.[4]

**2.4.2.** *Semantics* can refer to logical relationships between constituents of a clause. "Existence," "description," "identity," "agent," "experiencer," "undergoer," "location," "aspect," and "tense" are all semantic categories. Predication frames and the dictionary are also part of the semantic domain of language.

**2.4.3.** *Pragmatics* refers to the communication situation. I am specifically interested in constituents that have been *signaled in the language system*, in

---

1. *Semantically* is a technical term and will be contrasted with *pragmatically* below. Examples (2a) and (2b) do not contrast semantically, but they do contrast pragmatically.

2. Serious theoretical linguistic work often uses whimsical phraseology to lighten what can become quite dry material. Biblical scholars should interpret "comes in many flavors" accordingly.

3. See my "Functional Grammar, Hebrew and Aramaic: An Integrated, Textlinguistic Approach to Syntax," in *Discourse Analysis of Biblical Literature: What It Is and What It Offers* (SBLSS 27; ed. Walter R. Bodine; Atlanta: Scholars Press, 1995) 77–102.

4. In BH the Subject is regularly marked by grammatical concord in a governing verb.

the grammar, so that they carry additional information beyond the syntactic or semantic information just mentioned. For example, the commonly used terms *Topic* and *Focus* fit here. The larger pragmatics of Relevance theory do not fit here because they go beyond what the grammar system marks or manipulates and deal with the overall "interpretation" of a text.

**2.4.3.1.** Pragmatically, a Topic is a specially signaled[5] constituent for the purposes of relating the clause to the larger context. Because a pragmatic Topic is not limited to the Subject of a clause, yet the name Subject and Topic are synonymous in informal English as well as in many other languages, I prefer to call the less-salient pragmatically marked constituent a *Contextualizing Constituent* (CC), that is, a constituent that orients the clause to the larger context.[6] The Subject is simply the local, primary point of view within the clause and is grammatically bound by the rules of the syntactic domain.

**2.4.3.2.** *Focus* refers to a specially signaled constituent for highlighting salient information of a clause.[7] This information may be contrastive. It may be contraexpected, that is, the speaker/writer assumes his or her audience may be expecting something different and so marks it for Focus. It may also be new information that is specially marked to fill in, or to complete, assumed missing information. It may also be old information that needs special reinforcement, through repetition.

Three English examples will illustrate these terms before we proceed to Hebrew material.

(3) From my perspective   the horse   is beautiful.
    CC                       Subject    Predicate

The prepositional phrase orients the clause to a larger framework. For example, the sentence may be spoken in a discussion about whether a horse, or a particular horse, fits in a picture scene. The 'horse' is the primary, grammatical point of reference for the clause, the Subject, and is indexed in the verb by the form 'is' [instead of 'are', 'am'].

(4) The horse   is beautiful from my perspective.
    Subject    Predicate (prep. phrase is part of the predicate)

---

5. That is, *marked* in the popular sense of the term, or *explicit*. A Topic is also marked in the sense of markedness theory by being a more specialized constitutent than an unmarked constituent.

6. Randall Buth, "Contextualizing Constituent as Topic, Non-sequential Background and Dramatic Pause: Hebrew and Aramaic Evidence," in *Function and Expression in Functional Grammar* (ed. Elisabeth Engberg-Pedersen, Lisbeth Falster Jakobsen, and Lone Schack Rasmussen; Berlin: Mouton/de Gruyter, 1994) 215–31.

7. This relates to Praguian rheme material in a theme-rheme dichotomy, or to comment material in the topic-comment dichotomy, though Focus is limited to *specially marked* rhemic material. Focus does not equal rheme; Focus usually only marks a part of the rheme.

The clause has neutral or basic intonation. Neither a CC nor Focus constituent is included in (4). The clause/sentence may be spoken as a basis of agreement before going on to another point or aspect of a discussion.

(5) From my perspective   the *horse*            is beautiful.
      CC                          Subject + Focus   Predicate

The capital letters symbolize high-low intonation in English, which marks focus. Syntactically and semantically, the clause is identical to (3). Example (5) could be spoken by a man looking at a barn with a horse in a corral, selecting one for his comment, and contrasting the two.

All three examples (3)–(5) reveal similar semantics and even similar syntax, but they differ in pragmatics. Example (5) shows that it is possible for more than one pragmatic function to be marked in a clause. Hebrew also allows this, as the next examples show.[8]

(6) Qoh 1:4

והארץ לעולם עמדת    and the earth remains forever

'The land/earth' relates to the larger context of 'under the sun' and 'generations of people'. It is not just the Subject of the clause.[9] Rather, it is in a fronted position, which also marks it pragmatically. Here the Subject is serving to relate the clause to the context, so it is a Topic or, as I prefer, Contextualizing Constituent (CC).

If only 'forever' were fronted and marked pragmatically the order would have been:

(7)        עמדת        הארץ        לעולם
      Predicate    Subject    Pragmatic Constituent

For such a regular, one-pragmatic-constituent order compare:

(8) Judg 9:36

הנה־עם יורד מראשי ההרים    Look,  a-people are-descending
                                                from-the tops-of-the-mountains!

---

8. The order Subject–Adverb–Participle is quite rare in BH; cf. Gen 13:7. Most nominal clauses with two pragmatic constituents can be analyzed as Theme, Pragmatic Constituent, Subject–Predicate, where Theme is an extraclausal Contextualizing Constituent. Likewise, verbal clauses with two pragmatically marked constituents are quite rare in narrative, though less so in legal texts and poetry. For examples in prose, see Gen 14:10d, 17:6c, 9b (cf. 17:16b, 35:11e), 28:13d (Theme, Focus–Verb); Lev 25:4; and Judg 21:25. In poetry, see Isa 1:15e, 27a; Ps 2:7d; 3:5a; 51:5a, 8b.

9. Here, the concord with feminine-singular עמדת shows that הארץ is Subject. It is also marked pragmatically, since it does not occur immediately before the verb in the Subject–Predicate core of the clause. This clause illustrates how a generative approach helps clarify what is specially marked. That this clause is from Late Biblical Hebrew is incidental.

ויאמר אליו זבל     And Zevul said to him,

את צל ההרים אתה ראה     "You are seeing the shadow of the

כאנשים     mountains as men!"

Notice that the Subject (אתה 'you') precedes the participle (ראה 'see') and is not the salient information of the deceiving/taunting response: 'The shadow of the mountains is what you are seeing as though men'. 'Shadow of the mountains' is pragmatically marked and is a single constituent, here Focus, because it is both salient information and specially marked by the grammar.

Returning to Qoh 1:4 (6), לעולם is also marked by being placed in front of the verb. The function is probably Focus,[10] since this is salient information and it contrasts with the temporary nature of the context, where generation after generation disappears. Thus, Qoh 1:4 has two marked constituents because the Subject is not just in front of the verb—it is in front of another marked constituent, which is in front of the verb.[11]

**2.5.** We must also recognize that ambiguities sometimes exist, and our theory should describe and include them as well. This is particularly true where two noun phrases are juxtaposed as a predication.

For example, Exod 9:27 can be read in two different ways:

---

10. Thus, a sensitive reader would read this constituent with a high-tone (or in whatever manner ancient focal intonation patterned) Focal intonation pattern, which probably involved some kind of high tone, to judge from modern languages using intonation patterns.

We learn a great deal about the "biblical" language from what we know of Semitic languages and human language in general. Neither First-Temple Period nor Second-Temple Period Hebrew was a "tonal" language. That is, differences in vocabulary/lexicon were not regularly and systematically signaled by changes in acoustic pitch. Since Hebrew is a nontonal language, we can assume from language universals that certain pitch contours fit certain clause types and communication situations. Certain syntactic structures and even occasional lexical items may also be expected to be signaled by pitch contrasts. For example, a simple statement versus a question may be assumed to have had a different pitch contour. Similarly, and here we touch something germane to this paper, we can assume that special contours for focal information existed. (Syntactically, Focus functions are theorized to be universal to human language, though certainly marked in a variety of ways [for example, tone, lexicon, morphology, and/or syntax].) Since the existence of Focal contours in a nontonal language is the default situation, whose nonexistence would be quite surprising and need justification, we certainly cannot work from an artificial or false framework that ignores the existence of this category, even if we do not know precisely how such contours would have sounded. This is not very different from assigning vowels to an ancient text even if we do not know exactly what their phonetic quality was.

11. This assumes that positioning in front of the core predication is the mechanism being used for marking and not a complicated sandwich structure. The example from Judg 9:36 (8) was given to show the normal, one-constituent fronting, in which the item does not land between Subject and participle. It is by far the most common order for a constituent other than Subject or Verb to be fronted.

(9a)  Exod 9:27

            הַצַּדִּיק     יהוה      The LORD is the righteous one.
           Predicate  Subject

(9b)    הַצַּדִּיק             יהוה      The righteous one is *the* LORD.
    Subject  Predicate (Focus)

While we cannot know what the different intonations would have sounded like in the ancient world, it is reasonable to assume that some ambiguities are only the result of the graphic system. They would not have been ambiguous in speech and were not ambiguous in the grammar of the language. In most cases the context is sufficient for reconstructing the relationships, and a sensitive reader would have been expected to supply the correct intonation. (A modern reader will simply use an artificial reconstruction.)[12]

---

12. Some readers may wonder about the relationship between the Masoretic accents and potential intonation patterns. Each word in the Masoretic Text has an accent mark that gives a musical tone and a prosodic context. The musical tones reflect a chanted reading tradition whose relationship to intonation patterns in "natural" language situations can only be conjectured. However, the prosodic context that is indicated by the accents shows the reader where to make minor pauses and gives a general orientation to the rest of the verse. Thus, the accents are very useful for immediate constituent analysis in showing which words go together and, conversely, where clause and phrase boundaries occur. Unfortunately for the concerns of this paper, the accents are more sensitive to the length of an utterance than its pragmatic, informational structure and thus do not directly reflect syntactic, semantic, or pragmatic relations. See Bezalel Elan Dresher, "The Prosodic Basis of the Tiberian Hebrew System of Accents," *Language* 70 (1994) 1–52, especially p. 6: "This prosodic orientation helps to account for some of the well-known 'failings' of the accents as markers of logical and syntactic relations." See also the examples in Dresher and his comment: "In this way, what appear to be eccentric phrasings from a syntactic point of view turn out to have a prosodic basis" (p. 6).

It is possible that further study may find some restrictions that could partially interact with pragmatic analyses and interpretations. For example, the first pragmatic constituent of clauses with two pragmatic constituents before a Verb or before a Subject of a Subject-participle core consistently ends in a disjunctive accent, while the second pragmatic constituent may have a disjunctive or conjunctive accent. All of the examples in nn. 8 and 33 fit this observation.

On the other hand, longer single constituents before a Verb or a Subject-participle core sometimes have two disjunctive accents. See example (14), Deut 9:4, where one-half of the fronted constituent 'and because of the wickedness of' has a disjunctive *pashta* accent, and 'these nations' follows with a disjunctive *zaqep*. See also Num 34:14 and Judg 7:6 treated by Dresher ("The Prosodic Basis," 26). These doubly disjunctive constituents might be thought of as having a hint of confirmation of Focus. But such an analysis cannot be maintained absolutely since fronted constituents that are only one word in length would be negatively devalued because of their size rather than their informational value. See example (16b), Jer 1:12, where a fronted participle functioning as an obvious wordplay only has a conjunctive accent. Also, a lengthy constituent that is fronted as a Contextualization would necessarily receive two disjunctive accents, regardless of potential Focus value. See, for

**2.6.** Another question that needs to be cleared up before proceeding: do we need the distinction between grammatical Subject and pragmatic Topic (CC)? Some have said, "no."

**2.6.1.** Recently Tamar Zewi[13] at Hebrew University has argued that for verbless clauses Subject and Topic are the same thing; the Topic is the "true" Subject, and neither one is grammatically or morphologically marked. However, this homogenizes and collapses a necessary distinction, as points 2.6.2–2.6.5 will show.

**2.6.2.** Participial clauses have grammatical concord with a subject for gender and number. For example:

(10)             אני רואה   I am seeing

                 אתן רואות   you (f. pl.) are seeing

Both אני 'I' and אתן 'you (f. pl.)' require changes to the verb and are grammatical Subjects. However, a Praguian analysis does not tie a grammatical Subject to a logical Subject (theme) or a logical Predicate to the grammatical Predicate. The logical Predicate can be any part of a sentence. Since pragmatic marking does not obliterate the syntactic Subject marking, it is in the interests of clarity to preserve both aspects in a grammatical description. For this paper, both syntactic Subjects and Predicates and pragmatic *Contextualizing Constituents* and *Focus* are the preferred terminology.

**2.6.2.2.** Thinking of an alternative to Qoh 1:4 can help to illustrate the difference between an unmarked Subject and a pragmatically marked Subject-Contextualizing Constituent. For example, consider the sentence הארץ עמדת לעולם (same semantic translation as [6]). It has the same Subject as the biblical verse, but it does not show pragmatic movement or Topic/CC marking as does Qoh 1:4.[14]

---

example, 'the land that you are lying on' in Gen 28:13 (n. 8). These observations accord with accent patterns that are primarily sensitive to prosodic length and constituent position and only secondarily sensitive to informational structure or grammar. Further study will need to be made on the extent to which the Masoretic "chant" tradition may interact with pragmatic structure in general, first with verbal clauses where basic syntactic patterns are not disputed and second with verbless clauses. Finally, even if some patterns become useful for a part of the pragmatic analysis, the Masoretic reading will only be a single reading and not a grammatical statement about possible pragmatic, multireadings of the same sentence. Questions of syntax, semantics, and pragmatics need to be worked out within their own parameters.

13. Zewi has written a Ph.D. dissertation from such a functional perspective in which she brings out many points that are lacking in the identification/classification scheme of Andersen. Tamar Zewi, הההסבות התחביריות הכרוכות במבנה הפונקציונלי של המשפט בעברית מקראית (Jerusalem: Hebrew University, 1992). Her framework would have been improved by adding a generative perspective.

14. It is possible that Prague-style analysis and a generative-functional analysis will occasionally lead to conflicting interpretations. For example, in Qoh 1:4, a Praguian desire to

**2.6.3.** With strictly verbless clauses, keeping a distinction of Topic from Subject provides a rationale for the distinction between Topics (CC) and "resumptive" pronoun tags that remain after Topic/CC and Focus movement (see n. 42 below).

**2.6.4.** It allows structures of noun plus prepositional phrases to be labeled syntactically as Subject plus Predicate, regardless of which constituent, if any, is a Focus or CC.

**2.6.5.** It provides a framework for distinguishing complex clauses both syntactically and pragmatically:

| | | | |
|---|---|---|---|
| A | | + resumptive pronoun | + B |
| (CC) | | Subject (±Focus) | Predicate |
| versus A | + B | | + resumptive pronoun |
| (CC) | Predicate (Focus) | | Subject |

For example, a traditional Praguian analysis would label either יהוה 'Lord' or the הוא 'he' in the first clause of Ps 100:3 (11) as a logical predicate:

(11)   יהוה הוא אלהים      The LORD, *he* is God
      הוא־עשנו ולא אנחנו    *he* (is the one who) made us and not
                          we ourselves.[15]

As we see in the second clause (הוא־עשנו), the הוא can function as a Subject in Hebrew with Focus marking at the same time. That is the preferred reading of the first line as well. Setting off יהוה 'Lord' as a CC[16] and following with a resumptive Subject pronoun draws the pragmatic Focus marking. Semantically, exactly the same information could have been communicated without the pronoun:

(12)   יהוה אלהים      The LORD is God.

Now, if only two-place clauses were used in Hebrew, then a single category for Subject and Topic/CC would be enough, and a single category for Predicate/Comment/Rheme would be enough. However, with split Subjects and split Predicates and with participial clauses such as (10), we need to distinguish between a grammatical core and pragmatically marked constituents. The Praguian analysis is helpful, but it must be used in conjunction with the

---

keep themes and rhemes continuous, where possible, might lead to labeling עמדת as the most salient part of the sentence, although by that analysis a pragmatic Focal distinction on לעולם is lost. See example (19), Gen 15:14 below, where the explanatory power of fronting and special marking beyond predication is important.

15. Q: ולו אנחנו 'and we are *his*'.

16. Actually, within Functional Grammar, this Topic/CC should be viewed as outside the sentence proper and can be labeled *Theme*, an extrasentential Topic. In traditional grammars, such a construction may be called a *casus pendens* or *nominative absolute*.

full grammar of syntactic and semantic relationships and within a generative framework.

With this survey of linguistic terminology we can return to Hebrew data and the nominal clauses.

## 3. Participial Clauses in Biblical Hebrew

**3.1.** Because participial clauses have clearly marked Subjects, I begin the discussion of *nominal clauses* with them.[17] They are only a subset of the nominal clause,[18] but we will be able to see the mechanics of clause-generation most clearly, and we will also be able to demonstrate how a functional analysis will allow us to interpret what is going on. We need to recognize any pragmatic movement or placement.

First of all, there are many clauses with Predicate–Subject order and many more (approximately four times more) with Subject–Predicate order.[19] But raw statistics do not explain what is going on.

The tell-tale clue comes when something is put in front of a participle other than the Subject. Something quite different happens with participial clauses than when a clause with a finite verb has something fronted.[20] We need to

---

17. Some nominal clauses are susceptible to more than one interpretation of what is the Subject, and differing theories define differently what the Subject of a nominal clause might be. The participle as a verb is normally unambiguous in being at least part of the syntactic Predicate. The Subject as a grammatical category is also more sharply defined. With the participle we have the control of grammatical concord in number and gender between the participle and the Subject.

18. Semitists have long recognized the nominal nature of the participial clause. For one thing, the morphology of participles follows that of adjectives and nouns, not verbs. This study confirms that its syntax is part and parcel of the nominal clause, using the same rules and base patterns.

One colleague has suggested that participles and Subjects form a unit that is identical to the verb in a verbal clause (oral communication). This is an illusion based on the frequent use of pronouns as Subjects of participles. First of all, both the orders Subject–participle and participle–Subject occur. These orders must be differentiated, hopefully in a way as congruent as possible with the rest of the syntactical system. Second, when nouns are Subjects (whether indefinite, definite, possessed, or proper) they cannot be treated as enclitic parts of the verb constituent.

19. These numbers and ratio come from Jan Joosten, "The Predicative Participle in Biblical Hebrew," *ZAH* 2 (1989) 131, 140, 158. On p. 158 he lists all 110 examples of the order participle(verbal)–Subject in the Bible.

20. Finite verbal clauses and nominal clauses could be joined into one category if one were to layer the rules and stipulate that a Subject of a participial clause must first be put into a lower ordered pragmatic slot before other rules were allowed to operate. One pragmatic advantage of such a theory would be its ability to show and explain why participial clauses in narrative function similarly to Noun + verb clauses in breaking up the temporal

review briefly what happens with finite verbs in order to appreciate what happens with participles.

**3.2.** In a verbal clause,[21] a verb usually follows the pragmatically fronted, marked constituent and an explicit Subject follows the verb. In Gen 30:40, presented as a commonplace example, notice that the Subject יעקב remains after the verb הפריד.

(13) Gen 30:40

והכשבים הפריד יעקב    (Jacob separated the sheep.)

and-the-sheep (obj.) separated Jacob (subject)

With participles, the normal pattern is that when a constituent comes before the participle other than the Subject, then the Subject follows that element and the participle follows the Subject. This happens regularly and is not a result of double pragmatic marking. For one thing, the natural order of pragmatic marking (as a linguistic universal) when two elements are fronted is Topic/CC followed by Focus. However, with participles, we regularly find Focus information (that is, marked salient information) in front of an otherwise insipid Subject.

**3.3.** The direct conclusion from this is that we are seeing the default, base or neutral order[22] in clauses with a Pragmatic (Focus or Contextualizing) Constituent + Subject + Participle + X. Several examples follow:

---

succession. However, the placing of a Subject in a participial clause is normally immediately next to the verb, even when there are other fronted constituents. On the other hand, in finite-verbal clauses with a Subject and another marked constituent, a fronted Subject will usually precede another pragmatically marked constituent, usually a Focus, which then comes between the Subject and the main verb. Thus, an extra rule is still necessary to distinguish verbal clauses from nominal clauses if one wants to preserve functional explanatory power and correctly predict certain restrictions.

21. A verbal clause is one whose main verb is either a suffix-verb, prefix-verb, or imperative. Participles are excluded since they use adjectival morphology and a different word order syntax.

22. The neutral order should not be thought of as "context-free"; indeed, there is no such thing as context-free constructions. For example, initiating, intermediary, and ending propositions are all part of a larger context. Rather, a base or default order is an order that results without any pragmatic conditioning of word order. A neutral order is relative within the language system.

Unfortunately, one game that linguists can play is to divide and conquer by labeling particular constructions as context-bound and then to try to deal with a more obedient remainder, hopefully more "basic." Such approaches can be manipulated. For example, one can ignore all *waw ha-hippuk* clauses (sequential finite verb clauses) so that the Biblical Hebrew verbal clause can be labeled Subject–Predicate, an uninsightful analysis (see my "Functional Grammar, Hebrew and Aramaic"). Something similar may be going on with nominal clauses when "circumstantial" clauses are pulled out of the picture. The "circumstantial" clauses may in fact be those clauses without a need for Focus saliency marking.

(14) Deut 9:4

אל־תאמר . . .

בצדקתי הביאני יהוה לרשת
את־הארץ הזאת
וברשעת הגוים האלה יהוה
מורישם מפניך

Don't say . . .

because of my righteousness the LORD
brought me to possess this land
and because of the wickedness of
these nations the LORD is
dispossessing them before you.

This is a good example of the difference between verbal clauses and participial clauses. Both clauses have a fronted pragmatic constituent, 'because of my
righteousness' and 'because of the wickedness of these nations', respectively.
The verbal clause has a suffix-verb (הֱבִיאַנִי) and then an explicit Subject (יהוה)
(=x–V–S). The participial clause has an explicit Subject (יהוה) and then the
participle (מוֹרִישָׁם) (=x–S–Ptc).[23]

(15) Gen 37:15–16

מה תבקש
את־אחי אנכי מבקש
איפה הם רעים

What are you looking for?
My brothers I am seeking.
Where (are) they shepherding?

In the example from Genesis 37, Joseph could have answered with simply אחי
'my brothers' in a less formal conversation. The salient information is fronted
and thus is a result of a Focus function operation. The phrase אנכי מבקש 'I am
looking for' adds nothing except syntactic completeness.[24] The following
question also fronts the question word as a pragmatic function: איפה הם רעים.[25]

(16a) Jer 1:11

מה־אתה רֹאֶה ירמיהו
מקל שָׁקֵד אני רֹאֶה

What (do) you see, Jeremiah?
An almond stick I am seeing.

(16b) Jer 1:12

היטבת לראות
כי שֹׁקֵד אני על־דברי לעשתו

You have seen well
for diligent (am) I over my word to
do it.

---

23. Cf. Deut 18:12 for a similar clause and one without any resumptive pronoun of the
pragmatic constituent: ובגלל התועבת האלה יהוה אלהיך מוריש אותם מפניך 'and because of
these abominations the LORD your God is dispossessing them from before you' (=x–S–Ptc).

24. From an approach within Relevance Theory, this syntactic completeness may have
an implication of "formality" in order to fit a context of speaking with a stranger.

25. The interrogative may be either CC or Focus, depending on the intonation. A question word may be simply contextualizing in eliciting a later salient response. But there may
also be a Focal intonation which would then imply some special saliency—for example,
some kind of surprise or contraexpectation. A question word, in any case, normally triggers
a pragmatic fronting rule.

The LORD now makes a wordplay on the root of שקד. Notice that by recognizing Subject–Predicate as the unmarked order with participles, we are obliged to explain this order here. The participle שֹׁקֵד is pragmatically placed in front of the Subject. This completes the wordplay and should be read as a Focus function, drawing special attention to the slight difference in the word.

(16c) Jer 1:13

| | |
|---|---|
| מה אתה רֹאֶה | What (do) you see? |
| סיר נפוח אני רֹאֶה | A pot boiling I am seeing |
| ופניו מפני צפונה | and its face is toward the north. |

The examples from Jeremiah reinforce the general conclusion that the unmarked order is Subject–Predicate. In the repeated question, מה אתה ראה, is placed in front of the Subject–Predicate core by an obligatory pragmatic function (either CC or Focus).[26] Similarly, the answer מקל שקד is fronted by a Focus function; the rest of the clause is neutral. It could even have been dropped.

Jer 1:13 repeats these structures. Of added interest is the final clause that describes the condition of the pot, ופניו מפני צפונה. I would call this a neutral, descriptive, unmarked clause, though Andersen and Waltke and O'Connor and others would make it a special category called "circumstantial."[27]

### 3.4. Joosten's Aspectual Approach to Participles

**3.4.1.** Before summarizing how clauses with participles work, we need to discuss a proposal by Jan Joosten.[28] He claims that Predicate–Subject order signals a "factitive," aoristic present tense, while Subject–Predicate order signals a durative, real-present aspect. I will respond at length.

**3.4.2.** It is improbable on general linguistic grounds that a pragmatic structure would be strictly aspectual and semantic. As will be seen below, the Subject–Predicate, Predicate–Subject order is a loose generalization and not a restricted syntactic-pragmatic order as is, for example, verb-subject order in German conditional clauses.

---

26. Some question words obligatorily trigger pragmatic placement rules in many languages. Such is the case with מָה in Hebrew.

27. Francis I. Andersen, *The Hebrew Verbless Clause in the Pentateuch* (Journal of Biblical Literature Monograph Series 14; New York and Nashville: Abingdon, 1970); B. K. Waltke and M. O'Connor, *An Introduction to Biblical Hebrew Syntax* (Winona Lake, Ind.: Eisenbrauns, 1990). When we accurately define which constituents are moving and why, it turns out that categories such as "circumstantial" disappear. "Circumstantial clauses" (whether verbal or nominal) are already correctly generated by the grammar within a proper textlinguistic framework. The word *circumstantial* is useful for speaking with Semitists on a popular level, but grammatically it has no ontological status.

28. Joosten, "The Predicative Participle in Biblical Hebrew," 128–59.

**3.4.3.** Joosten's rules do not make room for additional pragmatic marking. So, for example, what happens if in a Predicate–Subject clause someone wants to Topicalize (= contextualize with CC) or put Focus on a Subject? Are these functions missing with the participle? Symmetry in a language that already clearly uses word order pragmatically in verbal clauses would argue against its widespread neutralization here.

**3.4.4.** The "facticity" of Joosten's Predicate–Subject order, for example, with yes/no questions, can just as easily be described as a reason for invoking fronting in questions. For example:

(17) Gen 18:17

המכסה אני מאברהם אשר   (= Should I hide from Abraham

אני עשה   what I am about to do?)

is-it-that hiding I-am from Abraham what I-am doing?

Here the potential contraexpectation suggests a Focus function. Notice the normal Subject–Predicate order inside the relative clause.

**3.4.5.** When a constituent separates particles such as אם 'if',[29] ה־ 'is-it?',[30] אשר 'that/which',[31] or הנה 'look, behold' from the core elements of the clause (that is, from the Subject and Predicate) then Subject–Predicate order normally follows. Again, this order is predicted from a functional-generative perspective. Otherwise, one would have to make them all special cases. One example follows as an illustration:[32]

---

29. Joosten writes (ibid., 136): "If the participle and its subject follow the particle *'im* immediately, then the sequence is always *'im* Ptcp-Su. . . . if any other element comes between the particle and the participle with its subject the sequence Su-Ptcp is used." He lists *'im Ptcp-Su* examples at Gen 27:46; Exod 7:27, 9:2, 10:4; Deut 5:22; Judg 11:9; Jer 26:15, 38:21, 42:13; Hos 4:15; Joel 4:4. He lists *'im-Su-Ptcp* [*sic*] examples at Num 11:15; Lev 3:1, 7; Judg 9:15; 1 Sam 7:3. These latter examples have obviously marked a constituent other than the participle (=x–S–Ptc).

30. "The sequence is $h^a$-*Ptcp-Su* unless an element separates $h^a$- from the participle with its subject. In the latter case the sequence Su-Ptcp is used, e.g., Jer 7:19. . . . If another element follows $h^a$- the weight of the question falls on this element and not on the action expressed by the participle" (ibid., 136–37). He lists direct questions with *ha-Participle-Subject* at Gen 18:17; Num 11:29; 2 Sam 10:3, 15:27(?); Ezek 8:6, 9:8; 1 Chr 19:3. Indirect questions with *ha-Participle-Subject*: Judg 2:22; Qoh 3:21, 22. Questions with *ha-X-Subject-Participle*: Exod 2:14, 2 Kgs 1:3, Jer 7:19.

31. Joosten (ibid., 135) writes, "In relative clauses introduced by *'asher* we find almost exclusively the sequence Su-Ptcp. However, it seems that in these clauses the sequences Su-Ptcp is not the expression of the actual present. . . . The only exception is Job 6:4."

32. All of the examples in Joosten (ibid., 135–37) will fit here, since we are both agreed on the data. Joosten merely lists these as a neutralized environment where his general rules do not apply. I would say that normal pragmatic functions must be assumed for all fronted constituents. Such an approach is more encompassing and symmetric within the language.

(18) Judg 9:15

אם באמת אתם משחים אתי     if in-truth you (are) anointing me as

למלך עליכם     a king over you . . .

This is a good "aoristic," nondurative, conditional clause with a constituent separating the conditional conjunction 'if' from the Subject–Predicate core. Joosten's aspect theory would have predicted a Predicate–Subject order. However, a Focus interpretation of the fronted constituent 'in truth' as a counterexpectation is fairly transparent in the contrafactual/sarcastic context. A functional-generative perspective has no problem recognizing the fronted constituent, interpreting it, and showing the remaining unmarked basic order of the default core.

**3.4.6.** According to Joosten's count, out of 550 participial clauses, not counting "circumstantial" (!) clauses, there are 7 ([sic] at least eight) examples in the Bible where a constituent precedes Participle + Subject. A functional approach predicts that this order occurs where Focus marking on the participle is desirable. That is, one constituent is pragmatically marked and fronted as a CC, and then the participle is pragmatically marked and fronted before the Subject. A CC followed by participle marked for Focus fits 7 out of the 8 examples.[33] These claims are illustrated by example (19). The one outstanding example, Gen 41:2 (20), probably has a double CC marking.

(19) Gen 15:14

וגם את־הגוי אשר יעבדו     (= as for the nation that they will

דן אנכי     serve I will certainly judge them too)

and-too, the-nation that they-serve *judging* I-am (CC–Focus–S)

The Object is fronted to serve as a new point of discussion in comparison to Abraham's descendents. It would be interpreted as a Contextualizing Constituent and would not receive "focal intonation." Pragmatically marking the verb 'judge' also makes sense in this context since 'judging the agent of justice' describes something contra-expected and can be interpreted as a Focus function. Here, a generative-functional approach leads us to recognize two special positionings and a functional approach requires us to explain two pragmatic functions operating on this clause. Furthermore, the distinction between a "nonemphatic" Contextualizing Constituent and an "emphatic" Focus provides necessary refinements for meaningfully dealing with complex sentences like Gen 15:14. More traditional approaches to syntax simply cannot help here. Compare Joüon and Muraoka's comment: "When a third element additional to a personal pronoun and a participle or some other element occupies

---

33. The examples are Gen 15:14 [also 41:2]; Jer 4:29; Ps 19:2, 31:24; Prov 17:17; Job 6:4; Qoh 1:6.

the first slot and attracts some prominence to itself, the pronoun commonly occupies the second slot. . . . There are, of course, exceptions to the rule: e.g., Gn 15.14."[34]

(20) Gen 41:2

| והנה מן־היאר עלת שבע פרות | and behold, from the Nile were- |
| יפות מראה ובריאת בשר | going-up seven cows pretty of sight and healthy of flesh. |

Both the prepositional phrase and the verb have been fronted and seem to be Contextualizing Constituents. This description can be viewed as a backward way of leaving the Subject to be the most salient part of the clause.[35] As such, the analysis would be congruent with a Praguian reading where the Subject has become the rheme.

**3.4.7.** Joosten's aspectual analysis of Subject-participle order ignores the relationship of the larger Predicate. A participle with an object or a prepositional phrase can follow a Subject (common). But the extra constituent (for example, object or prepositional phrase) can also come before the Subject + participle (common), between the Subject and the participle (rare; for example, Qoh 1:4; Gen 12:6, 26:29), or before the participle + Subject (rare, Gen 15:14), after a Participle + a Subject (common), or even between a participle + Subject (rare; cf. Isa 3:13).[36] A generative grammar demands a flexibility that can produce all of these orders, and a functional-generative grammar demands an interpretation. Something powerful is happening that is elusive from a strictly referential semantic point of view.

Is it just possible that whatever is moving or positioning the prepositional phrase is also working on the participle and Subject as part of its proper domain? If so, we are again drawn toward a pragmatic, functional explanation and away from a semantic explanation. (A semantic explanation would need to develop six aspects for all of the above orders and would create innumerable additional neutralized environments.)

---

34. Paul Joüon, *A Grammar of Biblical Hebrew* (2 vols.; trans. and rev. by Takamitsu Muraoka; Subsidia Biblica 14/1–2; Rome: Pontifical Biblical Institute, 1991) 571–72.

35. While it is true that there is a general tendency among languages to hold longer constituents toward the end of a clause, this explanation is not appropriate here. In Gen 41:6, in the second dream, a very long Subject is in front of the participle: והנה שבע שבלים דקות ושדופת קדים צמחות אחריהן 'and look, seven heads of grain thin and withered by the east wind are sprouting after them'.

36. Isa 3:13 נצב לריב יהוה 'the LORD is set for arguing'. The whole Predicate has been fronted and has apparently been treated as one Focal constituent. The phrase לריב 'for argument' does not seem to have been fronted by a separate pragmatic function. The Masoretic accents apparently support such an argument because the disjunctive accent is not on נצב but on לריב.

**3.4.8.** The bottom line for points 3.4.2–3.4.7 is that a functional-generative analysis must be preferred over Joosten's aspectual analysis. With the 110 clauses that have a participle preceding a Subject (almost always immediately preceding), we can say that a Focus function has caused considerable overlap with Joosten's "factitive" and "aoristic" semantics. But we need to follow the whole generative picture in order to recognize the insufficiency of an aspectual analysis. The aoristic fronted participle is based on an incomplete analysis and is ultimately illusory in comparison with the fully functioning pragmatics of Contextualization and Focus in participial clauses.

**3.5** A Conclusion for Participial Clauses

**3.5.1.** A grammatical template for participial clauses within the theoretical framework outlined here is

$$\pm \text{ (pragmatic slot[s])}^n + \text{Subject} + \text{participle} \pm \text{(predicate slots)}.$$

This template allows multiple pragmatic slots before the default core and has a number of advantages. It handles the biblical data. It leads a reader to interpret a text in a direct manner even when confronted with changing structural components. It is more complete than rival approaches by not requiring "neutralizations." Finally, it is integrated with general linguistic theory by incorporating insights from linguistic universals and Functional Grammar.

# 4. Verbless (Nonparticipial) Nominal Clauses

**4.1.** We may now turn to the nominal-verbless clause proper. Much discussion in North America during this past generation has been influenced by Andersen, followed by Waltke and O'Connor.[37] I will first explain why the problems and exceptions that develop in that system are sometimes counterintuitive to the way the language works. Then I will demonstrate how a generative-functional approach will handle the same data.

Andersen and Waltke and O'Connor analyze Predicate–Subject order as "classifying" and Subject–Predicate order as "identifying" clauses. These first two categories, "identification" and "classification," are semantic predications or relationships. Theoretically, such semantic relationships could be tied to word order rules in the grammar, and furthermore, "aspect" might have been connected to word order as well. Andersen and Waltke-O'Connor also group participles and circumstantial clauses as Subject–Predicate. Participles deal with morphology, and "circumstantial clauses" deal with an undefined text-linguistic relationship ("circumstantial"). However, as with the case of participles above, we will find that a complete examination of the data leads

---

37. Andersen, *The Hebrew Verbless Clause in the Pentateuch*; Waltke and O'Connor, *Introduction to Biblical Hebrew Syntax*.

straight to a pragmatic, generative-functional theory rather than a semantic or morphological one.

**4.2.** Andersen and Waltke-O'Connor do not try to explain why verbal participles reverse the proposed order of descriptive-classifying Predicate–Subject to Subject–Predicate. This is contrary to the nature of Hebrew verbal clauses that show a strong Verb-Subject syntax. Why would verbal participles produce a Subject-Verb order if both verbal clauses and classifying nominal clauses were predicate-initial? On the other hand, we did see that Subject–Predicate order is not absolute or fixed with participles and that Predicate–Subject order can be used for Focus marking.

**4.3.** Furthermore, Andersen and Waltke-O'Connor do not explain why frequently only a part of a predicate occurs before a Subject. To be fair, Waltke and O'Connor said that they would not deal with discontinuous or complicated predicates in their discussion. However, in this case the discontinuous predicates are highly suggestive of an alternative analysis from a generative grammatical model, an analysis not suggested within a model that lists different possible structures as proposed by Andersen and Waltke-O'Connor. Andersen also cannot explain why discontinuities predominate in Predicate–Subject orders.[38] The verbal clause shows that Hebrew, as an ordinary VSO language, allows a constituent to precede the verb. The constituent may be the Subject, Object, or other piece of the clause. (Less frequently, two constituents may be placed in front of a verb.) This means that the language included a mechanism for fronting a part of a verbal clause:

(21)         O   V   S   X
             S   V   O   X
             X   V   S   O
                 V   S   O   X
             [Pragmatic + V S O X]

The clause types in (21) all develop out of an underlying predication with a basic VSOX order[39] plus a slot before the verb for pragmatic marking by means of word order. The pragmatic, communication effect may have one of two functions, either marking special saliency, a Focus, or marking a less salient constituent as orienting the clause to the context. This Contextualizing Constitutent is the more common function in narrative.[40]

---

38. Andersen, *The Hebrew Verbless Clause in the Pentateuch*, 37. See discussion below, §4.3.2.

39. This is a simplification of the total word order system in which connectives, negatives, conjoined constituents, and postverbal pronouns fill some of the spaces between the major constituents or are part of a constituent.

40. The non-Focal character of a Contextualizing Constituent has confused many biblical grammarians. One does not need to read much text before discovering that *emphasis* is

This same process of fronting for pragmatic marking can explain the verbless clause with split predicates. An order "Predicate (partial) + Subject + Predicate (partial)" would be generated simply from a Subject–Predicate predication by marking a part of a Predicate constituent or word and placing it before the Subject. In this way a reader or hearer is able to work through a clause and distinguish special marking from normal order, processing the clause with little difficulty.

Discontinuous clauses, however, form an enormous task for analyses based upon lists of attested constituent orders, as would be the case if one followed Andersen and Waltke-O'Connor, because of endless complications requiring continual splitting and lumping of multiple lists.[41]

**4.3.2.** Despite my theoretical disagreement in this paper, I find Andersen's work generally very useful, especially for cataloguing the data on discontinuities. On p. 37 he says, "Table 5 shows that there are 185 clauses with a predicate of the kind in which discontinuity might occur; and of these, 153 have a predicate divided by the subject." This is a remarkable tendency that needs more of an explanation than saying that these are basic Predicate–Subject clauses. I submit that we are looking at pragmatic marking on only a part of the Predicate in 83% of the cases and on the whole predicate in 17%. A logical entailment follows. As soon as one recognizes a partial pragmatic marking on a fronted part of a predicate, what remains is a Subject–Predicate order at the core of the clause. This means that the language is not maintaining a Predicate–Subject core order but the reverse, Subject–Predicate. The discontinuous Predicate–Subject clauses show that pieces of the predicate may be fronted before the default Subject–Predicate core. Here is where generative grammar,

---

a misleading nomenclature for fronted constituents, yet a reader cannot just throw up hands in despair and treat word order functions as unrecoverable.

41. Andersen (pp. 52–108) distinguishes 555 structurally distinct nominal clause-types in the Pentateuch. He distills these into 9 rules or classes of rules (pp. 39–50). The functional-generative approach, in contrast, has one rule.

Andersen's rules (pp. 39–50), without listing the exceptions, are as follows: (1) The sequence is S–P in a clause of identification, in which both S and P are definite. (2) A pleonastic pronoun in a clause of identification comes before the predicate, in keeping with rule 1. (3) The sequence is P–S in a clause of classification, in which P is indefinite relative to S. (4) A pleonastic pronoun in a clause of classification comes after the predicate. (5) Circumstantial clauses of classification have sequence S–P, in contrast with rule 3. (6) When a suffixed noun is predicate, the sequence S–P (rule 1) is used for a clause of identification in which the suffixed noun is definite; the sequence P–S (rule 3) is used for a clause of classification in which the suffixed noun is indefinite. (7) When the predicate is a participle, the sequence is S–P in declarative clauses. (8) When the predicate is a participle, the sequence P–S is preferred in precative clauses. (9) The sequence P–S is used when the subject of a declarative clause is an infinitive; the predicate is always an indefinite noun. Finally, clauses with prepositional phrases have "no clear rules" (p. 50).

with its attention to the process of encoding a "thought" into a surface structure sentence, provides theoretical integration of these facts.

(22) Gen 34:21

האנשים האלה שלמים הם     These men, they are friendly with
אתנו     us.

This example has a compound predicate, שלמים אתנו. The most unmarked
clause would be האנשים האלה שלמים אתנו. A Focus on the whole predicate
could have produced שלמים אתנו האנשים האלה. A partial Focus on the predicate could have produced two forms, either שלמים האנשים האלה אתנו or
אתנו האנשים האלה שלמים. Finally, both the Subject and the Predicate could
have been fully marked pragmatically: האנשים האלה שלמים אתנו הם (CC +
Focus + Subject). Each order would need an appropriate communication environment. The clause in Genesis has used a CC (presumably to help introduce the topic being discussed)[42] and a Focus on the most salient piece of the
Predicate in the speaker's eyes.

(23) Num 14:7

הארץ אשר עברנו בה לתור     The land that we passed through it to
אתה טובה הארץ מאד מאד     see it, the land is very, very good.

This uses both a CC (technically an extraclausal Theme) and a Focus structure
followed by a Subject and two adverbs reinforcing the choice of 'good' as
Focus.

**4.4.** Finally, Waltke and O'Connor list further exceptions as ad hoc categories that "neutralize" word order patterns.[43] That is, both orders occur

---

42. These Contextualizing Constituents can also be treated as *casus pendens* and technically outside the grammar of the clause. Within Functional Grammar, such pragmatic
functions are called Theme, to distinguish them from Topic (= my CC). Pragmatically, there
is no difference in these contexts, because both Theme and Topic are marking a constituent
as a point of reference to the larger context. The question is whether or not the constituent
is part of the clause proper or is "sitting outside." With verbal clauses one can use resumptive pronouns as a means for defining when one or the other (Theme or Topic) is being employed as the clause is generated. With verbless/nominal clauses this distinction seems an
unnecesary complication, because a pronoun is usually necessary to mark the predication
core and to show that fronting of a constituent has occurred.

43. Their analysis hides one of the biggest problems with a nongenerative approach.
The patterns mentioned by Waltke and O'Connor are only statistical probabilities, not absolute rules, and they do not explain what is happening in any one instance. The "neutralized" patterns are really no different; it is just that the probabilities are less dominant. But in
either case, a reader or listener must interpret an individual instance. This is the same problem that Joosten ran into with his aspectual approach to word order with participles: several
environments were hypothesized to neutralize the word order distinctions so that "both"
could occur on a regular basis.

frequently. "Either order may be expected if the predicate is a numeral . . . , or an adverb . . . , or a prepositional phrase."[44] This analysis is inadequate. It certainly does not explain how any one clause would be generated at any one time. It is much better to assume that constituents in front of the Subject–Predicate are marked. It is the job of every reader/listener to interpret the marked constituents. In this way the same functions that are at work in other clause types can be applied in verbless clauses as well.

(24) Num 16:3

| | |
|---|---|
| כי כל־העדה כלם קדשים | because all of the congregation, all of them are holy |
| ובתוכם יהוה | and the LORD is in their midst |

This is a good example of ambiguity, where a theory helps us understand the possibilities but does not resolve the problem. The clause 'the LORD is in their midst' has P–S order and needs an explanation. 'In their midst' may be a Contextualizing Constituent relating to 'the congregation' and understood as spoken without any Focal intonation. Understood in this way, the clause would be subtle, a kind of soft-selling of the argument. On the other hand, the speakers may have added Focus intonation to the fronted phrase in order to drive home the point that all of the people were qualified. In any case, the clause has a fronted prepositional phrase in the opposite order from that in Gen 39:3. Recognizing a base structure (Subject–Predicate) and a marked structure (Predicate–Subject) leads to meaningful questions and possible interpretations. A statement that 'both orders can occur' may be accurate, but it is bankrupt as far as processing the language.

(25) Num 14:9

| | |
|---|---|
| כי לחמנו הם | for they are "meat on the table"; |
| סר צלם מעליהם | their shadow has left them |
| ויהוה אתנו | and the LORD is with us; |
| אל־תיראם | do not fear them |

These clauses start out with a colorful expression, 'they are our bread', which uses P–S order followed by two clauses that explain the saying more prosaically. One clause, 'their shadow has turned from them', is pragmatically unmarked. It appears that the following clause, 'the LORD is with us', is also pragmatically unmarked, confirming a Subject–Predicate order.

(26) Josh 9:16

| | |
|---|---|
| וישמעו כי־ | and they heard that |
| קרבים הם אליו | they were near to it |
| ובקרבו הם ישבים | and in its midst they were dwelling |

---

44. Waltke and O'Connor, *Introduction to Biblical Hebrew Syntax*, 134.

Again, we have two parallel clauses illustrating a pragmatic function. The last clause uses a fronted Focus constituent ובקרבו before a normal Subject-Participle core. It would appear that the "verbless" clause has likewise fronted the adjective קרבים 'near' as a Focus constituent before the Subject and the rest of the Predicate. The Predicate–Subject order is predicted by Andersen and Waltke-O'Connor for such a classifying clause. However, it is important to see that both the split Predicate and the parallel structure with the following clause strongly suggest that the real reason for the fronting is pragmatic (that is, as Focus) and that the construction is not a separate syntactic-semantic structure (as a "normal" classifying relationship).

**4.5.** There are examples where fronting one constituent in front of a Predicate–Subject core results in a Subject–Predicate order. This is predicted by the functional-generative approach of this paper but would contradict the expectations of Andersen and Waltke-O'Connor. Compare the following two examples from Judges 7.

(27a) Judg 7:2

רב העם אשר אתך   The people who are with you are (too) many.

(27b) Judg 7:4

עוד העם רב   Still the people are (too) many.

The difference between the two sentences involves the marked (fronted) constituents but not the semantic relationship between Subject and Predicate. Both clauses have a Predicate that describes or classifies the Subject. In Judg 7:2, the main point of the clause was the size of the people, and the appropriate part of the Predicate, רב 'many',[45] was fronted. Judg 7:4, by contrast, has marked the salient adverb 'still' as Focus. In so doing, the speaker/author no longer had any need to mark 'many' as Focus, and we find the order Subject–Predicate despite identical semantics with 7:2. A generative-functional approach not only handles these alternative word orders, it makes it easy to see what is happening in the grammar and leads an interpreter directly to the most salient points.

(28) Lev 25:55

| כי־לי בני־ישראל עבדים | The people of Israel are slaves for *me* |
| עבדי הם | They are *my slaves* |
| P(Foc)   Subj   Pred | |
| P(Foc)   Subj | |

---

45. The Predicate continues with מתתי את־מדין בידם 'from my giving Midian into their hand'.

The first clause is particularly interesting because it shows a "classifying" clause using a Subject–Predicate order (contra Andersen and Waltke-O'Connor) after a fronted constituent. This order is what a generative-functional approach would predict from a Subject–Predicate unmarked core with only one constituent pragmatically marked. It is the same thing that we saw with participles, and it helped us reject both an aspectual approach and an inflexible syntactic approach. As to the function of the fronted constituent, after the connector כי 'because' it is most probable that 'for me' is to be read as a Focus. The second clause continues with a Focus structure.

(29) Judg 16:5 (similarly Judg 16:6, 15)

| וראי | and find out |
| במה כחו גדול | with what his strength is great |
| ובמה נוכל לו | and with what we can prevail against him |

As in Deut 9:4 (14) above, we can see the pragmatic function used in two parallel clauses, one clause nominal and the other clause verbal. In both clauses the question word has been fronted. In the nominal clause the Subject follows first and then the Predicate. Notice that this clause is not identifying but descriptive and classifying (to use Andersen's terminology). This example follows the predictions of the functional-generative approach with a core, default Subject–Predicate order and contradicts the prediction of Andersen and Waltke-O'Connor.

## 5. A Proposal

The above discussion allows us to propose a simple strategy for interpeting nominal clauses in a Biblical Hebrew text, with several apparent advantages. Verbless clauses do not need to be separated from participial clauses, since both are using the same template. Extra categories such as "circumstantial clauses" disappear as unnecessary. "Complication" such as split Predicates are handled without a problem and are even predicted. The grammar becomes very simple to manipulate and describe while at the same time becoming very flexible and powerful. The grammar is capable of taking the same semantic relationships and generating more than one word order, as attested in the data.

**5.1.** In reading a text, the Subject will normally be identified as the more definite constituent. A ranking of first-second person pronoun, third person pronoun, proper name, definite noun phrase, suffixed noun phrase will provide a first indication of Subject. The Subject will also normally be the more presupposed constituent. When otherwise ambiguous (for example, two definite nouns), then a default order of Subject–Predicate can be used as a syntactic disambiguation.[46]

With a Subject and Predicate identified and a semantic "predication" deduced, the word order is examined to see which, if any, constituents are placed before the Subject–Predicate. All such fronted constituents are to be read as either Contextualizing Constitutents or Focus. (With pronoun Subjects and indefinite predicates, there is a strong tendency toward Focus function. This would make sense text-linguistically, since such clauses are often intrusive to the flow of a discourse. An author decides that the descriptive attribute is important enough for inclusion, while at the same time the subject matter has already been presented, hence the pronominal Subject.[47] Non-Focal material would follow the Subject.)

**5.2.** With these rules and guidelines, we might ask, "What can we generate?" or from the other perspective, "How can we read a text?"

**5.2.1.** As an example, we can put a simple definite Subject in a Subject position and a descriptive noun phrase in the unmarked Predicate position.

(30) Gen 46:32

והאנשים רעי צאן     and the men   (are) shepherds of flock
                Subject    Predicate

This Subject–Predicate clause is a descriptive "classifying clause," not "identification" or "circumstantial," and not in the Predicate–Subject order that Andersen's analysis would predict.[48] It is Subject–Predicate because it has not received any pragmatic marking. Andersen did not discuss this example but listed it in his comprehensive lists. Likewise, Andersen's identity/definite clauses fit this Subject–Predicate order because contrast and Focus are rarely

---

46. This explains why Andersen's identification clauses are so regularly Subject–Predicate. Both the Subject and Predicate are definite, so a fronting of the Predicate would create confusion in identifying the Subject. Nevertheless, such fronting was theoretically possible and used when the context was able to clarify the more "topicalized" constituent, the Subject. See Isa 5:7: כי כרם יהוה צבאות בית ישראל, ואיש יהודה נטע שעשועיו. The first clause uses the normal Subject–Predicate order, but the second line fronts the Predicate as a Focus, thus creating a chiasmus. 'His delightful plantation' is the more presupposed constituent and is parallel to 'the LORD of Host's vineyard' in the first line. See n. 49.

47. This description incorporates Andersen's insights on the frequency of Predicate–Subject clauses with indefinite Predicates but integrates them within a broader grammar. Andersen's problems and/or exceptions also disappear, since they are simply examples where Focus marking was not used.

48. The participle in Gen 46:32 is not functioning as a present tense but as a construct noun, 'shepherds of'.

useful in such an environment. (Of course, where they are useful, a Predicate (Foc)–Subject order is found.[49])

(31) Gen 41:31

כי־כבד הוא מאד

| for | severe | | it (is / will be) | very |
|-----|--------|--|-------------------|------|
| rel | Predicate-partial (Foc) | | Subject | Predicate-partial |

With a pronoun Subject ready from the context, a Focus function on the main adjective or characteristic is common as a salient point in an argument.

(32) Deut 14:2

כי עם קדוש אתה ליהוה    for you are a holy people to the LORD

This clause has the same pragmatics and split Predicate as (31).

(33) Ezek 9:9

עון בית־ישראל ויהודה    The guilt of Israel and Judah is
גדול במאד מאד    great in the extreme.

This verse begins a quotation with a classifying clause. It functions as a general description and builds some of the background toward a more specific judgment in v. 10. Thus, there is no need for a Focus function in this first clause. Someone with Andersen's perspective might try to call this "circumstantial," as though it were somehow different syntactically and semantically from classification and description. From a generative perspective this clause is simply unmarked and fits the general development of the argument in vv. 9–10.

(34) Exod 33:5

אתם עם־קשה־ערף    you are a people of a hard neck

Like Ezek 9:9 (33), this clause uses an unmarked order for a descriptive clause with an indefinite Predicate. Andersen listed this among his "real exceptions."[50] Again, it is simply an unmarked clause where there was no need for Focus. This clause serves as a reason clause for a threatened destruction. The point of the larger discourse is not that the people are stiff-necked but that they are about to be destroyed.

(35) Gen 33:13

אדני ידע כי־הילדים רכים    My lord knows that the children are
                              "soft."

---

49. For example, גלית שמו 'his name is Goliath!' (1 Sam 17:4), איוב שמו 'his name is Job!' (Job 1:1).

50. Andersen, *The Hebrew Verbless Clause in the Pentateuch*, 44.

This subordinated content clause also shows a basic Subject–Predicate order. A Focal order Predicate–Subject would certainly have been possible, had the speaker or author so chosen. (See the next example, [36], for the opposite order after the same verb.)

(36) Gen 3:7

וידעו כי עירמם הם    and they knew that they were naked

In Gen 3:7 the condition of the Subject is fronted by a Focus function. Of course, with a pronoun Subject such an order became so commonplace in Biblical Hebrew as to diminish its significance somewhat, yet it was not obligatory and still shows the functional movement. So the pragmatic function still needs to be interpreted, and a reader still needs to read with a Focus intonation.

(37) Gen 39:23

ואשר־הוא עשה יהוה מצליח    and what he was doing (Object) the
LORD (Subject) was prospering

This clause shows a typical Subject-participle core with a pragmatically front-positioned object. It may be read either as a Contextualizing Constituent or Focus, depending on whether the point falls on '*whatsoever* he was doing' (Focus on marked salient information) or on 'the LORD was *prospering*' (most salient [but unmarked] information, leaving the Object clause as CC). Notice the Subject–Predicate order inside the relative clause as well.

(38) Gen 39:3

וירא אדניו כי יהוה אתו    and his master saw that the LORD
(was) with him

This nominal clause is subordinated as the content of a perception verb 'saw'. It seems to exhibit a default order without any need for marking. The following clause in Gen 39:3 expanded the meaning of this clause and used a CC but without any Focus.

(39) Deut 2:7

זה ארבעים שנה יהוה    This (= for) forty years the LORD
אלהיך עמך    your God (is, has been) with you.

Here is another nominal clause using a prepositional phrase as the predicate, like (38), though with a Focal adverbial phrase/clause. The order after the Focal element is Subject–Predicate. See Gen 31:38 for a parallel.

(40) Deut 11:12

ארץ אשר־יהוה אלהיך דרש אתה    As for a land that the LORD your God
תמיד עיני יהוה אלהיך    seeks, the eyes of the LORD your God
בה מרשית השנה ועד    are always on it from the beginning
אחרית שנה    of the year to the end of the year.

This example is a parenthetical comment to the sentence before Deut 11:11. Verse 12 has a CC[51] followed by a Focus תמיד 'always' and then the default Subject–Predicate 'eyes of the LORD are on it' with additional material reinforcing 'always' at the end. This is a relatively complicated example and would cause some concern to grammarians trying to work with lists and multiple patterns. Within a functional-generative approach, the sentence can be processed without difficulty as long as one recognizes the need to interpret what is fronted and to accept the author's choice of what remains unmarked.

(41) Gen 47:6

ארץ מצרים לפניך הוא     The land of Egypt, it is in front of you.
Subject (CC [or Theme])  Predicate (Focus)  Subject

This is a relatively simple example with double pragmatic marking. The first constituent, 'the land of Egypt', relates to the larger context. A land for Joseph's family is under discussion, and the land of Egypt becomes the point of departure for the next sentences. The main point that Pharaoh makes is that the whole country is open for them. They may settle in the best land. This is expressed by the Focus constituent 'before you'. The following pronoun, הוא 'it/she', is the grammatical Subject. Its purpose is to anchor the core of the clause and show that the other constituents are placed by pragmatic functions. The order CC + Focus is quite common.[52] These two constituents by themselves would have produced a good clause, but without any marking. The pronoun at the end changes the construction into a marked one that would require a reader to use a Focal intonation on לפניך.

(42) Deut 31:3

יהוה אלהיך הוא עבר לפניך     The LORD your God *he* is going on
                                before you
הוא־ישמיד את־הגוים האלה     *he* will destroy these nations before
מלפניך                         you.

It is important to recognize that the Subject pronoun הוא 'he' can be used for Focus when it follows a Subject that has been fronted as a CC. The first clause in Deut 31:3 has a participial predicate, so there is no question as to its syntactic role. The pronoun הוא is a Subject, yet it is semantically and syntactically unnecessary. Pragmatically, it sets up יהוה אלהיך 'the LORD your God'

---

51. The indefinite CC is unexpected in this context (though explainable as an appositional parenthesis to the Predicate of the previous verse), and some manuscript traditions among the Samaritans, in Syriac, and the Targum have a definite noun phrase, 'The land. . . '.

52. Andersen (pp. 65–69) cites Gen 30:33; 40:12, 18; 41:25, 26; 42:11; 43:7; 49:20; Lev 11:12, 20; 13:15; 15:2; 23:27; 27:26, 28; Num 1:4; 8:4; 12:7; 13:32; 14:7; 18:9; 32:3–4; Deut 32:4; Josh 22:14.

as a Contextualizing Constituent. (It is what is popularly called a "topic.") The repetition of the Subject referent in the pronoun הוא becomes Focal and should receive Focus intonation. This is seen by the identical parallel use in the next clause, where it is also added as a Focus constituent. The following example (43) shows the same structure in a nominal clause.

(43) Deut 18:2

יהוה הוא נחלתו כאשר דבר־לו    The LORD *he* is his inheritance as he promised him.

The pronoun הוא 'he' has been added to the Subject–Predicate core, thus marking off יהוה as a CC that the pronoun follows as a Focus Subject. There is nothing that marks הוא as being in a pragmatic position, but its very existence signals a pragmatic function. Comparison with the participial clause and finite verb clause in (42) confirms this analysis.

(44) Isa 51:12

אנכי אנכי הוא מנחמכם    I, I am he, your comforter
Subject (CC), Subject (Foc) Predicate, Predicate (appositive-Tail)

This is a tricky example. The double first-person reference would seem to have at least one pragmatic marking. The first אנכי 'I' apparently orients the clause to the context, so it has been labeled CC (= "theme" in functional grammar). The core relationship אנכי הוא can be defined as Subject–Predicate on two grounds. First, Subject–Predicate is a default order when two definite constituents are used. Second, the doubling of אנכי makes the אנכי of the core clause more presupposed and thus a candidate for Subject. However, the use of הוא as the grammatical Predicate may suggest that the Subject should be given a Focus intonation as well. The pronoun is regularly used to fill a grammatical slot, so that a preceding constituent becomes pragmatically marked. The final phrase, 'your comforter', is an appositive to the grammatical Predicate. (In Functional Grammar this is what would be called a Tail function, which includes afterthoughts and extragrammatical intrusions.)

(45) Nah 1:2–3

אל קנוא ונקם יהוה    The LORD is a jealous God (Foc) and avenging (Foc),

נקם יהוה ובעל חמה    the LORD is avenging (Foc) and has wrath.

נקם יהוה לצריו    The LORD is avenging (Foc) against his foes,

ונוטר הוא לאיביו    he acts consistently (Foc) against his enemies.

יהוה ארך אפים וגדול־כח    The LORD is patient and very strong ('great of strength').

This passage in Nahum shows an interesting progression in its choice of grammatical structures. It begins with a clause with two fronted, Focus constituents.[53] It is followed by a clause that has two Predicate constituents, only one of which is marked as a Focus constituent. The other is an unmarked Predicate constituent after the Subject. The next two clauses only mark one part of the Predicate as Focus, with the remainder of the Predicate appearing after the Subject in the default position. Finally, the last clause uses an unmarked order Subject–Predicate with two Predicate constituents.

When we look more closely at the content, we notice that the clauses with a Focus constituent describe the LORD with aggressive attributes, and they diminish in grammatical intensity until reaching the grammatically neutral closing clause, which describes the LORD with a conciliatory attribute.[54] This provides an esthetic iconicity to the poem.

## 6. Areas for Further Research

**6.1.** The nominal clause and participles create a tension within Hebrew grammar because of their difference from the standard verbal clause. Conflicting patterns may pull a language in one direction or another over a period of time. For example, the participle came to be treated more and more as a verb and as an integral part of the verbal system. This fact could exert an influence on participial clauses toward the ordering P–S so as to mirror the order VSO that we see in verbal clauses. It remains to be established exactly when, how, and whether such a process transpired. Studies on Mishnaic Hebrew suggest that the process had not yet taken place during the time when Mishnaic Hebrew was a living language.[55]

---

53. It may be preferable to simplify these two constituents and treat them as a single Focus constituent unit, because one disjunctive accent marks the entire phrase. However, I have treated them in this paper as two constituents in order to reflect possible syntactic complexity. The next three clauses all have single, fronted words, and each receives a conjunctive accent. Presumably, this prevents an overly-heavy piling up of three disjunctive accents in each short clause. The last clause is similar to the first clause in having two descriptive phrases. It has two disjunctive accents for the two phrases following the Subject. These two phrases are made up of four words in the consonantal text, while the Masoretic tradition reads them as three metrical words.

54. While one may legitimately argue that poetry is not the place to define grammar, one must still read poetry and interpret what is there.

55. Abba Bendavid, לשון חז״ל לשון מקרא ושון (rev. ed.; 2 vols.; Tel Aviv: Dvir, 1967). See also Takamitsu Muraoka, "הפסוק השמני בלשון המקרא המאוחרת ובלשון חז״ל," in מחקרים בלשון ד' (ed. Moshe Bar-Asher; Jerusalem: Institute of Jewish Studies, Hebrew University, 1990) 219–52, especially 222: שמא ניתן ללמוד מזה, שלמרות התוכן הפועלי המובהק של הבינוני, מבחינה תחבירית, הוא היה מוחזק בתודעת בעלי לשון חז״ל כקטגוריה שמנית 'One might conclude from this that in spite of the pronounced verbal character of the participle, from a syntactic

**6.2.** In this study we have not discussed clauses of existence with שׁי 'there is' (138 examples in the MT) and אַיִן 'there is not' (over 700 examples). Both of these words lexicalize existence and often function like fronted, contextualizing Predicates.

**6.3.** The relative frequencies of various constructions and syntactic environments can be calculated according to genre and author. These distributions may be compared across time, though the incomplete nature of the biblical corpus vis-à-vis the living language will render results problematic. It will be difficult to establish which changes are the result of stylistic or grammatical drift in the language and which changes are accidental and idiosyncratic. It is important, however, to relate to a generative-functional framework so that illusionary grammatical constructions are not proposed and then traced through a corpus.

**6.4.** Most importantly, further text-linguistic work needs to be done in order to describe more precisely the ways in which the pragmatic functions are used within a text. This paper only attempts to establish the rationale for a generative-funtional approach and to establish how the grammar is generating the nominal clauses. This is a necessary first step. However there is a continuum from what might have been termed descriptive "circumstantial" clauses (that is, those with unmarked Subject–Predicate order) to those in which a part of the Predicate is made a Focus or in which all of the Predicate is Focus.

In addition, nominal clauses themselves play an interesting role within narrative to break up the sequencing of events. Both nominal clauses and finite verb clauses with XV(S)(O) order overlap at this point in breaking up the narrative flow.

## 7. Conclusion

The underlying order in nominal clauses is Subject–Predicate. This is clear from the pattern of fronted partial Predicates, from the patterns with participles, from patterns with "neutralized" order, from subordinate clauses that have one fronted constituent, from "circumstantial" clauses, and from descriptive clauses that have one fronted constituent.

Reading becomes a simple matter of interpreting pragmatically positioned material against the context, whether salient, Focus material; or orienting, Contextualizing material. The pattern can be abstracted for readers/students as:

(CC) (Focus) Subject Predicate

---

perspective it remained as a nominal category within the conciousness of Mishnaic Hebrew speakers'.

Such a way of reading and generating Hebrew nominal clauses corrects and reorganizes the suggestions of previous approaches based on multiple lists, patterns, and exceptions. The flexibility of the generative approach and the power of a functional approach provide a basis for better understanding and interpretation and for more productive future research.

# A Unified Analysis of
# Verbal and Verbless Clauses within
# Government-Binding Theory

VINCENT DeCAEN

*Hebrew Syntax Encoding Initiative*
*University of Toronto*

## 1. Introduction

It once was thought that the earth remained immobile at the center of the stellar dance. It was so obvious: all one had to do was look. And if looking were insufficient, there were the ancient authorities. That the finite verb remains immobile in the Standard Biblical Hebrew[1] clause is so obvious too. And if looking is insufficient, there are at least two centuries of Semitic philology behind this pillar of conventional wisdom.[2]

*Author's note*: This work is dedicated to Dr. Robert Fisher, my first instructor in Biblical Hebrew, on the occasion of his retirement from the Department of Religion and Culture, Wilfrid Laurier University (Waterloo, Ontario).

1. "Standard" is used here in the sense employed by E. J. Revell in, e.g., "The System of the Verb in Standard Biblical Hebrew," *HUCA* 60 (1989) 1–37, viz., with reference to the dialect found in the corpus of Judges, Samuel, and Kings.

2. It would appear that nowhere in the literature is there a suggestion that the Hebrew verb might move. Only nonverbal constituents are thought to move if "emphasized." A recent survey of Hebrew syntactic theory is provided by K. Jongeling, "On the VSO Character of Hebrew," in *Studies in Hebrew and Aramaic Syntax: Presented to Professor J. Hoftijzer on the Occasion of His Sixty-Fifth Birthday* (ed. K. Jongeling, H. L. Murre-van den Berg, and L. van Rompay; Studies in Semitic Languages and Literatures 17; Leiden: Brill, 1991) 103–11. The conventional wisdom outlined there is a VSO (verb-subject-object) basic word order supplemented by a spurious (as he explains, p. 106) psychological explanation relating linear precedence to relative importance or "emphasis": hence the notion that elements before the verb are promoted under "emphasis." His survey traces such a view back to the German pioneers Gesenius and Ewald, working in the early 1800s; presumably there are further antecedents. Jongeling does dwell on the one surprising exception in the

We now know that the earth moves, however counterintuitive and heretical the notion first appeared. The burden of my doctoral investigations was the analogous notion that the Biblical Hebrew verb *moves* in some sense, however counterintuitive that appears.[3]

There are a number of advantages resulting from such a dynamic model. By shifting responsibility to the syntactic component of the Biblical Hebrew grammar under a *verb-movement* analysis, the morphological inventory can be pared down to the two or three verb forms justified under independent morphological analysis; and the semantic analysis of the verb can be greatly simplified by means of enriched syntactic representations. An unexpected bonus is a model that can support the text-linguistic investigation of obligatory topicalization.[4]

A further advantage not yet fully explored is the unified treatment of nonfinite structures, including the so-called verbless constructions. Hitherto, conventional wisdom has arbitrarily fragmented Hebrew syntax into three unrelated theories treating of preverbal order, postverbal order, and the verbless clause. My account insightfully unites pre- and postverbal ordering; an extension of such an account that derives the verbless clause as a special case is greatly to be preferred.

A last advantage is obvious with even a brief perusal of the discourse-analytic investigations of the biblical texts.[5] An inadequate syntactic analysis is deeply embedded in all such frameworks (let alone an inadequate model of

---

literature, namely, the SVO view found in P. Joüon, *Grammaire de l'hébreu biblique* (Rome: Pontifical Biblical Institute, 1923) 474, §155 k I. This dissident view is rejected by Jongeling and in any case is subsequently eliminated in T. Muraoka's revision and translation of Joüon, *A Grammar of Biblical Hebrew* (2 vols.; Subsidia biblica 14/1–2; Rome: Pontifical Biblical Institute, 1991) 579, §155 k. While Joüon does not explain how derivations might proceed, it can easily be argued within a generative framework that a verb-movement analysis is implicit in Joüon's SVO ordering.

3. V. DeCaen, *On the Placement and Interpretation of the Verb in Standard Biblical Hebrew Prose* (Ph.D. diss., University of Toronto, 1995).

4. Perhaps the best treatment in the literature on "emphasis" and the reasonable analysis thereof as *topicalization* is found in B. L. Bandstra, "Word Order and Emphasis in Biblical Hebrew Narrative: Syntactic Observations on Genesis 22 from a Discourse Perspective," *Linguistics and Biblical Hebrew* (ed. W. Bodine; Winona Lake, Ind.: Eisenbrauns, 1992) 109–123.

5. A convenient summary of the standard canon of discourse-analytic works on Biblical Hebrew with bibliography is provided in D. A. Dawson, *Text-Linguistics and Biblical Hebrew* (JSOTSup 177; Sheffield: Sheffield Academic Press, 1994). Within this canon, the conventional model of Biblical Hebrew syntax outlined above (n. 2) is simply assumed. It should be added in passing that Dawson's offering, while providing a convenient summary, is probably the most problematic exemplar of biblical text-linguistics. A review of this work by M. Eskhult can be found in *Orientalia Suecana* 43–44 (1994–95) 93–103; see also S. Meier's brief notice in *JBL* 115 (1996) 723–24.

grammatical tense-aspect).[6] However, the required formalist corrective runs counter to the direction of the field with its functionalist bias and domination by the text-linguistic agenda.[7]

The present work is organized as follows: first, some data will be introduced to facilitate pretheoretical discussion of the inadequacies of Hebrew syntactic analysis, and basic conclusions will be drawn. Next, an introduction to the syntactic model and its notation will set the stage for entertaining the logical possibility of the verbless clause. A series of derivations extend the treatment. Remaining questions will be raised for further consideration in the conclusion.

## 2. Pretheoretical Considerations

The goal of this section is to lay out specific problems with the traditional analysis of the syntax and semantics of certain structures from 2 Kings, the most grammatically interesting text of the Standard Biblical Hebrew corpus, in my view. A summary will list the problems for which an adequate theory of Biblical Hebrew syntax and semantics must account.

Perhaps the most arresting section from a grammatical point of view begins around 2 Kgs 17:27 and extends to 18:4. This section is characterized by a syntactic structure that does not register or even exist in the textbook tradition represented by, for example, Weingreen, Lambdin, and his student Seow.[8] That structure contains the participle supported by *hyh* as if it were an

---

6. J. Joosten expressed similar sentiments in an unpublished paper presented at the Tilburg conference on narrative syntax (October, 1996). In his conclusion he writes, "existing morphosyntactic analyses of the BH verb . . . are not satisfactory. Central questions remain to be debated, at least some of which will not be solved on the level of discourse analysis. The present enthusiasm for the text-linguistic approach, in as far as it neglects morphosyntactic research, is a *fuite en avant*" (pp. 14–15).

7. The rapid convergence on the text-linguistic agenda is seen in such collections as R. Bergen (ed.), *Biblical Hebrew and Discourse Linguistics* (Dallas: Summer Institute of Linguistics, 1994). More recently, there was another major conference on narrative syntax; see E. J. van Wolde (ed.), *Narrative Syntax and the Hebrew Bible: Papers of the Tilburg Conference 1996* (Biblical Interpretation Series 29; Leiden: Brill, 1997).

8. J. Weingreen, *A Practical Grammar for Classical Hebrew* (2d ed; Oxford: Clarendon, 1959); T. O. Lambdin, *Introduction to Biblical Hebrew* (New York: Scribner's, 1971); C. L. Seow, *A Grammar for Biblical Hebrew* (Nashville: Abingdon, 1987). It could be argued that the construction is marginal, and even late (frequency increases with time); hence the absence is easily explained. However, the key to the model articulated in my doctoral study, *On the Placement and Interpretation of the Verb*, is that the construction is central, not marginal, and therefore crucial to a correct understanding of the verbal system. The structure is of course treated in passing in the most recent standard reference grammars: B. K. Waltke and M. O'Connor, *An Introduction to Biblical Hebrew Syntax* (Winona Lake, Ind.: Eisenbrauns, 1990) 628–30, §37.7.1; and Joüon and Muraoka, *A Grammar of Biblical Hebrew*, 409–13, §121c–g. Waltke and O'Connor assume somehow that the simple collocation of the

auxiliary verb in a verbal complex; indeed, I argue that this is in fact what we have here. Consider the representative structures in (1)–(3).

(1)  2 Kgs 17:41
     *wayyihyû haggôyîm hā'ēlleh yerē'îm 'et YHWH*

(2)  2 Kgs 17:41
     *wĕ'et-pĕsîlêhem hāyû 'ōbdîm gam-bĕnêhem . . .*

(3)  2 Kgs 18:4
     *kî 'ad-hayyāmîm hāhēmmāh hāyû bĕnê-yiśrā'ēl mĕqaṭṭĕrîm lô*

While these structures escape the traditional accounts, they are still exceedingly familiar. To see where this is going, German and English translations of (3) are given in (4) and (5).

(4)  Luther
     Denn bis zu dieser Zeit hatte ihr Israel geräuchert

(5)  NIV
     for up to that time the Israelites had been burning incense to it

The German syntax of (4) most closely parallels (3) (the placement of the clitic-like pronoun *ihr* immediately after the auxiliary *hatte* is strictly governed by independent principles and is irrelevant to the present account). In both (3) and (4), there is a major constituent placed before the inflection-bearing auxiliary, creating in both cases a characteristic verb-second structure. In both (3) and (4), the nonfinite form (which is arguably the main verb semantically) is separated from the auxiliary by the subject. I argue that an account of the German verbal syntax in (4) will apply mutatis mutandi to the Hebrew in (3).

Another syntactic factor not addressed in the grammars at all is the transformational relation between (3) and its equivalent in (6) without the finite verb.

(6)  *kî 'ad hayyāmîm hāhēmmāh bĕnê yiśrā'ēl mĕqaṭṭerîm lô*

It is fair to say that an account that does not relate (3) and (6) in an interesting way is missing a significant linguistic generalization about Biblical Hebrew.[9]

---

finite *hyh* with the predicative participle assigns a progressive aspectual index to the participle (628, §37.7.1b); whereas Muraoka suggests a virtual identity in value (durative) of participle and *yiqtol* (412, §121h).

9. The transformational relation is briefly addressed by J. Dyk, *Participles in Context: A Computer-Assisted Study of Old Testament Hebrew* (Applicatio 12; Amsterdam: Free University Press, 1994) 136–40, §5.2.2.3 and 211, §9.3.2. A technical comparison of the analysis sketched in the present work with Dyk's "reanalysis" analysis and the notion of the (non)lexical copula selecting for a small clause will be left as a research project and might best be embedded in a critical review of Dyk's monograph.

Turning to the semantic parallels between (3) and the English in (5), we see the clear analogue of the main verb appearing as a participle, adjectival in nature, supported by the auxiliary *be*. The analogy of the English progressive "tenses" does in fact appear to capture, as a first approximation, the semantics of the Hebrew.[10]

But such an analogy should be systematically ruled out by the traditional aspectual account and related discourse analyses.[11] Let us ignore for the moment the oddity of the inherently imperfective copula *hyh* being construed as a perfective.[12] The real difficulty is bringing a grammatical perfective together with the inherently imperfective (progressive) participle. Such a conjunction defies what we know independently of general aspectual principles.[13] Moreover, since the participle is apparently bearing the progressive aspect, what would otherwise be considered the principal grammatical aspectual axis of the system in cross-linguistic perspective, one would naturally assume as a null hypothesis that the auxiliary *hyh* is *not* bearing grammatical aspect. As a close first approximation, the finite inflection of the auxiliary appears to encode tense in line with the German and English analogues (with consequences for the analysis of the system as a whole).

Even more innocuous at first glance, but troubling upon further consideration, is the construction in (7).

(7)  2 Kgs 12:17
     *lakkōhănîm yihyû*

In the standard account, the construction in (7) is necessarily an emphatic transformation (that is, with emphasis on *lakkōhănîm*) of the more basic (8):

(8)  *yihyû lakkōhănîm*

---

10. "The participle, both as an attribute and as a predicate, usually indicates a continuing action, one in progress, and is best translated with the English progressive tenses" (Lambdin, 19; cf. Waltke and O'Connor, 628, §37.7.1b).

11. While the analogy of the English progressive tenses has been noted by Lambdin (p. 19) and Waltke and O'Connor (628, §37.7.1b), the failure of the aspectual account to explain the semantics of the structures does not register.

12. In my *Placement and Interpretation of the Verb*, chap. 6, I deal with arguments against perfectivity; and the particular point about the clash between the copula and the perfective is dealt with in passing on pp. 191–92, §6.5.4.1. I rehearsed these arguments at the Philadelphia conference of the SBL (1995) in a presentation entitled "Reconsidering the Aspectual Analysis of Biblical Hebrew." I recently argued in "Ewald and Driver on Biblical Hebrew 'Aspect': Anteriority and the Orientalist Framework" (*ZAH* 9 [1996] 129–51) that among other things the perfectivity analysis was a misunderstanding introduced in the first half of this century and best attributed to Carl Brockelmann, "Die 'Tempora' des Semitischen," *Zeitschrift für Phonetik und allgemeine Sprachwissenschaft* 5 (1951) 133–54.

13. Canonical works on aspect include B. Comrie, *Aspect* (Cambridge Textbooks in Linguistics; Cambridge: Cambridge University Press, 1976); and R. Binnick, *Time and the Verb: A Guide to Tense and Aspect* (Oxford: Oxford University Press, 1991).

This analysis, arising from the standard VSO (Verb-Subject–Object or verb-initial) account[14] is seriously flawed. Niccacci is apparently the first to notice what he aptly dubbed the "neglected point of Hebrew syntax," namely, that word order makes a crucial difference in the reading of the prefixed verb forms.[15] Indeed, his point directly contradicts the standard analysis, turning it on its head as it were (though he himself does not work out such a conclusion). To get a sense of the contradiction, the constructions in (7) and (8) are rendered in (9) and (10) respectively with the prefixed verb form in the singular, in which semantic contrasts are explicit.

> (9) *lakkōhănîm yihyeh*

> (10) *yĕhî lakkōhănîm*

In other words, all things being equal, the verb-initial *yiqtol* in (10) is marked by its modal reading; whereas, the verb-second *yiqtol* in (9) is the semantically neutral or unmarked.

Where is the contradiction? On the standard account, the only difference between (7) and (8) is the "emphasis" (whatever that might mean) on *lakkōhănîm*; there is no effect on the verbal semantics. Further, the logic of the standard account dictates that it is the syntactic structure in (8) that can be characterized as neutral.

Contrast this with the way Biblical Hebrew *actually* works. The neutral structure is actually (7) with no "emphasis" and no effect on verbal semantics. The verb-initial structure in (8) is anything but neutral: there is a clear modal element added by virtue of the verb's initial position. In point of fact, then, the Hebrew syntactic facts are a *mirror image* of what might be expected on the standard account.

Moreover, the finite verb in (7) is, under standard assumptions, a "future" of some description. What one would have naturally expected in context would have been the verbless construction in (11).[16]

> (11) *lakkōhănîm hēm*[17]

---

14. For discussion of the VSO account, with bibliography, see Jongeling, "On the VSO Character of Hebrew."

15. A. Niccacci, "A Neglected Point of Hebrew Syntax: Yiqtol and Position in the Sentence," *Liber Annuus* 37 (1987) 7–19. Niccacci's account is limited in scope because of his discourse genre considerations. The point has been established as a strong generalization for Standard Biblical Hebrew prose in my *Placement and Interpretation of the Verb*.

16. This little section employs the *yiqtol*, and not the usual narrative *qatal*, in alternation with the sequential *wayyiqtol*. Otherwise one might have expected *lakkōhănîm hāyû*.

17. I employ the shorter form *hēm* here because it is also used in close proximity to the example under consideration.

This creates at least two problems. Syntactically, we are missing a signifi-cant generalization if we cannot relate (7) to (11) instead of *hēm lakkōhǎnîm*. Semantically, we have to account for the semantics of the prefixed form of *hyh* in this narrative context; or to put it another way, we have to account for the alternation between the presence of the prefixed form of the copula *hyh* and its absence in verbless structures.

In summary, an adequate theory of Biblical Hebrew verbal syntax and se-mantics must account explicitly for the data briefly examined above. On the syntactic side, a theory must account for the neutrality of the verb-second *yiq-tol* construction as well as relate the verb-second *yiqtol* to the neutral verb-second *qatal*; and correctly assign the verb-initial *yiqtol* its modal reading. Further, a syntactic analysis should be able to capture the relation between the problematic structures with *hyh* and the verbless constructions.

On the semantic side, it appears that we have to account for a Biblical He-brew "progressive" paradigm and somehow connect it to the independent be-havior of the copula *hyh*. Further, such an account must explain how tense features can apparently be separated out both from aspectual features and the main verb. Finally, a semantic theory should be able to explain the presence or absence of the *yiqtol* of *hyh*, suggesting some sort of ellipsis under conditions yet to be ascertained.

## 3. Phrase Structure and Movement: An Introduction

The sort of facts just enumerated are best treated within the popular Gov-ernment-Binding (GB) framework.[18] There is much ferment and excitement in the field, which is already making GB appear quaint.[19] Nevertheless, GB is

---

18. Perhaps the best introduction is E. Cowper, *A Concise Introduction to Syntactic Theory: The Government-Binding Approach* (Chicago: University of Chicago Press, 1992). See also H. Lasnik and J. Uriagereka, *A Course in GB Syntax: Lectures on Binding and Empty Categories* (Current Studies in Linguistics 17; Cambridge, Mass.: MIT Press, 1988); A. Radford, *Transformational Grammar: A First Course* (Cambridge Textbooks in Linguis-tics 23; Cambridge: Cambridge University Press, 1988); L. Haegeman, *Introduction to Government and Binding Theory* (Oxford: Blackwell, 1991); and very recently P. Culi-cover, *Principles and Parameters: An Introduction to Syntactic Theory* (Oxford Textbooks in Linguistics; Oxford: Oxford University Press, 1997). Works on ancient Hebrew within this sort of framework, in addition to my own studies, include J. Naudé, "A Syntactic Analysis of Dislocations in Biblical Hebrew," *JNSL* 16 (1990) 115–30; idem, *Independent Personal Pronouns in Qumran Hebrew Syntax*, (D.Litt. diss., University of the Orange Free State, 1996); and Dyk, *Participles in Context*.

19. The excitement comes from a major convergence among theoretical and computa-tional linguists, cognitive scientists, and artificial intelligence theorists. Part of the excite-ment is embodied in the terms *unification* and *minimalism* and centers around a computa-tional theory of morphological parsing and the lexicon. See R. Jackendoff, *The Architecture*

adequate for our purposes, and the analysis can quite easily be recast and updated.

The two concepts of *phrase* or *constituent structure* and *movement* are not at all difficult to grasp, but the standard notation is in fact daunting to the non-specialist. In many ways, reading the notation is like reading a new alphabet: after a period of acclimatization, one hardly notices the new symbolism. It is hard to imagine Hebraists working on syntax in the next century without a familiarity with both the basic concepts and the standard notations.

Consider a fragment such as *going to the store at the corner*: intuitively we can identify the internal structure of such a fragment. Using brackets we can make a major division as in (12).

(12) ((going) (to the store at the corner))

Additionally, we could supply the brackets with labels for the constituents: participle and prepositional phrase. But the parsing obviously continues down into the prepositional phrase. A complete parsing is given in (13).

(13) ((going) ((to) ((the) ((store) ((at) ((the) (corner)))))))

With little imagination one can see that complex sentences are going to be difficult to read and understand, even with labels on the brackets.

Our eyes are not great at parsing structures suitable for machine reading. The inverted tree notation is easy to read and understand (in comparison) and permits a more conspicuous labeling of constituents. A parsing in tree notation is given in (14); the additional P is read "phrase": hence PP, for example, is read "prepositional phrase." It may not be necessary to show this much structure in a given discussion, so the abbreviation in (12) can be recast as (15).

(14)

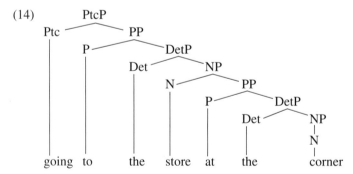

*of the Language Faculty* (Cambridge, Mass.: MIT Press, 1997); J. Pustejovsky, *The Generative Lexicon* (Cambridge, Mass.: MIT Press, 1995); N. Chomsky, *The Minimalist Program* (Cambridge, Mass.: MIT Press, 1995); M. Brody, *Lexico-Logical Form: A Radically Minimalist Theory* (Cambridge, Mass.: MIT Press, 1995); and C. Collins, *Local Economy* (Cambridge, Mass.: MIT Press, 1997).

(15)

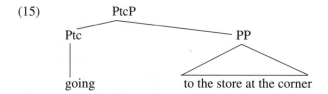

In (14) we can see the reason for the piling-up of brackets on the right in (13): English like Hebrew is *left-headed*, prepositions come before the objects that they govern, and modifiers follow the nouns they modify. Such observations can be captured using variables such as X, Y, Z in generalized schemas. Such a schema can be abstracted away from (14) as in (16).

(16)

The schema in (16), therefore, captures an important generalization governing English and, by extension, Hebrew syntax.

Such generalizations have been studied for some decades within the typological framework established by Greenberg and his many associates.[20] Both English and Hebrew display a strong *left-headedness* and so conform to the VO (Verb-Object) type. So, true to type, we find prepositions in Hebrew instead of postpositions; and we find the noun before both the genitive and the adjective.[21] We, therefore, reasonably expect the structure in (17) as an instantiation of the general schema in (16), where the noun phrase (NP) is the object of the verb (V).[22]

---

20. An entry point for "universals" and the typological study of languages is B. Comrie, *Language Universals and Linguistic Typology: Syntax and Morphology* (2d ed; Chicago: University of Chicago Press, 1989). The relevant chapter here is chap. 4 on word order parameters.

21. Ibid., 95 (12e).

22. Beyond establishing its VO character, the further *typological* question whether the basic word order of Biblical Hebrew is VSO like Welsh or SVO like English (and Dutch and German?) that occupies Jongeling ("On the VSO Character of Hebrew") is not relevant to my work, and in any case I do not find the question interesting. But for what it is worth, Biblical Hebrew is clearly SVO (see the most straightforward interpretation of P. Joüon, *Grammaire de l'hébreu biblique*, §155k), contra Jongeling. I offer a few notes to clarify my position, while recognizing that it will take much more to defend the view. I addressed the question in passing in chap. 5 of *On the Placement and Interpretation of the Verb*, 136–37, §5.1.3.

First, there are two distinct linguistic frameworks within which the question of basic word order is cast: *generative* and *typological* (Comrie, *Language Universals*, 89, §4.1); furthermore, within the typological framework, there are two senses of "basic" that are not

(17)               VP

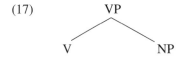

            V              NP

Equally clear but even more difficult to capture visually is the concept of
*movement*. A conspicuous case of movement in English is known as *auxiliary
inversion*, a special case of the general phenomenon of *verb movement*. Consider the contrast in (18)–(19) and the question embedded therein.

(18) Hebrew word order does make a difference.

(19) Does Hebrew word order make a difference?

I am convinced that Hebrew word order *does* make a difference, and in precisely the same manner through verb movement.

---

always clearly distinguished: *statistically prevalent* versus *dominant* (A. Siewierska, *Word
Order Universals* [London: Croom Helm, 1991], 8–14, §1.1.1).

In generative grammar the concern is to find basic or *underlying* representations on
which economical computations can be performed to derive *surface* structures. In large
part, then, "basic" will be abstract and theory-driven; and as can be seen below, GB virtually dictates an *underlying SVO* for Hebrew (as indeed it does for Welsh, as Jongeling notes
somewhat dismissively: "On the VSO Character of Hebrew," 104 n. 8).

Within the *typological* perspective, the concern is with significant cross-linguistic generalizations over *surface* structures. The naive and theoretically uninteresting sense of *statistically prevalent* is the basis for the standard VSO account of Biblical Hebrew; it is only
the sense in which Jongeling's crucial notion of *economy* of derivation can be understood
(p. 106). The more interesting typological sense in which criteria are supplied to define a
*dominant* word order (for example, basic word order obtains in a simple, declarative, main
clause that is prototypically transitive and contains full versus pronominal constituents, following A. Siewierska, *Word Order Rules*, 8, §1.1.1) leads necessarily to the SVO type on
the crucial assumption that the statistically prevalent, narrative construction with *wayyiqtol*
is morphologically, syntactically and semantically marked (DeCaen, *On the Placement and
Interpretation of the Verb*, 137, §5.1.3). No doubt such considerations influenced Joüon as
well (Jongeling suggests that Joüon adopted a *synchronic* versus *historical-comparative*
viewpoint ["On the VSO Character of Hebrew," 104], but I fail to see what meaning can be
given to this mysterious suggestion and how *synchronic* might correlate with SVO).

Second, if I understand the nature of typological argumentation, there is nothing to argue typologically for VSO over SVO (pace Jongeling). Generally, VSO and SVO pattern together along the major parameters (Comrie, *Language Universals*, esp. p. 95, §4.2.1).
Moreover, the relevant typological universals are *statistical* (that is, not necessary) and crucially *unidirectional*, from clause type to the other parameters (ibid., esp. 93, 100, §4.2.1;
see further Comrie's references to J. Hawkins, *Word Order Universals* [New York: Academic, 1983]). In other words, correlations with putative VSO Welsh along the parameters
of noun-adjective or adjective-adverb, for example, are irrelevant in determining basic
word order. The correlation only works the other way: if it can be established that a given
language is VSO (in what sense?), then it is predicted that adjectives follow nouns, and so
on. In summary, Jongeling's second line of argumentation is unsound, though no doubt
there is much to be learned from a comparison between Welsh and Hebrew.

It remains to find some sort of notation to capture the relation, which could be described as a *mapping*, from (18) to (19). One way to go about it is to introduce abstract, phonologically null elements (that is, elements present syntactically but unrealized phonologically) into the representation. In (20)–(21) an abstract *Q* for "question" and a *t* for "trace" are introduced to account for (19).

(20) *Q* Hebrew word order does make a difference?

(21) Does Hebrew word order *t* make a difference?

The pair of structures in (20)–(21) is related by a *mapping* or *transformation*. An abstract, phonologically null *Q* must be *lexicalized* or signaled somehow. The verb therefore *moves* to lexicalize or realize the abstract *Q*, leaving behind a *trace* to mark its original position. We characterize (20) as an *underlying representation* and the transformed (21) as a *surface* or *derived representation*.

Increasingly, linguists are making use of arrows to indicate such movements. The transformation in (20)–(21) might be represented in abbreviated form in (22).

(22) *Q* Hebrew word order does make a difference?

In summary, then, we have introduced the two basic concepts of phrase structure and movement. In traditional studies of Biblical Hebrew syntax, the internal structure of Hebrew constituents is not related to larger clausal relations; however, an analysis that relates structures at all levels is greatly to be preferred. Greater generalization over phrase structures can be achieved by introducing movement. The burden of theories in the generative linguistic tradition is to explain and constrain movement with general principles and parameters. The great attraction of GB is the leap to fully generalized structures and movements.

## 4. GB Phrase Structure and Movement

Two extensions of the general picture of phrase structure introduced above characterize the GB approach: X′ (read "X bar") notation, and functional heads and their projections. After extending the theory of phrase structure, we will be in a position to look at a sample derivation of Gen 1:1.

Briefly put, an XP has internal structure: an intermediate level headed by X, and the expanded or *maximal projection*. The X′ schema is given in (23).

(23)

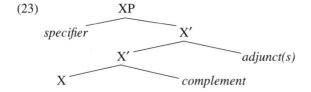

The schema captures the left-headedness of English and Hebrew. The head X has its sister[23] on the right, forming a minimal X′ projection. This structure can be expanded recursively to the right. The ordering of these constituents to the right is fixed and well understood both for English and Hebrew.[24] The specifier position is an innovation with a long history; suffice it to say that within a verb phrase (VP), the specifier or *spec-VP* is the home of the syntactic subject.

An underlying VP for Gen 1:1 can now be constructed as in (24).

(24)

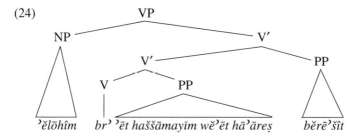

The verb, or more accurately, the uninflected verbal root, directly governs its object to the right, in this case a PP whose internal structure is not relevant. The temporal modifier, also a PP, is indirectly governed; it is a sister of V′. The subject is stationed to the left under the general schema and is also a sister of V′; the subject and V′ together form the maximal projection of V, that is,

---

23. It is common to speak of syntactic configurations in genealogical terms because of the common tree notation. In the structure

the dominant node A is the *mother*, while the direct dependents B and C are *daughters*. Following on with this analogy, we speak of the basic and important configurational relation between B and C in terms of *sisterhood*.

24. A thorough treatment of constituent ordering in the verb phrase is provided by L. Lode, "Postverbal Word Order in Biblical Hebrew: Structure and Function," *Semitics* 9 (1984) 113–64.

VP. The overall structure at this underlying level, then, is necessarily Subject-Predicate and SVO (Subject-Verb-Object).

Crucial to this picture is the fact that the verbal root is morphologically ill formed at this early stage of the derivation: it lacks inflection and so cannot be realized phonologically. Inflectional features are treated as syntactic heads, heading their own maximal projections. These "functional" projections form layers above the VP. There does not appear to be any need in Hebrew for more than two such functional heads, mood (M) and tense (T).[25] An abstract skeleton for the Hebrew clause will therefore have the complex structure in (25).

(25)

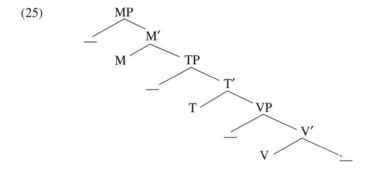

The resulting situation is this: abstract inflectional features are morphologically ill formed and need to be lexicalized; the verbal root is morphologically ill formed and requires inflection. The verb must move, therefore, to pick up inflection, thereby creating complex heads that can be morphologically interpreted or *spelled out*. Movement can create increasingly complex heads known as *adjoined* structures displayed in (26).

(26)     (a)   V          (b)   T          (c)   M

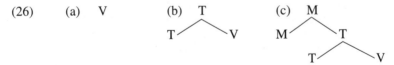

As an illustration, the derivation of Gen 1:1 will now be presented. The derivation begins with the underlying representation in (27); the MP is left out for convenience only, since modal features do not play a role in this case. Two transformations are applied in (28) and (29) to derive the surface representation.

---

25. The precise names of these heads are not important, but I have adopted labels that more accurately reflect the semantic functions in keeping with much current practice. In the standard GB notation, M(ood) is C(omplementizer), while T(ense) is I(nflection), formerly Aux(iliary).

(27)

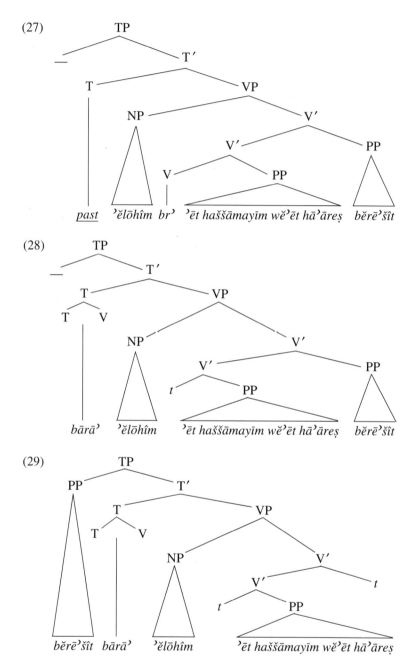

(28)

(29)

In (28) the verbal root *raises* to the tense feature, thereby creating the complex head which will be spelled out as *bārā'*. The morphological demands of the verbal root and the inflectional feature are both satisfied. This movement is responsible for the characteristic VS ordering. The spec-TP position is then filled by the movement of the temporal modifier in (29). The simplest assumption for Hebrew is the strong claim that a movement of one constituent to spec-TP is obligatory. Such an apparently discourse-functional transformation is generally termed *topicalization*, with possible discourse-structuring properties.

Notice what would happen if the verb further raised to M. A verb-initial structure would be created that would leave the topicalized constituent tucked *behind* the verb. Such obligatory topicalization trapped behind the verb would apparently account for the postverbal effects so ably described by Lode.[26] Notice also that there are two spec-positions, spec-MP and spec-TP, that could be used to separate such low-level topicalization and the so-called *casus pendens* phenomenon. The latter could be placed in spec-MP (the consequences of which pass beyond the scope of this work).

## 5. Feature Complexes and Their Interpretation

There are two steps remaining before we can capture the verbless clause in a unified model of Standard Biblical Hebrew. First, an integrated model of the creation of complex syntactic heads must be offered that supports both morphological and semantic interpretation. Second, the verbless structure must be shown to fall out naturally from such an account.

The simplest approach to the structure of the Hebrew clause is to assume as a null hypothesis that all three heads, Mood (M), Tense (T), and Verb (V), are present in the underlying representation.[27] Further, the simplest model will allow the presence or absence of material to vary independently for each head. On this basis the behavior of the Hebrew verb should be captured in a systematic and principled manner.

What this approach explicitly permits, then, is a variety of underlying *mismatches*. A verbal root may be present and require inflection, while there may be no inflectional features to satisfy the requirement. An inflectional feature

---

26. Lode, "Postverbal Word Order."

27. It might be argued that another approach would be to eliminate the V and its projection in a verbless construction; or in other words, to let the head of the predicate in the verbless construction project independently a maximal projection governed by T. However attractive this might appear, within the current framework it would cause a serious problem. Within this framework, only maximal projections and heads can move; but because of the movement in Predicate-Subject constructions, we would be forced into moving an X′ projection. To avoid this, we would have to add a further projection without independent motivation and to posit an additional series of movements. In my view, such an approach would abandon a simple, unified treatment and lack elegance.

may be present and require lexicalization in the absence of a verbal root. From
the simplest model we can expect complex interactions. The morphological
component will have to be able to interpret such defective representations;
and for this we can invoke *default* operations for the spell-out process.

The crucial point for our purposes is that such a model allows in principle
for the possibility of the absence of head material across the board: no inflectional features at M or T, and no verbal root at V. It is this logical possibility
that can account for the Hebrew verbless clause in such a way as to unify the
syntax of verbal and verbless clauses in an interesting way.

As a crude first approximation we can posit three primitives, one for each
head: *mood* (M), *past* (T), and *root* (V), where by *root* we understand a general variable. Since the logic of the system permits the absence of *mood* without consequences for spell-out, we require only two default mechanisms for T
and V. Let us stipulate that a default interpretation for T in the absence of *past*
is the prefixed conjugation or *yiqtol*; and further that a default interpretation
for V in the absence of a verbal root is the semantically null copula *hyh*. On
this basis we can generate a chart such as (30). Presence of a feature is marked
[+] and its absence by [∅]; verb-second is abbreviated V2 and verb-initial V1.

(30)

| *mood* (M) | *past* (T) | *root* (V) | spell-out | syntax |
|:---:|:---:|:---:|:---:|:---:|
| ∅ | ∅ | + | *yiqtōl* (long) | V2 |
| ∅ | + | + | *qātal* | |
| + | ∅ | + | *(w(ay))yiqtōl* (short) | V1 |
| + | + | + | *(wĕ)qātal* | |
| ∅ | ∅ | ∅ | *yihyeh* | V2 |
| ∅ | + | ∅ | *hāyāh* | |
| + | ∅ | ∅ | *(way)yĕhî / wîhî* | V1 |
| + | + | ∅ | *(wĕ)hāyāh* | |

In summary, then, this chart captures the verbal system with only three primitives in a principled and systematic manner. Crucially, it relates the presence
of *mood* to the verb-initial structures, thereby accounting for Niccacci's neglected point of Hebrew syntax. However, as yet there is still no verbless
clause.

There are aspects of this chart worth noting. First, it cannot be emphasized
enough that this is a crude first approximation. Second, it is not germane to
this discussion what the exact labels of the features are. One could, for ex-

ample, substitute *completed*, or even *fred*, for *past* without affecting the *formal*, syntactic structure of the model (though I am prepared to argue that the labels are in fact warranted). This leads to the third point, which also cannot be emphasized enough, that the precise semantic *interpretation* of this formal model is still an open question: this is especially true in the case of the modal analysis of the so-called consecutive forms, though in the light of cross-linguistic data, I believe this is the right sort of solution.[28]

The formal model in (30) is now assumed in the following discussion. A final and crucial step is now required, namely, the step from the chart in (30) to the generation of the *surface* verbless clause. Upon reviewing the chart in (30), it should be obvious that the zero feature row, with $\emptyset$–$\emptyset$–$\emptyset$ across the board, captures the representation of the verbless constructions. Let us assume that $\emptyset$–$\emptyset$–$\emptyset$ is in fact the source of the verbless clause and examine the consequences.

First, the purpose of the default rules is to *repair* defective representations by *satisfying* morphological demands. But an underlying $\emptyset$–$\emptyset$–$\emptyset$ representation has no demands to be satisfied, it does not violate any spell-out constraints. The simplest model, it would seem then, would omit altogether the realization of $\emptyset$–$\emptyset$–$\emptyset$, which is a promising result.

Second, however, the automatic mapping of $\emptyset$–$\emptyset$–$\emptyset$ to the surface verbless construction cannot be correct, or else the prefixed form of the copula *hyh* would never surface in this model.

Third, then, the model could be saved by identifying another condition that forces the spell-out of $\emptyset$–$\emptyset$–$\emptyset$, the *yiqtol* of *hyh* in this model. So we move to a second approximation and say that the default reading of $\emptyset$–$\emptyset$–$\emptyset$, the absence of features and verbal root, is phonologically null, as might reasonably be expected under a more rigorous interpretation of defaulting. It should not be spelled out, all things being equal. The surfacing of the long *yiqtol* of *hyh* must then be independently motivated. Consequently, within the formal model adopted, the lexicalization of $\emptyset$–$\emptyset$–$\emptyset$ must be syntactically optional though otherwise unmotivated; and we will naturally look to other components of the grammar for motivation(s).

Within other perspectives this optional behavior might be characterized in terms of suppression or *ellipsis* of the *yiqtol*; however, the ellipsis approach would appear to get the defaulting backward, as explained.

In summary, the general model can be saved but at the price of casting about for reasons why the *yiqtol* of *hyh* must be realized in the surface representation. Such a search constitutes an open-ended research project. There are in fact a few contexts that suggest that zero inflection must be realized under

---

28. The modal analysis, in light of data from, for example, Fula and Swahili, is laid out in my *Placement and Interpretation of the Verb*, chap. 9, esp. §§9.3–9.4.

certain conditions. The most salient example has already been introduced above from 2 Kgs 12:17, *lakkōhănîm yihyû* 'it belonged to the priests'. A number of factors that might be in play in this particular context include the use of *yiqtol* instead of *qatal* in alternation with the sequential *wayyiqtol* (genre, stylistics; pragmatics), and the absence of an overt subject perhaps requiring that subject agreement be realized by the verb form (formal semantic). Another example from the Standard corpus, *ḥōdeš yihyû ballĕbānôn* 'they spent a month in Lebanon' (1 Kgs 5:28[14]) suggests both links as well. An adequate account would also have to relate these instances of realization in some fashion to the ubiquitous "future" and "modal" contexts of *yiqtol* (again, semantic).

## 6. Sample Derivations

The sample derivation of Gen 1:1 presented above is sufficient to demonstrate the basic dynamic of the formal model. In this section, the derivation of the surface verbless constructions is worked through as an overall summary. Variations on *wayhî saʿar-gādôl bayyām* (Jonah 1:4) are followed by a derivation of the progressive construction.

The three structures in (31)–(33) are now derived. An underlying representation of (31)–(32) is given in (34), with respective derivations in (35)–(36). Underlying and derived representations of (33) follow in (37)–(38).

(31) *saʿar gādôl bayyām*

(32) *bayyām saʿar gādôl*

(33) *wayhî saʿar gādôl bayyām*

(34)

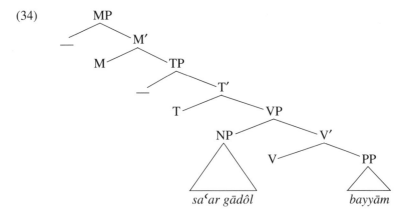

(35)

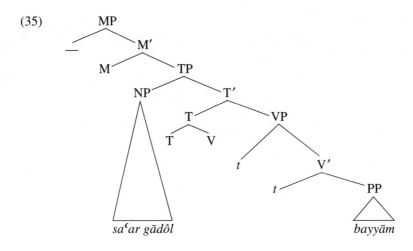

(36)

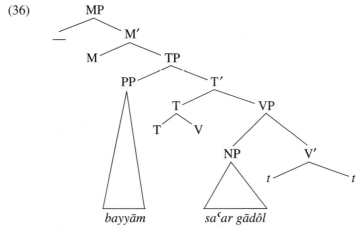

(37)

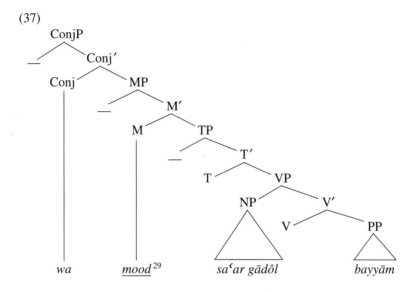

(38)

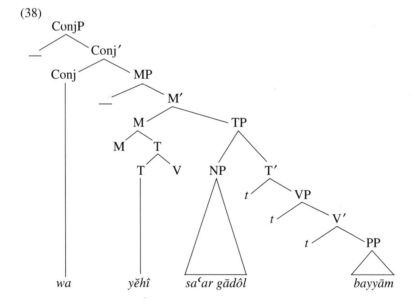

<hr />

29. To distinguish modal features that differentiate *wayhî* from *wîhî*, we could extend the primitives, for example, to mood 1 and mood 2, but this is not germane to the syntactic treatment here.

In reviewing these derivations, we should emphasize that Subject-Predicate and Predicate-Subject surface constructions are *equally derived*: one is not necessarily more "basic" than another, except at an abstract or underlying level (within this model, of course, Subject-Predicate is *underlying*). The two structures are related by an obligatory topicalization; they differ only in which element has been topicalized to spec-TP. As well, these derivations make predications about the realization, for example, of *past*, and specifically its surface location. It should follow, therefore, that the related constructions are (39)–(40).

(39) *saʿar gādôl hāyāh bayyām*

(40) *bayyām hāyāh saʿar gādôl*

Finally, the Hebrew progressive construction will be derived. The construction from 2 Kgs 18:4 is assigned an underlying and surface representation in (41) and (42), respectively.

(41)

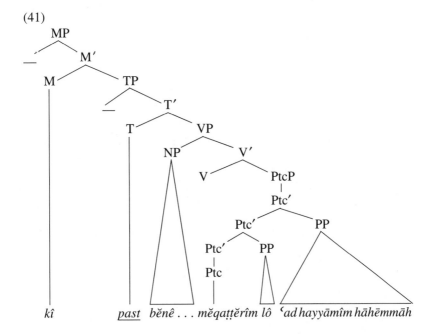

*kî*          *past bĕnê . . . mĕqaṭṭĕrîm lô ʿad hayyāmîm hāhēmmāh*

(42)

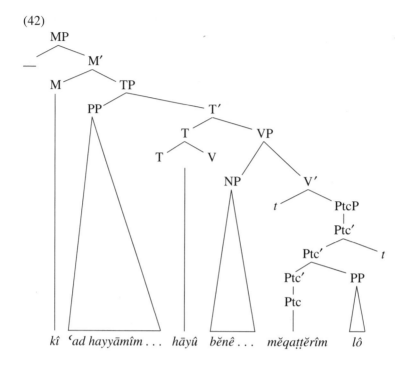

kî ʿad hayyāmîm . . . hāyû běnê . . . měqaṭṭĕrîm   lô

It should follow naturally that in the absence of the feature *past*, the derivation of the progressive construction will be identical except for the unlexicalized T head. From such structures the full complement of a Biblical Hebrew progressive paradigm will fall out straightforwardly.

## 7. Summary of Possible Ordering within the Verbless Clause

The model sketched above constrains quite narrowly the possible ordering among constituents within the surface verbless construction. If, for example, we were to schematize the underlying constituents in (41) minus the feature *past* as in (43), there are only three possible orders ex hypothesi, as given in (44)–(46).

(43) *underlying*

| M | NP$_{subject}$ | Ptc | PP$_{dative}$ | PP$_{temporal}$ |

(44) *subject topicalized*

| M | NP$_{subject}$ | Ptc | PP$_{dative}$ | PP$_{temporal}$ |

(45) *dative topicalized*

| M | PP$_{dative}$ | NP$_{subject}$ | Ptc | PP$_{temporal}$ |

(46) *temporal topicalized*

| M | PP$_{temporal}$ | NP$_{subject}$ | Ptc | PP$_{dative}$ |

Each ordering will be appropriate in different discourse contexts. According to my unpublished studies of topicalization in context,[30] (44) is actually quite rare, while (46) with the temporal constituent topicalized is almost obligatory. However, because the dative is pronominal, (45) is obligatory when the pronoun refers to the paragraph focus or discourse participant (in the actual context of [41], the principal participant under focus is Hezekiah).

## 8. Conclusion: A Formal Syntax and the Verbless Clause

A number of problems were raised at the outset of this paper that an adequate theory of Biblical Hebrew grammar must address. On the syntactic side, there is the neutrality of the verb-second constructions in the Hebrew main clause, both with *qatal* and crucially with *yiqtol*; and the marked modal nature of verb-initial *yiqtol*. The verb-second structures are derived under a verb-movement analysis together with an obligatory topicalization. The modal nature of the verb-initial *yiqtol* is accounted for by an additional movement to lexicalize a feature *mood*.

A model of interactions between the syntactic heads M(ood), T(ense), and V(erb) allows for the logical possibility of unlexicalized zero inflection, the so-called verbless clause. This model posits an explicit, direct relationship between the verbless clause, on the one hand, and clauses with *hyh*, on the other, which might reasonably be expected on semantic grounds. The model can also support an analysis of Biblical Hebrew with a full array of compound "progressive tenses" in light of the independent behavior of *hyh*.

The outstanding issue left to be resolved on this view is the independent motivation for the surfacing of the *yiqtol* of *hyh*. This issue constitutes an open-ended research project. It is not clear whether morphological, syntactic, semantic, or pragmatico-discourse factors or, even more likely, some combination thereof, are responsible. Though a major issue, admittedly, it does not detract in any way from the explanatory power of a unified morphosyntactic and semantic model of Standard Biblical Hebrew.

---

30. V. DeCaen, "Where is the Exegetical Pay-Off? Textlinguistic Applications of a Revised Syntax and Semantics for Standard Biblical Hebrew" (manuscript submitted for the Dahood Memorial Prize, SBL, 1996); idem, "On the Predictability of Word Order in Jonah: Toward a Topicalization Algorithm," *Hebrew Syntax Encoding Initiative Working Papers* 96.5; idem, "A Textlinguistic Analysis of Pronominalization and Coherence in the Book of Jonah," *Hebrew Syntax Encoding Initiative Working Papers* 96.7.

# Paradigmatic and Syntagmatic Features in Identifying Subject and Predicate in Nominal Clauses

JANET W. DYK and EEP TALSTRA

*Free University, Amsterdam*

## 1. Introduction

### 1.1. Definition of the Intended Topic

The topic *nominal clauses* may appear to be unambiguous; nonetheless, when one takes stock of various treatments of the subject, it becomes apparent that there is no a priori consensus about what exactly should be included or excluded. Constructions that receive an inconsistent evaluation about whether they belong to the topic or receive diverse analyses when they are included in the topic are at least the following:

> one-member nominal clauses
> constructions with the so-called copula pronoun
> structures containing the particles of being: *yš* and *'yn*
> structures containing the sentence modifiers: *hnh* and *'wd*
> participial constructions
> the verb of being: *hyh*
> complex structures involving embedding, extraposition, dislocation, stranding

The core data, on which it seems all would agree, are the constructions that consist of a predicative relationship between two nonverbal elements, of which one element is taken to be the S and one the P.

*Authors' note*: Our thanks are due to T. Walton for his critical comments on the text.

It is to this core that we initially and primarily direct our attention. Thereafter, on the basis of what comes to light in these constructions, other related structures will also be considered to see whether and to what extent the same syntactic processes are present and the same analysis, or a variation thereof, is applicable.

The initial data consist of simple nominal clauses, as defined above, gleaned from the following texts:

| | |
|---|---|
| Exodus 1–3 | narrative and direct speech |
| Numbers 22–24 | narrative, direct speech, and poetry |
| Deuteronomy 3–8 | rhetorical and embedded narrative |
| Judges 6–9 | narrative and direct speech |
| Isaiah 15, 16, 28 | poetry |
| Ruth 1–4 | narrative and direct speech |
| Esther 1–3 | narrative and direct speech |
| Qohelet 1–3 | rhetorical |

Occasional examples drawn from other texts will also be used.

### 1.2. Isolation of the Relevant Data

When constructing a database of grammatically analyzed data, one is generally confronted with a considerable number of complex constructions for which no consistent and unambiguous analysis is apparent. While in much grammatical discussion one starts from a set of selected examples belonging to the desired set of clause-types, our point of departure has been integral segments of texts with all of their idiosyncrasies.

Within integral portions of text, words, phrases, and clauses have been isolated from the basic morphological coding on the basis of formally recognizable patterns. This means that the resulting data are more ideal than the actual facts, due to the complexity of many of the syntactic possibilities. Nonetheless, at some level, the text can be divided into segments with not more than one internal predicative relation apiece. From this data, for the purposes of this paper, all segments containing a finite verbal form were rejected as irrelevant.

A closer look at the remaining segments revealed that a variety of structures do not meet the requirement of having a predicative relationship between the members. For example, it is not always obvious whether a segment is to be taken as an ellipse, dependent on an already-occurring verb, or an independent nominal clause. An illustration of this can be found in Judg 6:37:

| (1) Judg 6:37 | ᵓm ṭl yhyh ᶜl-hgzh lbdh |
|---|---|
| | wᶜl-kl-hᵓrṣ ḥrb |
| RSV | if there is dew on the fleece alone, |
| | and it is dry on all the ground |

Whether the second segment is to be taken as an independent nominal clause is unclear. What lies behind this uncertainty is the fact that the verb of being, *hyh*, takes the same constellation of elements in its environment as that which constitutes a nominal clause. The relation between clauses with *hyh* and nominal clauses will be discussed more thoroughly below (§3.5.2).

With other verbs, where the valency pattern imposes other relationships between the elements occurring with the verb, it is easier to conclude that an ellipse is present:

(2) Isa 16:11    *ʿl-kn mʿy lmwʾb kknwr yhmw*
               *wqrby lqyr ḥrś*
    RSV        Therefore my soul moans like a lyre for Moab
               and my heart for Kir-heres.

It is reasonable to assume that the two elements occurring after the main clause in the last example have a relationship to each other dependent on the significance of the verb in the main clause, not a relationship to each other as though they together composed a nominal clause.[1] Such segments do not represent independent nominal clauses and will not be included as examples.

Similarly, it is necessary to distinguish between one-element nominal clauses (see more on these below, §3.1) and cases of interjections, *casus pendens*, or vocatives.

Thus, *verbless clause* is not to be defined simply as the absence of a finite verbal form within a string, but there must also be a predicate relation among the elements. In rough approximation, Table 1 shows the proportions of the various types of structures found to be present in the texts used.

## 2. In Search of Paradigmatic Categories of Description

Limiting ourselves first to this narrowly delimited set of data, we will attend to the following questions:

- How is one to recognize which element present is the S and which is the P within an isolated simple nominal clause?
- What types of predicative relationships hold between the two elements?
- What linguistic explanation can be given for the constructions and for the predicative relationships encountered?
- Does one need to assume an underlying, unmarked default word order for simple nominal clauses from which one can deviate in order to express emphasis or focus?

---

1. Were the second half not an ellipse, that is, without the preceding verb and its accompanying valency pattern, it would be a nominal clause corresponding to the syntactic pattern usually translated as a possessive clause: 'my innermost belongs to Kir-heres'.

**Table 1.  Approximate Distribution of Types of Predicates
within the Selected Texts**

| Type \ Texts | verbal | | nominal | | | | leftovers[a] | | Total |
|---|---|---|---|---|---|---|---|---|---|
| | | | participles | | other | | | | |
| Exodus 1–3 | 247 | 83% | 10 | 3% | 24 | 8% | 18 | 6% | 299 |
| Numbers 22–24 | 362 | 80% | 28 | 6% | 33 | 7% | 31 | 7% | 454 |
| Deuteronomy 3–8 | 531 | 71% | 54 | 7% | 79 | 11% | 79 | 11% | 743 |
| Judges 6–9 | 587 | 77% | 30 | 4% | 90 | 12% | 54 | 7% | 761 |
| Isaiah 15, 16, 28 | 153 | 70% | 10 | 5% | 33 | 15% | 23 | 10% | 219 |
| Ruth 1–4 | 368 | 79% | 15 | 3% | 53 | 11% | 33 | 7% | 469 |
| Esther 1–3 | 166 | 61% | 37 | 13% | 35 | 13% | 36 | 13% | 274 |
| Qohelet 1–3 | 184 | 54% | 25 | 8% | 96 | 28% | 35 | 10% | 340 |
| Total | 2,598 | 73% | 209 | 6% | 443 | 12% | 309 | 9% | 3,549 |

a. These are neither nominal clauses nor verbal clauses but are segments that will be connected to larger units at a later stage in our database construction. They include vocatives, time phrases, the fronted element of a *casus pendens* construction, stranded NPs, and ellipses.

**2.1.** Recognition of S and P within a Simple Nominal Clause

The challenge inherent in building a database is to see whether the data itself presents enough formally recognizable information for the assignment of S and P to be done with the assistance of the computer. Developing a procedure by which a machine can be employed to make such decisions requires taking an inventory of relevant parameters and establishing a significant relative order among these parameters.

It appears that some authors prefer to base their decisions on the distribution of phrase-types alone. Others would add observations on clause-types, often relating these to patterns of word order. Still others add categories of logical and/or semantic relations between the S and P in order to be able to assign those labels.

It is thus necessary to make a number of decisions in answer to the following questions:

- Should S–P parsing be based only on the actual presence of phrase-types in a particular clause?
- Should the S–P parsing be related to word order?
- Should the S–P parsing be expressed in terms of logical and/or semantic relations?

In constructing a database of grammatically analyzed data, it is important to be clear about the type of arguments used to make decisions. In the absence of native-speaker competence for ancient Hebrew, it would appear preferable to avoid analyses based on our intuition about the effect or function of a specific language unit or about whether or not a particular word order is to be taken as exceptional. Rather, observations of a more distributional character should be used to reformulate insights arrived at by other means.

In searching for clues to help us in this analysis, the insights of others have been taken into consideration. In particular, the following approaches will be reviewed:

> textual-semantic relations (Muraoka)
> logical-semantic relations (Niccacci)
> nominal clause-types (Michel)
> functional and formal syntactic analysis (Andersen and Hoftijzer)
> clause-type patterns and phrase-types (Richter)

In spite of the heterogeneity in the approaches represented, we propose to search for underlying formal common denominators of the analyses given that would be helpful to us in constructing a database of grammatically analyzed data.

### 2.1.1. Niccacci on Logical-Semantic Relations

After defining a simple nominal clause as one "that does not contain any finite verb form—not even the verb *hyh*," Niccacci[2] addresses first the lack of criteria for determining what the S and P of a nominal clause are. Another aspect that he says needs to be treated is a clarification of the principle that lies behind word order.

Niccacci proposes to solve the first matter by taking two basic principles into consideration: first, the traditional doctrine of universals and particulars; second, the position in the sentence. The first principle involves distinguishing substances (or particulars), which function as Ss, and accidental properties (or universals), which function as Ps. The second principle involves recognizing as predicative a sentence in which the P occurs sentence-initially and as nominal a sentence in which the P does not occur sentence-initially. From these principles, Niccacci derives a division of possible nominal clause-types in which the major distinction is between unmarked and marked types.

The unmarked types include those where the S is an element representing substance and the P is an element representing accidence. There are three types of unmarked nominal clause structures: predicative, presentative, and

---

2. A. Niccacci, "Simple Nominal Clause (SNC) or Verbless Clause in Biblical Hebrew Prose," *ZAH* 6 (1993) 216–27.

circumstantial. The predicative has emphasis on the P as the first member, wherein the first position of the sentence is taken by an expression belonging to the class of the P (accidence): the sentence is predicative (unmarked, neutral) because class and function coincide; the emphasis is on that which is the P; the information involved is general. In the presentative sentence, the S, representing substance, comes first; there is no emphasis on this first element because "there is no predicative nexus in it between (grammatical) subject and (grammatical) predicate."[3] In these sentences characters are introduced, simultaneous happenings are described, events are reported, and so on. In circumstantial sentences, the P (accidence) can be either sentence-initial or after the S (substance); in both cases the word order is unmarked.

What these unmarked types of sentences have in common is that the P and the S follow Aristotelian terms quite nicely—that is, substances function as Ss while accidental properties function as Ps. Because the formal categories within our database do not have information on "substance" and "accidence," in order to utilize Niccacci's insights it is necessary to translate them, if possible, into formally recognizable grammatical categories. Of the 35 examples given by Niccacci for these 3 types (predicative, presentative, and circumstantial), 36 can be assigned S and P as proposed by Niccacci by coordinating substance and accidence with certain (limited) grammatical categories, as follows:

SUBJECT (substance)                  PREDICATE (accidence)
personal pronouns (13×)[4]           proper names (7×)[5]
                                     prepositional phrases (7×)[6]
                                     adjectives / stative participles (4×)[7]

Sometimes more than one of these determinative factors were simultaneously present, confirming the S–P analysis; there were no cases of conflict between criteria. For example, Niccacci's example 5 (Gen 29:4) has both a personal pronoun, which is consistently S, and a prepositional phrase, which is consistently P, within the unmarked sentence types:

---

3. Ibid., 220.

4. Niccacci's examples 1 (Lev 11:35), 2 (1 Kgs 20:32), 5a+b (Gen 29:4), 7 (Gen 28:13), 8 (Gen 24:65), 12a+b (Gen 24:23, 24), 13a+b (Gen 27:32), 16 (Lev 11:35), 17 (Num 9:7) and 22a (Gen 48:14).

5. Niccacci's examples: 20 (Gen 24:29 plus Gen 38:1, 2 mentioned in his text), 22 (Gen 48:14a plus 2 Sam 20:21 and 1 Kgs 13:2 mentioned in his text), and 22b (Gen 48:14b). It should be observed that all of the cases cited where a proper name is predicate involve sentences in which the subject is '[his/her] name'.

6. Niccacci's examples: 5a+b (Gen 29:4), 6 (1 Sam 17:41), 11b (Gen 19:31b), 14 (Gen 26:20), 15 (1 Kgs 2:14), and 23c (Num 22:22c); examples 5a+b are also counted as having a personal pronoun S.

7. Niccacci's examples: 1 (Lev 11:35), 11a (Gen 19:31a), 16 (Lev 11:35), and 17 (Num 9:7); examples 1, 16, and 17 are also counted as having a personal pronoun S.

(3) Gen 29:4    (P) *mḥrn*   (S) *ʾnḥnw*
    Niccacci     From Haran are we.

The above correlation between substance-accidence and formally recognizable grammatical categories covers the majority of the examples of the unmarked simple nominal clauses given. As one might imagine, within Niccacci's selected examples, not all possible syntactic combinations have been dealt with, and it would seem that a fuller range of combinatory possibilities should be proposed.

Of the remaining 9 not accounted for by these grammatical categories, 7 involve participles[8] that we are omitting at the present, to be discussed below (§3.3.1). The remaining 2 cases involve more complex structures that will be returned to below (§3.2).[9]

The matter becomes really exciting, however, when we arrive at cases where Niccacci assumes a switch of category assignment in the initial position. A member of the class S (substance) is interpreted as P. Thus, class and function diverge; there is emphasis on an expression that is not expected to be a P. These are marked constructions. As in the predicative sentences, the emphasis is on the first member; however, the first position of the sentence is occupied by an expression not belonging to the class of the P, that is, not accidence. These are nonpredicative sentences but also nonnominal, according to the definition above, nominal having the word order S–P. The information conveyed is not general but is concerned with a specific detail, for example (Niccacci's example 32b = Gen 27:24):

(4) Gen 27:24    (P) *ʾth* (S) *zh bny ʿśw* . . .
                (P) *ʾny*
    Niccacci     Are you (this, i.e.) my son Esau?
                (Jacob answered:) I am.

In order to come to such a reversal of assignment of P (for the S is merely the other element that occurs in noninitial position), the broader context must be taken into consideration, for "correct syntactic analysis is impossible if one remains bound to the sentence level; only on the larger level of the text are the relationships between sentences correctly understood."[10]

In Niccacci's approach, the examples given are determined to a large extent at least by the following three principles, which also hold true for all of Niccacci's examples:

---

8. Niccacci's examples: 4 (Gen 37:16), 9 (Gen 38:13), 10 (Num 11:27), 18a+b (Gen 45:12), and 23a+b (Num 22:22).

9. Niccacci's examples: 3 (Deut 3:21b) and 18c (Gen 45:12c).

10. Niccacci, "Simple Nominal Clause," 216.

- there is no pronoun copula in Hebrew[11]
- the verb *hyh* is not a copula but a normal verb[12]
- "when a verb form takes the second position, the sentence has the function of a noun phrase, i.e., it is used as a nominal or adverbial element of a larger unit of text."[13]

Summarizing Niccacci's 33 examples of nonpredicative, nonnominal, marked nominal clauses, it appears that they represent the following hierarchy of grammatical structures:

a question pronoun, when present, is always the P                                    4×[14]
   (it could be noted that it is also clause-initial in all cases)
demonstrative pronouns with other nominal elements:
- when sentence-initial, always the P                                                6×[15]
- when preceded by a nominal element, always S                                       3×[16]

in *casus pendens* constructions, after the initial nominal
element, a nominal construction occurs involving a pronoun:
- when the second element of this nominal construction
  involves any verbal form at all,[17] then the pronoun is the P    13×[18]
- when the second element of this nominal construction
  involves another Pronoun + Nominal structure, then the
  first pronoun is the P                                                             1×[19]
- when the second element of this nominal construction is a
  noun phrase, then the pronoun is the S                                            5×[20]

Thus, the interpretation of Niccacci is translatable into formal patterns, but the grammatical information present in the phrase-types is overruled by his insights concerning patterns of a higher abstraction.

In contrast to Niccacci, when we do take the broader context into account, we choose to maintain consistently the grammatical analysis based on the

---

11. Ibid., 224.

12. Ibid., 216, 224.

13. Ibid., 216.

14. Niccacci's examples: 35 (1 Chr 22:1), 36 (2 Chr 2:5b), 37 (Deut 4:7), and 38 (Exod 3:11).

15. Niccacci's examples: 19a (1 Sam 9:18), 31a+b+c (Gen 5:1, 20:13, 25:12), and 34a+b (1 Chr 22:1).

16. Niccacci's examples: 32a+b+c (Gen 27:21, 27:24, 32:3).

17. These include: participle, definite article + participle, finite verbal forms, and finite forms of *hyh*.

18. Niccacci's examples: 24a+b+c (Deut 9:3), 25a+b+c (Deut 31:3), 26a+b (Deut 31:8), 27a+b (Josh 22:22), 28a+b (Josh 23:3b, 5a), and 33b (2 Chr 20:6).

19. Niccacci's example: 33a (2 Sam 7:28).

20. Niccacci's examples: 29 (Gen 36:8b) and 30a+b+c+d (Gen 41:25, 26).

simpler structures. We will leave a discussion of the rest of Niccacci's treatment for what it is, something to be incidentally returned to in later sections.

### 2.1.2. Muraoka on Textual-Semantic Relations

Although Muraoka is concerned with emphasis and not primarily with nominal clauses, a major section of his chapter on word order is devoted to the nominal clause and supplies examples from which inferences can be made that pertain to our topic.[21] Unfortunately, Muraoka does not present criteria for determining which element is to be recognized as S or P, stating:

> I have no intention whatever to venture into the precarious and also dubious logico-grammatical argument as to whether the word-orders said to be normal in Semitic languages (if we know what they are) give in themselves any indication as to dominant emphasis on any specific group of ideas—action (in the case of the verbal clause) and subject (in the case of the nominal clause).[22]

From his examples, nonetheless, one can distill a more or less applied hierarchy of definiteness and/or of phrase-types by analyzing the elements that Muraoka has taken to be S or P. Thus, for example, when Muraoka states that

> the added *hu'* in an utterance like *yhwh ṣaddiq hu'* (as against *ṣaddiq yhwh*) does not affect the basic logical relation that obtains between the subject and its predicate; it only seems to indicate the force and stress laid upon the fact that Jahweh is righteous, for which purpose, it might be noted, a certain stress or accentual pattern may serve just as well . . . ,[23]

he seems to imply that the adjective *ṣaddiq* is to be taken as the P in both cases.

Muraoka's discussion of the category of nominal clauses that he calls "Response" is instructive. He argues against the idea of emphasis being involved because: "It may be thought rather natural that the substantial part of a reply to a question should be given at the beginning. Thus P–S is the regular pattern for it."[24] In spite of our inability to confirm or deny the claimed naturalness, it is sufficient to translate Muraoka's insights into the formal categories: a prepositional phrase is a P and a personal pronoun is an S. These two criteria alone are sufficiently decisive in all examples of "Response" given by him.

In presenting evidence of emphasis, Muraoka does use word order as an argument when he states that the data teach us that

---

21. T. Muraoka, *Emphatic Words and Structures in Biblical Hebrew* (Jerusalem: Magnes / Leiden: Brill, 1985).
22. Ibid., 3.
23. Ibid., xiii, xiv.
24. Ibid., 18.

there are places in which the preceding pron. subject receives greater or lesser emphasis. . . . In many of these places the intended contrast most probably accounts for the fronting of the pron. subject, while in the following ones, in which the second clause constitutent [*sic*] is determinate, we can certainly sense emphasis or stress placed upon the subject. . . . This group of examples stands in obvious contrast to those in the reverse order in which the predicate receives emphasis. . . .[25]

Nonetheless, in all examples given by Muraoka, it is the personal pronoun that is taken to be S, whether the second element involved is indefinite or definite.

Similarly, in other examples the following elements are taken to be the S:

- personal pronouns, whether sentence-initial or not
- definite NPs when occurring with an indefinite adjective or indefinite noun
- NPs when occurring with a prepositional phrase

The following elements are taken to be the P:

- adjectives
- indefinite nouns
- prepositional phrases

It is this type of formal information that is useful in constructing a procedure whereby a computer can be used to assist in language analysis.

### 2.1.3. Michel on Nominal Clause-Types

Michel proposes to rely primarily on the features "determination" and "nondetermination" for the parsing of (two-constituent) nominal clauses, analyzing them as formally observable features of the surface structure on which different categories of nominal clauses can be based.[26] From the presence of these elements, Michel draws conclusions concerning clause-functions. When two constituents are involved:

1. one determinated, one nondeterminated, the clause is a *nominale Mitteilung* (gives descriptive information);
2. both determinated, the clause is a *nominale Behauptung* (makes a statement or judgment);
3. both nondeterminated, the clause is a *nominale Einleitung* (describes a setting, makes an introductory statement).

---

25. Ibid., 11,12.
26. D. Michel, "Probleme des Nominalsätzes im biblischen Hebräisch," *ZAH* 7 (1994) 215-24, esp. 215.

In the article cited, Michel reports only on his research with respect to the first two categories mentioned.

For clause-type 1, Michel avoids the more traditional term *classification*, since he sees it as a term requiring too much background in philosophical logic. He prefers to describe the nominal clause-types in terms of their *Sprachliche Leistung*, that is, linguistic function, which is in this case to inform (*Mitteilung*).

When dealing with constituent labeling and word order, Michel again tries to avoid traditional terminology, which he considers to be too philosophical. Instead of the labels S and P, he prefers the labels "known" and "new," adopting names from Arabic grammar: *mubtada'* 'known' and *ḫabar* 'new'. In relation to the question of whether there is a default word order in type 1 clauses, Michel combines functional terminology with observations on textual surface structure. He concentrates first on clauses of type 1 introduced by *'m, 'šr, hnh, ky, 'wd*, in order to be able to isolate cases of obligatory word order.[27] He reports: *'m* and *ky* clauses have the order "new"–"known"; the others have "known"–"new." Analyzed in this way, however, word order appears to be fully dependent on the definition of "known" and "new." *Ky* clauses can be said to exhibit the order "new"–"known" only if one does not reason on the basis of grammatical phrase-type, as is clear from Michel's examples:

(5) Num 23:23  [*ky*] [*l'*] *nḥš* new (*ḫabar*:P)     *by'qb* known (*mubtada'*:S)
(6) Lev 21:18  [*'šr*] *bw* known (*mubtada'*:S)  *mwm* new (*ḫabar*:P)

Thus, from observations on determination and word order, Michel draws conclusions about clause-types and clause-functions. The possible relevance of the grammatical category of an element and the distribution of the phrase-types are ignored. The phrase-type as such does not appear to be decisive: PP, or even the adverb *šm*,[28] can be the 'known' (*mubtada'*) if connected by means of a suffix or by lexical reference to elements mentioned earlier in the text.

Given the fact that Michel does not rely on phrase-type but on data interpreted in terms of determined and nondetermined, "known" and "new," one can question how much of the text's surface structure is actually being used. One wonders whether it would not be more objective to base one's analysis more directly on the form and distribution of phrase-types.

This issue becomes more prominent in cases of a nominal clause with two determined phrases (which in Michel's view expresses a statement or judgment: *Nominale Behauptung*—type 2 listed above),[29] since it becomes difficult

---

27. Ibid., 217.
28. Ibid., 218 n.17.
29. Ibid., 219.

to determine which of the two is "known" and which is "new." Michel criticizes the statement made by some grammarians who, with reference to the traditional term *identification* for the function of clauses of this type, claim that the distinction between S and P in this case would be meaningless. In his approach, Michel considers it necessary to identify what type of statements are being made; however, since he does not use a paradigm based on phrase-types, in some cases Michel's analyses become more complicated than necessary. Because he qualifies the pronouns merely as "determined NPs," for example, the analysis of the clause *ky hw' zh* becomes problematic. Searching for the definition of what is "known" and what is "new" and the formulation of the *Sprachliche Leistung* of this clause-type, Michel draws further information from the context in order to identify the question to which this nominal clause is giving an answer:[30]

> (7) Exod 22:8    *ky-hw' zh* answers the question: *mh zh* 'What is this?'
>                  Answer: 'the thing I lost', mentioned earlier in the
>                       text, so *hw'* is new.
>                  The order is: *ḥabar-mubtada'*.
>
> (8) 1 Sam 16:12  *ky-zh hw'* answers the question: *my hw'* 'Who is the
>                       one we look for?'
>                  Answer: 'This one', so *zh* is new.
>                  The order is: *ḥabar-mubtada'*.

In our opinion, this type of analysis implies that language as a system of markers or signs is not given sufficient consideration. Textual interpretation begins to overrule the paradigm.

We question whether these examples are to be seen merely as two determined noun phrases. Things may be made less complicated if one recognizes that *zh* as a linguistic sign is distinct from *hw'* as a linguistic sign. In our proposal below (see §2.2), we will elaborate further on the suggestion that allowing for a difference in the deictic force of these two elements has advantages: *zh* refers to what is present in the situation of communication, it is determinated or "known" because it is there; *hw'* refers back to what has been mentioned previously in the text. Taking *zh* as having a higher level of determination or deictic power than *hw'* is based on the assumption that, in the communication situation, deixis has more force than textual reference. Moreover, *ky-hw' zh* in Exod 22:8 is not necessarily the answer to a question but may be merely a statement: it is the thing lost (P), that which you and I can see here (S). The text of 1 Samuel 16 also makes clear that *zh* refers to actual presence in the situation of communication. In vv. 8–10 it is reported that David's

---

30. Ibid., 220.

brothers are not being chosen by God: *gm-bzh l'-bḥr yhwh.* When David comes, God says: *ky-zh hw'* 'this one, in front of you' (S), is 'the one I look for' (P). Here again, no question is being answered; instead, a statement is made about someone referred to in the situation.

Working along these lines means that the assignment of P and S depends on a paradigm involving the level of determination. The order of the elements in a text, however, is syntagmatic, that is, either obligatory because of the elements involved (for example, interrogatives occur in clause-initial position) or related to the context. In 1 Sam 16:12 the S *zh* is clause-initial, similar to the order of the preceding negative clauses *gm-bzh l'-bḥr* 'this is the one . . .'. In Exod 22:8, the reversed statement is made: 'What I have lost' (referred to in the text by *dbr-pš‘*) 'is this one here'.

So, though we agree in general with Michel's proposal to start from surface structure features, we think that one should pursue those lines further than Michel actually did. The question for computer-assisted analysis is, of course, how much of the linguistic system is recognizable in the distribution of surface text phenomena. This theme is also present in the comments made by Hoftijzer on the work of Andersen.

### 2.1.4. Andersen and Hoftijzer on Formal and Functional Analysis

In this section, we refer to Hoftijzer's[31] extensive comments on the work of Andersen.[32] Hoftijzer made it clear that, in addressing the parsing of nominal clauses from a functional (tagmemics) approach, Andersen ran up against the problem of how, in the analysis of texts in ancient languages, one is to distinguish among contexts where it is possible to rely on a registration of forms, where one works from an assumption of linguistic function, and where there is a need to resort to semantic interpretation.

Hoftijzer notes that Andersen's analysis starts with surface-level linguistic registrations and then gradually deviates from this initial formal description. This movement to the more functional and semantic categories is, of course, deliberate, due to its background in the tagmemic approach, where the tagmeme is defined as a combination of a functional slot and the formal class of elements that can fill this slot. According to Hoftijzer, Andersen proceeds from the formal to the functional at an early stage in his research, as early as his data collection. For example, he sorts clause-types according to criteria of declarative, precative, subordinated, and coordinated,[33] and phrases according to a criterion of "grade of definiteness" that may even include semantic judgments: *bnw* may be indefinite, meaning 'a son of his', but also definite,

---

31. Hoftijzer, "The Nominal Clause Reconsidered," *VT* 23 (1973) 446–510.
32. F. I. Andersen, *The Hebrew Verbless Clause in the Pentateuch* (Journal of Biblical Literature Monograph Series 14; Nashville and New York: Abingdon, 1970).
33. Hoftijzer, "The Nominal Clause Reconsidered," 451.

meaning 'his (only) son'; in constructions of the type "*šmw* + Name," Andersen takes *šmw* to be the Subject "as if *šēm* in itself is definite."[34]

Generally speaking, Hoftijzer's criticism is that functional, tagmemic type of research tends to skip too quickly over the collection of data on the basis of inherent formal characteristics alone and thus too easily tends to present clause material "as if the meaning of the clauses in question is clear in every respect."[35] Therefore, contrary to certain claims made by Andersen, Hoftijzer is "not convinced that in Andersen's study 'formal considerations are given priority.' "[36]

In order to avoid mixing formal and functional categories, Hoftijzer himself proposes, first, not to work from assumptions concerning a default word order, a normal core sequence in nominal clauses in general or in certain groups of nominal clauses.[37] The core sequence does *not* determine the function of core constituents. Second, Hoftijzer proposes abandoning the use of the labels "predicate" and "subject," since they reflect analysis in logical or functional terms rather than in formal syntactic terms.[38] Hoftijzer prefers to use only formal labels, such as: Pr(onoun), NP (= noun phrase). Using these labels Hoftijzer then disusses a number of nominal clause-types:

- Two constituents, both formally definite.[39] There is no "normal" S–P sequence. The NP occurring initially received the emphasis: Gen 12:13: 'My sister is she (not something else)'.
- A definite and an indefinite NP.[40] The constituent in first position has the greater argumentative weight in the context: Gen 42:11.

We fully agree with Hoftijzer that one should pursue the inventory of linguistic forms as long as possible, both as to the phrase-types and as to the sequences in which they actually occur.

We also agree with Hoftijzer that it is this sequence of phrase-types that is determinative for clause-functions. It is not necessary, we believe, to avoid the use of the labels "predicate" and "subject" if one is prepared to apply them on the basis of the phrase-types and their patterns of combination in actual clauses rather than on the basis of the logic of the statements or propositions made by those clauses.

---

34. Ibid., 467.
35. Ibid., 457.
36. Ibid., 466; cf. Andersen, *The Hebrew Verbless Clause*, 29.
37. Hoftijzer, "The Nominal Clause Reconsidered," 486ff., 505.
38. Ibid., 487ff.
39. Ibid., 488ff.
40. Ibid., 495ff.

**2.1.5.** Richter on Clause-Type Patterns and Phrase-Types

The approach of Richter,[41] which concentrates on phrase-type features and formal clause-types, was helpful in our experimentation with procedures needed to meet the formal demands that the construction of a database entails. It is important to note that Richter distinguishes between the observation of features at the surface text level and the observations or conclusions to be made at the functional or semantic level.[42] The question as to what extent the observation of surface text phenomena can be maintained surfaces again.[43]

Richter starts his collection of data by using the elements of the text surface, that is, phrase-types, defined in terms of categories of parts of speech. When listing categories, he proposes a simplification (*Vereinfachung*) by assuming that certain parts of speech (pronouns, some adverbs, and deictic words) can be seen as *Pro-Elemente*; that is, they are able to replace nouns (*Hauptwörter*) in a position of equal grammatical value.[44] Because in our findings it appears that personal pronouns have their own unique influence on the S–P parsing, and because the interrogative pronoun also influences the order of constituents, we have some reservations about whether this can be maintained without further consequences to the formal definition of clause-types.

The second feature Richter uses in his analysis is determination,[45] defined in terms of lexical data (proper name, personal pronoun), morphological data (enclitic personal pronoun),[46] and morphosyntactic data (nominal forms with the definite article).

Once these observations have been made, it becomes possible within Richter's method to define patterns of phrase-type combinations. He states explicitly that the parsing of these patterns in terms of S and P is a matter of grammatical interpretation. So a third, indispensable tool is an *Urteil*, a judgment, based on the differences of determination in the various phrase-types ("das nachgeordnete Merkmal der Ungleichheit in der Determination").

---

41. W. Richter, *Grundlagen einer althebräischen Grammatik, B: Die Beschreibungs-ebenen, III: Der Satz (Satztheorie)* (ATSAT 13; St.Ottilien: EOS, 1980).

42. Ibid., 51, 73, 231ff.

43. For a further discussion of Richter's approach to syntax in relation to computer-assisted linguistic analysis, see: E. Talstra, "Towards a Distributional Definition of Clauses in Classical Hebrew: A Computer-Assisted Description of Clauses and Clause Types in Deut. 4, 3–8," *ETL* 63 (1987) 95-105.

44. Richter, *Grundlagen*, 70 n. 181.

45. Ibid.

46. Here Richter (ibid., 72 n. 186) refers to Andersen's statement that sometimes phrases of the type Nominal + Pronominal Suffix may be semantically nondetermined. It is not clear, however, to what extent Richter agrees with Andersen on this point.

Using the categories of phrase-type and determination, Richter presents the (theoretically) possible types of nominal clauses. He does not indicate S and P in those cases where a clause contains constituents of equal determination. The result is the distinction of four formally different clause-types:

| I | (with NPs only)[47] |
|---|---|
| II | (NP and PP)[48] |
| III | (AdjP and NP/PP)[49] |
| IV | (one constituent is a participle or an infinitive)[50] |

Allowing for all of the possible variations in the order of constituents, the matrix displayed in Table 2 emerges (the numbers refer to Richter's clause-types and their subcategories; cases of clause-type IV are skipped for the moment; see §§3.3.1 and 3.3.2).

#### Table 2.  Richter's Possible Types of Nominal Clauses

| pos1 \ pos2 | *detNP* | *indetNP* | *detPP* | *indetPP* | *indetAdj* | *detAdj* |
|---|---|---|---|---|---|---|
| detNP | ..-..  I.1 | S–P  I.2.1 | ..-..  II.1.1 | ?  II.2.1 | S–P  III.1.1 | S–P  III.3.1 |
| indetNP | P–S  I.2.2 | ?  I.3 | ..-..  II.3.1 | ?  II.4 | S–P  III.2.1 | – |
| detPP | ..-..  II.1.2 | ..-..  II.3.2 | ..-..  II.7 | – | – | – |
| indetPP | P–S  II.2.2 | – | – | – | – | – |
| indetAdj | P–S  III.1.2 | P–S  III.2.2 | – | – | – | – |

? the clause-type is not attested in the textual corpus selected by Richter.

..-.. identification of P and S on the basis of grammatical type of the constituents is not possible.[51]

– S–P analysis considered by Richter not to be applicable.

Richter's approach is useful for our aims because his observations of form make clear which features are being registered. Furthermore, Richter's dis-

---

47. Ibid., 75ff.
48. Ibid.
49. Ibid., 78ff.
50. Ibid., 79ff.
51. See the discussion in ibid., 225ff.

tinction between the basic pattern and an expansion or modification of that pattern offers a promising perspective. The clause and/or the separate constituents can be expanded by the personal pronoun, *yš*, *'yn*, and the verb *hyh*. The clause can be modified by clause-level modifiers, that is, the adverb *ʿwd* and the interjection *hnh*. All of these matters will be treated below in §§3.5 and 3.6.

**2.2.** Proposal for a Paradigm (a Procedure) for
Computer-Assisted S–P Analysis

Our specific goal in concentrating on the parsing of nominal clauses is that we need a controllable procedure for parsing elements of the text surface, rather than a fully explanatory linguistic theory on what certain types of nominal clauses might signify within a text. The labeling should not only be explicit with regard to the linguistic information on which it is based but also allow for further research within different theoretical frameworks.

We start, therefore, from an inventory of the parameters used in the various discussions of nominal clauses treated above. One difficulty in attempting to do so is that not all of the authors reviewed above have S–P parsing as a primary aim. It is understandable that for a majority of researchers, the linguistic interpretation of the various types of nominal clauses in their context appears to be the real goal. Some researchers make the assignment of the labels S and P dependent on previously established clause-function, while others go so far as to avoid the use of the terms P and S altogether. Nevertheless, we propose to continue using the traditional labels P and S for the core constituents of two-element nominal clauses, under the condition that the formal connection is between these labels and the distribution of the phrase-types involved is made explicit, rather than making the labels dependent on explanatory semantic or logical models. Thus, the schema presented in Table 3 may not do full justice to the research of some colleagues: what appears in the schema is what we have gleaned from their work, as described in the preceding paragraphs, while searching for the parameters used in S–P parsing.

When thus presented, it appears that there is a gradual shift from left to right in the importance attached to argumentation based on formally recognizable grammatical information. From this overview and from our own findings, one can conclude that the first four parameters listed are the most important, or at least the most frequently used, for the parsing of verbless clauses:

1. phrase-type of the constituents
2. level of determination of those phrases
3. order of the constituents in a clause
4. clause-type and function.

**Table 3.  Parameters Used in Proposals for**
**the Parsing of Nominal Clauses**

|  | Niccacci | Muraoka | Michel | Andersen | Hoftijzer | Richter | Our Proposal |
|---|---|---|---|---|---|---|---|
| 1. Phrase-Type | ? | ? |  | x | x | x | x |
| 2. Determination |  | ? | x | x | x | x | x |
| 3. Order of Constituents | x | x | x | x | x | * | * |
| 4. Clause-Type/Function | x | x | x | x | * | * | * |
| 5. Semantic info.: "known"–"new" |  | x | x |  |  |  |  |
| 6. Logical Cat.: Substance-Accidence | x |  |  |  |  |  |  |
| Avoid the Labels P and S |  |  | x |  | x |  |  |

x = categories that are taken as input for determining S and P
* = categories that are calculated in combination with the parsing
? = although it appears that the use of phrase-types may be deduced from the presentation, this is not explicitly stated by the author

Because these parameters cover features of various linguistic levels, from morpheme and lexeme up to syntax, it is important to investigate the ways that these levels integrate with one another to provide the information necessary for a correct analysis of the structures involved. The various authors are not unanimous regarding where to begin and where to conclude: some argue on the basis of P–S parsings to explain word order; some argue on the basis of determination to explain the P–S parsing; still others take the clause-function as providing the clue that determines what is P and what is S.

The computer-assisted parsing of verbless clauses requires a grammatical model that is based on the observation of the distribution of grammatical and lexical features. This corroborates Hoftijzer's argument that analyzing texts of ancient languages requires an approach starting from the inventory of grammatical forms, rather than from assumptions about linguistic functions, since a researcher, unable to rely on native speakers' knowledge, is obliged to build up linguistic competence with the help of a precise inventory of formal linguistic data. Therefore, our line of argumentation runs from the "distribution of forms" to the "conclusions concerning functions." This is the same line of research that is proposed by Richter. We propose that parameters 1 and 2 are sufficient to determine the S–P parsing. Parameter 3, the order of the constituents, we take to be a syntagmatic rather than a paradigmatic feature and therefore not contributing to the S–P parsing itself. Parameter 4, the function of a nominal clause, requires an explanation in terms of the P and S order and the position of the clause in a text.

With respect to the use of parameters 1 and 2, one additional remark is needed. For the greater part of the data, observations of a paradigmatic type are sufficient to produce the S–P parsing, that is, the registration of particular sets of clause-level data, such as the co-occurrence of two nonidentical phrase-types in one clause. In other cases, additional information of a syntagmatic sort is needed—for example, when there are two constituents of formally identical type within one clause, one has to search for morphosyntactic or lexical references in the context (see §3.6). For the parsing of nominal clauses one can start from one basic paradigm, namely, a matrix that combines parameters 1, "phrase-type," and 2, "determination."

The effectiveness of such a matrix is based on two further assumptions:

1. The presence of a *hierarchical order of phrase-types* that can receive the label S. For example: a suffix on an element like *yš*, *'yn*, *hnh*, or *ʿwd* or on the locative interrogative always takes the label S; if this kind of suffix is not present in a clause, a demonstrative pronoun will be present; otherwise a personal pronoun; etc. The next constituent in the hierarchy, when present in the actual clause, will take the label P. The hierarchical order is based on a decreasing level of "determination."

2. *Determination* is defined not in terms of grammatical features alone but somewhat broader, in terms of *"referred to or not yet referred to in the situation of communication."*[52] In this way one can combine into one category "presence in the situation" (deixis, marked by a demonstrative pronoun) and "presence in the text" (marked by phrase-type [proper name], grammatical features [definite article, pronominal suffix], syntactic features [attributive clauses assigning textual information to one of the constituents], or lexical features [repetition of lexeme]).

If these assumptions are correct, they result in a schema presenting a hierarchy based on phrase-types and relative determination from which the S–P labeling of constituents can be deduced. The schema presented below is presently being employed in automatic parsing procedures.

For the construction of the schema, we combine the findings of our own experiments with the emphasis on a "formal approach" advocated by Hoftijzer and with observations on phrase-type and determination made by Richter, though we treat certain matters slightly differently from Richter:

• Pronouns are inserted as a separate phrase-type category. Because pronouns in combination with other constituents appear to operate differently from NPs, we do not treat them paradigmatically as mere

---

52. Cf. Muraoka, *Emphatic Words*, 8, 9. See more on this topic in §4.1.

replacements of NPs. We propose that allowing them an independent
position results in a clearer assignment of P and S.

- We exclude for the moment clauses with participles and infinitives. At
  a higher syntactic level, the participle and the infinitive often do have a
  nominal function, but this is dependent on the embedding in the
  broader context; we will return to these clauses in §§3.3.1 and 3.3.2.

#### Table 4.  Basic Paradigm for Deciding S–P
#### Based on Phrase-Type and Definiteness

| (1) | (2) | (3) | (4) | (5) | (6) | (7) | (8) | (9) | (10) |
|-----|-----|-----|-----|-----|-----|-----|-----|-----|------|
| suf | demPro | persPro | defNP | PN | indefNP | interrPro | Adj | PP | Loc |
| S | P | P | P | P | P | P | P | P | P |
|   | S | P | P | P | P | P | P | P | P |
|   |   | S | P | P | P | P | P | P | P |
|   |   |   | S | P | P | P | P | P | P |
|   |   |   |   | S | P | P | P | P | P |
|   |   |   |   |   | S | P | P | P | P |
|   |   |   |   |   |   | S | P | P | P |
|   |   |   |   |   |   |   | S | P | P |

| | | |
|---|---|---|
| suf | = | suffix on *yš*, *'yn*, *hnh*, *'wd*, Loc |
| demPro | = | demonstrative pronoun |
| persPro | = | personal pronoun |
| defNP | = | definite noun phrase |
| PN | = | proper noun; name |
| indefNP | = | indefinite noun phrase |
| interrPro | = | interrogative pronoun (NPs) |
| Adj | = | adjective |
| PP | = | prepositional phrase |
| Loc | = | locatives; locative interrogative |

The schema lists the phrase-types ranking from high to low in definiteness as
defined above. According to their level of determination, the phrase-types can
be divided into three subsets, each of them also being ordered hierarchically,
based on the level of definiteness:

1. Phrase-types that are always S: this includes only the suffix attached to
   *yš*, *'yn*, *hnh*, *'wd*, and the locative interrogative (category 1).
2. Phrase-types that are capable of being either the S or the P. From the
   phrases found in a clause, the phrase that is highest in rank takes the S
   position. Lower-ranking phrases take the P slot (categories 2–8).
3. Phrase-types that are normally only P (categories 9–10); an exception
   is formed by certain idiomatic expressions (see §3.6).

The actual assignment of the S–P labels can be done automatically in all cases fitting into the above schema; for other cases the assignment will be partly dependent on a reader's knowledge of the context. We attempt thus to rely on paradigmatic information first and only later to adduce syntagmatic data for the parsing or for the interpretation of the clause-type. Aspects relating to syntagmatic information will be treated in §3. From all of the information thus gathered, the type of S–P relation expressed by the nominal clause can be established.

Examples in decreasing order of determination (using the labels in Table 4):

*With a suffix as subject*[53]
    (1)–(10) suf–Loc
    Exod 2:20        *w'yw*
    RSV            And where is he?

*With a demonstrative pronoun as subject*
    (2)–(3) demPro–persPro
    1 Kgs 18:7      *h'th zh*
    RSV            Is it you?

    (2)–(4) demPro-defNP
    Deut 4:44       *wz't htwrh*
    RSV            This is the law

    (2)–(5) demPro-PN
    Ruth 1:19       *hz't n'my*
    RSV            Is this Naomi?

    (2)–(6) demPro-indefNP
    Qoh 2:19        *gm-zh hbl*
    RSV            This also is vanity

    (2)–(7) demPro-interrPro
    Gen 48:8        *my-'lh*
    RSV            Who are these?

    (2)–(9) demPro-PP
    Exod 2:6        *myldy h'brym zh*
    RSV            This is one of the Hebrews' children.

---

53. For examples with *yš*, *'yn*, *hnh*, and *'wd*, see §§3.4.1 and 3.4.2.

*With a personal pronoun as subject*

    (3)–(4) persPro-defNP

    Judg 8:19       *ʾḥy bny-ʿmy hm*

    RSV              They were my brothers

    (3)–(5) persPro-PN

    Esth 2:7        *hyʾ ʾstr*

    RSV              that is Esther

    (3)–(6) persPro-indefNP

    Ruth 3:11       *ky ʾšt ḥyl ʾt*

    RSV              that you are a woman of worth

    (3)–(7) persPro-interrPro

    Exod 3:11      *my ʾnky*

    RSV              Who am I . . . ?

    (3)–(8) persPro-Adj

    Exod 1:19      *ky-ḥywt hnh*

    RSV              for they are vigorous

    (3)–(9) persPro-PP

    Qoh 2:24       *ky myd hʾlhym hyʾ*

    KJV              that it *was* from the hand of God

*With a definite NP as subject*

    (4)–(5) defNP-PN

    Exod 1:15      *ʾšr šm hʾḥt šprh*

    KJV              the name of the one *was* Shiphrah

    (4)–(6) defNP-indefNP

    Deut 4:6       *rq ʿm-ḥkm wnbwn hgwy hgdwl hzh*

    RSV              Surely this great nation is a wise and understanding
                       people.

    (4)–(7) defNP-interrPro

    Exod 3:13      *mh-šmw*

    RSV              What is his name?

    (4)–(8) defNP-defAdj

    Judg 6:15[54]    *hnh ʾlpy hdl bmnšh wʾnky hṣʿyr bbyt ʾby*

    RSV              Behold, my clan is the weakest in Manasseh, and I am
                       the least in my family.

---

54. For the treatment of *hnh*, see §3.4.2.

(4)–(8) defNP-Adj
Isa 28:21      *nkryh ʿbdtw*
RSV           alien is his work

(4)–(9) defNP-PP
Num 22:22    *wšny nʿryw ʿmw*
RSV           and his two servants were with him

(4)–(10) defNP-Loc
Judg 6:13     *wʾyh kl-nplʾtyw*
RSV           And where are all his wonderful deeds . . . ?

*With a proper name as subject*
  (5)–(6) PN-indefNP
Deut 4:31     *ky ʾl rḥwm yhwh ʾlhyk*
RSV           for the LORD your God is a merciful God

(5)–(7) PN-interrPro
Judg 9:28     *my-ʾbymlk*
RSV           Who is Abimelech . . . ?

(5) (8) PN-Adj
Num 24:20    *rʾšyt gwym ʿmlq*
RSV           Amalek is the first of the nations

(5)–(9) PN-PP
Judg 6:12     *yhwh ʿmk*
RSV           The LORD is with you

*With an indefinite NP as subject*
  (6)–(7) indefNP-interrPro
Deut 4:7      *ky my-gwy gdwl*
RSV           for what great nation is there?

(6)–(8) indefNP-Adj
Esth 1:7      *wyyn mlkwt rb kyd hmlk*
RSV           and the royal wine was lavished according to the bounty
              of the king

(6)–(9) indefNP-PP
Isa 15:2      *bkl-rʾšyw qrḥh*
RSV           On every head is baldness

*With an interrogative pronoun as subject*
  (7)–(8) interrPro-Adj
Mic 6:8       *hgyd lk ʾdm mh-ṭwb*
RSV           He has showed you, O man, what is good

(7)–(9) interrPro-PP
1 Kgs 17:18          *mh-ly wlk*
RSV                  What have you against me?

*With an adjective as subject*
(8)–(9) Adj-PP
Qoh 2:24             *ʾyn-ṭwb bʾdm š. . .*[55]
RSV                  There is nothing better for a man than that . . .

This approach has two further implications:

1. Word order does not determine the S–P parsing.[56] It is not part of the paradigm. The order of the constituents is to be studied in combination with the syntagmatic relations, that is, the position and function of the clause-types in their context.
2. The linguistic interpretation of the S–P relations found is a matter of interpretation afterward, in terms of functional or semantic categories (see §2.3). The possible functional or semantic relations do not determine the parsing itself.

### 2.3. A Linguistic Explanation for the Predicative Relations Encountered

While still focusing on the simple nominal clause, we now take a diversion to look at what is being predicated of the S, that is, what types of relationships are represented between the S and the P. Our motivation for doing so is to see whether it is legitimate to treat all of these structures as variants of one linguistic pattern or whether it is necessary to posit different structures in order to reflect the relationships between the elements correctly.[57]

A closer look at the data shows that a wide range of relationships is predicated within nominal clauses.[58]

locative:            Judg 6:37   *wʿl-kl-hʾrṣ ḥrb*
                     literally:  and upon all the earth dryness
                     RSV         and it is dry on the ground . . .

---

55. See §3.4.1 for discussion of *ʾyn*.
56. Cf. Hoftijzer, "The Nominal Clause Reconsidered," 487–88.
57. The legitimacy of a unified treatment of all cases where Indo-European languages employ a form of the verb "to be" has been questioned, particularly by various philosophers and logicians. Cf. C. H. Khan, *The Verb "Be" in Ancient Greek* (The Verb "Be" and Its Synonyms: Philosophical and Grammatical Studies, Part 6; ed. J. W. M Verhaar; Dordrecht: Reidel, 1973), chap. 1: "Introduction: The Problem of the Verb 'Be,'" 1–37.
58. A list of the functions of "to be" can be gleaned from, e.g., J. Lyons, *Theoretical Linguistics* (Cambridge: Cambridge University Press, 1971), 388–89; C. H. Khan, *The Verb "Be" in Ancient Greek*, chap. 2: "Subject, Predicate, Copula," 38–59. The existential function of the copula will be treated in §3.1 on one-member nominal clauses and in §3.5.2 on the verb "to be."

| possession: | Exod 2:16 | *wlkhn mdyn šbʿ bnwt* |
| | literally: | and for the priest of Midian were seven daughters |
| | RSV | Now the priest of Midian had seven daughters |
| property assignment: | Exod 2:2 | *ky-ṭwb hwʾ* |
| | literally: | that he was good |
| | RSV | that he was a goodly child . . . |
| identity: | Ruth 1:19 | *hzʾt nʿmy* |
| | RSV | Is this Naomi? |
| class membership: | Ruth 4:10 | *ʿdym ʾtm hywm* |
| | RSV | you are witnesses this day |
| class inclusion: | Ps 8:5 | *mh-ʾnwš* |
| | RSV | what is man . . . ? |

The above types of relationships are often discussed as functions of the verb "to be" and indeed, in translating such examples into English, the use of 'to be' is usually required. Hebrew does not require the verb 'to be' in such cases; in this Hebrew is not unique among the languages of the world.[59]

Though the diversity of predicative relationships possible within a simple nominal clause has led some linguists to posit more than one copula in the lexicon,[60] L. Heggie argues for a "unified approach" to copular constructions involving the verb "to be."[61] Her motivation for this proposal is the observation that copular structures have much in common syntactically: the similarities considerably outweigh the differences.[62]

Of particular interest to us here is that, using data from Modern Hebrew, Heggie extends her analysis of copular constructions to include structures in

---

59. Some think that the copulative function of the verb "to be" is a secondary development even in the Indo-European languages. Cf. J. Lyons, *Theoretical Linguistics*, 322. Cf. also A. C. Graham, "'Being' in Classical Chinese," in *Classical Chinese / Athapaskan / Mundari* (The Verb "Be" and Its Synonyms: Philosophical and Grammatical Studies, Part 1; ed. J. W. M. Verhaar; Dordrecht: Reidel, 1967) 15: "There is no concept of Being which languages are well or ill equipped to present; the functions of 'to be' depend upon a grammatical rule for the formation of the sentence, and it would be merely a coincidence if one found anything resembling it in a language without this rule."

60. Cf. L. Heggie (*The Syntax of Copular Structures* [Dissertation of the Graduate Students in Linguistics, University of Southern California, 1988]), who reviews other authors who have suggested differentiating various copulas on the basis of the syntactic combinations in which they appear. See also C. H. Kahn, *The Verb "Be" in Ancient Greek*, chap. 2: "Subject, Predicate, Copula," 38–59.

61. Heggie, *The Syntax of Copular Structures*, 47, 50.

62. Ibid., 2.

which no overt copula is present. These correspond to the structures considered here as simple nominal clauses, that is, verbless strings in which predication is present. When present, the verb "to be" serves as a syntactic place for marking tense, mood, and aspect.

Heggie proposes that the lexical "to be" copula (or its non-overt counterpart) selects a small clause as complement.[63] The copula would be listed in the lexicon

> as a verbal element which must coindex a constituent which becomes the predicate position of a small clause. Its entry would be the following:
>
> be:   [ ___$_i$ . . . XP$_i$ ]
>
> This definition of the copula captures the intuition that *be* is like a verbal operator which creates predicates.[64]

The index on the P of the small clause spreads by predication to the S. Heggie argues that this structure "accurately describes that the predicate selects its subject, i.e., the appropriateness of the subject is determined by the predicate."[65] The ability of the copula to coindex with any phrasal category, which then selects its subject, allows for "unusual combinations for the subject-predicate relation."[66] The agreement between the S and P is explained by the lexical properties of "to be," as given above. It is thus not necessary for the variety of combinations of elements within a nominal clause to be accounted for in the syntax, since specification of elements that may co-occur belongs to the domain of the lexicon.[67]

Thus, the subtleties of the predicative relationships obtaining between the S and the P in nominal clauses need not be attributed to various functions of an overt or non-overt form of "to be" but can be ascribed to the broad range of relationships that the two elements involved can have to one another. The copula, lexical or nonlexical, is neutral in itself in regard to predicative relationships but requires as complement a small clause in which the semantic fields of the S and the P involved determine which so-called "function" of "to be" is

---

63. Cf. also R. Jackendoff (*X′ Syntax: A Study of Phrase Structure* [Cambridge, Mass.: MIT Press, 1977] 66, 67), who maintains that copulas, just like other verbs, can be treated syntactically in the base component. Thus, instead of having to posit exceptional structures for copular constructions, the copula would subcategorize the necessary component, that is, a small clause.

64. Ibid., 121.

65. Ibid., 50; cf. also 122–23.

66. Ibid., 123.

67. Heggie (ibid., 123–53) explains the differences between straightforward predication, specificational, pseudoequatives, and equatives on the basis of various types of "focus movement," whereby the members of the small clause end up in different positions within the structure.

present. This diversity can then indeed be treated syntactically in a unified approach.

This approach has the advantage of treating the verb "to be" in the lexicon in a manner similar to the treatment of other verbs; that is, like other verbs, "to be" has its own specific lexical frame, while allowing for the formal similarities between structures in Hebrew in which "to be" appears and those in which it is not present (nominal clauses).[68]

## 3. Variation in and Extension of the Paradigm: The Contribution of Syntagmatic Features

Not all nominal clauses occurring in our material are two-membered: some have more members; some have less. Some structures, like the one-member nominal clauses, present a variation of the material presented in the basic paradigm. Other constructions can best be described as an extension of the paradigm to include syntagmatic information and processes.

### 3.1. One-Member Nominal Clauses

#### 3.1.1. Subject Only

One function of "being" not discussed above is the existential function, that is, cases where the mere existence of the subject is being affirmed rather than something being predicated on it. An example of this function of "being" occurring with the verb "to be" is

| (9) Gen 1:3 | *wy'mr 'lhym yhy 'wr wyhy-'wr* |
| literally: | And God said, "Light shall be," and light was. |
| RSV | And God said, "Let there be light"; and there was light. |

In order to make this example into a sentence in English, it is necessary to add the dummy locative *there*; in other such constructions in English, *it* is added as a dummy pronoun S of the construction. In Hebrew, no dummy pronouns or locatives are necessary.

Niccacci calls *hyh* in such cases "a 'full' verb of complete predication," in contrast to the structures where *hyh* "is a verb of incomplete predication," needing a predicate complement to complete the predication of the verb.[69]

---

68. The first part of this statement is in agreement with Niccacci ("Simple Nominal Clauses," 216): "Contrary to most grammarians, I think that, first, the verb *hyh* is not a copula but a normal verb since its presence is not optional in a main sentence. . . ." But Niccacci makes no allowance for the formal similarities between clauses with *hyh* and nominal clauses (cf. also pp. 223–24).

69. Ibid., 224.

It appears that this mere assertion of the existence of the S is also to be found in verbless clauses:

(10) Qoh 3:2     *ʿt lldt wʿt lmwt*
                 [there is] a time to be born and a time to die[70]

(11) Isa 28:8    *bly mqwm*
     KJV         [*so that there is*] no place *clean*

This type of simple assertion of existence occurs more often in combination with clause modifiers and particles of existence (§3.4) and with the verb *hyh* 'to be' (§3.5.2), to which we will return below.

**3.1.2.** Predicates Only

When a nominal P occurs without an S, some type of dependent structure is involved. A considerable number of these structures involve relative clauses in which the S to which the P refers is outside of the relative clause itself, being referred to by the relative pronoun (the portion intended as illustration is underlined below).

(12) Exod 3:7    *wyʾmr yhwh rʾh rʾyty ʾt-ʿny ʿmy ʾšr bmṣrym*
     RSV         Then the LORD said, "I have seen the affliction of my
                 people *who are in Egypt*"

Others involve attributive clauses lacking the introductory relative pronoun,

(13) Deut 4:38   *lhwryš gwym gdlym wʿṣmym mmk mpnyk*
     RSV         driving out before you nations *greater and mightier
                 than yourselves,*

or appositional clauses at some distance from the noun that they modify,

(14) Deut 4:24   *ky yhwh ʾlhyk ʾš ʾklh hwʾ ʾl qnʾ*
     RSV         For the LORD your God is a devouring fire, *a jealous
                 God.*

Still others are ellipses, with the subject understood from the context. In the following example, the Ss belonging to the Ps *gmwly mhlb* and *ʿtyqy mšdym* are to be found in the preceding sentences; the Ps are the answers to the phrase *ʾt-my*:

---

70. Were one to choose an alternative analysis, namely, that the infinitive is the predicate complement, the translation would be 'to be born has a time and to die has a time'. In order to maintain this, it would be necessary to find other examples where the infinitive is unquestionably the possessor. Even were such cases to be found, analyzing the infinitive as a further specification of the time whose simple existence is being stated remains a viable alternative.

(15) Isa 28:9   *'t-my ywrh d'h w't-my ybyn smw'h <u>gmwly mḥlb 'tyqy</u>*
                   *<u>mšdym</u>*

    KJV       Whom shall he teach knowledge? and whom shall he make to understand doctrine? [*them that are*] *weaned from the milk,* [*and*] *drawn from the breasts.*

### 3.2. Embedding and Recursion: Elements within the Nominal Clause Predication

As noted in the introduction, many nominal clause structures are not merely two-membered but involve more extensive structures. A variety of re-lationships are present between the main predication and the various other elements occurring within the same nominal clause. Beside the usual addi-tional elements that can occur in a clause, such as time phrases, negatives, clause questioners (*h-, mdw'*), adjuncts of comparison, extra information, and so on, there are other elements that have a closer structural bond to the main nominal predication.

The need for elegance and consistency in building up a database of gram-matically analyzed text motivates us to search first for underlying simpler units with transparent relationships and then for patterns of combinations of the simpler units. At the higher level, the simpler units have an analysis in conformity to their function at that level, which can be seen as an adaptation of their function within the simpler unit.

Joüon and Muraoka remarked on the structural similarity between two nouns in apposition and a nominal clause.[71] It seems that what makes the one a nominal clause and the other a case of apposition or attribution is the fact that in the latter situation the structure occurs within another predicative re-lationship so that the potential predication between the two elements is em-bedded and is realized as apposition or attribution, that is, purely nominal relationships.

A similar shift can be detected within nominal clauses: a potential predi-cate relation between nominal elements can occur within a structure where an-other S or P takes over as the main S or P, yielding one S–P relation embedded within another. Examples:

(16) Num 22:9    *my*   *h'nšym h'lh*    *'mk*
     potential NC   |    S          P    'these men are with you'
     actual NC     P     S        (further specification of S)
     RSV        Who are these men with you?

---

71. P. Joüon, *A Grammar of Biblical Hebrew* (trans. and rev. by T. Muraoka; 2 vols.; Subsidia Biblica 14/1–2; Rome: Pontifical Biblical Institute, 1990) 447, §131a. Cf. J. W. Dyk, *Participles in Context: A Computer-Assisted Study of Old Testament Hebrew* (Applicatio 12; Amsterdam: Free University Press, 1994) 20–21, for an extension of this analysis to include attributive relationships.

The embedding can occur recursively:

| (17) Deut 6:15 | *ky* | *ʾl qnʾ* | *yhwh* | *ʾlhyk* | *bqrbk* | |
|---|---|---|---|---|---|---|
| potential NC | | I | P | S | I | YHWH is your God |
| potential NC | | I | | S | (App) | P | YHWH your God is in your midst |
| actual NC | | | P | S | (App) | (specification) |
| RSV | | | | for the LORD your God in the midst of you is a jealous God |

Recognizing the possibility of recursive embedding would provide an alternative way of arguing Niccacci's *casus pendens* structures which, in his analysis, have a finite verbal element as S. At a lower level, the finite verbal form is indeed P but can function at a higher level as the S (in his analysis). Embedding also leads to a somewhat more nuanced analysis of Gen 45:12, Niccacci's example (18), which he states to be "very similar to (3)," that is Deut 3:21b:

| (18) Deut 3:21b | (P) *ʿynyk* | (S) *h-* | *rʾt* | *ʾt kl-ʾšr ʿśh yhwh ʾlhykm* |
|---|---|---|---|---|
| embedding: | I | | I | Ptc    verbal object of Ptc |
| | I | | | [relative clause                    ] |
| | P | | S | |
| Niccacci | (To Joshua I said . . .) "It is your eyes which have seen all that Yahweh your God" (did to those two kings . . .) |

Niccacci explains his designation of *ʿynyk* as predicate as follows:

> [this] illustrates cases where a particular term (a substantive with a personal pronoun . . .) . . . functions as a predicate . . . the information is not general, or unmarked, or neutral, but rather detail-oriented, or marked.[72]

In his analysis, an S–P order would indicate a presentative or circumstantial nominal clause, which would not fit into his perception of this text. Therefore, Niccacci is forced to switch the P–S assignment labels.

Turning to Niccacci's example (18), we see:

| (19a) Niccacci's analysis: | | |
|---|---|---|
| Gen 45:12 | (S) *hnh ʿnykm* | (P) *rʾwt* |
| | (S) *wʿny ʾhy bnymyn* | (P) . . . |
| | (P) *ky-py* | (S) *hmdbr ʾlykm* |
| Niccacci | (Joseph said to his brethren:) "And, behold, your eyes see, as do the eyes of my brother Benjamin, that it's my mouth that speaks unto you." |

---

72. Niccacci, "Simple Nominal Clause," 219.

Ignoring for the moment the introductory *hnh* (see §3.4.2), an analysis using recursive embedding would give

(19b) Our analysis:

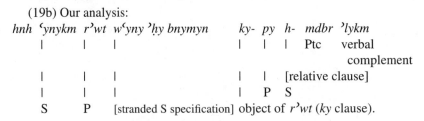

Though we would agree on the similarity, both in outward form and in analysis, of the final part of Gen 45:12 to Deut 3:21b, the verbal element *r'h* (participial or not) requires a direct object. This direct object is present in Deut 3:21b in the *'t kl-'šr* clause and in Gen 45:12 in the *ky* clause. Thus Gen 45:12 is not three simple nominal clauses, two with S–P and one with P–S, as Niccacci analyzes. Rather, it is one clause of the type defNP-indefNP,[73] the complement of the particle *hnh*, in which the main predication is *'ynykm r'wt*, and the embedded *ky* object clause contains a structure comparable to Deut 3:21b.[74]

By using an analysis that recognizes embedding, we offer an alternative analysis for Deut 9:3 (Niccacci's example 24). Niccacci presents it as follows, though it is not clear whether this is his own proposal or that of S. R. Driver,[75] with whom Niccacci heartily agrees (in the following, Pd = *casus pendens*):

(20a) Niccacci's analysis:

Deut 9:3  (Pd)  *wyd't hywm ky yhwh 'lhyk*
      (P)  *hw'*  (S)  *h'br lpnyk*
      (Pd)  *'š  'wklh*
      (P)  *hw'*  (S)  *yšmydm*
      (P)  *whw'*  (S)  *ykny'm lpnyk*

Niccacci: And so you shall experience today that Yahweh your God, it's Him that is about to go over before you; a consuming fire, it's Him that will destroy them; it's Him that will bring them down before you.

Alternative analysis with recursive embedding:

---

73. For the treatment of the participle as an NP, see §3.3.1.

74. If *r'wt* were to have an article here, as in Deut 3:21b, the clause would be a case of defNP-defNP, in which the second-person suffix on *'ynykm* ranks higher as S than does the person-neutral participle; see further §3.6.

75. S. R. Driver, *A Treatise on the Use of the Tenses in Hebrew and Some Other Syntactical Questions* (3d ed.; Oxford: Oxford University Press, 1892; repr., Biblical Resource Series; Grand Rapids, Mich.: Eerdmans / Livonia, Mich.: Dove, 1998) §§198–201.

(20b) Our analysis:

| *wydᶜt* | *hywm* | *ky* | *yhwh* | *ʾlhyk* | *hwʾ* | *h-* | *ᶜbr* | *lpnyk* | *ʾš* | *ʾklh* |
|---------|--------|------|--------|---------|-------|------|-------|---------|------|--------|
| \| | \| | \| | \| | \| | \| | \| | \| | \| | S | P |
| \| | \| | \| | \| | \| | \| | \| | Ptc | VComp | \| | \| |
| \| | \| | \| | \| | \| | \| | \| | [relative clause] | | \| | \| |
| \| | \| | \| | \| | \| | S | P | | | \| | \| |
| \| | \| | \| | P | S | (specification of S) | | | | \| | \| |
| \| | \| | \| | S | (App) (specification of S) | | | | | P | (attributive) |
| P | Ti | object of *ydᶜ* (*ky* clause) | | | | | | | | |

And know this day that YHWH your God, he who goes before you, is a consuming fire.

This analysis renders a translation at variance with the one presented in Niccacci (see [20a] above) but one that is defensible in its consistent treatment of the various syntactic relationships involved.

The embedded nominal clauses can function as a further specification of a nominal element within a more complex sentence structure. Thus, Ruth 1:1b–2a can be read as one sentence in Hebrew, in which the nominal clauses give further information within the larger structure. The main argument in favor of considering these two verses to be a single whole is the fact that the phrase "Ephrathites from Bethlehem in Judah" refers to the further specification of the subject occurring at the end of v. 1:

(21) Ruth 1:1b–2a   *wylk ʾyš mbyt lḥm yhwdh lgwr bśdy mwʾb*
                     |
                     *hwʾ wʾštw wšny bnyw*
                     |   *wšm hʾyš ʾlymlk*
                     |   *wšm ʾštw nᶜmy*
                     |   *wšm šny-bnyw mḥlwn wklywn*
                     *ʾprtym mbyt lḥm yhwdh*

It would be interesting to research whether there are formal constraints on the choice of element to take precedence over another as the main P when embedding occurs, but this is beyond the scope of the present undertaking.

**3.3.** Other Elements Functioning as P and S

Not all elements that can function as P or S in nominal clauses are included in our basic paradigm for determining the parsing. A number of these will be considered in the paragraphs that follow.

**3.3.1.** Participles

Because of their nominal morphology, participles can formally be included in the class of nominal predicates. Most treatments of nominal clauses do include participles, albeit at times with a critical note.

> One generally treats the participle as one of the form-classes which serve as the predicate of a nominal clause. On the other hand, it is a well known fact that in course of time the participle in many Semitic languages, particularly in the Northwest branch, tended to evolve as the third tense form beside the perfect and imperfect.[76]

Joosten, taking the opposite approach, wrote an entire article only on the verbal uses of the participle.[77]

The crux of the matter is, of course, the double nature of the participle: its full verbal potential encased within its nominal form with full nominal potential. It is undeniable that the participle later came to be used as a part of the verbal system and that the start of this development is discernible within the Hebrew Bible; nonetheless, it should be remembered that a participle never became only a verb but, rather, preserved its double potential. Though there are formal restrictions concerning when it is syntactically possible for a participle to be taken as the main verbal predication,[78] a difference should be maintained between stating that the formal syntax allows for a participle to be interpreted as being the main verbal predication and stating that in a particular instance it actually was intended as the main verbal predication. The first is dependent on the formal syntactic pattern (concrete and observable), while the second would be a deduction or interpretation on the basis of relative distribution of verbal forms and frequency of their occurrences within texts.

Obviously, something would be missed if one were to treat the participle merely as a nominal form, for example, in the following sentence, in spite of the fact that besides question markers and prepositions all forms are nominal:

| (22) Jer 7:17 | *hᵓynk rᵓh mh hmh ʿśym bʿry yhwdh* |
|---|---|
| RSV | Do you not see what they are doing in the cities of Judah . . . ? |

Nonetheless, for the purposes of this paper, it is not necessary to determine whether the participle is to be taken as a verbal or a nominal predicate. The participle can be taken as a nominal form that fits the basic paradigm for determining S and P, that is, as a defNP or an indefNP. With the participle delineated as an NP, the elements related to its verbal valency can be taken as further specifying the participle in a way similar to nouns reflecting the valency pattern of their related verbal form. Cf. the noun 'king' in the following example:

---

76. Muraoka, *Emphatic Words*, 20–21.

77. J. Joosten, "The Predicative Participle in Biblical Hebrew," *ZAH* 2 (1989) 128–59.

78. See Dyk (*Participles*, 136–40) on the possibility of reanalysis of the participle as the main verbal predicate of a clause.

(23) Num 22:4    *wblq bn-ṣpwr mlk lmwʾb bʿt hhwʾ*
    KJV        And Balak the son of Zippor was king of the Moabites
                at that time.

We encounter the participle not only as the P, as it is usually treated, but also as the S.

Participle as P:

persPro + Participle:

(24) Ruth 3:2    *hnh- hwʾ    zrh    ʾt-grn hšʿrym    hlylh*
                  S     P    specification   time
    RSV       See, he is winnowing barley tonight at the threshing floor.

defNP + Participle:

(25) Exod 2:5    *wnʿrtyh hlkt    ʿl-yd hyʾr*
                S        P    specification
    RSV       and her maidens walked beside the river

(26) Prov 12:22  *wʿśy ʾmwnh       rṣwnw*
                P    specification  S
    RSV       but those who act faithfully are his delight

PN + Participle:

(27) Gen 9:25    *ʾrwr    knʿn*
                P    S
    RSV       Cursed be Canaan

Participle as S:

Definite Participle + Indefinite Participle:

(28) Prov 3:18    *wtmkyh  mʾšr*
                 S     P
    RSV       those who hold her fast are called happy

Definite Participle in Construct State + Indefinite Participle:

(29) Prov 10:19  *wḥśk śptyw    mśkyl*
                 S        P
    RSV       but he that restrains his lips is prudent

Thus, it is possible to fit the participle qua form into the basic paradigm for deciding S and P as presented above.

**3.3.2.** Infinitive Constructions as S and P

Just as they do within verbal clauses, infinitives can serve various functions within nominal clauses. From the examples we encountered, it appears that, in order to be parsed acceptably, an infinitive must be placed after the interrPro and before the Adj in the basic paradigm for deciding S and P. Examples:

demPro + Inf: S–P

| | | |
|---|---|---|
| (30) Gen 11:6 | | *wzh hhlm lʿśwt* |
| | RSV | and this is only the beginning of what they will do |

defNP + Inf: S–P

| | | |
|---|---|---|
| (31) Prov 14:8 | | *hkmt ʿrwm hbyn drkw* |
| | KJV | The wisdom of the prudent *is* to understand his way |

irgP + Inf: S–P

| | | |
|---|---|---|
| (32) Esth 1:15 | | *kdt mh-lʿśwt bmlkh wšty* |
| | RSV | According to the law, what is to be done to Queen Vashti . . . ? |

Adj + Inf: P–S

| | | |
|---|---|---|
| (33) Gen 2:18 | | *lʾ-twb hywt hʾdm lbdw* |
| | RSV | It is not good that the man should be alone |

It should be noted that, for the purposes of parsing, it does not appear to matter whether or not the infinitive is introduced by the preposition *l*-:

| | | |
|---|---|---|
| (34) Prov 21:9 | | *twb lšbt ʿl-pnt-gg mʾšt mdynym wbyt hbr* |
| | Prov 25:24 | *twb šbt ʿl-pnt-gg mʾšt mdwnym wbyt hbr* |
| | RSV | It is better to live in a corner of the housetop than in a house shared with a contentious woman |

With ellipsis:

| (35) 1 Sam 15:22 | *šmʿ* | *mzbh* | *twb* | *lhqšyb* | *mhlb ʾylym* |
|---|---|---|---|---|---|
| | S | adjunct | P | S | adjunct |
| RSV | To obey is better than sacrifice, and to hearken than the fat of rams | | | | |

The infinitive construction involved may in itself be a many-membered clause embedded in the nominal clause construction:

Adj + Inf: P–S:

> (36) Judg 18:19  *ḥṭwb*  *hywtk*        *khn lbyt ʾyš ʾḥd*
>               Inf 'to be'+ S  PComp
>                   *ʾw hywtk khn lšbṭ wlmšpḥt byśrʾl*
>                   . . . (conjoined extension of S)
>           P      S
> RSV        Is it better for you to be priest to the house of one
>                man, or to be priest to a tribe and family in Israel?
>
> (37) Jer 2:19    *ky-rʿ wmr*  *ʿzbk*     *ʾt-yhwh ʾlhyk*
>                   Inf+S    obj. of Inf
>           P        S
> RSV        that it is evil and bitter for you to forsake the LORD
>                your God

### 3.3.3. Dependent Clauses as S and P

There are also cases where dependent clauses function as a main element within a nominal clause. Both examples occur with an adjective that functions as the predicate, making the dependent clause the subject:

> (38) Ruth 2:22   *ṭwb*     *bty*    *ky tṣʾy ʿm-nʿrwtyw*
>              P       Voc   S
> RSV        It is well, my daughter, that you go out with his
>                maidens
>
> (39) Ruth 3:13   *ʾm-ygʾlk*   *ṭwb*
>              S         P
> RSV        if he will do the part of the next of kin for you, well

Within our material, there were not sufficient occurrences of this type of construction to draw more detailed conclusions.[79]

### 3.4. Expansion and Modification: Elements outside of the Nominal Clause Predication

As indicated by Richter, within the basic nominal clauses identified by means of their phrase-type, either the separate elements or the whole clause can be expanded by the particles of being: *yš* and *ʾyn*; by the verb of being: *hyh*; and by the personal pronoun. They also be modified by the clause-level modifiers *ʿwd* and *hnh*. The verb of being, *hyh*, is dealt with separately in §3.5.2 and the expansion of a nominal clause by personal pronoun is discussed in §3.5.1.

---

79. See also Qoh 1:9 for an example of a relative clause as P, as treated in §3.5.1.

**3.4.1.** Expansion: *'yn* and *yš*

According to Muraoka, the "fundamental significance" of these words is "nonexistence" or "existence."[80] Richter's treatment of these elements as expansions of the nominal clause allows for a simple and elegant analysis of the constructions in which they occur. The parsing of elements in the nominal clause follows the principles outlined above, and the particle of existence is an expansion of the nominal clause. Examples:

| (40) Judg 6:13 | *wyš* | *yhwh* | *ʿmnw* |
|---|---|---|---|
| | Ex | S | P |
| RSV | if the LORD is with us | | |

| (41) Esth 2:7 | *ky* | *'yn* | *lh* | *'b w'm* |
|---|---|---|---|---|
| | | negEx | P | S |
| RSV | for she had neither father nor mother | | | |

When the S within the nominal clause is a pronoun, it may occur as a suffix on these particles of being:

Suffix + Participle: S–P

| (42) Judg 6:36 | *'m-* | *yšk* | *mwšyʿ* | *hydy* | *'t-yśr'l* |
|---|---|---|---|---|---|
| | | Ex+S | P | specification | specification |
| | | | | | (object of participle) |
| RSV | If thou wilt deliver Israel by my hand | | | | |

An element may be fronted and repeated as a suffix on the particle of being:

| (43) Qoh 1:7 | *whym* | *'ynnw* | *ml'* |
|---|---|---|---|
| | fronted | negEx+S | P |
| RSV | but the sea is not full | | |

Just as with the other nominal clauses treated in §3.1.1, the nominal clauses occurring with the particles of existence can be one-member clauses. In these cases, the existence or nonexistence of the subject is being stated:

| (44) Deut 8:15 | *'šr 'yn-mym* |
|---|---|
| RSV | where there was no water |

| (45) Esth 1:8 | *'yn 'ns* |
|---|---|
| literally | nonexistence one who compels |
| KJV | none did compel |

This S can be expanded by other elements that further specify or modify it but do not have a predicative relationship to the S:

---

80. Muraoka, *Emphatic Words*, 78.

S expanded by infinitive clause:

> (46) Num 22:26  *ʾšr   ʾyn-    drk   lntwt ymyn wśmʾwl*
>                 negEx  S     specification
>
>   RSV          where there was no way to turn either to the right or to
>                the left

S expanded by relative clause:

> (47) Qoh 1:10   *yš   dbr   šyʾmr . . .*
>                 Ex    S     attributive relative clause
>
>   RSV          Is there a thing of which it is said . . .

S expanded by dependent nominal clause:

> (48) Judg 7:14  *ʾyn        zʾt   blty ʾm-ḥrb gdʿwn bn-ywʾš ʾyš yśrʾl*
>                 negEx       S     dependent nominal clause (P only)
>
>   RSV          This is no other than the sword of Gideon the son of
>                Joash, a man of Israel.

Elements of the total clause can appear in various positions, with some member of the nominal clause occurring before the particle of being:[81]

Particle of being at the end:

> (49) Qoh 3:19   *wmwtr hʾdm mn-hbhmh ʾyn*
>
>   RSV          and man has no advantage over the beasts

Particle of being in the middle:

> (50) Judg 6:5   *wlhm wlgmlyhm    ʾyn       mspr*
>                 P                 negEx     S
>
>   KJV          both they and their camels were without number

> (51) Gen 41:15  *wptr ʾyn ʾtw*
>
>   RSV          there is no one who can interpret it

In this last example, the object of the participial subject occurs after the negative particle of existence but still belongs to the S. In spite of the verbal valency of this participle, it is a nominal S whose (negative) existence is being affirmed.

At times the particles of existence can occur without an explicit S but with further specifications referring to an impersonal S:

> (52) Ruth 4:4   *ky ʾyn zwltk lgʾwl*
>
>   RSV          for there is no one besides you to redeem it

---

81. What effect various word orders have is not the topic of discussion in this paragraph.

(53) Prov 11:24  *yš mpzr wnwsp ʿwd*
    KJV          there is that scattereth, and yet increaseth[82]

The negative particle of existence can occur alone: "it simply negates the veracity of the proposition,"[83] meaning, a preceding proposition understood from the context:

(54) Judg 9:15  *wʾm ʾyn . . .*
    RSV          [If in good faith you are anointing me king over
                 you, then come and take refuge in my shade;] but
                 if not, [let fire come . . .]

(55) Gen 30:1  *wʾm ʾyn . . .*
    KJV          [Give me children,] or else [I die]

In the various cases where the nominal clause in which a particle of existence occurs is a one-member clause (S only), it is tempting to read the particle of existence itself as the predicate, certainly since the assumed Ø-copula predicates existence and the actually present particles of existence do the same. Though the significance of the whole is not distorted by doing so and it would appear more practical and natural to interpret the particle of existence as the P in such cases, it is not necessary to assign two different analyses to the particles themselves. It has already been necessary to assume a Ø-copula for other nominal clause constructions; therefore, this is not an element added merely for the analysis of the particles of existence. Thus we do not find it necessary to posit that the particle *ʾyn* "has two distinct syntactic functions, that of simply negating a statement and that of indicating non-existence or absence."[84] Rather, it and its positive counterpart both have a single function of indicating existence or nonexistence in the clause to which they are attached. The clause itself can be of diverse structure, and it is this that effects a supposed difference in the syntactic functioning of the particles of existence.

Because of the semantic overlap between these S-only clauses predicating mere existence and the significance of the particles of existence, one might prefer to label the particles of existence as the Ps in these specific cases; computer programs could be constructed to parse the particle of existence as the P under these specified syntactic circumstances.

---

82. This example could be translated 'there is a scatterer and one who increases more', that is, assuming the forms present are the explicit subject; but the above suggestion that the S is an impersonal unmentioned "someone" further specified by the forms present remains a possibility.
83. Muraoka, *Emphatic Words*, 109.
84. Ibid.

To discover what the effect is of the presence or absence of these particles in a construction would involve a comparison of the various syntactic possibilities for expressing the same predicative functions (see comments on this topic in §3.5.2).

**3.4.2.** Modification: *ʿwd* and *hnh*

The analysis suggested above for the particles of existence can be applied here as well. One difference here, however, is that the significance of these particles does not have a semantic overlap with the predication of being. Richter's differentiation between the particles of existence as expansions of the nominal clause and *ʿwd* and *hnh* as clause-level modifiers could have been motivated by this difference in semantic overlap as well as by the fact that the latter two particles occur freely with verbal clauses, while the particles of existence occur principally with nominal forms. When *ʿwd* and *hnh* occur with nominal clauses, the parsing of elements within the nominal clause follows the principles outlined in the basic paradigm given above.

(56) Deut 3:11   *hnh*      *ʿrśw*    *ʿrś brzl*
                 CMod       S        P

RSV              behold, his bedstead was a bedstead of iron

With embedding:

(57) Ruth 1:11   *h-*  *ʿwd-*  *ly*  *bnym*  *bmʿy*
     potential NC |     |       |     S       P       sons are in my womb
     potential NC |     |       P     S       spec    I have sons in my womb
     actual NC    Q     CMod    P     S       spec
     RSV          Have I yet sons in my womb . . . ?

When the S within the nominal clause is a pronoun, it may occur as a suffix on *ʿwd* and *hnh*:[85]

(58) Judg 8:20   *ky*    *ʿwdnw*     *nʿr*
                 CMod+S              P

RSV              because he was still a youth

The clauses occurring with *ʿwd* and *hnh* can be one-member nominal clauses, and this S may be simply the suffix. These cases belong with what has already been proposed concerning S-only nominal clauses:

---

85. That it is not obligatory for the S pronoun to occur as a suffix in such a construction can be seen in Isa 65:24: *ʿwd hm mdbrym* (cf. Esth 6:14: *ʿwdm mdbrym ʿmw*). See Richter (*Grundlagen*, 175) with reference to *ʿwd*: "Das erste Syntagma kann durch ePP [enclitic personal pronoun] vertreten sein."

(59) Exod 3:4     *hnny*
      RSV            Here I am.

(60) Num 22:30   *mʿwdk*
      literally     from yet you [being]
      RSV            all your life long

(61) Judg 8:15   *hnh zbḥ wṣlmnʿ*
      RSV            Behold Zebah and Zalmunna

The S can be expanded by other elements that further specify or modify it but do not have a predicative relationship to the S:

(62) Num 22:11   *hnh*      *hʿm*    *hyṣʾ mmṣrym*
               CMod   S      attributive relative clause
      KJV            Behold, there is a people come out of Egypt

As is true of the particles of being, *ʿwd* and *hnh* also do not obligatorily occur at the beginning of a construction:

(63) Judg 6:24   *ʿd hywm hzh*    *ʿwdnw*       *bʿprt ʾby hʿzry*
               time phrase    CMod+S   P
      RSV            To this day it still stands at Ophrah, which belongs to
                         the Abiezrites.

In our data, a defective or truncated form occurs:

(64) Deut 4:35   *ʾyn*      *ʿwd*      *mlbdw*
               negEx   CMod   adjunct
      RSV            there is no other besides him

(65) Deut 4:39   *ʾyn ʿwd*
      RSV            there is no other

In these examples, only the extension (*ʾyn*) and the clause modifier (*ʿwd*) are present in the text's surface structure. They could be seen as parallel to the nominal clauses whose S is understood from the context (see §3.1.2). Here not only is the S to be understood from the context, but the Ø-copula is to be understood as asserting the existence of the S.

## 3.5. Related Structures

### 3.5.1. So-Called Pronominal Copula and *Casus Pendens* Constructions

In some constructions, an initial nominal element is followed by a nominal clause, one element of which is a pronoun. Opinions differ as to what the correct analysis of such a construction should be. The pronoun is variously taken to be a mere dummy pronoun, to be an element of focus, or to function as a copula.

Niccacci is quite clear on his rejection of the possibility of the pronominal copula in Hebrew:

> The copula is not a category of the Biblical Hebrew syntax. This conclusion is drawn from two facts: first, the verb *hyh* behaves as any other verb and not as the copular verbs; second, the pronoun (personal independent or demonstrative) which is sometimes found in the SNC [simple noun clause] does not function as a copula, either.[86]

These constructions are analyzed by Niccacci as ones in which the initial element is a *casus pendens*, followed by an independent nominal clause in which the first element (in his examples, always the pronoun) is taken to be the predicate.

Muraoka, on the other hand, does use the term *copula* when discussing the particles of being, the verb of being, and the pronoun in *casus pendens* constructions, though he warns against the "careless use of the misleading term 'copula.'"[87] He defines the pronominal copula as "one of the third person personal pronouns used in a nominal clause alongside its subject and predicate."[88] According to Muraoka:

> Formally speaking, there are three ways of looking at the construction. 1) The resumptive pronoun may be considered pleonastic, one of the formal features characterizing emphatic construction [*sic*]. 2) The possible emphasis may be due to the initial position occupied by the extraposed word. 3) Extraposition does not affect the basic inner structure of an utterance; it does not, for instance, turn a subject into an object or vice versa, and emphasis, if any, is something superimposed on this basic structure.[89]

Muraoka sees "little point in arguing as to which is the real subject of the two elements connected by the copula,"[90] since he takes the elements other than the pronoun to be the S and the P. Richter treats the pronoun in such constructions as an extension of the nominal clause, which agrees with Muraoka's remarks cited above.

In order to maintain a unified approach to the data in building up our database and in order to give a consistent analysis of formally similar structures, our preference goes to a formal treatment of these structures in a manner that incorporates, as much as possible, the insights gained in the analysis of nominal clause constructions seen thus far. Before one researches the effect of the use of a particular element or construction, there must be an analysis of the syntax as such.

---

86. Niccacci, "Simple Nominal Clause," 223.
87. Muraoka, *Emphatic Words*, 77.
88. Ibid., 69.
89. Ibid., 93–94.
90. Ibid., 74.

Li and Thompson and Junger[91] illustrate how, in many languages, such a copular construction with a pronoun can originate historically from a marked topic–comment (or theme–predication) construction, with pausal intonation, the topic being the element in initial position and the comment being the clause consisting of the pronominal subject and the predicate NP. This marked form with "pronominal support" (Junger) was used in contrast to the unmarked S–P sequence in nominal clauses. Because the marked structure was also used to express meanings that in themselves are not pragmatically marked but could be more clearly conveyed by the marked form (for example, clauses with long and complex subject NPs and situations where, if the pronoun were absent, the whole could appear to be one term instead of a complete sentence), a gradual "unmarking" of the marked construction occurred. Thus, there came to be two unmarked structures available: S–P and S-pronoun-P without pausal intonation. In the latter case, the pronoun has been reanalyzed as a copula morpheme, and a new marked construction is needed to replace the old one, which has become unmarked. In Modern Hebrew this occurs in constructions having both a personal pronoun and a demonstrative particle:

(66) *ywsp   wdn   ʾlh   hm   ʾḥy*
            these   they   my brothers
     Joseph and Dan, they are my brothers.

Within Classical Hebrew, the constructions could be read either as a marked topic–comment (*Casus pendens* + Nominal Clause) construction with pausal intonation or as a nominal clause with a pronoun as copula. The problem with written texts is that it is not certain when a pausal intonation is present and, therefore, when a pronoun intervening between two nominal elements is to be interpreted as a subject pronoun or as a copula.

We choose, therefore, to give a consistent analysis of the syntactic patterns; this results in labeling constructions as

Fronted Element + Nominal Clause

in which the members of the nominal clause receive their S–P parsing according to the basic paradigm in §2.2.

Whether, or at which exact point the "marked" structure became "unmarked," is a matter to be determined by an investigation of the relative frequency of occurrence of alternative structures. Thus, for the database, consistent syntactic marking can still be applied, without necessarily stating what the effect of a particular construction is in the text.

---

91. C. Li and S. Thompson, "A Mechanism for the Development of Copula Morphemes," in *Mechanisms of Syntactic Change* (ed. C. Li; Austin: University of Texas Press, 1977) 419–44; J. Junger, "Copula Constructions in Modern Hebrew," *GLOT: Leids Taalkundig Bulletin* 3 (1980) 117–34.

(67) Deut 4:35   *ky   yhwh      hwʾ   hʾlhym*
                 fronted  S       P
KJV              that the LORD he *is* God

It is not necessary that the pronominal element involved occur between the other two elements:

(68) Qoh 2:23    *gm-zh    hbl   hwʾ*
                 fronted   P     S
RSV              This also is vanity

This approach allows for treating the same type of construction, but with an NP instead of the pronoun, in the same manner:

(69) Qoh 2:14    *ḥḥkm    ʿynyw   brʾšw*
                 fronted  S       P
RSV              The wise man has his eyes in his head

(70) Qoh 3:16    *mqwm hmšpṭ   šmh   hršʿ*
                 fronted      P     S
RSV              in the place of justice, even there is wickedness

With embedding:

(71) Deut 4:4    *wʾtm      hdbqym byhwh ʾlhykm   ḥyym   klkm   hywm*
                 fronted    attributive RC         P      S      time
RSV              but you who held fast to the LORD your God are all
                 alive this day

(72) Qoh 1:9     *mh-      šhyh             hwʾ    šyhyh*
                 S         P                 |      |
                 fronted   attributive RC   S      P
RSV              That which has been is what will be

The fact that a particular construction may have gained prominence through time and thus may have shifted in its effect or interpretation need not hinder us from choosing a formally consistent analysis for a construction without denying that the interpretation of a construction may shift in various texts through time. The fact that one text makes more frequent use of such constructions than another is an encouragement to do research on the quantitative aspect of this construction without undermining the formal analysis given.

**3.5.2.** Variation in Syntactic Possibilities
According to Niccacci,

> the situation of the verb *hyh* is not comparable with that of the copular verbs of the classical languages which are optional elements of the sentence. The situation of the verb *hyh* is different since its occurrence in the sentence is governed by definite rules. It is mandatory when there is a need to indicate a time setting

for the information which is different from the present. . . . The nominal complement found with the verb *hyh* functions as a predicative complement since it completes the predication of the verb. In fact, in such cases, *hyh* is a verb of incomplete predication (it can also be a "full" verb of complete predication, as in Gen 1:3).[92]

In taking this position, it appears that Niccacci is ignoring the similarities between the nominal clause structures treated above and the clauses containing the verb *hyh*. Exactly the same types of logical relationships between the S and P are in effect with or without the presence of the verb of being. Not infrequently, identical clauses occur within a passage, once with the verb of being and once without. Compare

| (73) Gen 48:5 | *šny-bnyk hnwldym lk bᵓrṣ mṣrym ᶜd-bᵓy ᵓlyk mṣrymh* |
|---|---|

                                                                     *ly-hm*

                    fronted element                                        P  S

      RSV           your two sons, who were born to you in the land of Egypt before I came to you in Egypt, are mine

with

| (74) Gen 48:6 | *wmwldtk ᵓšr-hwldt ᵓḥryhm lk*     *yhyw* |
|---|---|

                    Fronted Element                   PComp   Verb of Being + S

      RSV           And the offspring born to you after them shall be yours

In the following example, use of the principle of embedding preserves a consistent treatment of the elements in these clauses. Compare

| (75) Isa 28:10 | *ky ṣw lṣw ṣw lṣw qw lqw qw lqw zᶜyr šm zᶜyr šm* |
|---|---|

                                              S   P   S   P  . . .

      RSV           For it is precept upon precept, precept upon precept,
                          line upon line, line upon line,
                          here a little, there a little.

with

(76) Isa 28:13

| *whyh* | *lhm* | *dbr-yhwh* | *ṣw* | *lṣw* | *ṣw* | *lṣw* | *qw* | *lqw* . . . |
|---|---|---|---|---|---|---|---|---|
| I | I | I | S | P | S | P | S | P |
| P | sc[93] | S | PComp | spec | PComp | spec | PComp | spec |

      RSV           Therefore the word of the LORD will be to them
                       precept upon precept, precept upon precept,
                       line upon line, line upon line,
                       here a little, there a little

---

92. Niccacci, "Simple Nominal Clause," 223–24.

93. In "to be" constructions where a *l*+suffix constituent is present as the predicate complement, a possessive relation is expressed. If this possessive relation is not to be taken as the main P, the *l*+suffix element can be labeled a *supplementary constituent* (sc).

We have also seen that what Niccacci calls a "full" verb of complete predication is also applicable to one-member nominal clauses with S only (see §3.1.1). Without going into the function and effect of the presence of the verb of being in a construction, we would argue for a unified formal treatment of structures with and without the verb of being, such as advocated in §2.3.

The same logical relation between two elements can be expressed in various ways. This possibility of syntactic variety should not obscure a consistent analysis of the constructions involved. Example:

(77) Judg 6:12     *yhwh ʿmk*
     RSV            The LORD is with you

(78) Judg 6:13     *wyš yhwh ʿmnw*
     RSV            if the LORD is with us

(79) Judg 6:16     *ky ʾhyh ʿmk*
     RSV            But I will be with you

The variety of syntactic possibilities to express the same logical relation can extend even to an NP being parallel to a nominal clause:

(80) Qoh 2:13     *yš  ytrwn  lḥkmh  mn-hsklwt*
                  *k-  ytrwn  hʾwr   mn-hḥšk*
     RSV          wisdom excels folly as light excels darkness

The possessive is expressed in the first clause by the *l* + NP predicate as possessor, with an NP subject as the item possessed, and in the second by the construct state structure in which the possessor is the governed NP and the item possessed is in construct state.[94]

The variety possible in syntax motivates us to give a consistent formal account of the data first and only thereafter to look for the function that the constructions considered might have. Research into the effects of expressing the same logical relationship in differing syntactic expressions goes beyond the scope of the present paper.

**3.6.** Cases of Clauses with Two Formally Identical Constituents

A more extensive differentiation of phrase-types—for instance, placing the personal pronoun separately in the basic paradigm—leaves us with fewer cases to be discussed here; however, some do occur. We suggest continuing

---

94. See Dyk, "Who Shepherds Whom?" (in *Een boek heeft een rug: Studies voor Ferenc Postma op het grensgebied van theologie, bibliogie en universiteitsgeschiedenis* [ed. M. Gosker; Zoetermeer: Uitgeverij Boekencentrum B.V., 1995] 166–72), for an analysis of the possessive construct state construction using the Government-Binding theory of syntax.

the type of analysis already presented, that is, to work with a definition of *determination* in terms of the marking of linguistic communication, either by deixis or by pronominal or lexical reference. Muraoka defines a determinate as

> a noun or noun phrase that can be conceived by virtue of the context as already known to the speaker(s) or hearer(s), chiefly because it has been mentioned earlier in the flow of speech, so that it can be referred to by means of an anaphoric pronoun or because it indicates something which is part of the common knowledge of participants in a given speech situation.[95]

First, examples of two personal pronouns occurring together will be considered. In these, it appears that if one were to recognize a hierarchy of deixis within the personal pronouns, a suitable S–P parsing would result, namely: first person ranks above second person in deixis within the context, and second person ranks above third. This insight can be extended to apply to nominal clauses comprising two definite NPs or two PPs in which pronominal suffixes are the only formal distinction. Examples:

First-Person Pronoun—Third-Person Pronoun:

    (81) Deut 32:39[96]   *ky*   *ʾny*     *ʾny*   *hwʾ*
                        fronted    S      P

        RSV            that I, even I, am he
                     that is: I, the one referred to in the situation

NP + First-Person Pronominal Suffix—NP + Second-Person Pronominal Suffix:

    (82) Ruth 1:16    *ʿmk*   *ʿmy*   *wʾlhyk*   *ʾlhy*
                      P     S    P       S

        RSV            your people shall be my people, and your God my God

which we would understand as meaning:

              [What I call] my people (S) is your people (P).

The fronted (P) in the Hebrew text could be giving extra emphasis to the fact that it is Naomi's people that are to be seen from now on as the ones whom Ruth will call 'my people'. Ruth's people had already been mentioned in the context when Naomi told her daughter-in-law to return, as her sister-in-law had done, to her people and to her gods. Ruth's people are thus contextually already known and the new information is the predication that they will henceforth be identified with Naomi's people. Thus the meaning of her reply we would read as:

---

95. Muraoka, *Emphatic Words*, 8, 9.
96. For the treatment of *casus pendens*, see §3.5.1.

[not Moab,] but your people (P) are [what I call] my people (S) and
your God (P) is [what I henceforth choose to call] my God (S)[97]

PP + First-Person Pronominal Suffix—PP + Second-Person Pronominal
Suffix:

(83) 1 Kgs 22:4   *kmwny   kmwk   kᶜmy   kᶜmk   kswsy   kswsyk*
                  S        P      S      P      S       P
RSV               I am as you are, my people as your people, my horses
                  as your horses.
                  that is: I, the one referred to in the context, I am,
                  as you are

PP + Second-Person Pronominal Suffix—PP + Third-Person Pronominal
Suffix:

(84) Judg 8:18    *kmwk   kmwhm*
                  S       P
RSV               As you are, so were they

In these last two examples, an idiomatic expression is apparently involved (*k
. . . k*) that allows a PP to be an S.

Second, there are a number of remaining examples for which the broader
linguistic context can at times be helpful in deciding which one of the two
phrases of identical types is referring to what is present in the text or the situation of communication. Each of the following examples merits separate comment because of the variety of factors involved:

(85) Num 23:19   *lʾ  ʾyš  ʾl*
RSV              God is not a man

Though formally both 'god' and 'man' are indefinite NPs, an understanding
of the context indicates that 'god' refers here to a specific person, to be compared with a proper name, rather than with an indefinite NP. This is in contrast
to the context around Isa 31:3, where the term 'god' is used parallel to 'human', and 'spirit' is used parallel to 'flesh':

(86) Isa 31:3    *wmṣrym ʾdm wlʾ-ʾl wswsyhm bśr wlʾ-rwḥ*
                 The Egyptians are human and not a god, and their
                 horses are flesh and not spirit

---

97. Though we do not presume to have a native speaker's competence for Biblical Hebrew, we suggest that if the speaker were wanting to express the opposite, that is, if he
would want to state that something belonging to another (non-first person as subject) is the
speaker's own (first person as predicate), thus going against our proposed hierarchy of S-
determination, the speaker might then use a construction such as Benhadad did in 1 Kgs
20:3: *kspk wzhbk ly-hwʾ*, in which a fronted element is repeated in the simple NC as a pronoun with a possessive prepositional predicate.

The following example appears at first to be a case of two PPs following each other:

(87) Num 23:22  *ktw‘pt r’m lw*

RSV          they have as it were the horns of the wild ox

A look, however, at the preceding verse offers a case of similar syntax:

(88) Num 23:21  *wtrw‘t mlk bw*

RSV          and the shout of a king is among them

The parallel construction would lead to parsing Num 23:22 as a single PP, a one-member nominal clause with the S understood from the context, as is correctly reflected in the RSV translation.

The following case of two PPs reflects yet another set of extenuated circumstances:

(89) Exod 1:14  *’t kl-‘bdtm ’šr-‘bdw bhm   bprk*
                 S                            P

RSV          in all their work they made them serve with rigor

In this verse the first PP can be explained as a case of movement of the object marker *’t* related to the valency of the verb *‘bd*, thus resulting in complex internal syntax of the S, while the second PP has no such complex syntax but is a simple PP that can simply be taken to be the P.

The following example involves two indefinite participles within one clause:

(90) Prov 10:5  *’gr bqyṣ bn mśkyl*
                 *nrdm bqṣyr bn mbyš*

KJV          He that gathereth in summer *is* a wise son;
             *but* he that sleepeth in harvest *is* a son that causeth shame.

RSV          A son who gathers in summer is prudent,
             but a son who sleeps in harvest brings shame.

alternative  A wise son gathers in summer
             and a son who causes shame slumbers in the harvest.[98]

It appears that information from outside of the clause structure is needed to resolve the indeterminancy in this case, probably global information on dominant S–P patterns or frequency of occurrence of the reanalysis of participial constructions.

Thus, apparently the hierarchy of formally recognizable grammatical elements for assigning S–P relations needs to be enriched with information from the broader context, such as information from parallel syntactic constructions

---

98. Cf. Dyk, *Participles*, 157.

in the context, participant tracking, or general information concerning language usage in a particular passage or book.

There is a limit to what the paradigm with its syntagmatic extensions can cover; nonetheless, we maintain that the paradigm should be applied first, where possible, and thereafter the context can be observed for further clues.

This standpoint appears to be in conflict with Niccacci's approach in some instances. One example used by Niccacci[99] is as follows:

> (91) 1 Sam 9:18  (P)  *ꜣy-zh*  (S)  *byt hrꜣh*
>      1 Sam 9:19  (P)  *ꜣnky*  (S)  *hrꜣh*
>      Niccacci    (Saul) said: Please tell me, which is the seer's house?
>                  Samuel answered: It's me the seer.

Niccacci analyzes the personal pronoun in v. 19 as the predicate because

> Samuel does not simply identify himself; rather he qualifies himself as the one Saul is looking for. This . . . is not a "self-presentation formula."

This is similar to his argumentation for a P–S in Deut 3:21b and in the last clause of Gen 45:12 (see §3.2). It appears that in his analysis Niccacci indeed is reacting to factors present in the broader context—for example, the fact that in 1 Sam 9:19 *hrꜣh* had already been mentioned in a previous clause and that therefore *ꜣnky* could be taken as the new element; however, his reaction to the context takes precedence over a consistent application of formally described paradigmatic features. Because of this approach, Niccacci's analyses and insights tend at times to have an unverifiable character.

His analysis of 1 Sam 9:19 resembles his analysis of *casus pendens* constructions in that the personal pronoun is labeled P (see §3.5), with the difference being that there is no fronted element here. The second clause of this example is indeed not a case of *casus pendens*. The word *ꜣnky* is the S, we would maintain, due to its higher rank in the paradigm. The defNP *rꜣh* is the P: 'It is I, this *rꜣh*'. Niccacci's remark, that Samuel does not simply identify himself, remains true, but one is not thereby forced to change the parsing paradigm: the word order (S initial) and the lexical repetition of *rꜣh* + Definite Article are sufficient clues: 'you speak of the *rꜣh*? I am that one'.

## 3.7. The Question of Word Order

As will have been noted, our proposal is independent of word order. In other words, the syntactic category and degree of definiteness appear to be sufficiently decisive in defining the element that is the S and the P in cases where the two elements have diverse formal characteristics. In order to speak of alternative syntactic order and the effect of it in emphasis and so forth,

---

99. Niccacci, "Simple Nominal Clause," 222, example 19.

there must be a default order. This cannot be a simple S–P or P–S underlying order but must entail a subtle interrelation between the types of constituents involved. Muraoka reminds us that

> It is of great importance to remember that there exists fundamental disagreement among the leading Hebraists as to the validity of the prevalent assumption as to the alleged word-order polarity discernible in the two main sentence types, namely the nominal clause shows the order S–P and the verbal clause V–S. Thus, Joüon, König, and Schlesinger do not recognize any correlation between the sentence type and the word-order pattern while the majority of scholars do recognize such a correlation.[100]

Before one can discuss word order, one must take the following factors into account:

1. In general accordance with widely valid cross-linguistic principles of *wh*-movement, the interrogatives tend to occur sentence-initially whether they are S or P. It would thus skew the statistics to count these cases, as though an alternative word order were possible.
2. Occasionally the relative length of the S seems to be the reason that the P occurs initially, since, as is generally true in languages, "heavy" or longer NPs tend to "sink," that is, occur later in the sentence.
3. Stylistic factors, such as chiasm, also determine the word order, particularly in poetic portions. Chiasm affects the word order in Isa 15:2 (but the S–P order seems to follow the rules Richter proposes):

(92) Isa 15:2[101]   *bkl-rʾšyw*   *qrḥh*   [P–S]
           *kl-zqn*     *grwʿh*   [S–P]

    RSV      On every head is baldness,
                 every beard is shorn

4. Further, account should be taken of the effect, for example, of particles like *ky* that appear to have a preference for a P–S word order.[102] Andersen observes that, when the P is a participle, the dominant pattern is S–P; in contrast, when the P is an indefinite noun, the sequence is P–S, which according to him is normal in such cases.[103] Thus, certain lexical properties of the elements involved may have a standard effect on word order.
5. In addition, one should allow for the possibility that certain genres may betray a preference for one word order above another.

---

100. Muraoka, *Emphatic Words*, 4–5.
101. For the treatment of participles, see §3.3.1.
102. Cf. Muraoka, *Emphatic Words*, 17.
103. Andersen, *The Hebrew Verbless Clause*, 34, 47ff.

In general, word order is often obligatory or context-dependent; therefore, we choose not to assume that a certain word order should be seen as "marked," that is, as having a special meaning in its deviation from some default order.

The order of the S and P can be established once they have been parsed with the help of the paradigm. The word order can be explained as a feature of interaction with linguistic context. Compare

(93) Judg 7:2     *rb   hᶜm   ʾšr   ʾtk*
                   P     S     attributive relative clause
     RSV           The people with you are too many

with

(94) Judg 7:4[104]  *ᶜwd     hᶜm   rb*
                    CMod    S     P
     RSV            The people are still too many

The different order of S and P in these two references should not be explained too quickly as emphasis or markedness. The word order in the first could be influenced by the fact that the S has an attributive relative clause attached to it, making it "heavy" and therefore tending to occur later. The word order in the second could be influenced by deixis: 'the people' about whom this has been spoken, 'they are too many'. Quite correctly, in our opinion, the RSV translation does not make a distinction in emphasis between these two word orders in Hebrew.

After considering these and perhaps more factors that have an effect on word order, one is left with a truncated but much more nuanced standpoint concerning what is actually significant in word order variation. Word order can allow for differences in emphasis but should not be confused with a paradigmatic assignment of the S–P parsing.

## 4. Conclusion

Our aim has been to compose programs capable of parsing verbless clauses. In doing so, it was necessary to define which parameters we took to be decisive and what parsing procedures could be used.

First, we struggled with a problem that is often simply skipped in grammatical discussion, namely, the question of how to isolate a set of nominal clauses from the larger set of verbless constructions. Whereas most discussion is restricted to a neat set of chosen examples, we discovered that we had to reckon with a complex interplay of criteria, both distributional (patterns of elements) and functional (identification of P).

---

104. For the treatment of *ᶜwd*, see §3.4.2.

Second, we have tried to identify what linguistic parameters are being used for S–P parsing in a number of existing theories and proposals. We have argued for a parsing procedure that analyzes from the distribution of forms and progresses to the assignment of functions.

Third, it became apparent that for a parsing paradigm, two parameters—phrase-type and determination—were sufficient if arranged in a hierarchically meaningful manner along an axis of relative deictic power. Phrase-types were listed according to their appearance in the text's surface structure. This resulted in pronouns being treated as a separate category. The phrase-types were sorted according to their level of determination, ranking from high to low, as defined in terms of linguistic communication, that is, deictic and referential force. In the patterns of combination of phrase-types in actual clauses, the phrase that has the highest level of determination takes the S position.

Fourth, a recursive application of the paradigm made it possible to explain clauses with complex structure.

Fifth, the similarity between related constructions can be made transparent by maintaining the formal parameters of the paradigm.

Sixth, the contribution of the broader linguistic context can be used to solve examples with formally identical phrase-types and to gain insight into the significance of the word order in a particular instance.

In our view it is possible to base the S–P parsing on formal, syntactic data, arguing from form to function and from simple to complex, using one paradigm. Extension, recursion, and embedding help to explain the actual surface structure of nominal clauses. An explanation in terms of categories of semantics or propositional logic is not needed for the linguistic procedure to find the S–P parsing itself but is useful to describe what kind of statements these clauses make in their context.

# The Tripartite Nominal Clause Revisited

## Takamitsu Muraoka
### Leiden University

## 1. Introduction

Since 1877–88 when Albrecht published his classic article on the subject, the Hebrew nominal clause (henceforth NC)[1] has received a considerable amount of attention from Hebraists. This interest in the Hebrew NC has been quite evident during the last three or so decades. A comparison of the number of pages devoted to the subject in the French original of Joüon's grammar (1923) and in its revised, English version (Joüon and Muraoka 1991) testifies to this intense interest: 7 pages compared with 17. Neither have a number of other languages cognate to Hebrew remained untouched during the same period: notably Classical Syriac (Muraoka 1975, 1987; Goldenberg 1983; Pennacchietti 1987; Joosten 1996), Modern Hebrew (Rubinstein 1969; Glinert 1989),[2] Biblical Aramaic (Naudé 1994), Targumic Aramaic (Golomb 1983), Akkadian (Kraus 1984; Huehnergard 1986), and Semitic in general (Cohen 1984). Nonetheless, there remains many an area of uncertainty.[3] For this reason, I suppose, a session of the SBL meeting in November, 1996, was dedicated to this topic. Furthermore, no really systematic and comprehensive study has been undertaken on the nominal clause in the limited corpus of Biblical Hebrew. In the light of this and in addition to exploratory forays

*Author's note*: The substance of this paper was presented at a series of seminars on the nominal clause in Semitic languages convened by Dr. K. Jongeling of Leiden University.

1. For a reason why the term *nominal* is preferable to *verbless*, see Joüon and Muraoka (1991: §153 n. 2) and Gibson (1994: 52).

2. Geller (1991: esp. 16 n. 9) stresses that "reference to Modern Hebrew . . . is particularly meaningless." We find such a complete break regrettable and unproductive, and the same applies to specialists on Modern Hebrew ignoring studies on earlier forms of Hebrew.

3. In addition to the literature mentioned in Joüon and Muraoka (1991), the following ought to be added: Baasten 1997; Geller 1991; Gibson 1994; Kraus 1984; Huehnergard 1986; Michel 1994; Joosten 1996; Naudé 1994; Niccacci 1993; Pennacchietti 1987; Rosén 1965; Zewi 1994, 1996.

launched from various angles by actual participants in the session, it appears sensible to me to undertake a thorough investigation into specific and well-defined parts of the entire complex. In this contribution, then, I will focus on the tripartite nominal clause.[4]

The formal criterion for identifying tripartite nominal clauses is that one of the three components is a third-person independent personal pronoun. One of the remaining two components may not be a noun phrase (NP) but an adverbial or a prepositional phrase. Unlike Niccacci I shall not regard as nominal the clauses that contain a finite verb as the second or later clause constituent.[5] Given these qualifications, then, the tripartite nominal clause in Biblical Hebrew appears in two distinct patterns: namely, one with a pronoun in the second slot and the other with a pronoun in the last slot:

$$(A)\ NP_1–Pro–NP_2$$
$$(B)\ NP_1–NP_2–Pro$$

First, I present the data according to various patterns[6] and then discuss a few salient points arising from them.

## 2. The Data

**2.1.** Pattern A: $NP_1–Pro–NP_2$

**2.1.1.** Pattern Aa: indetNP–Pro–indetNP (7×)

(1) Prov 30:29

שְׁלֹשָׁה הֵמָּה מֵיטִיבֵי צָעַד     three are those that walk gracefully

Also with a numeral in Prov 6:16; 30:15, 24; Cant 6:8.

---

4. This type of nominal clause did receive due attention in my *Emphasis in Biblical Hebrew* (1969: 11–12, 49-62) and in its subsequently revised form, *Emphatic Words and Structures in Biblical Hebrew* (1985: 17–18, 67–82), as well as in Andersen (1970) and Joüon and Muraoka (1991: §154 i–j), though our corpus was rather limited.

5. Niccacci's approach is, as is well known, that of native Arab grammarians. For an objection to such an approach, see my review of Niccacci (Muraoka 1989: esp. 188–89); and see Gibson (1994: 54). Note that Reckendorf's definition as applied to Classical Arabic is the conventional one (Reckendorf 1921: 1, 10 n. 1). On a description of how native Arab grammarians perceived the sentence structure of Arabic, see Trumpp 1879.

6. Contrary to Revell (pp. 297–319 in this volume), I believe that it *is* important to take the nature of both NPs into consideration. For instance, an interrogative word, pronoun, or adverb is by definition the predicate of a nominal clause. No less important is the feature of definiteness or determinateness. Hoftijzer (1973: 446–510) virtually elevated it to the status of the single most important formal parameter. On this issue I concur with Zewi (1994: 151). Michel (1994) also uses the feature of definiteness as the only classificatory parameter. He further replaces the traditional S and P with *mubtadaʾ* and *ḫabar*, terms taken from Arabic grammar, but surely a sequence *ḫabar–mubtadaʾ* is a total contradiction in terms since *mubtadaʾ*, by definition, cannot fill the second slot.

(2) Prov 10:18

מוֹצָא דִבָּה הוּא כְסִיל     one who utters slander is a fool

(3) Prov 28:26

בּוֹטֵחַ בְּלִבּוֹ הוּא כְסִיל     one who trusts in his own wits is a
וְהוֹלֵךְ בְּחָכְמָה הוּא יִמָּלֵט     fool; and one who walks in wisdom
                    will be spared

**2.1.2.** Pattern Ab: indetNP–Pro–detNP (9×)

(4) Lam 1:18

צַדִּיק הוּא יהוה     righteous is the Lᴏʀᴅ

(5) Cant 6:9

אַחַת הִיא יוֹנָתִי     one is my dove

With a numeral also in Isa 51:19.

(6) Ezek 27:22

רֹכְלֵי שְׁבָא וְרַעְמָה הֵמָּה     the merchants of Sheba and Raama
רֹכְלָיִךְ     are your merchants

See Ezek 27:13, 17, 21.

(7) Isa 9:14

זָקֵן וּנְשׂוּא־פָנִים הוּא הָרֹאשׁ     an elderly person and dignitary is
וְנָבִיא מוֹרֶה־שֶּׁקֶר הוּא הַזָּנָב     the head and a false teacher-prophet
                    is the tail

See also Isa 51:19.

**2.1.3.** Pattern Ac: detNP–Pro–indetNP (4x)

(8) Job 28:28

יִרְאַת אֲדֹנָי הִיא חָכְמָה     the fear of the Lord is wisdom

(9) Josh 2:11

יהוה אֱלֹהֵיכֶם הוּא אֱלֹהִים     the Lᴏʀᴅ your God is a god in
בַּשָּׁמַיִם מִמַּעַל וְעַל־הָאָרֶץ     heaven above and on the earth
מִתָּחַת     below

(9a) 2 Chr 20:6

הֲלֹא אַתָּה־הוּא אֱלֹהִים בַּשָּׁמַיִם     art thou not God in heaven?

is parallel to

(9b) Deut 4:39

. . . הָאֱלֹהִים

(10) Lev 14:13

כִּי כַּחַטָּאת הָאָשָׁם הוּא לַכֹּהֵן     for the guilt-offering, like the sin-
                    offering, belongs to the priest

**2.1.4.** Pattern Ad: detNP–Pro–detNP (54×)

(11) Deut 4:39

יהוה הוּא הָאֱלֹהִים בַּשָּׁמַיִם     The LORD is the God in heaven
מִמַּעַל וְעַל־הָאָרֶץ מִתָּחַת     above and on the earth below.
אֵין עוֹד     There is none other.

(12) Deut 4:35

יהוה הוּא הָאֱלֹהִים אֵין עוֹד     the LORD is the God; there is (none)
מִלְבַדּוֹ     except him

Very often in similar credo-like confessions of monothesism; for example, Deut 7:9, 10:17,

Deut 10:20–21

אֶת־יהוה אֱלֹהֶיךָ תִּירָא אֹתוֹ     the LORD your God thou shalt fear,
תַעֲבֹד וּבוֹ תִדְבָּק וּבִשְׁמוֹ     Him thou shalt serve, and by His
תִּשָּׁבֵעַ     name thou shalt swear

1 Kgs 8:60, 18:39 (2×); Ps 44:5, 100:3; Neh 8:10; 9:6, 7; 1 Chr 17:26; 2 Chr 33:13.

(12a) Deut 3:22, Josh 23:3

כִּי יהוה אֱלֹהֵיכֶם הוּא     for the LORD your God is the one
הַנִּלְחָם לָכֶם     who fights for you

(13) Deut 9:3

כִּי יהוה אֱלֹהֶיךָ הוּא־הָעֹבֵר     for the LORD your God is the one
לְפָנֶיךָ אֵשׁ אֹכְלָה הוּא     who goes before you, a consuming
יַשְׁמִידֵם וְהוּא יַכְנִיעֵם לְפָנֶיךָ     fire; He will annihilate them and He
    will subdue them

See Deut 31:6, 8; Josh 24:17.

(14) Gen 2:14

הַנָּהָר הָרְבִיעִי הוּא פְרָת     the fourth river is Euphrates

with which compare,

(15) Josh 11:10

כִּי־חָצוֹר לְפָנִים הִיא רֹאשׁ     for Hazor was previously the chief
כָּל־הַמַּמְלָכוֹת הָאֵלֶּה     of all these kingdoms

and

(16) Gen 9:18

וְחָם הוּא אֲבִי כְנָעַן     and Ham was the father of Canaan

and

(16a) 1 Sam 17:14

דָּוִד הוּא הַקָּטָן   David is the youngest.

(17) Deut 10:9, 18:2 (similarly Josh 13:33)

יהוה הוּא נַחֲלָתוֹ   the LORD is his inheritance

(18) 2 Kgs 19:15 (= Isa 37:16)

אַתָּה־הוּא הָאֱלֹהִים לְבַדְּךָ   you only are the God

With personal pronoun as NP₁ also in 2 Sam 7:28; Isa 51:9 (similarly 51:10), 52:6; Jer 14:22; Ezek 38:17; Ps 44:5; Neh 9:6, 7; 1 Chr 17:26, 21:17.

(19) Isa 51:12

אָנֹכִי אָנֹכִי הוּא מְנַחֶמְכֶם   I, I comfort you[7]

See also Isa 43:25,

אָנֹכִי אָנֹכִי הוּא מֹחֶה פְשָׁעֶיךָ   I, I wipe out your transgressions.[8]

(20) Gen 36:8

עֵשָׂו הוּא אֱדוֹם   Esau is Edom

A parenthetical gloss, with which compare

(21) 1 Chr 8:13

בְּרִעָה וָשֶׁמַע הֵמָּה רָאשֵׁי   Beriah and Shema (they were heads
הָאָבוֹת . . .   of ancestral houses) . . .

in a long genealogical list. Compare with (27) below.

(22) Dan 8:21

הַקֶּרֶן הַגְּדוֹלָה אֲשֶׁר בֵּין־עֵינָיו   the large horn between his eyes is
הוּא הַמֶּלֶךְ הָרִאשׁוֹן   the first king

See Lev 25:33.

(23) Ezek 11:7

חַלְלֵיכֶם הֵמָּה הַבָּשָׂר וְהִיא   your slain . . . are the meat and it is
הַסִּיר   the pot

The pronoun brings out the difference in viewpoint held by the corrupt authorities of the city and God on the situation there and its future. The prophet is responding to the leaders' assessment: הִיא הַסִּיר

---

7. The absolute state form מֹחֶה, and not מֹחָה, in Isa 43:25 with a similar syntactic structure suggests that the participle is here better interpreted as verbal rather than substantivized, 'your comforter'. On the emphatic repetition of the pronoun, see below, example (60).

8. The emphatic pronoun matches the equally emphatically fronted אֹתִי in v. 22, וְלֹא אֹתִי קָרָאתָ יַעֲקֹב 'and me you have not called, O Jacob'.

וַאֲנַחְנוּ הַבָּשָׂר 'it is the pot and we are meat' (v. 3). The first half of their statement may be right but not the second: it is none other than the victims slain by themselves that fit the metaphoric description. The author places the corrected alternative up front.

**2.1.5.** Pattern Ae: demPro–Pro–NP (11×)

(24) 1 Sam 4:8

אֵלֶּה הֵם הָאֱלֹהִים הַמַּכִּים . . .      these are the gods who struck . . .

(25) Gen 25:16 (= 1 Chr 1:31)

אֵלֶּה הֵם בְּנֵי יִשְׁמָעֵאל      these are the Ishmaelites

Following אֵלֶּה תֹּלְדֹת יִשְׁמָעֵאל 'these are the generations of Ishmaelites' and אֵלֶּה שְׁמוֹת בְּנֵי יִשְׁמָעֵאל 'these are the names of the Ishmaelites'.

(26) Num 3:20

אֵלֶּה הֵם מִשְׁפְּחֹת הַלֵּוִי      these are the families of the Levites
לְבֵית אֲבֹתָם      according to their ancestral house

Summing up a series of sentences with אֵלֶּה . . . . but without a Pro. See also Num 3:21, 27, 33.

(27) 1 Chr 8:6

אֵלֶּה הֵם רָאשֵׁי אָבוֹת לְיוֹשְׁבֵי      these are the heads of the house-
גֶבַע      holds of the inhabitants of Geba

A parenthetical gloss; cf. (20) and (21). Mostly NP$_2$ = detNP, but Qoh 1:17,

גַּם־זֶה הוּא רַעְיוֹן רוּחַ      this is also a feeding on wind,

clearly an S–P clause; compare (52) and Qoh 2:15, 19,

גַּם־זֶה הָבֶל      this is also vanity

and Qoh 2:26,

גַּם־זֶה הֶבֶל וּרְעוּת רוּחַ      this also is vanity, a feeding on
wind

See also Lev 23:2 and 1 Chr 22:1.

**2.1.6.** Pattern Af: Interr–Pro–detNP (5×)

(28) Gen 27:33

מִי־אֵפוֹא הוּא הַצָּד־צַיִד      who is then the one who hunted
game?

(29) Gen 21:29

מָה הֵנָּה שֶׁבַע כְּבָשֹׂת הָאֵלֶּה      what are these seven sheep?

(30) Ps 24:10

מִי הוּא זֶה מֶלֶךְ הַכָּבוֹד     who is the king of glory?

Compare with (59).

(31) Zech 1:9

וָאֹמַר מָה־אֵלֶּה אֲדֹנִי וַיֹּאמֶר     and I said, "What are these, my
אֵלַי . . . אֲנִי אַרְאֶךָ מָה־הֵמָּה     lord?" and he said to me . . . , "I
אֵלֶּה     shall show you what these are."

Compare with (57).

(32) Zech 4:4–5

(וָאֹמַר . . . לֵאמֹר מָה־אֵלֶּה     (and I said . . . saying, "What are
אֲדֹנִי . . . וַיֹּאמֶר אֵלַי הֲלוֹא     these, my lord? . . ." and he said to
יָדַעְתָּ) מָה־הֵמָּה אֵלֶּה     me, "Didn't you know) what these
are?"

## 2.2. Pattern B: NP₁–NP₂–Pro

**2.2.1.** Pattern Ba: indetNP–indetNP–Pro (28×)

(33) Prov 18:9

גַּם מִתְרַפֶּה בִמְלַאכְתּוֹ אָח     also one who is slack in work is
הוּא לְבַעַל מַשְׁחִית     kindred to a vandal

Compare with (3).

(34) Lev 20:21

אִישׁ אֲשֶׁר יִקַּח אֶת־אֵשֶׁת     a man who takes the wife of his
אָחִיו נִדָּה הִוא     brother is impurity[9]

(35) Qoh 3:15

מַה־שֶּׁהָיָה כְּבָר הוּא     what once occurred has been
around for quite a while

Compare with Qoh 1:9.

מַה־שֶּׁהָיָה הוּא שֶׁיִּהְיֶה     what once was is that which is
וּמַה־שֶּׁנַּעֲשָׂה הוּא שֶׁיֵּעָשֶׂה     going to be and what was once done
is that which is going to be done

(36) Jer 10:8

מוּסַר הֲבָלִים עֵץ הוּא     the instruction of idols is but wood
(NRSV)

---

9. More plausibly ⟨a *casus pendens* + P + S⟩, where הוּא would be impersonal. Likewise
Prov 18:13, מֵשִׁיב דָּבָר בְּטֶרֶם יִשְׁמָע אִוֶּלֶת הִיא־לוֹ 'one who answers before he has heard
[someone] out, it is counted as folly for him'.

(37) Lev 27:28

כָּל־חֵרֶם קֹדֶשׁ־קָדָשִׁים הוּא     every devoted thing is exceedingly
לַיהוה     holy to the LORD

Opening with כל and followed by a rather long P, especially in
Leviticus:

(38) Lev 11:27

כל . . . [8 words] . . . טְמֵאִים     all . . . are impure to you
הֵם לָכֶם

Similarly at Lev 11:10, 12, 20, 23, 41; Num 19:15; Deut 14:19.

(39) Josh 6:19

כֹּל כֶּסֶף . . . קֹדֶשׁ הוּא לַיהוה     all silver . . . is sacred to the LORD

(40) Gen 30:33

. . . כֹּל אֲשֶׁר־אֵינֶנּוּ נָקֹד     all that which is not speckled . . .
גָּנוּב הוּא אִתִּי     shall be regarded as stolen property
in my possession

(41) Ezek 3:7

כָּל־בֵּית יִשְׂרָאֵל חִזְקֵי־מֵצַח     the whole house of Israel are of a
וּקְשֵׁי־לֵב הֵמָּה     hard forehead and a stubborn heart

Likewise Prov 28:24 and Hag 2:14.

**2.2.2.** Pattern Bb: detNP–indetNP–Pro (52×)

(42) 1 Chr 29:16

. . . כֹּל הֶהָמוֹן הַזֶּה אֲשֶׁר     all this multitude . . . is from your
מִיָּדְךָ הוּא וּלְךָ הַכֹּל     hand and to you belongs all

(43) 2 Sam 21:2

הַגִּבְעֹנִים לֹא מִבְּנֵי יִשְׂרָאֵל     the Gibeonites are not part of the
הֵמָּה     Israelites

(43a) Gen 34:23

מִקְנֵהֶם וְקִנְיָנָם וְכָל־בְּהֶמְתָּם     their livestock and possessions and
הֲלוֹא לָנוּ הֵם     all their cattle are surely ours?

See also Gen 31:16, 43, 45:20, 47:6, 48:5; Exod 39:5; Lev 17:11,
27:30; Deut 1:17; 1 Kgs 20:3 (2×); Isa 49:21; Ezek 18:2; Ps 39:8; Job
41:3.

(44) Gen 41:25

חֲלוֹם פַּרְעֹה אֶחָד הוּא     Pharaoh's dream is one

(45) Deut 4:24

כִּי יהוה אֱלֹהֶיךָ אֵשׁ אֹכְלָה הוּא     for the LORD your God is a consuming fire

(46) Gen 34:21

הָאֲנָשִׁים הָאֵלֶּה שְׁלֵמִים הֵם אִתָּנוּ     these men are at peace with us

Dream interpretation: $NP_1$ = symbol. Compare with (7) and (22).

(47) Gen 40:18

שְׁלֹשֶׁת הַסַּלִּים שְׁלֹשֶׁת יָמִים הֵם     the three baskets are three days

Also Gen 40:12; 41:26 (2×), 27.

(47a) Jer 10:3

כִּי־חֻקּוֹת הָעַמִּים הֶבֶל הוּא     for the laws of the nations are a sham

(48) 2 Kgs 7:9

הַיּוֹם הַזֶּה יוֹם־בְּשֹׂרָה הוּא     this day is a day of good tidings

(49) 1 Kgs 20:31

מַלְכֵי בֵּית יִשְׂרָאֵל כִּי־מַלְכֵי חֶסֶד הֵם     the kings of the house of Israel are indeed gracious kings

(50) Exod 34:14

יהוה . . . אֵל קַנָּא הוּא     the LORD . . . is a jealous god

following

לֹא תִשְׁתַּחֲוֶה לְאֵל אַחֵר     you shall not worship another god

but—

(51) Neh 8:9

הַיּוֹם קָדֹשׁ־הוּא לַיהוה אֱלֹהֵיכֶם     the day is sacred to the LORD your God

is parallel to

Neh 8:11

הַיּוֹם קָדֹשׁ     the day is sacred

See also Exod 3:5, 16:36, 32:16 (2×), 39:5; Lev 13:15, 15:2, 17:11; Num 11:7, 13:32, 32:4; Deut 11:10; Josh 5:15; Jer 10:3; Ezek 48:15; Zeph 2:12; Mal 1:7, 12; Ps 50:6; Dan 8:26.

(52) Qoh 2:23

גַּם־זֶה הֶבֶל הוּא　　this is also vanity

is parallel to

Qoh 2:15, 19, 21, 26

גַּם־זֶה הֶבֶל

The same pattern as in Qoh 2:23 is to be found in Qoh 4:8, 5:18, and 6:2.

**2.2.3.** Pattern Bc: detNP–detNP–Pro (5×)

(53) Lev 17:14a

כִּי־נֶפֶשׁ כָּל־בָּשָׂר דָּמוֹ בְנַפְשׁוֹ　　for the life of every creature—its
הוּא　　blood is its life

with a *casus pendens*.[10]

(53a) Lev 17:14b

נֶפֶשׁ כָּל־בָּשָׂר דָּמוֹ הוּא　　the life of every flesh is its blood

(54) Num 21:26

כִּי חֶשְׁבּוֹן עִיר סִיחוֹן מֶלֶךְ　　for Heshbon is the city of Sihon, the
הָאֱמֹרִי הוּא　　Amorite king

(55) Jer 31:9

כִּי . . . אֶפְרַיִם בְּכֹרִי הוּא　　for . . . Ephraim is my firstborn

(56) Ezek 37:11

הָעֲצָמוֹת הָאֵלֶּה כָּל־בֵּית　　these bones are the entire house of
יִשְׂרָאֵל הֵמָּה　　Israel

(57) Zech 4:10

שִׁבְעָה־אֵלֶּה עֵינֵי יהוה הֵמָּה　　these seven are the eyes of the
מְשׁוֹטְטִים בְּכָל־הָאָרֶץ　　Lord going round in the entire land

**2.3.** Miscellaneous

(58) Isa 50:9

מִי־הוּא יַרְשִׁיעֵנִי　　who could condemn me?

See also Job 4:7, 13:19, 17:3, 41:2.

---

10. In the light of Lev 17:14b, נֶפֶשׁ כָּל־בָּשָׂר דָּמוֹ הוּא 'the life of every flesh is its blood', and Deut 12:23, הַדָּם הוּא הַנָּפֶשׁ 'blood is the life', one would follow Jenni (1992: 84–85), who interprets the preposition here and in similar places such as Lev 17:11, נֶפֶשׁ הַבָּשָׂר בַּדָּם הוּא . . ., and Gen 9:4, אַךְ־בָּשָׂר בְּנַפְשׁוֹ דָמוֹ לֹא תֹאכֵלוּ, הַדָּם הוּא בַּנֶּפֶשׁ יְכַפֵּר, as *beth essentiae*.

(59) Jer 30:21

מִי הוּא־זֶה עָרַב אֶת־לִבּוֹ . . .     who is it that would risk his life . . . ?

Compare with (30). See further below.

(60) Deut 32:39

אֲנִי אֲנִי הוּא

Followed by וְאֵין אֱלֹהִים עִמָּדִי.[11] This, however, is most likely not a
real tripartite NC, the second pronoun being a mere emphatic repetition of the first. Then the concluding הוּא must bear its full force, definitely no mere copula: 'I am He'. The initial position of the אֲנִי also
confers prominence on 'I', which is further reinforced by the following וְאֵין אֱלֹהִים עִמָּדִי as well as by the very same personal pronoun
present in the immediately following affirmation: אֲנִי אָמִית וַאֲחַיֶּה
מָחַצְתִּי וַאֲנִי אֶרְפָּא וְאֵין מִיָּדִי מַצִּיל 'I shall kill and give life. I smote and
I shall heal and there is none to rescue from my hand'. A similar sen-
timent on the omnipotence and the sovereignty of the God of Israel is
echoed in a number of Deutero-Isaianic passages with basically the
same syntactic structure: for example, Isa 43:10–13, 'so that you may
. . . understand that *I* am he (אֲנִי הוּא). Before me no god was made,
nor shall there be any after me. *I, I* am the LORD (אָנֹכִי אָנֹכִי יהוה), and
beside me there is no savior. *I* declared (אָנֹכִי הִגַּדְתִּי) and saved . . . *I*
am God (אֲנִי־אֵל), and also henceforth *I* am He (אֲנִי הוּא); there is none
who can deliver from my hand; I work and who can hinder it?' Other
examples of this theologically charged אֲנִי הוּא may be found in Isa
41:4, 46:4 (with the pronoun repeated four times in the same verse
with four different finite verbs), 48:12, and once with אַתָּה in Ps
102:28 אַתָּה־הוּא.[12] Another plausible interpretation of these passages
would be to view them as elliptical tripartite NCs, whereby the NP$_2$ is
to be supplied from the context.[13]

(61) Job 3:19

קָטֹן וְגָדוֹל שָׁם הוּא     The small and the great are there.

A difficult case, though the general sense is not in doubt. Some take
the pronoun in the sense of 'the same', which, however, Driver
(Driver and Gray 1921: II, 21) rightly finds questionable, pointing out

---

11. 'I, even I, am he' (NRSV); 'I myself am he' (NIV); 'moi, moi je Le suis' (Bible de
Jérusalem); 'dat Ik, Ik het ben' (Nederlands Bijbelgenootschap).

12. See Driver 1902: 378.

13. A similar problem in Classical Syriac has been discussed in my "On the Nominal
Clause in the Old Syriac Gospels" (1975: 37).

that such an idea would be expressed by כְּגָדוֹל כְּקָטֹן or כֵּן קָטֹן. See also
Driver 1892: 271 n. 2.

(62) Num 16:11

וְאַהֲרֹן מַה־הוּא כִּי תַלִּונוּ          what is Aaron that you should
עָלָיו                                      complain against him?

This is basically an example of pattern Bb. So also

Ps 39:5

קִצִּי וּמִדַּת יָמַי מַה־הִיא          what is the extent and span of my
                                           life?[14]


## 3. Discussion

### 3.1. Is the Pronoun a Copula?

The nature of the personal pronoun as a third constituent of the nominal
clause has been one of the central issues. There are two diametrically opposed
views: one school regards it as a copula, which is here defined as an overt and
formal means of indicating the logical relationship of equation between the
subject and the predicate, and the other assigns to it some other function, such
as emphasis or prominence.

One of the principal advocates of the copula school is Brockelmann, who
writes: "Doch verschiebt das Sprachgefühl das pron. schon in die Stellung
eines Bindegliedes."[15] Sappan concurs.[16] For Andersen such a pronoun is pleonastic and therefore void of any function.[17] The proof for Brockelmann's position may be found in cases where such a pronoun can follow a predicate, as
in (4) Lam 1:18, צַדִּיק הוּא יהוה 'the LORD is righteous'; (5) Cant 6:9, אַחַת הִיא
יוֹנָתִי 'one is my dove'; Lev 23:2, אֵלֶּה הֵם מוֹעֲדָי 'these are my appointed times';
(30) Ps 24:10, מִי הוּא זֶה מֶלֶךְ הַכָּבוֹד 'who is the king of glory?'[18] That the use
of the pronoun appears to be optional can be seen in pairs such as 1 Kgs 18:21,
אִם־יהוה הָאֱלֹהִים 'if the LORD is the God' // 1 Kgs 18:39, יהוה הוּא הָאֱלֹהִים 'the
LORD is the God'; and Qoh 2:26, גַּם־זֶה הֶבֶל וּרְעוּת רוּחַ 'this also is vanity and
a feeding on wind' // Qoh 1:17, גַּם־זֶה הוּא רַעְיוֹן רוּחַ 'this is also a feeding on
wind'. It is quite likely that a suprasegmental or prosodic feature such as intonation played some role, which is particularly true of the first pair. One could
say that what had been indicated by a prosodic feature in 1 Kgs 18:21 was lex-

---

14. Zewi (1996: 5) also mentions Gen 23:15 and Zech 1:5.
15. Brockelmann 1956: §30a.
16. Sappan 1981: 92.
17. Andersen 1970: 42. In *Emphasis in Biblical Hebrew* (1969) and *Emphatic Words
and Structures* (1985: 82–83), I still retained the term "copula," but its use was rather se-
verely qualified. In Joüon and Muraoka (1991), we took leave of the term for good.
18. Brockelmann 1913: 104.

icalized and given overt linguistic expression in 1 Kgs 18:39. Another objection to Brockelmann's analysis is that he fails to distinguish between an indeterminate predicate, as in the first two examples cited by him, and a determinate one, as in the remaining cases.

An argument against the view taken by Brockelmann and others is provided by a case such as (13) Deut 9:3, יְהוָה אֱלֹהֶיךָ הוּא־הָעֹבֵר לְפָנֶיךָ אֵשׁ אֹכְלָה הוּא יַשְׁמִידֵם וְהוּא יַכְנִיעֵם לְפָנֶיךָ 'the LORD your God is the one who passes before you, a burning fire; he will destroy them and he will bring them to their knees before you', where a tripartite nominal clause is followed by a verbal clause of kindred theological import by which the reader is reminded by means of the same pronoun that no other than his God will take care of his potential enemies.[19] Even Brockelmann recognizes an emphatic function of such a pronoun in the verbal clause.[20] It seems to me, then, that this kind of third-person pronoun carries a similar semantic load irrespective of clause-type, whether nominal or verbal. See also Deut 31:8, יְהוָה הוּא הַהֹלֵךְ לְפָנֶיךָ הוּא יִהְיֶה עִמָּךְ 'the LORD is the one who goes before you. He will be with you'. Likewise 2 Chr 20:6, quoted on p. 201. In Gen 42:6, וְיוֹסֵף הוּא הַשַּׁלִּיט עַל־הָאָרֶץ 'and Joseph was the ruler of the land', the pronoun introduces an element of surprise: 'no other than Joseph was the ruler', *ausgerechnet* in German and דַּוְקָא in Modern Hebrew.[21]

I doubt that one can prove the existence of the copula in any Semitic language. The notion undoubtedly originated with Indo-European languages in which a nominal clause without a copula in the present tense is virtually nonexistent.[22] Classical Syriac (in which the tripartite NC is the rule, especially when both S and P are nonpronominal NCs, and the bipartite NC is a rarity) can hardly be said to possess such a copula, as Goldenberg and I argued.[23] Even a heavily Europeanized language such as Modern Hebrew does not appear to us to use הוא as a genuine copula fully comparable to its Indo-European namesake.[24]

A view somewhat related to the copula theory sees in the intervening pronoun in question a means of avoiding logical and syntactic confusion, for

---

19. More examples of this nature may be found in Driver (1892: 270 n. 2) and Zewi (1994: 152).

20. Brockelmann 1956: 31.

21. Geller (1991: 27), who is also interested in the literary reading of the biblical text, regards this as one of the most artful hinges in the Hebrew Bible.

22. See, however, Jespersen 1924: 120–22. Some Indo-Europeanists went so far as to assert that even clauses containing *verba finita* as the kernel of the predicate can be analyzed as tripartite nominal clauses: *sol oritur* = *sol oriens est*, a view also taken by some Semitists. See a discussion in Wackernagel 1926: 28. That in its earlier phases Indo-European also admitted copula-less, bipartite nominal clauses is well known: see, for instance, Benveniste 1951: 151–67.

23. Goldenberg 1983: 97–140, esp. §8; Muraoka 1987: 61 n. 122.

24. This is contrary to Glinert (1989: 169), for instance.

without such a pronoun the two juxtaposed determinate NPs could be wrongly analyzed as cases of apposition or attribution—in other words, as an expanded *single* NP.[25] This is also Driver's view: "the pronoun at once makes it plain which of the two terms is the subject, and at the same time gives effect to the emphasis, which . . . in these cases belongs to it."[26] Such a view is indicated by the term used by native Arab grammarians: *ḍamīru l-faṣli* 'the pronoun of separation'. But Reckendorf makes it quite plain that the use of such a pronoun is far from being the rule.[27] In any case, the fundamental difference between Arabic and Hebrew must be duly recognized: namely, that pattern B is unknown to Arabic.[28] A systemic, structural, not atomistic, comparison is required. Moreover, one needs to ask whether the assumed separating function is the intention of the speaker/writer or is perceived by the hearer/reader as having such an effect.

In most of the A syntagmas, where the pronoun stands between the two NP's, the former appears to be more than a mere linguistic marker of the logical relation of predication between the two core constituents. Driver holds that such a pronoun adds emphasis to the preceding constituent.[29] Quoting a Greek example, τὸ πνεῦμά ἐστι τὸ ζῳοποιοῦν, he says that the implication is that nothing besides τὸ πνεῦμα can claim the epithet τὸ ζῳοποιοῦν. On this point I am in full agreement with Driver. In my earlier studies I have introduced the notion of "selective-exclusive," which highlights and underlines one of the semantic functions assignable to various NC patterns—namely, "identificatory."[30] The appropriateness of this analysis, which is eminently applicable to

---

25. Huehnergard (1986: 247), though admitting the possibility of the pronoun emphasizing the predicate, takes the view that its function in Akkadian lies in "delineating the end boundary of the clause and thereby ensuring that the two nouns or noun phrases are understood to constitute a complete predication rather than simple apposition."

26. Driver 1892: 269. So also Groß 1987: 125: "dient auch der Deutlichkeit des Ausdrucks und zeigt die Grenze zwischen determiniertem Subjekt bzw. dessen Apposition und determiniertem Prädikat an."

27. Reckendorf 1895–98: 389–90; 1921: 1–2, §141. Where the predicate is indeterminate, the pronoun is called *ḍamīru t-taʾkīdi* 'the pronoun of intensification' (Brockelmann 1913: 2.103).

28. Accordingly Saadia (see Derenbourg 1893) translates Gen 34:23 (43a above), . . . הלוא לנו הם as . . . *'innamā hiya lanā*, and occasionally as a bipartite NC, as in Gen 41:25 (44), חלום פרעה אחד as *raʾyu farʿauna wāḥidun*.

29. Driver 1892: 269.

30. See my *Emphasis in Biblical Hebrew* (1969: 53) and *Emphatic Words and Structures* (1985: 72). At the first introduction of this scheme of analysis, we made it quite plain that what we mean by "identification" or "identificatory" is significantly different from the usual use of the term, for the term is usually used where the two core constituents are co-extensive, both being determined. But, according to our analysis, only זאֹת אִשְׁתּוֹ 'this is his wife' is identificatory, and not אִשְׁתּוֹ זאֹת 'this is his wife', the latter of which is, according to our analysis, "descriptive," also called "classificatory" by some (see Muraoka 1969: 5 and n. 16; 1985: 7–8; Joüon and Muraoka 1991: §154 *ea* and n. 3).

many examples of pattern Ad, is obvious in some of the credo-like Deuterono-
mistic utterances, such as (11) Deut 4:39, יהוה הוּא הָאֱלֹהִים בַּשָּׁמַיִם מִמַּעַל וְעַל־
הָאָרֶץ מִתָּחַת אֵין עוֹד 'the LORD is the God in heaven above and on the earth below. There is none other'. Likewise (12) Deut 4:35 and (18) 2 Kgs 19:15.
Comparing Deut 4:39 with (9) Josh 2:11, יהוה אֱלֹהֵיכֶם הוּא אֱלֹהִים בַּשָּׁמַיִם מִמַּעַל
וְעַל־הָאָרֶץ מִתָּחַת 'the LORD your god is a god in heaven above and on the earth
below', one could suggest that Rahab's acceptance of the invaders' monothe-
ism left something to be desired.[31] Even theological statements where an explicitly identificatory word such as לְבַד 'only' is absent can be interpreted in
similar fashion: for example, 2 Chr 20:6, הֲלֹא אַתָּה־הוּא אֱלֹהִים בַּשָּׁמַיִם 'surely
you are God in heaven?' This is a statement found in a context full of similar
utterances stressing the uniqueness of the God of Israel: 'Do you not rule over
(אַתָּה מוֹשֵׁל, with the subject preceding[32]) all the kingdoms of the nations? In
your hand are power and might (וּבְיָדְךָ כֹּחַ וּגְבוּרָה, with the prepositional phrase
preceding[33]). . . . Did you not drive out (הֲלֹא אַתָּה אֱלֹהֵינוּ הוֹרַשְׁתָּ with the explicit pronoun subject[34]) the inhabitants of the land?' Likewise Deut 3:22;
Josh 23:3, 10 (12a); Deut 9:3 (13), 10:9, 18:2 (17); Isa 51:12 (19).[35] All instances of pattern Af with an interrogative pronoun as NP$_1$ may be, by definition, brought under this rubric.

### 3.2. Topicalization

The force of "identificatory" or "selective-exclusive" discussed in the foregoing paragraph is identifiable when both NPs are semantically determinate.
The label "cleft sentence" can also be applied here. But even in cases that do
not include cleft sentences, a greater or lesser degree of prominence of some
sort appears to be conferred by a third-person personal pronoun on the preceding constituent.[36] Let us first look at examples of pattern Ad, the identificatory
pattern par excellence.

---

31. See also Keil and Delitzsch 1988: 37.

32. Joüon and Muraoka 1991: §145 *fd.*

33. See Muraoka 1991: 147–48.

34. Muraoka 1985: 47–59.

35. A similar situation prevails in bipartite NCs as well: e.g., Isa 45:18, אֲנִי יהוה וְאֵין עוֹד
'I am the LORD; there is none other'; v. 21, הֲלוֹא אֲנִי יהוה וְאֵין־עוֹד . . . מִי הִשְׁמִיעַ זֹאת מִקֶּדֶם
אֱלֹהִים מִבַּלְעָדַי אֵל־צַדִּיק וּמוֹשִׁיעַ אַיִן זוּלָתִי 'who told this long ago? . . . Surely I the LORD? For
there is no other god than I. A righteous and saving god—there is none except me'; v. 22, אֲנִי
אֵל וְאֵין עוֹד 'I am God and there is not another'. These NCs are to be compared with other
clauses in the immediate context with a fronted prepositional phrase: v. 22, בִּי נִשְׁבַּעְתִּי 'on
myself do I swear'; v. 23, לִי תִּכְרַע כָּל־בֶּרֶךְ 'to me shall kneel every knee'; vv. 24–25, אַךְ
בַּיהוה לִי אָמַר צְדָקוֹת וָעֹז עָדָיו יָבוֹא . . . בַּיהוה יִצְדְּקוּ '. . . but in the LORD, he said to me, righteousness and might. To Him shall he come . . . in the LORD they will be found justified'.

36. That Geller (1991: 19–21) can assign emphasis with confidence only to slightly less
than half of his samples is due to the fact that he defines "emphasis" in terms of contrast,
whether explicit or implicit.

The pronoun is hardly "selective-exclusive" in (14). Rashi, however, was probably conscious of the syntactic feature in question when he commented that the Euphrates is mentioned as the most important of the four rivers on account of its connection with the Land of Israel. Note also that the way the Euphrates is presented differs from the way the other three rivers are presented with the formula "the name of the xth river is y," which is further supplemented by some salient geographical feature of the river. The fourth river, however, is presented as "the fourth river is the Euphrates," as if to say that there was no need to inform the reader about it. After having been told that the river flowing out of the garden of Eden had four tributaries, the reader had been anticipating that the Euphrates, a river known for its significance as marking the northern border of the Land of Israel, was going to be mentioned.[37]

The pronoun is not "identificatory" in (16), either. However, the passage is suggestive: Gen 9:18, "and Noah's sons who came out of the ark were Shem and Ham and Japheth, and Ham is the father of Canaan." Of Noah's three sons, Ham alone is singled out for an additional piece of information. The writer is preparing the reader for a subsequent story on the disgraceful act with which Ham would incur his father's displeasure and bring down a curse upon Canaan. See also Rashi (ad loc.).

In (16a) David is introduced as the unlikely opponent of the Philistine giant, after the author has mentioned that David had seven older brothers, three of whom were experienced warriors still in Saul's army.

The strategic importance of Hazor is duly stressed in the historical gloss of (15).

In all of these cases we can speak of the topicalizing function of the pronoun.[38] This is certainly true of (22), which is a case of vision interpretation. We must note, however, that an interpretation of a dream or vision can be presented in three distinct structures:

Meaning–Pronoun–Symbol, as in (7)
Symbol–Pronoun–Meaning, as in (22)
Symbol–Meaning–Pronoun, as in (47)

The topicalizing function of the pronoun is also recognizable in other A syntagmas where one or both of the remaining NC constituents is indeterminate and $NP_1$ is S: for example, Aa (2) and (3). Example (3) shows yet again

---

37. See also Geller's exposition on this verse (1991: 32).
38. See Cohen (1984: 194), who thinks that the pronoun as the third constituent in Classical Ethiopic is a mere separator between the two core constituents: "le rôle de la copule dans la résolution des ambiguïtés inhérentes à la structure de la proposition nominale." However, he is forced to admit a topicalizing function of the pronoun when it follows the subject (p. 197).

that this particular function of the pronoun is not confined to the nominal clause.

The examples in Ac and Ae are also topicalizing.

The optional nature of such a topicalizing pronoun is evident in a long list of Tyre's trading partners in Ezekiel 27 with the pattern ⟨trading partner– "your partner"⟩. The tripartite NC is found in vv. 13 (יָוָן תֻּבַל וָמֶשֶׁךְ הֵמָּה רֹכְלָיִךְ 'Greece, Tubal, and Meshech were your trading partners'), 17, 21, 22, and the bipartite pattern in vv. 15 (בְּנֵי דְדָן רֹכְלָיִךְ 'the Dedanites were your trading partners'), 16, 18, 20, 23. Compare also Zech 4:4–5 מָה־אֵלֶּה . . . הֲלוֹא יָדַעְתָּ מָה־ and הֵמָּה אֵלֶּה and Zech 4:13 הֲלוֹא יָדַעְתָּ מָה־אֵלֶּה.

### 3.3. Prominence

When $NP_1$ is an adjective or an indeterminate numeral, the pronoun obviously can be neither identificatory nor topicalizing. At the risk of being subjective, we may say that such a pronoun gives prominence to the preceding constituent.[39] Example (1) can be interpreted this way, as well as other "numerical" proverbs mentioned above: Cant 6:8 and (5).

This interpretation seems to apply to most examples of the B syntagmas, except passages in pattern Bb where the $NP_2$ is a prepositional phrase. In such cases, the pronoun appears to be almost identificatory, for example, (42) and (43a) and all of the passages listed above after (43a).

There is another syntactical detail peculiar to the B type: an $NP_2$ that is further modified by a prepositional phrase is split by the prepositional phrase after the pronoun, as in (33), (38), and the other passages listed there, (39), (40), Prov 28:24, Hag 2:14, (46), and (51).

### 3.4. *"Casus pendens"*

Some authors view the tripartite NC as examples of *casus pendens*: the $NP_1$ is in *casus pendens*—better perhaps, *nominativus pendens*. Driver (1892: 267–74), for instance, discusses the whole issue in an appendix entitled "The casus pendens," as does Groß (1987).[40] Let us set aside for now the question of whether one can meaningfully talk about cases in Biblical Hebrew and the fact that I would prefer seeing a *casus pendens* only in cases such as Ps 11:4, יהוה בַּשָּׁמַיִם כִּסְאוֹ 'the LORD—his throne is in heaven', where the "hanging" NP is later resumed by a pronoun in a different "case."[41] The general idea of *casus pendens* is familiar. In our case, the $NP_1$ is perceived, according to this view, as hanging, with the implication that the rest of the clause, Pron–$NP_2$, constitutes by itself a complete clause. The notion of *extraposition* is akin to

---

39. According to Cohen (1984: 206–7) this—"mise en relief"—is the basic function of the "copulaic" pronoun in Classical Ethiopic.

40. On *casus pendens*, see also Backhaus 1995.

41. See my treatment in Muraoka 1985: 93–111.

*casus pendens*, though extraposition is broader in scope, since an element other than a noun phrase can be extraposed. Some authors speak of delayed—that is to say, not fronted—extraposition.[42]

The case for *casus pendens* is particularly convincing in a passage such as 2 Kgs 15:36, ... וְיֶתֶר דִּבְרֵי יוֹתָם אֲשֶׁר עָשָׂה הֲלוֹא־הֵם כְּתוּבִים עַל־סֵפֶר דִּבְרֵי הַיָּמִים 'the rest of the deeds done by Jotham—are they not recorded in the Book of the Annals?' where the position of the rhetorical הֲלוֹא is striking as well as that of הֵם. This standard annalistic formula is attested quite often: see 1 Kgs. 11:41, 14:29, 16:5, and so on.

A notion kindred to *casus pendens* is the *cleft sentence*, such as English *It is in these questions that I am interested.* Although the terms *cleft sentence* and *casus pendens* have much in common, they differ significantly on the surface level, and not every Hebrew clause with a *casus pendens* is translatable as a cleft sentence.[43]

### 3.5. Identification of S and P

Our classification has not taken subject–predicate opposition into account, though for a reason other than the one that prompted Hoftijzer not to allow this feature to play a role in his study of the Biblical Hebrew NC. The reason for his exclusion of the term was the occasional difficulty of determining which is which.[44] Subject–predicate opposition is an important feature, however, and cannot be left totally without consideration.

When one of the two principal constituents is indeterminate and the other determinate, the former is P and the latter is S: consequently, patterns Ab, Ac, and Bb.[45]

When the core constituents are both determinate or both indeterminate, ambiguity can arise. When both are determinate, they are P–S if the pronoun can be considered identifying. This is certainly true in pattern Af[46] and mostly so in pattern Ad. Otherwise, the sequence is most likely S–P, including pattern Bc. If both core constituents are indeterminate, they are S–P for pattern Ba. In pattern Aa the nature of the NP$_1$ is the decisive factor: P–S if it is an adjective or numeral; otherwise, S–P. According to these maxims then, in all of the B-syntagmas the sequence is S–P and thus S–P–Pro.

---

42. For example, Zewi 1994: 150.

43. Thus here I take exception to the view held by Geller (1991: 16–17).

44. Hoftijzer 1973: 446–510. Driver (1892: 269) is oversimplifying when he says, "the subject, though as a rule the one which from its position is the first to be apprehended *definitely* by the mind, will be most naturally so regarded."

45. Backhaus (1995: 3–4) also takes the initial, demonstrative pronoun as S, though I fail to see why the personal pronoun in the final slot should be regarded as stressed (*betont*).

46. See Reckendorf (1895–98: 387), who regards a personal pronoun after an interrogative as "verstärkend": *man huwa hāḏā*.

When Driver states that in a case such as (12) (יהוה הוּא הָאֱלֹהִים) the pronoun resumes the subject, his notion of subject (and predicate) is different from mine.[47] I define the subject as given (something known) and the predicate as being new. Note that these terms are not the same as "determinate/definite" and "indeterminate/indefinite," respectively.[48] The failure to keep the two sets of terms separate leads to the dilemma rightly pinpointed by Zewi.[49]

On the other hand, the analysis presented by Zewi of a clause such as Gen 42:6, וְיוֹסֵף הוּא הַשַּׁלִּיט עַל־הָאָרֶץ, is highly problematic.[50] She distinguishes two kinds of A pattern: her type C represents the sequence S–Pro–S, and her type D, exemplified by Gen 42:6, represents the sequence S–Pro (= P)–S. Furthermore, she holds that the complex [Pro–S] is a predicate clause within which the pronoun constitutes its predicate. The major difficulty with this complicated analysis is that the initial subject, יוֹסֵף, referring to a personal entity, cannot possibly have as its predicate what amounts to a self-contained utterance of predication expressed in the form of a complete clause, a clause indicating a logical relationship of predication between "the governor of the land" (subject) and "he" (predicate). A similar difficulty arises from her perception of the logical structure of type C: Predicate clause [= P–S]–Subject. Moreover, it is not clear to me on what grounds type C and type D are considered distinct from each other.[51] Another example of her type D, Deut 3:22, כִּי יהוה אֱלֹהֵיכֶם הוּא הַנִּלְחָם לָכֶם, translated by her 'for it is the LORD your God that will battle for you', is comparable to an example of type C with the sequence P–Pro–S: Ezek 38:17, הַאַתָּה־הוּא אֲשֶׁר־דִּבַּרְתִּי בְּיָמִים קַדְמוֹנִים, translated by her as 'Is it you that I have spoken of in ancient times?' If אַתָּה of the second example is P, why not יהוה אֱלֹהֵיכֶם of the first also? Moreover, Zewi maintains that the predicate clause of type D is constructed after the manner of type A: for example, Gen 3:19, כִּי־עָפָר אַתָּה 'for you are dust'. But, as she herself would readily admit, type A is one of classification or description, and its first constituent is essentially indeterminate, which is patently not the case with type D.

---

47. Driver 1892: 270.

48. Driver's position in this regard appears to fluctuate. In discussing a clause such as Ps 44:5, אַתָּה־הוּא מַלְכִּי, he states that the pronoun anticipates the predicate (1892: 271), whereas elsewhere and later ("הוּא 4," BDB 216a), he calls it a "subject," though his translation remains the same, 'thou art *he*—my king'. For an elucidation of this theoretical question, see most recently Baasten 1997: 1–3.

49. Zewi 1994: 153.

50. Zewi 1994: 162–63.

51. Zewi's analysis of a quadripartite Syriac nominal clause as exemplified by the Peshitta translation of our Genesis passage is equally questionable: *wyawsef huyu šalliṭ ʿal ʾarʿaa*. According to her, the predicate clause is of Type C and within this predicate clause there is another predicate clause, the first pronoun being P and the second being S. What is *šalliṭ ʿal ʾarʿaa* then?

### 3.6. Congruence

Praetorius, a Semitist who made a fundamental statement on the nominal clause in Classical Ethiopic, said that in a descriptive NC the copulaic pronoun agrees in person, gender, and number with the subject and follows the predicate, whereas in an identificatory NC[52] the pronoun agrees with the predicate and precedes it.[53]

The only meaningful way to investigate this question is by studying clauses in which the gender and number of S differs from the gender and number of P. If we further narrow down our investigation by focusing on S–P–Pro clauses, which are all descriptive, as I have pointed out, we then see that the pronoun by definition *follows* the predicate as in Ethiopic but that the picture in respect to congruence is mixed; that is, Pro may agree with either S or P:

*Agreement with S:* Exod 3:5, הַמָּקוֹם אֲשֶׁר אַתָּה עוֹמֵד עָלָיו אַדְמַת־קֹדֶשׁ הוּא 'the place on which you are standing is a holy land' (similarly, Josh 5:15); Exod 32:16 הַלֻּחֹת מַעֲשֵׂה אֱלֹהִים הֵמָּה 'the tablets are God's making'; Lev 11:10 (mentioned in [38]), כֹּל אֲשֶׁר אֵין־לוֹ סְנַפִּיר . . . שֶׁקֶץ הֵם לָכֶם 'but anything that does not have fins . . . is detestable to you',[54] (45) Deut 4:24 כִּי יהוה אֱלֹהֶיךָ אֵשׁ אֹכְלָה הוּא, (53a) Lev 17:14b נֶפֶשׁ כָּל־בָּשָׂר דָּמוֹ הוּא 'the life of every flesh is its blood,' and (57) Zech 4:10 שִׁבְעָה־אֵלֶּה עֵינֵי יהוה הֵמָּה מְשׁוֹטְטִים בְּכָל־הָאָרֶץ 'these seven are the eyes of the LORD, going round in the entire land'.[55] In this last example, Praetorius would see a case of Gleichsetzung, but the pronoun agrees with S and follows the predicate.

*Agreement with P:* (47a) Jer 10:3 כִּי־חֻקּוֹת הָעַמִּים הֶבֶל הוּא 'for the laws of the nations are a sham'; Neh 8:10 חֶדְוַת יהוה הִיא מָעֻזְּכֶם 'the joy of the LORD is your strength'. Cases such as these make it difficult to go along with Zewi, according to whom the pronoun is the subject of the predicate clause (P–Pro) and represents the extraposed subject.[56] In (34) Lev 20:21 אִישׁ אֲשֶׁר יִקַּח אֶת־אֵשֶׁת אָחִיו נִדָּה הִוא 'a man who takes the wife of his brother is impurity', however, we probably have a *casus pendens*: 'as regards a man . . . , that is a case of impurity', for in a down-to-earth legal statement one can hardly say, 'He is

---

52. *Identificatory* is used in the conventional way: "Gleichsetzung zweier bekannter Dinge."

53. Praetorius 1886: 159–60. Cohen (1984: 192–209) represents a substantial advance on his predecessors, Praetorius and Dillmann, as far as the structure of the nominal clause in Classical Ethiopic is concerned. He has found examples in which, contrary to Praetorius's second rule, the pronoun follows the complex S–P (Cohen 1984: 200).

54. The plural form of the pronoun is *ad sensum*. In vv. 12, 20, 23, 41, comparable in content and wording, we find שֶׁקֶץ הוּא. This noun, unlike שִׁקּוּץ, is never used in the plural. A similar variation is found also in Lev 11:27 טְמֵאִים הֵם, as against Num 19:15 טָמֵא הוּא. Note also Deut 14:19 טָמֵא הוּא לָכֶם לֹא יֵאָכֵלוּ.

55. The *atnaḥ* is best moved backward from אֵלֶּה to זְרֻבָּבֶל. The masculine participle מְשׁוֹטְטִים cannot be construed with עֵינֵי.

56. Zewi 1994: 159.

impurity'. Likewise, Prov 18:13, מֵשִׁיב דָּבָר בְּטֶרֶם יִשְׁמָע אִוֶּלֶת הִיא־לוֹ 'as for a man who answers before having heard [someone] out, such a behavior would be regarded folly on his part'.

When we extend our enquiry further to include the A type, it appears that the picture is just as mixed.

*S–Pro–P*

Pro agreeing with S: (15) Josh 11:10 חָצוֹר לְפָנִים הִיא רֹאשׁ כָּל־הַמַּמְלָכוֹת הָאֵלֶּה.

Pro agreeing with P: (22) Dan 8:21 הַקֶּרֶן הַגְּדוֹלָה אֲשֶׁר בֵּין־עֵינָיו הוּא הַמֶּלֶךְ הָרִאשׁוֹן and Lev 25:33 בָּתֵּי עָרֵי הַלְוִיִּם הוּא אֲחֻזָּתָם 'the houses in the cities of the Levites are their possession'. So also (26).

*P–Pro–S*

Pro agreeing with S: (29) Gen 21:29 מָה הֵנָּה שֶׁבַע כְּבָשֹׂת הָאֵלֶּה. So also (31) and (32).
Pro agreeing with P: (17) Deut 10:9, 18:2 (similarly Josh 13:33) יהוה הוּא נַחֲלָתוֹ; also (23).

Examples such as (22) Dan 8:21 הַקֶּרֶן הַגְּדוֹלָה אֲשֶׁר בֵּין־עֵינָיו הוּא הַמֶּלֶךְ הָרִאשׁוֹן; and Josh 13:14 כִּי־חִקְקוֹת הָעַמִּים הֶבֶל הוּא; and (47a) Jer 10:3 אִשֵּׁי יהוה אֱלֹהֵי יִשְׂרָאֵל הוּא נַחֲלָתוֹ 'the offerings by fire to the LORD God of Israel are their inheritance' are particularly instructive.[57] They seem to lend support to the position that I tentatively aired in 1985 that the essential function of the pronoun in the tripartite NC lies in according some sort of prominence to the immediately preceding constituent.[58] In 1987 I raised the same issue, this time less tentatively, in my attempt to come to grips with the tripartite NC in Classical Syriac, which is far more common than in Biblical Hebrew.[59] As I intimated a couple of times above, the use of such a pronoun is not confined to the nominal clause, and it is not obligatory. This interpretation can be also applied to (61)[60] and (60), as well as to examples of possible elliptical tripartite NCs. The

---

57. This striking mode of congruence is also illustrated in Saadia's rendition (Derenbourg 1893) of Deut 10:9 (17), יהוה הוא נחלתו = *ʾallāhu hiya naṣibuhum* (*naṣibun* is masculine), and Deut 18:2 *ʾallāhu hiya* נחלתו.

58. Muraoka 1985: 82.

59. Muraoka 1987: 60.

60. Similarly in Classical Syriac, an enclitic *(h)u* can highlight any part of speech. Compare Geller's (1991: 30) attractive interpretation of Isa 53:4 אָכֵן חֳלָיֵנוּ הוּא נָשָׂא 'yet it was our sickness that he bore', and 53:11 עֲוֹנֹתָם הוּא יִסְבֹּל 'it is their punishment that he suffered'. See also clauses in Classical Ethiopic adduced by Cohen (1984: 208–9), such as *kama-zawəʾatu ʾasmātihomu* 'the following are [lit.: is] their names', *wa-mangaštu-ssa la-salomon ʾəm-mədr wəʾatu* 'as for Solomon's kingdom [f. noun], it [m.] is from the earth', and *mənt wəʾatu ḥalamihu* 'what are his dreams?'

highly frequent choice of the third-person enclitic pronoun following the first- or second-person disjunctive personal pronoun in Classical Syriac becomes more easily understandable in this light.[61] Examples such as (18) 2 Kgs 19:15 (= Isa 37:16) אַתָּה־הוּא הָאֱלֹהִים לְבַדְּךָ can be viewed in this light.[62] I have also suggested that *'enaa ('ناa* and the like with the repetition of the identical pronoun is a secondary analogical development, in contrast to *'enaa(h)w* < *'enaa hu*. One could perhaps consider a similar development in Hebrew as well. Analyzing these pronouns as subjects, even if we symbolize them with lowercase *s*, seems to me a shade too formal and mechanical. In a case like Zeph 2:12, גַּם־אַתֶּם כּוּשִׁים חַלְלֵי חַרְבִּי הֵמָּה 'you, O Ethiopians, are also casualties of my sword', we see the pronoun assimilated to the preceding P with respect to number.

It is also clear that the position of Driver, who writes of "its [= the pronoun's] power of resuming and reinforcing the subject," is untenable, for in the above-quoted (22) the pronoun is *not* resuming the subject.[63]

### 3.7. Statistics[64]

Contrary to Driver, who writes that the A structure is "much less common" than the B structure, my statistics show that exactly the opposite is the case: A 90 versus B 85.[65]

These 175 cases are spread fairly evenly over the entire Bible:

Pentateuch—72 (Genesis: 23, Exodus: 6, Leviticus: 17, Numbers: 10, Deuteronomy: 16)
Former Prophets—23 (Joshua: 9, Samuel: 5, Kings: 9)
Latter Prophets—35 (Isaiah: 11, Jeremiah: 4, Ezekiel: 12, Minor Prophets: 8)
Writings—45 (Psalm: 5, Proverbs: 8, Job: 5, Chronicles: 9, Nehemiah: 5, Daniel: 2, Canticles: 2, Lamentations: 1, Qohelet: 8)

---

61. Here one should compare cases in Classical Ethiopic adduced by Cohen (1984: 198–99), such as *'antəmu wə'ətu bərhānu la-ʿālam* 'you are the light of the world' and *'antəmu wə'ətu liqāwəntihā la-beta krəstiyān qəddəst* 'you are the scholars of the holy church,' where a second-person plural pronoun is followed by a third-person masculine singular pronoun. But his reasoning, that the use of a third-person pronoun after a first- or second-person pronoun is explicable on the ground that the former is the substitute of the second core constituent and not of the first, is not convincing in view of the second example quoted above, where the second constituent is plural.

62. More examples are found in (18) and (19) above.

63. Driver 1892: 269.

64. In an appendix, Sappan (1981: 175–76) purports to provide a complete list of passages with a pronominal copula, but the list, with a total of 138 cases, appears to be deficient.

65. Driver 1892: 269. According to Groß (1987: 127–28), the A type "ist die typische Konstruktion für betonte Identifikation zweier determinierter Größen," and the B type "ist ... das typische Satzmodel für pendierendes Subjekt in nominalen Klassifikations- und Qualifikationssätzen."

The relative infrequence in the books of Psalms, Proverbs, and Job, however, suggests that we are not dealing with an eminently poetic feature of Biblical Hebrew syntax.

**3.8. זֶה as the Clause-Medial Constituent**

The demonstrative pronoun זֶה appears fairly frequently as the clause-medial constituent of a tripartite NC. As such it is indeclinable irrespective of the gender or number of either of the other two constituents. Furthermore, and again unlike הוּא, it is hardly ever found as the clause-final core constituent. Nonetheless, its function is rather similar to the function of הוּא: namely, it accords some degree of prominence to the preceding constituent.

This kind of זֶה is most commonly placed immediately after an interrogative:

(63) 1 Sam 9:18

אֵי־זֶה בֵּית הָרֹאֶה    where is the house of the seer?

(64) 2 Kgs 3:8

אֵי־זֶה הַדֶּרֶךְ נַעֲלֶה    where is the way we should go up?

(65) 1 Kgs 22:24

אֵי־זֶה עָבַר רוּחַ־יהוה מֵאִתִּי    where is it that the spirit of the
LORD passed from me?'

The cohesion of the interrogative and the pronoun is indicated by the *maqqep*, which almost invariably joins the two. Another step further, the combination is virtually a new interrogative as in later Hebrew, in which it is an interrogative of choice: 'which?'[66] Compare Job 28:12, 20 אֵי זֶה מְקוֹם בִּינָה 'where is the place of intelligence?' with Isa 66:1 אֵי־זֶה מָקוֹם מְנוּחָתִי 'which place is my resting place?' And compare these with Qoh 11:6 אֵינְךָ יוֹדֵעַ אֵי זֶה יִכְשָׁר 'you do not know which is going to prosper'.

Examples of texts with other interrogatives are:

(66) 1 Sam 17:55

בֶּן־מִי־זֶה הַנַּעַר    whose son is the youth?

(67) Job 42:3

מִי זֶה מַעְלִים עֵצָה    who is he that conceals counsel?

(68) 1 Sam 10:11

מַה־זֶּה הָיָה לְבֶן־קִישׁ    what is it that has come over the son
of Kish?

---

66. Cf. Arabic *māḏā* and Syr. *mānaw* < *mānā hu*, *ʾaykaw*, etc.

(69) Gen 18:13

לָמָּה זֶּה צָחֲקָה שָׂרָה     why is it that Sarah laughed?

Five times the demonstrative follows אַתָּה:

(70) Gen 27:21

הַאַתָּה זֶה בְּנִי עֵשָׂו     whether *you* are my son Esau

(71) 2 Sam 2:20

הַאַתָּה זֶה עֲשָׂהאֵל     are *you* Asahel?

Likewise, Gen 27:24; 1 Kgs 18:7, 17.

In all of these five cases the speaker is attempting to reassure himself that he has correctly established the identity of the other party. The context is thus highly personal and characterized by a ring of immediacy, which is suitably expressed by the 'here' deictic element.

In three places we find זֶה in the third slot, each time in the form מִי הוּא זֶה:

(72) Jer 30:21

מִי הוּא־זֶה עָרַב אֶת־לִבּוֹ     who is it that would dare?

(73) Ps 24:10

מִי הוּא זֶה מֶלֶךְ הַכָּבוֹד     who is the king of glory?

(74) Esth 7:5

מִי הוּא זֶה וְאֵי־זֶה הוּא     who is it and where is he?

Ps 24:10 is preceded by 24:8 מִי זֶה מֶלֶךְ הַכָּבוֹד. In v. 8 the demonstrative pronoun has clearly been triggered by v. 7, 'Lift up your heads, O gates! and be lifted up, O ancient doors! And let the king of glory come in'. Thus the demonstrative echoes 'the king of glory' in v. 7 and therefore is more than a mere enclitic—it is the subject, followed by מֶלֶךְ הַכָּבוֹד in apposition. The same applies to v. 10, where, however, the interrogative is highlighted by הוּא, just as in Esth 7:5. The syntactic value of the demonstrative זֶה in these five passages is distinct from that of מָה זֶה, מִי זֶה, and so on.

## Bibliography of Works Cited

Andersen, F. I.
    1970    *The Hebrew Verbless Clause in the Pentateuch.* Journal of Biblical Litera-
            ture Monograph Series 14. Nashville and New York: Abingdon.
Baasten, M. F. J.
    1997    Nominal Clauses Containing a Personal Pronoun in Qumran Hebrew.
            Pp. 1–16 in *Studies on the Hebrew of the Dead Sea Scrolls and Ben Sira,*
            ed. T. Muraoka and J. F. Elwolde. Leiden: Brill.

Backhaus, F. J.
  1995     Die Pendenskonstruktion im Buch Qohelet. *Zeitschrift für Althebraistik* 8: 1–30.
Benveniste, É.
  1951     La phrase nominale. Pp. 151–67 in É. Benveniste, *Problèmes de linguistique générale*. Paris: Gallimard. Originally published in *Bulletin de la Société Linguistique de Paris* 46 (1950): fasc. 1, no. 132.
Brockelmann, C.
  1913     *Syntax*. Vol. 2 in *Grundriss der vergleichenden Grammatik der semitischen Sprachen*. Berlin: Reuter & Reichard.
  1956     *Hebräische Syntax*. Neukirchen-Vluyn: Neukirchener Verlag.
Brown, F.; Driver, S. R.; and Briggs, C. A.
  1907     *A Hebrew and English Lexicon of the Old Testament*. Oxford: Clarendon.
Cohen, D.
  1984     *La Phrase nominale et l'évolution du système verbal en sémitique: Études de syntaxe historique*. Leuven: Peeters.
Derenbourg, J.
  1893     *Œuvres complètes de R. Saadia ben Iosef fayyoûmî: Version arabe du Pentateuchi*. Paris: Leroux.
Driver, S. R.
  1892     *A Treatise on the Use of the Tenses in Hebrew and Some Other Syntactical Questions*. 3d ed. Oxford: Clarendon.
  1902     *A Critical and Exegetical Commentary on Deuteronomy*. 3d ed. International Critical Commentary. Edinburgh: T. & T. Clark.
Driver, S. R.; and Gray, G. B.
  1921     *A Critical and Exegetical Commentary on Job Together with a New Translation*. International Critical Commentary. Edinburgh: T. & T. Clark.
Geller, S. A.
  1991     Cleft Sentences with Pleonastic Pronoun: A Syntactic Construction of Biblical Hebrew and Some of Its Literary Uses. *Journal of the Ancient Near Eastern Society* 20: 15–33.
Gibson, J. C. L.
  1994     *Davidson's Introductory Hebrew Grammar: Syntax*. 4th ed. Edinburgh: T. & T. Clark.
Glinert, L.
  1989     *The Grammar of Modern Hebrew*. Cambridge: Cambridge University Press.
Goldenberg, G.
  1983     On Syriac Sentence Structure. Pp. 97–140 in *Arameans, Aramaic and the Aramaic Literary Tradition*, ed. M. Sokoloff. Ramat Gan: Bar Ilan University Press.
Golomb, D.
  1983     Nominal Syntax in the Language of Codex Vatican Neofiti 1: Sentences Containing a Predicate Adjective. *Journal of the Ancient Near Eastern Society* 42: 181–94.
Groß, W.
  1987     *Die Pendenskonstruktion im biblischen Hebräisch: Studien zum althebräischen Satz I*. Arbeiten zu Text und Sprache im Alten Testament 27. St. Ottilien: EOS.

Hoftijzer, J.
1973    The Nominal Clause Reconsidered. *Vetus Testamentum* 23: 446–510.
Huehnergard, J.
1986    On Verbless Clauses in Akkadian. *Zeitschrift für Assyriologie* 76: 218–49.
Jenni, E.
1992    *Die Präposition Beth.* Vol. 1 in *Die hebräischen Präpositionen.* Stuttgart: Kohlhammer.
Jespersen, O.
1924    *The Philosophy of Grammar.* London: Allen & Unwin.
Joosten, J.
1989    The Predicative Participle in Biblical Hebrew. *Zeitschrift für Althebraistik* 2: 128–59.
1996    *The Syriac Language of the Peshitta and Old Syriac Versions of Matthew: Syntactic Structure, Inner-Syriac Developments and Translation Technique.* Studies in Semitic Languages and Linguistics 22. Leiden: Brill.
Joüon, P.
1923    *Grammaire de l'hébreu biblique.* Rome: Pontifical Biblical Institute.
Joüon, P.
1991    *A Grammar of Biblical Hebrew.* Trans. and rev. by T. Muraoka. 2 vols. Subsidia Biblica 14/1–2. Rome: Pontifical Biblical Institute.
Keil, C. F., and Delitzsch, F.
1847    *Joshua.* Vol. 2 in *Commentary on the Old Testament.* Reprinted, 1987. Grand Rapids: Eerdmans.
Kraus, F. R.
1984    *Nominalsätze in altbabylonischen Briefen und der Stativ.* Mededelingen der Koninklijke Nederlandse Akademie der Wetenschappen, Afd. Letterkunde, Nieuwe reeks 47/2: 21–71. Leiden: Nederlandse Akademie der Wetenschappen.
Michel, D.
1994    Probleme des Nominalsatzes im biblischen Hebräisch. *Zeitschrift für Althebraistik* 7: 215–24.
Muraoka, T.
1969    *Emphasis in Biblical Hebrew.* Ph.D. Dissertation. Jerusalem: The Hebrew University.
1975    On the Nominal Clause in the Old Syriac Gospels. *Journal of Semitic Studies* 20: 28–37.
1985    *Emphatic Words and Structures in Biblical Hebrew.* Jerusalem: Magnes / Leiden: Brill.
1987    *Classical Syriac for Hebraists.* Wiesbaden: Harrassowitz.
1989    Review of *Sintassi del verbo ebraico nella prosa biblica classica,* by A. Niccacci (Jerusalem, 1986) in *Abr-Nahrain* 27: 187–93.
1991    Biblical Hebrew Nominal Clause with a Prepositional Phrase. Pp. 143–51 in *Studies in Hebrew and Aramaic Syntax,* ed. K. Jongeling, H. L. Murre-van den Berg, and L. Van Rompay. Studies in Semitic Languages and Linguistics 17. Leiden: Brill.
Naudé, J. A.
1994    The Verbless Clause with Pleonastic Pronoun in Biblical Aramaic. *Journal for Semitics* 6: 74–93.

Niccacci, A.
1993    Simple Nominal Clause (SNC) or Verbless Clause in Biblical Hebrew Prose. *Zeitschrift für Althebraistik* 6: 216–27.
Pennacchietti, F. A.
1987    La struttura della frase nominale tripartita di identificazione in ebraico e in siriaco. Pp. 157–74 in *Atti della 4ªgiornata di studi camito-semitici e indo-europei*, ed. G. Bernini and V. Brugnatelli. Milan: Unipoli.
Praetorius, F.
1886    *Aethiopische Grammatik mit Paradigmen.* Leipzig: Harrassowitz.
Reckendorf, H.
1895–98  *Die syntaktischen Verhältnisse des Arabischen.* Leiden: Brill.
1921    *Arabische Syntax.* Heidelberg: Carl Winter's Universitätsbuchhandlung.
Rosén, H. B.
1965    On Some Types of Verbless Sentences in Biblical Hebrew. *Report of the Third World Congress of Jewish Studies: Jerusalem, 1961.* Jerusalem: World Union of Jewish Studies. [Heb. with an Eng. abstract]
Rubinstein, E.
1969    *The Nominal Clause.* Tel Aviv: Ha-kibbuts ha-meʾuchad. [Heb.]
Sappan, R.
1981    *The Typical Features of the Syntax of Biblical Poetry in Its Classical Period.* Jerusalem: Kiryat-Sefer. [Heb.]
Trumpp, E.
1879    Über den arabischen Satzbau nach der Anschauung der arabischen Grammatiker. Pp. 309–98 in *Sitzungsberichte der Königlichen bayerischen Akademie der Wissenschaften zu München. Philos.-philol. und hist. Classe.* Munich: Straub.
Wackernagel, J.
1926    *Vorlesungen über Syntax mit besonderer Berücksichtigung von Griechisch, Lateinisch und Deutsch.* Erste Reihe. Basel: Birkhäuser.
Zewi, T.
1994    The Nominal Sentence in Biblical Hebrew. Pp. 145–67 in *Semitic and Cushitic Studies*, ed. G. Goldenberg and S. Raz. Wiesbaden: Harrassowitz.
1996    Subordinate Nominal Sentences Involving Prolepsis in Biblical Hebrew. *Journal of Semitic Studies* 41: 1–20.

# Types and Functions of the
# Nominal Sentence

ALVIERO NICCACCI

*Studium Biblicum Franciscanum, Jerusalem*

It is my intention to show that the common designation *verbless clause* is inadequate for two reasons. First, it may let people think that a verb is missing when it is simply not needed. Second, it does not account for the fact that a finite verb may be used with the function of a noun. Because of these two facts, a distinction based on the presence or absence of the finite verb is not useful for a comprehensive description of the sentence in BH. On the contrary, the sentence, both with and without a finite verb, can be adequately described from the point of view of syntactical predication.[1]

Before coming to the actual analysis of some types and functions of the nominal sentence, it is necessary to discuss the constituents of a sentence (§1.1). I will then examine the main problems and theories concerning the so-called verbless, or nominal, sentence (§1.2).

## 1. Preliminaries

### 1.1. Constituents and Satellites in the Sentence

A definition of the constituents of the sentence as well as their order is a major problem of BH syntax and is still not agreed upon. Until there is a

---

1. Predication is distinct from a verbal predicate because it may be realized even without a finite verb. This distinction helps solve the problem of the relationship between the sentence with a finite verb and the one without a finite verb as discussed by modern linguists. It also explains this relationship without annulling the distinction between noun and verb. See exposition and discussion in R. Contini, *Tipologia della frase nominale nel Semitico nordoccidentale del I Millennio a.C.* (Pisa: Giardini, 1982), chap. 1. Contini surveys the research of A. Meillet, J. Vendryes, C. Bally, O. Jespersen, L. Tesnière, L. Hjelmslev, and É. Benveniste. Also see D. Cohen, *La phrase nominale et l'évolution du système verbal en sémitique: Études de syntaxe historique* (Leuven: Peeters, 1984) 1–22.

solution to this problem, no coherent description of the BH sentence can be achieved. Here, I wish briefly to explain my position with the help of examples, while also discussing the opinions of others.[2]

First, the two central constituents of a sentence are the predicate and subject. Ordinarily, optional satellites are also present in the sentence—for example, different complements and adverbs—but they are not obligatory constituents.[3] Second, we need to distinguish a grammatical and a syntactical level in the sentence. This distinction is clearly seen in cases where the subject is represented by a complete sentence. One such case is (13a) below, where the nominal sentence יְהוָה אֱלֹהֶיךָ שֹׁאֵל מֵעִמָּךְ 'the LORD your God requires of you' occupies the same slot of a noun such as מַשְׂכֻּרְתֶּךָ 'your wages' in (9) below. In both cases the predicate is the interrogative pronoun מָה 'what'. Thus, I distinguish a syntactical predicate (P) and a syntactical subject (S), on the one side, and a grammatical predicate (gP) and a grammatical subject (gS), on the other, as appears in the following diagram:

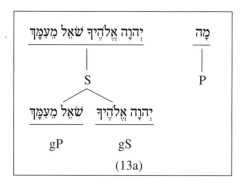

(13a)

The whole sentence (13a) is called superordinate; it is composed of P and S. The subject clause (S) is called embedded; it is composed of a gS (יְהוָה אֱלֹהֶיךָ) and a gP (שֹׁאֵל).[4] A grammatical complement (מֵעִמָּךְ) is also present in

---

2. I have already expressed my opinion in *The Syntax of the Verb in Classical Hebrew Prose* (Sheffield: Sheffield Academic Press, 1990) §6; and more recently in, "Marked Syntactical Structures in Biblical Greek in Comparison with Biblical Hebrew," *Liber Annuus* 43 (1993) 9–69, §3 (on subject and the predicate); §6 (non-verbal stressed elements becoming the predicate); §8 (two main slots in the sentence).

3. Similarly, F. I. Andersen (*The Hebrew Verbless Clause in the Pentateuch* [Journal of Biblical Literature Monograph Series 14; New York and Nashville: Abingdon, 1970] 29–30) speaks of "core" or "nucleus" and "optional margins" or "modifiers."

4. The distinction of grammatical and syntactical predicate and subject also holds for sentences having a finite verb form; see my paper, "On the Hebrew Verbal System," *Biblical Hebrew and Discourse Linguistics* (ed. R. D. Bergen; Dallas: Summer Institute of Linguistics, 1994) 117–37.

S. Thus, P and S are the syntactical constituents of the sentence, while the grammatical complement is an optional satellite.[5]

An additional slot can be added at the beginning or at the end of a complete sentence (that is to say, one composed of P and S). At the beginning, one finds the so-called *casus pendens* (for example, [5] below); at the end, the apposition (for example, [6]–[8] below).[6] There is clear evidence to show that the *casus pendens* constitutes a sentence by itself, separate from and dependent on the following main sentence. The *casus pendens* is the protasis, and the following main sentence is the apodosis; together, they constitute a *double sentence.*[7]

There is a great deal of discussion and misunderstanding about what in traditional terms are called *subject* and *predicate.*[8] Apart from individual people who would avoid this kind of analysis altogether,[9] most of modern grammarians reject the traditional pair "subject/predicate"; they propose instead "topic/comment" or "reference/predication" or "thème/propos" or "theme/rheme" or "given/new information."[10] They also criticize a criterion adopted in the present paper, namely *emphasis*, although this term was and still sometimes is used by competent scholars.[11]

---

5. Besides the syntactical level of the sentence, we need to posit the higher syntactical level of the text, involving the relationships among sentences. For instance, a sentence having a finite verb in second position (that is, x-*qatal*, or x-*yiqtol* in historical narrative) depends on another, preceding or following, having a finite verb in first position (that is, *wayyiqtol* in historical narrative). This is the case with the tense shifts *wayyiqtol* → x-*qatal* and vice versa, x-*qatal* → *wayyiqtol*. On this topic, see my paper, "Basic Facts and Theory of the Biblical Hebrew Verb System in Prose," *Narrative Syntax and the Hebrew Bible: Papers of the Tilburg Conference 1996* (Biblical Interpretation Series 29; Leiden: Brill, 1997) 167–202, esp. §3.

6. Consult my discussion in "Marked Syntactical Structures," §8.3.

7. See more on this in §3.3 below.

8. For an early, general linguistic discussion on subject and predicate, consult O. Jespersen, *The Philosophy of Grammar* (rev. ed.; London: Allen & Unwin, 1935), chap. 11. For a similar discussion in the field of Semitic studies, see Contini, *Tipologia*, 13–20. Contini, who uses the terms "subject" and "predicate," mentions Revell, Hoftijzer, and Michel among those who opposed such a terminology in the analysis of BH. However, a more recent essay of E. J. Revell ("The Conditioning of Word Order in Verbless Clauses in Biblical Hebrew," *JSS* 34 [1989] 1–24) does use these terms. For his part, D. Michel ("Probleme des Nominalsatzes im biblischen Hebräisch," *ZAH* 7 [1994] 215–24) adopts the Arabic designations *mubtada*ʾ and *ḫabar* for subject and predicate respectively (see n. 108 below).

9. E.g., S. Geller, "Cleft Sentence with Pleonastic Pronoun: A Syntactic Construction of Biblical Hebrew and Some of Its Literary Uses," *JANES* 20 (1991) 15–33, esp. n. 8; see my paper, "On the Hebrew Verbal System," 122 n. 16.

10. Consult J. Lyons, *Semantics* (Cambridge: Cambridge University Press, 1977), vol. 2, §§11–12; and Contini, *Tipologia*, 12, 27 n. 93. A full discussion of both the general linguistic and the Medieval Arabic terminology is found in Cohen, *La phrase nominale*, 22–57.

11. While T. Muraoka (*Emphatic Words and Structures in Biblical Hebrew* [Jerusalem: Magnes / Leiden: Brill, 1985]) accepts the phenomenon of *emphasis* and tries to classify it,

In the present essay, the term *emphasis* is equivalent to *stress* and *focus*.[12] In my understanding, emphasis characterizes P as defined above.[13] In other words, the stressed constituent is the reason why the sentence has been produced; it is the new information and the predicate.[14] Thus understood, emphasis can hardly be qualified as a vague and a nonsyntactical criterion, as is much too often affirmed by linguists who want to be "modern" at any cost.

---

Andersen (*The Hebrew Verbless Clause*) rejects it altogether; see Contini, *Tipologia,* 49. Andersen has been rather influential upon young grammarians; consult recent discussions, among others, by B. L. Bandstra, "Word Order and Emphasis in Biblical Hebrew Narrative: Syntactic Observations on Genesis 22 from a Discourse Perspective," *Linguistics and Biblical Hebrew* (ed. W. R. Bodine; Winona Lake, Ind.: Eisenbrauns, 1992) 109–23; by C. H. J. van der Merwe, "Discourse Linguistics and Biblical Hebrew Grammar," *Biblical Hebrew and Discourse Linguistics* (ed. R. D. Bergen; Dallas: Summer Institute of Linguistics, 1994) 13–49, esp. §3.2; and by T. Zewi, "The Nominal Sentence in Biblical Hebrew," *Semitic and Cushitic Studies* (ed. G. Goldenberg and S. Raz; Wiesbaden: Harrassowitz, 1994) 145–67, esp. 147–48. The term "emphasis" is still used by W. R. Garr (*Dialect Geography of Syria–Palestine 1000–586 B.C.E.* [Philadelphia: University of Pennsylvania Press, 1985] 189–91), as he reviews word order in Northwest Semitic dialects, as well as by Contini (*Tipologia*, 51), who mostly proceeds on the basis of statistical criteria. See also my paper "The Stele of Mesha and the Bible: Verbal System and Narrativity," *Or* 63 (1994) 226–48, esp. 240 n. 45.

12. See description by T. Givón, *Syntax: A Functional-Typological Introduction* (Amsterdam: Benjamins, 1990) 2.704. Also consult my "Marked Syntactical Structures," §5. In the latter, H. J. Polotsky is mentioned, who identified the correct function of "second tenses" in Coptic and of "emphatic forms" in ancient Egyptian as corresponding to "cleft sentences" in English (see §3.1 below). H. B. Rosén, who applied this insight to Greek, is also mentioned there.

13. From the survey of the different scholarly stands found in Jespersen, *The Philosophy* (pp. 147ff.), it appears that the opinion maintained here was held by Høffding, who proposed to identify the "logical predicate" on the basis of stress (or tone). As Jespersen notes, this opinion is similar to that of Paul, who proposed to identify the "psychological predicate" of the 19th-century tradition (G. von der Gabelentz) on the basis of novelty and importance. Jespersen also mentions Bloomfield and Wundt along similar lines. For my part, I prefer to call this predicate *syntactical* instead of *logical* or *psychological*. The reason is that it is identified on the basis of definite grammatical constructions and their function (that is, in this essay, the constructions with a pronoun in the first place of the sentence, §2 below).

14. Emphasis, new information, and predicate are considered equivalent here. From this perspective, it is difficult to understand the claim that sometimes the predicate receives no emphasis. Contini (*Tipologia*, 50) makes this remark concerning 1 Sam 24:18[17] צַדִּיק אַתָּה מִמֶּנִּי 'You are more righteous than I'. However, it seems obvious that the emphasis of the sentence does fall on צַדִּיק, which is the new information and the predicate. The emphasis is not easily recognized in this and other similar cases because it falls on a *universal* term (an adjective in 1 Sam 24:18[17]), which is expected to play the role of the predicate; vice versa, it is more evident in other cases where it falls on a personal pronoun, which is not expected as the predicate. The situation in a sentence with a finite verb is the same. If the verb is in the first place, the emphasis falls on it; it is the predicate as expected. However, the emphasis is more easily felt when it falls on a nonverbal element that is not expected as the predicate. See the discussion in §3.3 below.

What matters is the analysis, rather than the terminology adopted.[15] Besides, the fact that new terms—for example, *topic*—are used for different levels of analysis (that is, for single-sentence and intersentence relationships, as well as for text and large literary composition) does not improve clarity.[16]

Jespersen, one of the main linguists who criticized the traditional conception of subject and predicate,[17] wrote as follows:

> The subject is sometimes said to be the relatively familiar element, to which the predicate is added as something new. . . . This may be true of most sentences, but not of all, for if in answer to the question "Who said that?" we say "Peter said it," Peter is the new element, and yet it is undoubtedly the subject. The "new information" is not always contained in the predicate, but it is always inherent in the *connexion* of the two elements,—in the fact that these two elements are put together, i.e., in the "nexus.". . .[18]

It seems, first, that Jespersen's doctrine of "nexus" hardly explains sentences with only one member—that is, a sentence in which S is implied (see §3.3 below).[19] Second, in the example given by Jespersen, Peter is undoubtedly the new element. However, Peter is the subject if the sentence "Peter said it" is a reply to a question like "*Did* Peter *say* it?" In this case, the reply is a plain or unmarked sentence; in it the main information is the verb itself, as expected.

---

15. For example, the only difference between H. J. Polotsky's analysis and mine is terminological; that is, I prefer "syntactical predicate / subject" instead of "logical predicate / subject." Otherwise, I follow his lead in maintaining that what raises the interest, or the new element, is the predicate, while what is already known, or the given element, is the subject. Consult his epoch-making essay *Etudes de syntaxe copte. Première étude: La forme dite «finale»; Deuxième étude: Les temps seconds* (Cairo: Société d'Archéologie Copte, 1944) = *Collected Papers* (Jerusalem: Magnes, 1971) 102–207; and idem, "Les transpositions du verbe en égyptien classique," *IOS* 6 (1976) 1–50. See my "Marked Syntactical Structures," §§3, 5.

16. For example, G. Brown and G. Yule (*Discourse Analysis* [Cambridge Textbooks in Linguistics; Cambridge: Cambridge University Press, 1983], chap. 3) speak of "Sentential topic," "Discourse topic," and so forth. See discussion by Cohen, *La phrase nominale*, 22–46.

17. Other scholars are mentioned in Contini (*Tipologia*, 21 n. 19)—Ries, Hjelmslev, and Martinet—on the basis of S. Stati, *Teoria e metodo nella sintassi* (Bologna: Il Mulino, 1972; orig. 1967).

18. Jespersen, *The Philosophy*, 145; italics in the original.

19. In the section entitled "Final Words on Nexus," Jespersen surveys different cases of "one-member nexus" (*The Philosophy*, 141–44) without encountering any problem for his theory. From the examples that he quotes, it appears that the unexpressed member of the nexus is what he calls "the primary" part of the nexus—that is, the subject. The fact that he calls the predicate "the secondary part" of the nexus is due to practical reasons; that is, it is simply due to the fact that in plain English sentences the predicate comes after the subject. Still, it is noteworthy that his terminology formally contradicts the position taken in this paper, that is, that syntactically the main element of the sentence is the predicate not the subject. In BH, the P even occurs sentence-initially; see §3.3 below.

On the other hand, if the question is *"Who* said that?" it does not concern the *fact* of saying something but *who* said something, in which case the sentence—both the question and the answer—is marked. In other words, Peter is the subject in the plain sentence but is the predicate[20] or the new information in the marked sentence.[21] Besides, an acceptable reply to the question "Who said that?" would also be "Peter" (without any verb), while such a reply would be unacceptable for the question "Did Peter say it?"[22]

At this point it is useful to compare interrogative sentences in BH. In BH, as in English and in other languages, interrogatives can be general (that is, concern the action or event in itself) or specific (that is, concern a detail of the action or event such as who, what, when, why, and so on).[23] Compare the following sentences:

| S (Syntactical Subject) | P (Syntactical Predicate) |
|---|---|
| (a) | הַאֶעֱלֶה בְּאַחַת עָרֵי יְהוּדָה |
| (b) | עֲלֵה |
| (c) אֱעֱלֶה | אָנָה |
| (d) — | חֶבְרֹנָה |

---

20. Pace W. Groß, *Die Satzfolge im Verbalsatz alttestamentlicher Prosa: Untersucht an den Büchern Dtn, Ri und 2Kön* (A. Diße and A. Michel, collaborators; Tübingen: Mohr, Siebeck, 1996) 11–12 n. 49. He finds "absurd" my analysis of Deut 9:3c in "Simple Nominal Clause (SNC) or Verbless Clause in Biblical Hebrew Prose," *ZAH* 6 (1993) 216–27, esp. 224. See my detailed review of Groß's volume, to be published in *Henoch*. Also see discussion of Zewi's essay in §1.2 below.

21. There is misunderstanding among scholars concerning the concept of "new information." The fact that a piece of information is "new" does not mean that it is totally absent in the previous context; it can be already present and still be taken up again as the "new" element in order to be emphasized or specified in some way. Consult my "Basic Facts," example 9 (Job 32:2–3). Similar examples are Gen 1:27; 17:24–27; 41:12b; Exod 7:6; 12:28, 50; 2 Kgs 18:10.

22. I agree with the opinion of C. F. Stout (criticized by Jespersen, *The Philosophy*, 146) that "All answers to questions are, as such, predicates, and all the predicates may be regarded as answers to possible questions"; see my paper "On the Hebrew Verbal System," 125 and 135 n. 21, where J. Lyons is quoted. One may add the opinion of Garvin who, discussing how to distinguish "theme" or subject from "rheme" or predicate, writes as follows: "A suggested approach would be the formulation of the question to which the utterance under investigation would be an appropriate answer. It might then turn out that the theme is that portion of the utterance which is held in common by both question and answer, and the rheme is the portion of the utterance which constitutes the actual answer to the question" (P. L. Garvin, "Czechoslovakia," *Current Trends in Linguistics* [ed. P. L. Garvin, H. Lunt, and E. Stankiewicz; The Hague: Mouton, 1963] 499–522, esp. 503 n. 11). I also agree with the opinion of H. Sweet, which Jespersen criticizes as follows: "But curiously enough Sweet, NEG [i.e., *A New English Grammar*] §215, says that 'an interrogative pronoun is always the predicate of the sentence it introduces' " (Jespersen, *The Philosophy*, 153 n. 1).

23. For the so-called "x-question" or "WH-question" in English, consult Givón, *Syntax*, §18.4.2.4; for BH and Biblical Greek, see my "Marked Syntactical Structures," §§3, 5.

(a) (David inquired of the LORD) Shall I go up into any of the cities of Judah?
(b) (The LORD said to him) Go up.
(c) (David said) To which shall I go up?
(d) (The LORD answered) To Hebron. (2 Sam 2:1)

This passage beautifully illustrates both the general (a–b) and the specific interrogative sentence (c–d). The general question concerns the going up in itself; therefore, הַאֶעֱלֶה is the predicate, both grammatical and syntactical, of the question (a), as is עֲלֵה in the answer (b). Both sentences are verbal and plain. However, in the case of the specific question (c–d), the new information and P is אָנָה, while the finite verb אֶעֱלֶה is the given information and S. Both sentences (c–d) are marked. Since the adverb אָנָה clearly resumes the complement בְּאַחַת עָרֵי יְהוּדָה, we witness a complete reversal of roles: what is the grammatical complement in the plain sentence (a) becomes P in the marked sentence (c), and the finite verb that is the predicate in the plain sentence (a–b) becomes S in (c) and is implied in (d). This is further proof that in the marked sentence the finite verb is not P; otherwise it could not be implied.

What has been observed for the interrogative sentence similarly applies to sentences having a personal or a demonstrative pronoun with the function of P in first position (see §3 below).

**1.2.** Problems and Theories concerning the Nominal Sentence
The first problem regarding the nominal sentence is its structure. The view expressed in §1.1 takes into account my earlier treatment of the subject in 1993.[24] It is now time to compare this view with other scholars' views. I do this by discussing the recent and totally new presentation of the nominal sentence by Zewi.[25]

Before coming to the actual description of the nominal sentence, Zewi discusses (mostly following her professor, G. Goldenberg) the role of the independent personal (and demonstrative) pronoun in the nominal sentence; the relation between nominal and verbal sentence; and the function of definite nouns in the nominal sentence. I mention three positive results of her discussion. First, she does not accept the role of copula usually attributed to the pronoun; the pronoun is either the subject or the predicate.[26] For this rather unusual proposal, Zewi relies on studies by Polotsky (on Coptic) and Goldenberg (on Syriac). Second, the grammatical phenomena of topicalization and focalization are both nominal. In Zewi's view, we have topicalization when a part of a verbal sentence is isolated as theme; we have focalization when a part of a verbal sentence is isolated as rheme, while the rest, including the verb,

---

24. Niccacci, "Simple Nominal Clause."
25. Zewi, "The Nominal Sentence."
26. Consult Zewi's discussion of the opinions of different scholars (ibid., 146–49).

becomes the theme (the result is called a "cleft sentence"). An important consequence is stated as follows:

> That is to say that when phenomena like topicalization or focalization happen to be identified in a sentence, the sentence itself should not be treated anymore as a verbal sentence but rather as a nominal sentence.[27]

Third, concerning the rather commonly accepted distinction between clauses of classification (that is, those with an indefinite predicate and a word order of predicate–subject) and clauses of identification (that is, those with a definite predicate and a word order of subject–predicate), Zewi retains the first but rejects the second. Because the principle of definiteness/indefiniteness is useful but insufficient as the basis of the analysis, Zewi incorporates it into a more comprehensive system.

The three points just mentioned are positive, in my view, though some problems still remain. With reference to the second point, it seems to me that Zewi's understanding of topicalization or extraposition is hardly correct.[28] For her, the subject is extraposed at the beginning or at the end of a sentence, and the rest of the sentence is "the predicate clause," consisting of predicate and subject. In order to understand the meaning of "predicative clause," one has to bear in mind that, following Goldenberg, Zewi maintains that every finite verb is a "self-contained complete sentence." That is, it "includes three components: personal marker, predicate lexeme, and a nexus in between" (p. 150). This analysis will be discussed later on in connection with Zewi's nominal sentence "Type B." For the moment, suffice it to say that the extraposed element or *casus pendens* constitutes a sentence by itself, as observed in the previous section; therefore, it cannot be taken as the "logical subject" of the following "predicative clause," simply because the two belong to different sentences.

With reference to the third point mentioned above, I agree that the principle of definiteness/indefiniteness is insufficient, as is the distinction between

---

27. Ibid., 150.

28. I must say that scholars generally agree with this analysis of topicalization/extraposition. The extraposed element is identified as the "logical subject," the rest as the "logical predicate." See, e.g., Contini, *Tipologia*, 58–59, 83 n. 150. He refers to Driver, Gesenius-Kautzsch-Cowley, Muraoka, Andersen, and Bravmann (who applied this analysis to Arabic). Also see G. Goldenberg, "Tautological Infinitive," *IOS* 1 (1971) 36–85, esp. 37; idem, "Imperfectly-Transformed Cleft Sentences," *Proceedings of the Sixth World Congress of Jewish Studies*, vol. 1: *Division A: The Ancient Near East* (Jerusalem: World Union of Jewish Studies, 1977) 127–33, esp. 127. A similar analysis of what is also called *casus pendens* is found in H. B. Rosén, "אנכי and אני: Essai de grammaire, interprétation et traduction," H. B. Rosén, *East and West. Selected Writings in Linguistics, Edited for the Occasion of His Sixtieth Birthday by a Group of Friends and Disciples, Part Two: Hebrew and Semitic Linguistics* (Munich: Fink, 1984) 262–81, esp. 268–69 (originally published in *Mélanges André Neher* [Paris: Adrien-Maisonneuve, 1975] 253–72).

clauses of classification and clauses of identification.[29] In order to describe the nominal sentence in a comprehensive way, we need to combine two criteria: (1) the "universal term" (that is, the class of the predicate) versus the "particular term" (that is, the class of the subject), and (2) first position versus second position in the sentence.[30]

Zewi establishes five types of nominal sentences: Type A, predicate–subject; Type A2, subject–predicate; Type B, subject–predicate clause; Type C, predicate clause–subject; Type D, subject–predicate clause.[31] Types A and A2 are the basic types, while the others involve extraposition; the extraposed element is called the "subject" and the rest of the sentence is called the "predicate clause." Further, extraposition is either frontal (as in Types B and D) or rear (as in Type C). The difference between Types B and D is that a personal pronoun is the subject in B, while in D it is the predicate.

In the following discussion I compare Zewi's analysis (a) with Muraoka's (b) and my own (c).[32] I limit myself to Zewi's Types B–D, which involve extraposition (or topicalization or *casus pendens*) because what has been said in §1.1 above about subject and predicate is sufficient for Types A and A2.

---

29. Michel ("Probleme") defends the importance of "determination/indetermination" for the analysis of the nominal sentence, but the evidence remains inconclusive. The second part of his paper, where he uses a different approach, is much more interesting. He proposes a test by inversion of the components of the nominal sentence ("Methode der 'Umstellungsprobe,'" 220). In other words, he chooses sentences with the same basic elements, for example a pronoun and a noun, and tries to understand the function of the various word orders in the given speech-situation (*Sprechsituation*). He correctly notes that word order is not simply a question of style but a question of syntax.

30. See my paper, "Simple Nominal Clause," 216–17. As I wrote there, "In Biblical Hebrew . . . when the first position of the sentence is taken by an expression belonging to the class of the predicate [that is, a universal term] the sentence is predicative, or unmarked, or neutral; on the contrary, when the first position is taken by an expression not belonging to the class of the predicate [that is, a particular term], the sentence is non-predicative, or marked, or detail-oriented" (p. 217). See further §3.2 below.

31. Strangely enough, Zewi employs the same letter for the two basic types that show reversed word order (A with predicate–subject and A2 with subject–predicate), while she uses different letters for the other three types (B, C, D), which supposedly are also Type A (the "predicate clause," consisting of predicate and subject) but with the addition of an extraposed element (called "subject") at the beginning or end of the sentence. Another strange thing is that she distinguishes examples with "short predicates" from those with "long predicates," a distinction that may have a practical justification but, from the point of view of syntax, is of course meaningless.

32. Reference is made to Muraoka, *Emphatic Words*. His more recent treatment, "The Biblical Hebrew Nominal Clause with a Prepositional Phrase" (in *Studies in Hebrew and Aramaic Syntax Presented to Professor J. Hoftijzer on the Occasion of His Sixty-Fifth Birthday* [ed. K. Jongeling, H. L. Murre-van den Berg, and L. van Rompay; Leiden: Brill, 1991] 143–51), does not seem to change things. While Muraoka represents the standard traditional analysis of the nominal sentence, Zewi and I represent new proposals. Revell ("The Conditioning") and Contini (*Tipologia*) are along similar lines as Muraoka.

*Type B*, כֻּלָּנוּ בְּנֵי אִישׁ־אֶחָד נָחְנוּ (Gen 42:11):

| | | |
|---|---|---|
| כֻּלָּנוּ (S) | { בְּנֵי אִישׁ־אֶחָד (P) | נָחְנוּ (S) } | (a) |
| כֻּלָּנוּ (S) | בְּנֵי אִישׁ־אֶחָד (P) | נָחְנוּ (Cop) | (b) |
| כֻּלָּנוּ (Pd) | { בְּנֵי אִישׁ־אֶחָד (P) | נָחְנוּ (S) } | (c) |

(a)　　All of us {we are sons of one man}.
(b)　　We are all of us sons of one man.
(c)　　All of us, {we are sons of one man}.

*Type C*, אֵלֶּה הֵם בְּנֵי יִשְׁמָעֵאל (Gen 25:16):

| | | |
|---|---|---|
| אֵלֶּה (P) | { הֵם (S) | בְּנֵי יִשְׁמָעֵאל (S) } | (a) |
| אֵלֶּה (P) | הֵם (Pd) | בְּנֵי יִשְׁמָעֵאל (Cop) | (b) |
| אֵלֶּה (P) | { הֵם (S) | בְּנֵי יִשְׁמָעֵאל (App) } | (c) |

(a)　　{These are they} the sons of Ishmael.
(b)　　These are the sons of Ishmael.
(c)　　These are they, that is, the sons of Ishmael.

*Type D*, וְיוֹסֵף הוּא הַשַּׁלִּיט עַל־הָאָרֶץ (Gen 42:6):

| | | |
|---|---|---|
| וְיוֹסֵף (S) | { הוּא (P) | הַשַּׁלִּיט עַל־הָאָרֶץ (S) } | (a) |
| וְיוֹסֵף (S) | הוּא (Cop) | הַשַּׁלִּיט עַל־הָאָרֶץ (S) | (b) |
| וְיוֹסֵף (Pd) | { הוּא (P) | הַשַּׁלִּיט עַל־הָאָרֶץ (S) } | (c) |

(a)　　And Joseph {it was he the governor over the land}.[33]
(b)　　And Joseph was the governor over the land.
(c)　　And Joseph, {it was he the governor over the land}.

For Zewi in (a), Type B is a two-member sentence composed of a front-extraposed subject and a "predicate clause," which in turn is composed of predicate and subject. For Muraoka in (b), Type B is a three-member sentence with subject, predicate, and copula. In my analysis in (c), Type B comprises two sentences, the *casus pendens* with the function of protasis and the following sentence (composed of predicate and subject) with the function of apodosis.

For Zewi in (a), Type C is a two-member sentence composed of a "predicate clause" with predicate and subject and of a rear-extraposed subject (that is, the two members are in reverse order vis-à-vis Type B). For Muraoka in (b), Type C is a three-member sentence with predicate, copula, and subject (in different word order vis-à-vis Type B). In my analysis in (c), Type C comprises a two-member sentence with predicate and subject and a phrase in apposition (in reverse order vis-à-vis Type B).

---

33. Zewi's actual translation is as follows: 'And Joseph, it was he who was the vizier of the land'. This translation seems to reflect exactly the analysis I propose, that is, a *casus pendens* ('And Joseph') placed before a cleft sentence ('it was he . . .'). See (5a) below.

For Zewi in (a), Type D is like Type B, a two-member sentence composed of a front-extraposed subject and a "predicate clause" with predicate and subject, the difference being that in Type B the personal pronoun is the subject of the "predicate clause," while in Type D it is the predicate. For Muraoka in (b), Type D is a three-member sentence like Type B with a difference in word order: subject, copula, and predicate instead of subject, predicate, and copula. In my analysis in (c), Type D is the same as Type B, the only difference being that in Type D the predicate is a particular term (a personal pronoun). This is not expected in such a function, and therefore the sentence is marked. In Type B the predicate is a universal term as expected, and therefore the sentence is unmarked.

I agree with Zewi, against Muraoka, that the personal pronoun is not the copula but is either a subject as expected (the result is an unmarked sentence) or a predicate as not expected (the result is a marked sentence).[34] I also agree that the nominal sentence has two main constituents, predicate and subject, not three. Therefore, the so-called "three-member nominal sentence" is to be rejected. It should instead be analyzed as a two-member structure with an extra element added either at the beginning ("front-extraposition" for Zewi, equivalent to what I call *casus pendens*) or at the end ("rear-extraposition" for Zewi, equivalent to what I call *apposition*).

I disagree with Zewi in the analysis of the front-extraposed element as the "logical subject" of a "predicate clause" for two reasons. First, I object to the fact that a predicate has two coreferential (that is, not different, coordinated) nominal subjects (see her analysis of Types B and C above).[35] For Zewi, this is not a problem because (following Goldenberg) she thinks that every finite verb is "a self-contained complete sentence" including "the personal marker, predicate lexeme and a nexus in between." As a consequence, in every sentence with a finite verb the subject is expressed twice, once by the verb itself, once by the nominal subject (either a noun phrase or a pronoun). However, it seems to me that this analysis is hardly correct. On the one hand, it is of course true that every finite verb expresses the subject (in Zewi's words, it bears "the personal marker"), but it is also true that the finite verb constitutes a sentence by itself only when a nominal subject is expressed or is recoverable from the context. In other words, a finite verb indicates the subject in an implicit way; it needs a specific subject phrase in order to constitute a well-formed sentence.

---

34. I would add that the copula is not a category of BH syntax, since neither the pronoun (whether personal or demonstrative) nor the verb היה plays this role. For pronouns, see my "Simple Nominal Clause," 223–25; for the verb היה, see A. Niccacci, "Sullo stato sintattico del verbo *hāyâ*," *Liber Annuus* 40 (1990) 9–23.

35. In Type B the predicate has two subjects, one in front-extraposition, the other in its place; and in Type B again the predicate has two subjects: one in its place and the other in rear-extraposition. Of course the two subjects would not constitute any problem if they referred to different entities.

On the other hand, the position of the subject phrase in the sentence makes a difference both grammatically (for example, וַיֹּאמֶר יְהֹוָה versus יְהֹוָה אָמַר) and syntactically (that is, there result two different types of sentence, "verb-x" and "x-verb" respectively).[36] Second, there is clear evidence to show that the front-extraposed element (*casus pendens*) constitutes a sentence by itself as indicated above.

If then the front-extraposed element is not part of the following nominal sentence, and if the finite verb cannot have two coreferential subject phrases, Zewi's types of nominal sentence need revision.

A further problem concerning Type B, which is traditionally called a sentence with a "pronominal copula,"[37] involves the difference that exists between this three-member structure and the corresponding two-member structure without the "pronominal copula." Gen 25:16, already quoted in part, shows the two constructions one after the other:

| App | S | P |
|---|---|---|
| בְּנֵי יִשְׁמָעֵאל | הֵם | אֵלֶּה |
| | שְׁמֹתָם | וְאֵלֶּה |

These are the sons of Ishmael and these are their names.

Though the basic meaning of the two sentences is of course the same, some difference must still be present.[38] In order to understand it, we may compare the same sentence with a finite verb. From the point of view of grammar, the subject phrase may or may not appear after the finite verb when it is recoverable from the context. However, from the point of view of pragmatics, the illocutionary effect changes accordingly.[39]

---

36. Position of the finite verb in the sentence is one of the two main criteria I used for describing the BH verb system; see, e.g., *Syntax*, §135. This criterion is also important for Zewi, at least in some cases, because she states that sentences with extraposition or cleft sentences are nominal even though they contain a finite verb, and the verb is nominalized either with אֲשֶׁר or without it. The latter is what Goldenberg called "imperfectly-transformed cleft sentences"; see Zewi, "The Nominal Sentence," 150. Zewi never explicitly states that the nominalization happens because of the second position of the finite verb, but I do not see any other reason for it.

37. For this *vexata quaestio* of Semitic syntax, see Contini, *Tipologia*, 58–59.

38. This problem has been discussed with great skill, as usual, by H. J. Polotsky, "Nominalsatz und Cleft Sentence im Koptischen," *Or* 31 (1962) 413–30 (= *Collected Papers*, 418–35). He gives a full description of this phenomenon and concludes that the difference between the two constructions is difficult to determine.

39. See, e.g., F. I. Andersen, "Salience, Implicature, Ambiguity, and Redundancy in Clause–Clause Relationships in Biblical Hebrew," *Biblical Hebrew and Discourse Linguistics* (ed. R. D. Bergen; Dallas: Summer Institute of Linguistics, 1994) 99–116.

## 2. Analysis

I would like to show the paradigmatic interchangeability of: (a) a noun (that is, a substantive or adjective or morphologically nominal form of the verb, namely the participle); (b) a finite verb explicitly nominalized with אֲשֶׁר; and (c) a finite verb functionally nominalized by being placed second in the sentence.

For this purpose, I have chosen three forms of a cleft sentence that has one of the following pronouns in first position: (1) independent personal, (2) interrogative, or (3) demonstrative.

### 2.1. Independent Personal Pronoun

Hereafter, several examples are analyzed, having an independent personal pronoun in first position with the function of P (syntactical predicate) and different constructions in second position with the function of S (syntactical subject).

|       | S | P |
|-------|---|---|
| (1a)  | הַצַּדִּיק | יְהֹוָה |
| (1b)  | הָרְשָׁעִים | וַאֲנִי וְעַמִּי |
| (2)   | הַנֹּתֵן לְךָ כֹּחַ לַעֲשׂוֹת חָיִל | כִּי הוּא |
| (3)   | אֲשֶׁר הֵסִיר חִזְקִיָּהוּ אֶת־בָּמֹתָיו | הֲלוֹא־הוּא |
| (4a)  | שְׁלַחְתֶּם אֹתִי הֵנָּה | וְעַתָּה לֹא־אַתֶּם |
| (4b)  | —[40] | כִּי הָאֱלֹהִים |

(1) (Pharaoh said to Moses and Aaron) It is the LORD that is in the right, and it is I and my people that are in the wrong. (Exod 9:27)[41]

(2) (You shall remember the LORD your God,) for it is he that gives you power to do great deeds. (Deut 8:18)

(3) Is it not he (that is, the God of Israel) whose high places . . . Hezekiah has removed . . . ? (2 Kgs 18:22 = Isa 36:7)

(4) (Joseph said to his brothers) In fact, it was not you that sent me here, but God. (Gen 45:8)

---

40. The verb is implied here because it is not the "new" but the "given" element of the sentence. The contrastive pattern 'not you . . . but the LORD' is clearly concerned with the "who" did it rather than with the "doing" itself. In other words, the grammatical subject becomes P (see §1.1 above).

41. The translation of the examples is taken from the RSV, with modifications.

This basic pattern with an independent personal pronoun as P and the rest as S also occurs preceded by a *casus pendens* (5a) and followed by an appositive (6)–(8). I take *apposition* in the broad sense, as indicated by the following definition:

> Apposition is used for a variety of constructions where one form (an NP in the central cases) is "placed alongside" another, to which it is in some sense equivalent. Such equivalence puts apposition at the margin of the dependency, subordination relation—and in some cases, perhaps, beyond it.[42]

| S | P | Pd |
|---|---|---|
| (5a)   הַשַּׁלִּיט עַל־הָאָרֶץ | הוּא | וְיוֹסֵף |
| (5b)   הַמַּשְׁבִּיר לְכָל־עַם הָאָרֶץ | הוּא | |

(5)   Now as for Joseph, it was he the governor over the land; it was he the one who sold food to all the people of the land. (Gen 42:6)

Clearly, (5) is similar to (1) (S = noun[43]) with the addition of a *casus pendens* at the beginning (5a). Other passages, also preceded by *casus pendens*,[44] are as follows:

Similar to (1)—Gen 24:44; Num 16:7;[45] Deut 9:3;[46] 12:23; 31:3, 8; 1 Kgs 8:60 = 18:39.[47]

---

42. R. Huddleston, *Introduction to the Grammar of English* (Cambridge: Cambridge University Press, 1984) 262. See my "Marked Syntactical Structures," §8.

43. *Noun* comprises both *adjective* and *substantive*.

44. Most of the examples quoted by Zewi ("The Nominal Sentence," §11.2) are of this type. Zewi also gives poetic examples, which I am not considering. More recently ("Subject-Predicate Word Order of Nominal Clauses in El-Amarna Letters," *UF* 27 [1995] 657–93), she affirms that the "construction involving extraposition," that is, the sentence with *casus pendens*, in the El-Amarna Letters is due to West Semitic influence.

45. The phrase הָאִישׁ אֲשֶׁר־יִבְחַר יְהוָה is *casus pendens*, not the subject of וְהָיָה. This verb form renders the whole sentence verbal, instead of nominal. The sentence in its entirety is composed of the main verb (וְהָיָה), the *casus pendens* (consisting of the relative clause just quoted) with the function of the protasis, and the apodosis (consisting of הוּא הַקָּדוֹשׁ). A literal translation is as follows: 'and it will happen: as for the man whom the LORD shall choose, he shall be the holy one'. A similar "verbalizing" function is played by וַיְהִי. Without a form of the verb היה, the whole construction would be nominal instead of verbal. On this two-member construction, or double sentence, see my *Syntax*, §127; idem, "Sullo stato sintattico del verbo *hāyâ*"; and more recently, idem, "Finite Verb in the Second Position of the Sentence: Coherence of the Hebrew Verbal System," *ZAW* 108 (1996) 434–40, esp. 436–38.

46. In "Simple Nominal Clause" (pp. 224–25), I have studied Deut 9:3; 31:3, 8; Josh 22:22; and 23:3, 5, in order to prove that the "copula" does not have a place in BH, as already noted by S. R. Driver, *A Treatise on the Use of the Tenses in Hebrew and Some Other Syntactical Questions* (3d ed.; Oxford: Clarendon, 1892) §§198–201, esp. p. 270 n. 2. The proof consists in the parallelism between הוּא־הָעֹבֵר 'it is he the one who is about to go over' and הוּא יַשְׁמִידֵם 'it is he that will destroy them'.

47. Literally, 'As for the LORD (*casus pendens*), it is He [P] God [S]' (repeated twice in

Similar to (2) (S = participle)—Deut 3:22; 31:6; Josh 23:3, 10.
Similar to (3) (S = אֲשֶׁר + finite verb)[48]—Gen 42:14; Exod 16:23; Lev 10:3; Josh 24:17; 2 Kgs 18:22 (= Isa 36:7); 1 Chr 5:36; 2 Chr 22:9.
Similar to (4a) (S = finite verb)—Gen 3:12; 15:4; 44:17; Num 35:16; Deut 1:38; 1 Sam 6:9; 17:37; 2 Sam 14:19; 24:17 (cf. [7]); 1 Kgs 5:19.

|  | App | S | P |
|---|---|---|---|
| (6) | הָאֱלֹהִים | הוּא | אַתָּה־ |
| (7a) | אָמַרְתִּי לִמְנוֹת בָּעָם | | הֲלֹא אֲנִי |
| (7b) | אֲשֶׁר־חָטָאתִי וְהָרֵעַ הֲרֵעוֹתִי [49] | הוּא | וַאֲנִי־ |
| (8) | ( . . . ) אֲשֶׁר־רָכַבְתָּ עָלַי | אֲתֹנְךָ | הֲלוֹא אָנֹכִי |

(6) (David said to God) It is you the only God. (2 Sam 7:28)[50]

(7) (David said to God) Is it not I that gave command to number the people? It is I who have sinned[51] and done very wickedly. (1 Chr 21:17; cf. 2 Sam 24:17)

(8) (The ass said to Balaam) Am I not your ass, upon which you have ridden (all your life long to this day)? (Num 22:30)

Other passages are as follows:
Similar to (6) (S = independent personal pronoun, App = noun)—2 Chr 20:6.
Similar to (7b)[52] (S = independent personal pronoun, App = אֲשֶׁר + finite verb)—Ezek 38:17.
Similar to (8) (S = noun, App = אֲשֶׁר + finite verb)—Judg 13:11, 2 Kgs 15:12.[53]

---

1 Kgs 18:39). Compare 1 Kgs 18:24: 'And it will happen: as for the God who will answer by fire, it is he God'.

48. The same construction is attested in Phoenician (with relative pronoun *'š* + finite verb): *w'nhn 'š bnn bt l'šmn* 'It is we that built a temple to Eshmun' (*KAI* no. 14:16–18); in Yaudic (with demonstrative pronoun *zy* + finite verb): *'nk pnmw br qrl mlk y'dy zy hqmt nṣb zn lhdd* 'It is I, PNMW, son of QRL, king of Yaudi, that erected this statue for Hadad' (*KAI* no. 214:1); and in Ugaritic (with demonstrative pronoun *d* + finite verb): *'aḥdy.dymlk.ʿl.'ilm* 'It is I alone that will rule over the gods' (*CTA* 4 VII 49–50). Consult Contini, *Tipologia*, 65–66.

49. For the next sentence of 1 Chr 21:17 // 2 Sam 24:17 (not quoted here), see (42c) below.

50. Literally, 'It is you that are he, namely the (only) God'.

51. Literally, 'It is I he, namely the one who have sinned'. Note the parallelism between this sentence and the previous one, 'It is not I that gave the command to number the people', which does not interpose the הוּא as the subject. See discussion below, §3.1.

52. Example (7a) is similar to (4a); in both, S is a finite verb.

53. Compare: 'It is this (P) the word of God (S), which he said (App)' (2 Kgs 15:12), with: 'It is this (P) what the LORD said (S)' (Lev 10:3; see [3] above).

Similar to (7b) with the difference of having a noun as P instead of an independent personal pronoun—Gen 48:9;[54] Lev 25:42, 55;[55] 1 Sam 26:16;[56] 1 Kgs 8:51; 13:26; 2 Kgs 9:36; 2 Chr 8:11b.[57] Finally, Exod 34:10b is also similar to (7b), with the additional difference of having a nonverbal clause instead of a *qatal* after אֲשֶׁר.[58]

**2.2.** Interrogative Pronoun

| | S | P |
|---|---|---|
| (9) | מַשְׂכֻּרְתֵּךְ | מַה־ |
| (10a) | אַתָּה | לְמִי־ |
| (10b) | תֵלֵךְ [59] | וְאָנָה |
| (10c) | אֵלֶּה לְפָנֶיךָ | וּלְמִי |
| (11) | הַהֹלְכִים | מִי וָמִי |
| (12) | לָךְ | מַה־ |
| (13a) | יהוה אֱלֹהֶיךָ שֹׁאֵל מֵעִמָּךְ | מָה |
| (13b) | —[60] | כִּי אִם־לְיִרְאָה אֶת יהוה אֱלֹהֶיךָ |
| (14a) | הֲלַכְתֶּם | אָן |

54. Literally, 'They are (S) my sons (P), namely the ones God has given me here (App)'.

55. An identical sentence is found in these two verses: 'They (S) are my servants (P), whom I brought out of the land of Egypt (App)'. In Lev 25:55, this sentence is preceded by another one showing the same pattern P–S: 'It is to me (P) that the children of Israel belong as servants (S)'. Despite the similarity in pattern, the latter sentence is marked because P is represented by a prepositional phrase (לִי), which is not expected to play such a role, while the first sentence is unmarked because P is a universal term (עֲבָדַי), which is expected in such a role.

56. Literally, 'you (S) are sons of death (that is, you deserve to die) (P), you who have not kept watch over your lord (App)'.

57. Literally, 'for they (S) are holy (P), namely the (places) to which the ark of the LORD has come (App)'.

58. Literally, 'for it is (S) a terrible thing (P), namely what I am going to do with you (App)'.

59. This *yiqtol* occupies the slot of a noun (9), of a personal pronoun (10a) or of a demonstrative pronoun (10c). The fact that they interchange means that they play the same function. There is, however, a difference in aspect (§3.2 below).

60. Example (13b) comprises P only; S is implied from the previous sentence. In (13a) S consists of a complete nonverbal sentence with the pattern "grammatical subject–grammatical predicate" (see diagram in §1.1 above). This nonverbal sentence is embedded in the superordinate interrogative sentence with the function of subject clause; literally, 'What is (P) the fact that the LORD God requires of you? (S)'.

| (14b) | —[61] | לְבַקֵּשׁ אֶת־הָאֲתֹנוֹת |
|-------|-------|------------------------|
| (15a) | דָּבָר לִי אֵלֶיךָ הַשָּׂר | |
| (15b) | — | אֶל־מִי מִכֻּלָּנוּ |
| (15c) | —[62] | אֵלֶיךָ הַשָּׂר |

(9) (Laban said to Jacob) What are your wages? (Gen 29:15)

(10) (When Esau my brother meets you, and asks you) To whom do you belong? Where are you going? And whose are these before you? (Gen 32:18 [17])[63]

(11) (Pharaoh said to Moses and Aaron) But who are exactly (literally, 'who and who') those who are going? (Exod 10:8)

(12) (Caleb asked his daughter) What do you wish? (Josh 15:18)

(13) (And now, Israel) What does the LORD your God require of you,[64] but to fear the LORD your God . . . ? (Deut 10:12)

(14) (Saul's uncle said to him and to his servant) Where did you go? (And he answered) To seek the asses. . . . (1 Sam 10:14)

(15) (During the council of the commanders of the army, the son of the prophets said) I have an errand to you, O commander. (Jehu asked) To which of us all? (He replied) To you, O commander. (2 Kgs 9:5)

Other passages are:

Similar to (9) (S = noun)—Exod 12:26, 1 Sam 29:3, Jonah 1:8.

---

61. In the answer (14b), the verb is implied from the preceding question; it can be implied because it is S, not P; see §3.3 below.

62. Example (15a) is a presentative sentence conveying news. In the presentative sentence there is no syntactical predication, only the grammatical one; see my "Simple Nominal Clause," 220–22; idem, "Marked Syntactical Structures" §7.3. The question in (15b) consists of P alone, exactly as does the answer in (15c). In both cases, S is implied from (15a).

63. The reply to these questions (Gen 32:19[18]) comprises three sentences: '(a) To your servant Jacob; (b) they are a present sent to my lord Esau; (c) and moreover he is behind us'. Sentence (a) consists of the predicate only; the subject 'they belong' (in BH a personal pronoun) is implied from the preceding question, 'To whom do you belong?' Sentence (b) has the same pattern, "syntactical predicate–syntactical subject" ( . . . מִנְחָה הִוא), as the question; see (10). Sentence (c) is "presentative," that is, announces news, and shows the pattern "grammatical subject (personal pronoun)–grammatical predicate (prepositional phrase)" (גַּם־הוּא אַחֲרֵינוּ).

64. Literally, 'What is (P) the fact that the LORD your God requires of you? (S)'. See discussion in §1.1 above.

Similar to (10a) (S = personal pronoun)[65]—Josh 9:8; 1 Sam 25:11,[66] 30:13;
   2 Kgs 18:7.
Similar to (11) (S = participle)—1 Sam 11:12.
Similar to (12) (S = prepositional phrase)—Judg 1:14, 18:24; 2 Sam 14:5.
Similar to (13a) (S = nonverbal sentence)—Gen 28:17; Josh 5:14; Judg 9:2,
   16:5; 1 Sam 10:27; 1 Kgs 12:16 (= 2 Chr 10:16); 2 Kgs 7:3; Jonah 1:7–9.[67]
Similar to (14) (S = finite verb; cf. [10b] above)—Gen 3:13, 38:29; Josh 9:8;
   1 Kgs 20:14; 2 Kgs 3:8;[68] Jonah 1:8.

As with the personal pronoun, an additional slot is added in some examples
at the end of the sentence with a interrogative pronoun playing the function of
apposition (App).

|  | App | S | P |
|---|---|---|---|
| (16) | שֶׁבַע כְּבָשֹׂת הָאֵלֶּה | הֵנָּה | מָה |
| (17) | הַצַּד־צַיִד | הוּא | מִי־אֵפוֹא |
| (18a) | זֶה | הוּא | מִי |
| (18b) | אֲשֶׁר־מִלְאוֹ לִבּוֹ לַעֲשׂוֹת כֵּן | הוּא | וְאֵי־זֶה |
| (19) | לִי בְּכֹרָה | זֶה | וְלָמָּה־ |
| (20a) |  | [69] ------------------- | וְאַיּוֹ |
| (20b) | עֲזַבְתֶּן אֶת־הָאִישׁ | זֶה | לָמָּה |
| (21a) | רוּחֲךָ סָרָה | זֶה | מַה־ |
| (21b) | וְאֵינְךָ אֹכֵל לָחֶם[70] | — | — |
| (22a) | פִּשְׁעִי | | מַה־ |
| (22b) | כִּי דָלַקְתָּ אַחֲרָי | חַטָּאתִי | מַה |

---

65. The personal pronoun is usually in the independent form, but the suffix form is also
attested—for example, in (20a).

66. אֵי מִזֶּה is a compound interrogative pronoun; literally, 'Which-of from-this?'

67. See my paper, "Syntactic Analysis of Jonah," *Liber Annuus* 46 (1996) 9–32, §2.

68. P is אֵי־זֶה הַדֶּרֶךְ (interrogative adjective and noun) and נַעֲלָה is S.

69. Here the subject is represented by the suffix pronoun after a "quasi-verb" (GKC
§100o).

70. Two complete sentences follow one another in apposition; literally, 'What is (P) this
(S), namely the fact that your spirit has gone away (App), and the fact that you do not eat
food? (App)'. Despite the accent in the last syllable (מלרע in the *masora parva*), סָרָה is
probably *qatal*, not a participle.

(16) (Abimelech said to Abraham) What mean ('are') these seven ('they, namely these seven') ewe lambs . . . ? (Gen 21:29)

(17) (Isaac said) Who is it then that hunted game . . . ? (Gen 27:33)[71]

(18) (King Ahasuerus said to Queen Esther) Who is that man, and which is he, whose heart has filled him to do this? (Esth 7:5)[72]

(19) (Esau said) Of what use is a birthright to me? (Gen 25:32)[73]

(20) (Reuel said to his daughters) And where is he? Why have you left the man? (Exod 2:20)[74]

(21) (Jezebel his wife said to Ahab) Why has your spirit gone away, and you eat no food? (1 Kgs 21:5)

(22) (Jacob said to Laban) What is my offense? What is my sin, that you have hotly pursued me? (Gen 31:36)

Other passages are as follows:

Similar to (17) (App = participle)—Deut 10:12.
Similar to (18b) (App = אֲשֶׁר + finite verb)—Gen 37:10, 44:15; Deut 6:20; Josh 22:16; Judg 10:18, 20:12; 1 Sam 3:17; 1 Kgs 9:13; 2 Kgs 18:19 = Isa 36:4; 2 Kgs 20:8.
Similar to (19) (App = nonverbal sentence)—Exod 18:14; Num 13:19, 14:41; Josh 7:10; 1 Sam 26:18; 2 Sam 12:23, 18:22; 1 Kgs 14:6; 2 Kgs 23:17.
Similar to (20b) and (21a) (App = finite verb)—Gen 18:13, 27:20; Exod 5:22, 17:3; Num 11:20; Judg 8:1,[75] 13:18, 18:24; 1 Sam 10:11,[76] 17:28, 20:8,[77] 26:14;[78] 2 Sam 3:24, 19:43; 2 Kgs 1:5.[79]

---

71. Literally, 'Who is (P) he (S), namely the one who hunted the game? (App)'.

72. Apart from this remarkable passage, I never used Esther because it might not always be written in classical prose. Despite the similarity with Qoh 8:11 (where verb מלא is intransitive), the meaning is the same as the phrase 'whose heart (or, spirit) incited' to do something (with verb נדב or נשא); see Exod 25:2; 35:21, 29, and compare 1 Chr 29:9, 31. With (18b) compare an Imperial Aramaic passage from Ahiqar 107: *mn hw zy yqm qdmwhy* 'Who is (P) he (S), that is, the one who could stand up in front of him? (App)'; see Contini, *Tipologia*, 66.

73. Literally, 'Why is this, namely, the fact that I have a birthright?'

74. Literally in (20b), 'Why is this, namely, the fact that you have left the man?'

75. Literally, 'What is this thing, namely, the fact that you have done to us?'

76. Literally, 'What is this, namely, the fact that it happened to the son of Kish?'

77. The phrase וְעַד־אָבִיךָ is a *casus pendens* placed before the interrogative pronoun—a rare case. Literally, 'and (as for) to your father, why is this, namely the fact that you should bring me (to him)?' See (20b) and (21a).

78. Literally, 'Who are you, namely, the fact that you have called to the king?'

79. Literally, 'What is this, namely, the fact that you have returned?'

Similar to (22b) (App = כִּי + finite verb)—Gen 37:26; Exod 3:11, 32:21, etc.[80]

In some cases, a slot for *casus pendens* (Pd) is added before the sentence P–S. In (25)–(26) both the slot of *casus pendens* and apposition (App) are present.

| | App | S | P | Pd |
|---|---|---|---|---|
| (23a) | | ‎----אֵינֶנּוּ[81] | | הַיֶּלֶד |
| (23b) | | אֲנִי־בָא | אָנָה | וַאֲנִי |
| (24) | אוֹלִיךְ אֶת־חֶרְפָּתִי | | אָנָה | וַאֲנִי |
| (25) | כִּי תִלּוֹנוּ ‎[qere תַלִּינוּ] עָלָיו | הוּא | ‎־מַה | וְאַהֲרֹן |
| (26) | כִּי תִלּוֹנוּ ‎[qere תַלִּינוּ] עָלֵינוּ | ‎[82]— | מָה | וְנַחְנוּ |

(23) (Reuben said) As for the lad, he is not there; and as for me, where shall I go? (Gen 37:30)

(24) (Tamar said to Amnon) As for me, where could I carry my shame? (2 Sam 13:13)

(25) (Moses said to Korah and his company) As for Aaron, what is he that you murmur against him? (Num 16:11)[83]

(26) (Moses and Aaron said to the people) As for us, what are we, that you murmur against us? (Exod 16:7; cf. 16:8)[84]

In at least one case, *casus pendens* and apposition are attested one after the other before the interrogative sentence P–S. In the following example, the interrogative sentence is indirect; this, however, makes no difference in terms of sentences structure:

---

80. Among the many texts with כִּי + *qatal* or *yiqtol*, one finds several variant constructions, such as אֲשֶׁר + *yiqtol* (Exod 5:2), *wĕyiqtol* (1 Sam 20:4), *waw-x-yiqtol* (2 Sam 15:4), and *wĕqatal* (2 Sam 21:3). Each construction, of course, plays a distinctive function.

81. Since אֵינֶנּוּ is a complete sentence, composed of the "quasi-verb" אֵין and the pronominal suffix as its subject, the preceding noun הַיֶּלֶד is a *casus pendens*; literally, 'As for the lad, he is not there'.

82. In the light of (25), S is implied here.

83. What precedes in Num 16:11 is difficult to analyze. One possibility is to take הַנֹּעָדִים עַל־יְהוָה as S and the previous phrase אַתָּה וְכָל־עֲדָתְךָ as the syntactical predicate. Literally, 'Therefore, it is you and all your company (P) that gathered together against the LORD (S)'. If so, it is a cleft sentence because the usual roles are reversed; that is, the pronoun and the noun are the predicate instead of the subject and, vice versa, the participle is the subject instead of the predicate.

84. Other cases similar to (24)–(26) are 1 Sam 20:8 and 1 Chr 21:17 = 2 Sam 24:17 (see [7] above).

|  | S | P | Pd / App |
|---|---|---|---|
| (27a) |  |  | כִּי־זֶה מֹשֶׁה (Pd) |
| (27b) |  |  | הָאִישׁ אֲשֶׁר הֶעֱלָנוּ מֵאֶרֶץ מִצְרַיִם (App) |
| (27c) | הָיָה לוֹ | לֹא יָדַעְנוּ מֶה־ |  |

(27) (The people said to Aaron, Up, make us gods . . .) for, as for this Moses, the man who let us come up from the land of Egypt, we do not know what happened to him. (Exod 32:1)

**2.3.** Demonstrative Pronoun

|  | App | S | P |
|---|---|---|---|
| (28) | בְּהִבָּרְאָם | תּוֹלְדוֹת הַשָּׁמַיִם וְהָאָרֶץ | אֵלֶּה |
| (29) | אֲשֶׁר־אֲנִי נֹתֵן בֵּינִי וּבֵינֵיכֶם | אוֹת־הַבְּרִית | זֹאת |
| (30) | אֲשֶׁר הֲקִמֹתִי | אוֹת־הַבְּרִית | זֹאת |
| (31) | לַעֲשׂוֹת | הַחֲלֹם | וְזֶה |
| (32) | מִשְׁפַּחַת הַלֵּוִי לְבֵית אֲבֹתָם | הֵם | אֵלֶּה |
| (33) | עוֹד עָצוּר מִפְּנֵי שָׁאוּל בֶּן־קִישׁ | הַבָּאִים אֶל־דָּוִיד לְצִיקְלַג | וְאֵלֶּה |
| (34) |  | אֲשֶׁר לַלְוִיִּם | זֹאת |
| (35) |  | אֲשֶׁר תַּעֲשֶׂה אֹתָהּ | וְזֶה |
| (36a) |  | בְּנֵי־נֹחַ | שְׁלֹשָׁה אֵלֶּה |
| (36b) |  | נָפְצָה כָל־הָאָרֶץ | וּמֵאֵלֶּה |
| (37a) | מֶלֶךְ הָאָרֶץ | דָּוִד | הֲלוֹא־זֶה |
| (37b) |  | יַעֲנוּ בַמְּחֹלוֹת לֵאמֹר | הֲלוֹא לָזֶה |

(28) These are the generations of the heavens and the earth when they were created. (Gen 2:4)[85]

(29) (God said to Noah) This is the sign of the covenant that I am going to make between me and you. . . . (Gen 9:12)

(30) (God said to Noah) This is the sign of the covenant that I have established (between me and all flesh that is upon the earth). (Gen 9:17)

---

85. This type of sentence is headed by a demonstrative pronoun whose referent is presented in the following context (that is, it is a cataphoric demonstrative). The pronoun is P as recognized, for example, by Contini, *Tipologia*, 49–50.

(31) (The LORD said) And this is their beginning to do (things). (Gen 11:6)

(32) These are the families of the Levites,[86] by their fathers' houses. (Num 3:20)

(33) And these are those who came to David at Ziklag, while (David) was still barred from the presence of Saul the son of Kish. (1 Chr 12:1)

(34) (The LORD said to Moses) This is what pertains to the Levites. (Num 8:24)[87]

(35) (God said to Noah) It is this how you shall do it. (Gen 6:15)[88]

(36) These three were the sons of Noah; and from these the whole earth was peopled. (Gen 9:19)[89]

(37) (The servants of Achish said to him) Is not this David the king of the land? Is it not of this that they sang to one another in dances saying . . . ? (1 Sam 21:12 [11])[90]

Other examples are as follows:

Similar to (28) (S = noun)—Gen 5:1, 6:9, 40:12.
Similar to (29)–(30) (S = noun, App = אֲשֶׁר clause)—Gen 17:10, 25:12, 35:26, 36:5.
Similar to (31) (S = infinitive)—Ruth 2:7.[91]

---

86. Literally, 'These are they, namely the families . . .'. A similar expression is found without the personal pronoun as S; see Num 26:14, 18, 22, 25, 27, etc. The two constructions, with and without a personal pronoun, are found one after the other in 1 Chr 8:6: 'These are the sons of Ehud (וְאֵלֶּה בְּנֵי אֵחוּד). They were heads of fathers' houses (אֵלֶּה הֵם רָאשֵׁי אָבוֹת) of the inhabitants of Geba'; and 22:1: '(Then David said) This is the house of the LORD God (זֶה הוּא בֵּית יְהֹוָה הָאֱלֹהִים 'this is it, namely the house of the LORD God') and this is the altar (וְזֶה־מִּזְבֵּחַ) for burnt offering for Israel'. See discussion in §1.2 above.

87. The rest of the sentence has the structure x-*yiqtol*, which puts emphasis on the "x" element (the new element, or the predicate), and therefore it is a cleft sentence; literally, 'It is from twenty-five years old and upward that they shall go in (the verb is singular in Hebrew) to perform the work in the service of the tent of meeting'.

88. Literally, 'It is this what-you-shall-do-it'. Compare, without אֲשֶׁר, 'It is thus and thus (P) the fact that Micah has done to me (כָּזֹה וְכָזֶה עָשָׂה לִי מִיכָה) (S)' (Judg 18:4).

89. The S is a noun in (36a) as in (28)–(30), while it is a *qatal* in (36b). See (37) and discussion in §3.1 below.

90. As in (36), S is represented by a noun in (37a) and by a finite verb, this time *yiqtol*, in (37b).

91. Literally, 'And this is (P) her sitting aside (?) for a while (S)'; see my "Syntactic Analysis of Ruth," *Liber Annuus* 45 (1995) 69–106, esp. 82 n. 24.

Similar to (32) (S = personal pronoun)—Gen 25:16;[92] Num 3:20, 21, 27, 33;
1 Sam 4:8; 1 Chr 1:31.

Similar to (33) (S = participle)—2 Sam 18:26, 1 Chr 6:18.[93]

Similar to (34) (S = nonverbal clause)—2 Chr 19:2.[94]

Similar to (35) (S = אֲשֶׁר + finite verb)—Gen 44:5,[95] 49:28; Exod 29:38; Num
34:29; Deut 14:12; Josh 13:32, 14:1; Jer 33:16;[96] 1 Chr 6:16.

Similar to (36b) and (37b) (S = finite verb)—Gen 34:15, 22; 37:32; 42:15,
33; Exod 7:17; Judg 7:4;[97] Gen 42:18; 43:11; 45:17, 19; Lev 20:23; Num
4:19.[98]

---

92. See an analysis of this passage in §1.2.

93. In 1 Kgs 3:22–23, the phrase זֹאת אֹמֶרֶת 'this one was saying' (in 3:22, historical narrative) or 'this one says' (in 3:23, direct speech) is a different type of sentence from the sentence we are studying. It is a presentative sentence, that is, the narrator in 1 Kgs 3:22, or the
speaker in 3:23, is describing the situation. In 3:23, we find a contrast between 'She says
(זֹאת אֹמֶרֶת) . . . while she says (וְזֹאת אֹמֶרֶת)'; however, the speech situation shows that the
king is simply presenting the state of affairs, not putting any emphasis on the demonstrative
pronoun occurring in the first place of the sentence. Indeed, the claim of the two mothers is
interesting to analyze. It is expressed by two contrastive sentences with the pattern P–S.
Both P and S are definite—a noun with pronominal suffix and a participle or adjective with
article, respectively. Here is 1 Kgs 3:23: 'The one says, "It is this my son (P) the one alive
(S; זֶה־בְּנִי הַחַי), and it is your son (P) the one dead (S; וּבְנֵךְ הַמֵּת)"; while the other says, "No;
but it is your son (P) the one dead (S; בְּנֵךְ הַמֵּת), and it is my son (P) the one living (S;
וּבְנִי הֶחָי)" '.

94. Literally, 'For, it is because of this (P) that wrath from before the LORD is upon you
(S; וּבָזֹאת עָלֶיךָ קֶצֶף מִלִּפְנֵי יְהוָה)'. The previous sentences also interest our research: '(Jehu
the seer said to King Jehoshaphat) Is it the wicked (P) that one shall help (S; הֲלָרָשָׁע לַעְזֹר),
and is it to those who hate the LORD (P) that you shall show love (S; וּלְשֹׂנְאֵי יְהוָה תֶּאֱהָב)?'
Both sentences show a P–S pattern; in the first sentence, S is a prepositional phrase with an
infinitive (לַעְזֹר), while in the second it is a finite verb (תֶּאֱהָב). We have here a further proof
that the finite verb in the second position of the sentence plays a nominal function. Its English equivalent is the cleft sentence, that is, a sentence split into two, the second one being
relative ('it is . . . that . . .'). In BH, however, there is only one sentence; see discussion in
§3.1 below.

95. Literally, 'Is it not this (P) what-my-lord-used-to-drink-from-it? (S; הֲלוֹא זֶה אֲשֶׁר
יִשְׁתֶּה אֲדֹנִי בּוֹ)'.

96. Literally, 'And it is this (P) what one shall call it (S) (וְזֶה אֲשֶׁר־יִקְרָא־לָהּ)'.

97. The opposition 'This man shall go (זֶה יֵלֵךְ) with you' / 'This man shall not go (זֶה
לֹא־יֵלֵךְ) with you' shows that emphasis falls on the demonstrative pronoun found in first
position in the sentence. However, this is not always the case with x-*yiqtol* constructions because the indicative (nonvolitive) *yiqtol* is a second-position verb form per se (that is, x-
*yiqtol*); see my paper, "A Neglected Point of Hebrew Syntax: Yiqtol and Position in the Sentence," *Liber Annuus* 37 (1987) 7–19, §1. For instance, in the sentence זֶה יְנַחֲמֵנוּ 'He will
comfort us' (Gen 5:29), no emphasis appears to fall on the demonstrative pronoun; it simply
predicts the future.

98. In Gen 42:18; 43:11; 45:17, 19; Lev 20:23; and Num 4:19, the finite verb is an
imperative.

## 3. Summary and Evaluation

### 3.1. Marked Sentence and Cleft Sentence

Three sentence patterns have been examined having a pronoun—personal (persPro), interrogative (interrPro), or demonstrative (demPro)—in the first place of the sentence with the function of P. Different grammatical elements were found to fill the slot of S. They are as follows:

1. noun (adjective or substantive): (persPro) (1); (interrPro) (9), (22a); (demPro) (28)–(30);
2. pronoun: (persPro) (6); (interrPro) (10a); (16); (17)–(19); (20b); (21a); (25); (demPro) (32);
3. participle: (persPro) (2); (interrPro) (11); (demPro) (33);
4. infinitive: (demPro) (31);
5. nonverbal clause: (interrPro) (13a); (23b); (demPro) (34);
6. אֲשֶׁר + finite verb: (persPro) (3); (demPro) (35);
7. finite verb: (persPro) (4a); (interrPro) (14a); (24); (27c); (demPro) (36b); (37b);
8. prepositional phrase: (interrPro) (12).

For the principle of paradigmatic substitution, the constructions that fill the same slot are interchangeable from the point of view of their syntactical function; however, because they are grammatically different, they are not entirely equivalent (see [38]–[41] below).

The fact that a finite verb form (no. 7) interchanges with a noun or a noun equivalent (nos. 1–4), including a prepositional phrase (no. 8), with a nonverbal clause (no. 5), and with a finite verb form nominalized with אֲשֶׁר (no. 6) means that in this position (second in the sentence) and with this function (of S), a finite verb is equivalent to a noun. Therefore, the sentence is nominal although it contains a finite verb form.

To express this fact more stringently, let us compare some specific cases. The general question "What have you done?" is attested in the following forms:

|        | S | P |
|--------|---|---|
| (38)   | הַדָּבָר הַזֶּה אֲשֶׁר עָשִׂיתָ | מָה־ |
| (39)   | הַדָּבָר הַזֶּה עָשִׂיתָ | מָה־ |
| (40)   | זֹאת עָשִׂיתָ | מַה־ |
| (41)   | עָשִׂיתָ | מֶה |

(38) What is    this thing, which you have done? (2 Sam 12:21)

(39) What is    the-fact-that-you-have-done-this-thing? (Judg 8:1)

(40) What is    the-fact-that-you-have-done-this? (Gen 12:18)[99]

(41) What is    the-fact-that-you-have-done? (Gen 4:10)[100]

A parallel passage from 2 Sam 24:17 (42) and 1 Chr 21:17 (already quoted in part above, [7]) is worth notice:[101]

| | S | P | Pd |
|---|---|---|---|
| (42a) | חָטָאתִי | הִנֵּה אָנֹכִי | |
| (42b) | הֶעֱוֵיתִי | וְאָנֹכִי | |
| (42c) | עָשׂוּ | מֶה | וְאֵלֶּה הַצֹּאן |
| (7a) | אָמַרְתִּי לִמְנוֹת בָּעָם | הֲלֹא אֲנִי | |
| (7b) | הוּא אֲשֶׁר־חָטָאתִי . . . | וַאֲנִי־ | |
| (7c) | עָשׂוּ | מֶה | וְאֵלֶּה הַצֹּאן |

(42) Lo, it is I    that sinned,
   and it is I    that did evil, while these sheep,
   what    have they done?

(7) Is it not I    that gave command to number the people,
   and it is I    this, namely the one who have sinned . . . while these sheep,
   what    have they done?

Clearly, אָנֹכִי חָטָאתִי (42a) is equivalent to אֲנִי־הוּא אֲשֶׁר־חָטָאתִי (7b). This means that a finite verb form (see [41], [42], and [7a, c]) is used exactly with the same function as a noun or pronoun (see [38]–[40] and [7b]).

What has been observed in sentences with a finite verb form is similarly attested in sentences without a finite verb form. For instance, the question "What are you doing?" is expressed as follows:

| | S | P |
|---|---|---|
| (43) | הַדָּבָר הַזֶּה אֲשֶׁר אַתָּה עֹשֶׂה | מָה־ |
| (44) | אַתָּה עֹשֶׂה | מָה־ |

(43) What is    this thing, which you are doing? (Exod 18:14)

(44) What is    the-fact-that-you-are-doing? (Judg 18:3, Ezek 24:19)

---

99. Cf. Gen 26:10, 29:25; Exod 14:11; Judg 15:11; Jonah 1:10.
100. Cf. Gen 20:9, 31:26; Num 23:11; Josh 7:19; 1 Sam 13:11, 14:43; 2 Sam 3:24.
101. I have drawn the attention of scholars to this text more than once; see my *Syntax*, 26, §6; idem, "Marked Syntactical Structures," §§1–2; idem, "Finite Verb," 435 (example 2).

The function of these types of sentences is to emphasize the nonverbal element occurring in the first place and at the same time to nominalize the finite verb. As a consequence, the finite verb is demoted to the role of S, while the nonverbal element is promoted to the role of P.[102] The corresponding syntactical structure is the *cleft sentence* in English, the *phrase coupée* in French, and the *frase scissa* in Italian.[103] This correspondence applies not only to a sentence with an interrogative pronoun but also to a sentence with a personal and a demonstrative pronoun in first position (see analysis in §2 above). The most explicit or "analytical" type of sentence attested in BH can be translated almost word-by-word into English:

| (3) | הֲלוֹא־הוּא | It is not he |
| | אֲשֶׁר הֵסִיר הִזְקִיָּהוּ אֶת־בָּמֹתָיו | whose high places . . . Hezekiah has removed? |
| (35) | וְזֶה | It is this |
| | אֲשֶׁר תַּעֲשֶׂה אֹתָהּ | that you shall make it. |
| (38) | מַה־ | What is |
| | הַדָּבָר הַזֶּה אֲשֶׁר עָשִׂיתָה | this thing, which you have done? |
| (43) | מָה־ | What is |
| | הַדָּבָר הַזֶּה אֲשֶׁר אַתָּה עֹשֶׂה | this thing, which you are doing? |

The corresponding plain or unmarked sentences are as follows: for (3), 'Hezekiah removed the high places *of the* LORD'; for (35), 'You shall make it *that way*'; and for (38) and (43), 'He did / is doing *something*'. A marked sentence is employed in each case to highlight a nonverbal element of the plain sentence; the highlighted element (in italics above) is the grammatical complement in (3) and (35), and the grammatical object in (38) and (43).

---

102. Rosén (" אנכי and אני") correctly accords predicative value to אָנֹכִי in some specific cases. However, it seems difficult to believe that אֲנִי cannot have the same value; see, for example, (7) and (42). Further, Rosén only discusses the first-person pronoun, and his criterion of analysis is purely semantic. Therefore, several of his proposals may be questionable.

103. As already mentioned, the structure of the "cleft sentence" served as a model for H. J. Polotsky to explain the function of "emphatic forms" in ancient Egyptian and "second tenses" in Coptic; see his second essay in *Etudes de syntaxe copte*. In his last major study, "Les transpositions du verbe," he explains that the French terms "construction 'plane'" and "vedette" correspond to "plain sentence" and "cleft sentence," respectively (Polotsky borrows them from J. Damourette and E. Pichon, *Des mots à la pensée*: *Essai de grammaire de la langue française* [7 vols.; Paris: Collection des linguistes contemporains, 1926–49], vol. 4, §1554). Polotsky writes as follows: "Pareille mise en vedette implique un revirement des valeurs syntactiques. Le membre non verbal à mettre en vedette est élevé au rang de prédicat, tandis que le verb est dégradé à celui de sujet" (p. 15). He then goes on to show that old Egyptian and Coptic produce this transformation from plain to cleft sentence by means of morphologically nominal verb forms.

The main difference between BH and English in sentences with a personal pronoun (3) or a demonstrative pronoun (35) in first position is that in English (as well as in French and in Italian) the marked sentence is "clefted" into two sentences. The first sentence is constructed "It is . . ."; the second "that . . ." ("c'est . . . que" in French; "è . . . che" in Italian). On the other hand, in BH we have just one sentence, with a pronoun in first position as P and the rest as S.[104] As shown above, the syntactic subject can be a noun, noun phrase, or even a complete clause, with a grammatical subject and predicate embedded in the superordinate sentence (see diagram, §1.1 above). However, the structure of the sentence with an interrogative pronoun in the first place (see [38] and [43]) is exactly the same in BH and in English. The English sentence is not "clefted" in this case, because P ("what") is co-referential to the following S.

This comparison of the corresponding marked structures of BH and other languages shows that the most notable phenomenon is the nominalization of the verb. This is done by prefixing the relative "that/which" in the English cleft sentence (and the corresponding relative pronoun in the French and Italian constructions). In BH the verb is nominalized in different ways, that is, either morphologically by using the participle (no. 3 above) or the infinitive (no. 4), or syntactically by prefixing the relative particle אֲשֶׁר (no. 6). A further way, distinctive of BH, of nominalizing a finite verb is by simply putting it in second place in the sentence (no. 7).[105] This is possible because the word

---

104. According to Goldenberg ("Tautological Infinitive," 67), BH lacks "explicit cleft sentences." However, if, in his words, "the syntactical structure for turning any part of the sentence into a 'logical predicate' is that of the fairly common, though not always adequately analyzed, Cleft Sentence," then BH does have such a structure. In fact, if (as H. J. Polotsky has shown for ancient Egyptian and Coptic; see previous footnote) the way to turn a nonverbal element of the sentence into a "logical (or syntactical, in my terminology) predicate" is nominalizing the verb, then BH does this both explicitly (with אֲשֶׁר) and implicitly, but equally effectively, by putting the verb in second position in the sentence. Further, in regard to Goldenberg's discussion on p. 51, I would say that in BH the cleft sentence does not concern the finite verb. In fact, the way of turning the verb into the "logical (or syntactical) predicate" is simply to put it in sentence-initial position. The cleft sentence serves to transform a nonverbal element into the "logical (or syntactical) predicate."

105. See my *Syntax*, 29, §6. BH may share this characteristic with other Semitic languages that show an unmarked type of sentence with the finite verb initial and a rather fixed word order (the so-called "VSO word order"). See, e.g., A. Gianto, *Word Order Variation in the Akkadian of Byblos* (Rome: Pontifical Biblical Institute, 1990) 5 n. 8. Gianto lists a number of studies on word order in different Semitic languages (Hebrew, Aramaic, Ugaritic, Arabic, comparative Semitic, classical Ethiopic, Akkadian, and Northwest Semitic). The Mesha inscription shows the same syntax of the verb as BH; see my paper "The Stele of Mesha and the Bible." The cases, for example, where some grammarians of Semitic languages consider a noun to be placed before a finite verb for the sake of emphasis are actually marked sentences and are appropriately translated with cleft sentences in English. According to Zewi ("Subject–Predicate"), the word order of the nominal sentence in El-Amarna Letters is not fixed. Still, the distinction between predicative and nonpredicative, presentative sentences may be useful; see (15a) above; Gen 32:19 (n. 63 above); 1 Kgs 3:22–23

order in BH is fixed, and the first position in the sentence belongs to the predicate.[106] The basic tenet is that two fundamental sentence-types exist in BH: (1) finite verb–x ("x" being any nonverbal element: subject, object, indirect complement, or adverb); and (2) x–finite verb. Type (1) underlies the unmarked sentence and type (2) the marked sentence.[107]

I should note that the marked type of sentence "x–finite verb" is different from the construction with *casus pendens*. While the "x" nonverbal element of the marked type is part of the sentence (it is P in the cases examined in the present paper), the *casus pendens* constitutes a sentence by itself—it is not part of the following sentence, which is complete without it. This results from the previous analysis; see (5a), (23)–(26), (42c), and similar passages quoted in connection with these examples.[108]

Finally, the syntactical equivalence between a subject represented by a noun or noun phrase and another represented by a finite verb does not annul the grammatical difference that exists between the two constructions. Compare, for instance, the following examples:

| | S | P |
|---|---|---|
| (45) | בְּנֵי עָדָה אֵשֶׁת עֵשָׂו | אֵלֶּה |
| (46) | הָיוּ בְּנֵי בָשְׂמַת אֵשֶׁת עֵשָׂו | אֵלֶּה |
| (47) | יִהְיֶה לָכֶם גְּבוּל נֶגֶב | זֶה־ |

---

(n. 93 above); Gen 24:25 (n. 119 below). Presentative sentences are also found in Moabite (see n. 125 below) as well as in other languages. Concerning this formula in the El-Amarna Letters, 'I am your servant . . . / your loyal servant' (see Zewi, "Subject–Predicate," §3), I would observe that it can have a predicative as well as a nonpredicative, presentative function. Accordingly, the word order is predicate–subject and subject–predicate, respectively, exactly as we find in Gen 24:24 (predicate–subject) versus Gen 27:32 (subject–predicate); see my "Simple Nominal Clause," 220. (In the latter article, ad loc., read "(S) *'nky*" instead of "(P) *'nky*," under Gen 24:24.)

106. See discussion in §3.3 below. This analysis does not correspond to Goldenberg's, in "Imperfectly-Transformed Cleft Sentences," which is adopted by Zewi (n. 36 above). With or without אֲשֶׁר, the finite verb is functionally nominalized when it occupies second position in the sentence.

107. As I have repeatedly observed, from these two basic patterns all types of sentence are generated and all kinds of intersentence relationships in prose texts can be analyzed. See my paper "Finite Verb."

108. Contini (*Tipologia*, 12) discusses the Semitic type of construction called "double-faced sentence" by native, especially Arab, grammarians. It is composed of *mubtada'* ('what begins, the inchoative') and the *habar* ('the enunciative, the declaration'). In a special type of this structure, the *mubtada'* is nominal and the *habar* is a nominal sentence. Contini correctly criticizes D. Cohen, who maintains that this "double-faced sentence" and the construction "subject + verb" are similar. But Contini's own analysis is hardly correct, because he thinks that the *casus pendens* is the "logical subject" of the following sentence.

(48)                         גְּבוּל נֶגֶב            זֶה

(45) These are      the sons of Adah, Esau's wife. (Gen 36:12b)

(46) These were     the sons of Basemath, Esau's wife. (Gen 36:13b)

(47) This shall be   your south boundary. (Josh 15:4)

(48) This is        the southern border. (Josh 18:19)

Without a finite form of verb היה (examples [45], [48]), the sentence refers to the present;[109] however, with a *qatal* form of this verb, the sentence refers to the past (46), and with a *yiqtol* form of the same verb, it refers to the future (47). Indeed, the verb היה is not an optional element of the sentence, and its function does not correspond to the function of a copula in classical languages. Further, it is not a fossilized auxiliary, not even when it introduces a circumstance.[110] In most cases, the verb היה is an incomplete predication, meaning 'to be(come) (such and such)', just as other verbs are, for example, 'to do, to model (in such and such form)', 'to see, to find (in such and such state)', and so on, but היה is also found as a complete predication, meaning 'to exist'.[111] A further consequence, with direct reference to our topic, is that a sentence with a finite form of the verb היה is not nominal per se but is verbal or nominal as is any other verb form.

### 3.2. Defining the Nominal Sentence

We are now in a position to define a nominal sentence. Grammatically, only a sentence without a finite verb form (including a form of the verb היה) is nominal, but syntactically a sentence with a finite verb form in second position is also nominal because the verb plays the role of a noun.[112] The

---

109. When it is independent in direct speech, a sentence without a finite verb (in other words, a "simple noun clause") indicates present tense; only when it is circumstantial is it atemporal per se and assumes a time reference from the main verb form to which it relates. See my *Syntax*, §53; idem, "Essential Hebrew Syntax," *Narrative and Comment: Contributions Presented to Wolfgang Schneider* (ed. E. Talstra; Amsterdam: Hebraica Amstelodamensis, 1995) §2.1; idem, "Basic Facts," §9.2.

110. Reference is made here to the "macrosyntactic" function of וַיְהִי and וְהָיָה introducing a "double sentence" composed of protasis and apodosis, called "two-element syntactic construction (2SC) (protasis-apodosis)" in my *Syntax*, chap. 8. The function of וַיְהִי and וְהָיָה is to render the "double sentence" (which is nonverbal per se) verbal. See ibid., §127.

111. Full exposition is found in my paper "Sullo stato sintattico del verbo *hāyâ*."

112. This analysis confirms the definition put forward by Arab grammarians. On this definition, consult G. Goldenberg, "Subject and Predicate in Arab Grammatical Tradition," *ZDMG* 138 (1988) 39–73. On the problems posed by this definition for word order in a sentence without a finite verb, see Cohen, *La phrase*, 53–56. Contrary to what Cohen, among others, assumes (pp. 37, 56), the neutral or unmarked word order in this kind of sentence is predicate–subject as is the sentence with a finite verb. This means that the marked word order is subject–predicate, not vice versa.

three types of sentence illustrated above (§§2.1–3) prove this in an unequivo-cal way.[113]

One should carefully distinguish nominal and verbal function, on the one hand, from syntactical predication, on the other. According to the evidence presented in this paper, a sentence is nominal when it contains no finite verb form or contains a finite verb form in second position. However, a sentence can be predicative both with and without a finite verb form. In other words, predication is not the exclusive function of the finite verb; we have real predi-cation even without a finite verb form.[114]

It is more important to determine the difference between unmarked and marked types of sentences. A sentence with a finite verb is (a) unmarked, or plain, when the verb appears initially; it is (b) marked when the verb appears second. In (a), the emphasis falls on the verb itself, and the sentence is verbal. A verbal sentence conveys information at the main level of communication (according to H. Weinrich's textlinguistics). In (b), the sentence is nominal. In this case, either the emphasis falls on the nonverbal element that occupies the first place, or the sentence as a whole is made syntactically dependent. A nominal sentence conveys information at a secondary level of communication (according to H. Weinrich's textlinguistics).[115]

---

113. The problem remains how to explain the many sentences of the marked type (that is, with a finite verb in second position, x-*qatal*, or x-*yiqtol*) that, according to the speech situation or context, do not signal any emphasis on the "x" element (that is, "x" is not P but keeps its grammatical function of subject, object, complement, or adverb, according to its nature). I have suggested that in these cases the sentence is syntactically dependent. In other words, the very fact of putting the finite verb in second position demotes it from its normal role of P to that of S. At the same time, it promotes a nonverbal element from its grammati-cal role of subject, object, complement, or adverb to that of P (when the nonverbal element is emphasized); alternatively, the whole sentence is made dependent on another one having the finite verb in first position, that is, a syntactically verbal sentence (when the nonverbal element is not emphasized). On this, consult my "Marked Syntactical Structures," §6; idem, "Finite Verb"; and §3.3 below.

114. É. Benveniste clearly distinguished "verbal function" from the verb; see Contini, *Tipologia*, 8. Because of this fact, I prefer to speak of *predicative function* instead of *verbal function*. See n. 1 above.

115. I have illustrated this position with selected examples as well as with complete texts in, besides *Syntax*, the following publications: *Lettura sintattica della prosa ebraico-biblica: Principi e applicazioni* (Jerusalem: Franciscan Printing Press, 1991) (on Joshua 1–6; Judges 1–4, 6; 2 Samuel 5–7 // 1 Chronicles 11–17); idem, "Diluvio, sintassi e metodo," *Liber Annuus* 44 (1994) 9–46 (on Gen 6:9–8:22); idem, "Analysis of Biblical Narrative," *Biblical Hebrew and Discourse Linguistics* (ed. R. D. Bergen; Dallas: Summer Institute of Linguistics, 1994) 175–98 (on Genesis 1–3); idem, "Syntactic Analysis of Ruth," 69–106 (on the whole book); idem, "Workshop: Narrative Syntax of Exodus 19–24," *Narrative Syn-tax and the Hebrew Bible: Papers of the Tilburg Conference 1996* (Biblical Interpretation Series 29; Leiden: Brill, 1997) 203–28 (on Exod 19:1–20:17, 20:18–23:33, 24:1–8); and in idem, "Syntactic Analysis of Jonah" (on the whole book).

In the sentence that contains no finite verb, the situation is similar, with the difference being that the criterion is not the position of the verb but the quality of its constituents. In fact, the constituent playing the function of P and S can be a "universal term" (that is, an indefinite common noun, an abstract term, a participle, or an adjective) or a "particular term" (that is, a proper name, a pronoun, or a definite noun). When the element occupying first place (which is the position of the predicate in BH) is a universal term, the sentence is unmarked; the emphasis falls on the universal term, which is expected in the function of the predicate. On the other hand, when the element occupying first place is a particular term, the sentence is marked; the emphasis falls on the particular term, which is not expected in the function of the predicate.

Unmarked sentences, both with and without a finite verb form, put emphasis on an element that belongs to the class of the predicate by definition—that is, the verb and the universal term, respectively; marked sentences, both with and without a finite verb form, put emphasis on an element that does not belong to the class of the predicate—that is, a nonverbal element and a particular term, respectively.

**3.3.** Discussion of the Constituents of the Nominal Sentence

The sentence, both with and without a finite verb, consists of two main slots: P and S.

We mentioned above that two additional slots can be appended to a nominal sentence: *casus pendens* and apposition (see §1.1). *Casus pendens*, on the one hand, does not belong to the sentence to which it is prefixed, although it is closely associated with it; it constitutes a separate sentence that plays the role of the protasis while the following main sentence plays the role of the apodosis.[116] Apposition, on the other hand, is placed at the margin of a sentence for the sake of specification.[117] Both *casus pendens* and *apposition* are traditional terms. In modern terminology they are called *topicalization* or *left-* (or *front-*) *dislocation* and *right-* (or *rear-*)*dislocation*, respectively.[118] I still prefer to use

---

116. The so-called *casus pendens* is a frequently misunderstood construction; see my discussion in "Marked Syntactical Structures," esp. §8, and C. Bally's correct analysis, which I quoted on p. 49 in "Marked Syntactical Structures." The fact that the *casus pendens* functions as the protasis is demonstrated, among other things, by comparing two parallel passages in Num 21:8–9. In this passage, כָּל־הַנָּשׁוּךְ 'every one who shall be bitten' is equivalent to אִם־נָשַׁךְ הַנָּחָשׁ אֶת־אִישׁ 'if the serpent would have bitten someone'; consult my "Finite Verb," 437 (read there 'would have bitten' instead of 'would bite' because the verb form, a *qatal*, indicates anteriority).

117. Remember R. Huddleston's definition of apposition quoted above (§2.1); and see my "Marked Syntactical Structures," §8.2, where examples are quoted from the Hebrew Bible, the LXX, and the NT.

118. Some linguists posit a difference between *topicalization* (with a resumptive pronoun) and *left-dislocation* (without a resumptive pronoun); see W. A. Foley and R. D. van

the traditional terminology, especially *casus pendens*, for the sake of clarity. In fact, considerable complexity (not to say confusion) reigns among modern linguists. This is due to the fact that the difference between the lower level of grammar and syntax (in other words, the sentence and the text) and the higher level of literary composition is not infrequently disregarded or mixed up. Clearly, I do not speak in terms of literary composition but of grammar and syntax only.

P and S are the main constituents of a sentence.[119] However, the subject can be implied in the finite verb form, or it can be inferred from the context. There is no need to cite examples of the first possibility; for the second possibility, see (4b), (13b), (14b), (15b–c), (26). By definition, P cannot be implied because it is precisely what the sentence is all about, or the new information. This is an indirect proof that the finite verb, when it is implied (as in the examples just mentioned), is not P.

A final statement on word order in BH, which is a very controversial issue, is appropriate.[120] The controversy arises from insufficient syntactical analysis

---

Valin, Jr, "Information Packing in the Clause," in *Language Typology and Syntactic Description* (ed. T. Shopen; Cambridge: Cambridge University Press, 1985) 1.282–364, §3.1. If one accepts this distinction, one has to say that *casus pendens* is usually "topicalization" but sometimes "front-dislocation," while "apposition" is "right-dislocation." If one speaks of "left/right-dislocation" instead of "front/rear-dislocation," the indications "right" and "left" need, of course, to be reversed in BH.

119. While the syntactical predicate cannot be implied, the grammatical predicate (gP) can be in, for example, the presentative sentence, which shows no syntactical predication. Consider: גַּם־תֶּבֶן גַּם־מִסְפּוֹא רַב עִמָּנוּ גַּם־מָקוֹם לָלוּן 'We have (gP) plenty of straw as well as of provender (gS), and room to lodge in (gS)' (Gen 24:25). Clearly, in the second sentence the grammatical predicate, עִמָּנוּ, is implied.

120. J. Joosten ("The Predicative Participle in Biblical Hebrew," *ZAH* 2 [1989] 128–59) stresses the importance of the participle for expressing present tense in BH. This is not the first time that I have voiced reservations against such a claim; see my "Basic Facts," 198 n. 81. It is significant that Joosten does not deal with nominal sentences not comprising a participle. This choice is not only arbitrary, it also spoils his research. He writes: "I leave aside the so-called nominal clauses. In a sense it is correct to say that the notion of 'tense' is relevant only to verbal clauses. The term 'present tense' is used for statements which refer to time contemporary with the moment of speaking. The use of this term for Biblical Hebrew is not quite exact, see n. 102" (ibid, 128 n. 2). On p. 155 n. 102, Joosten affirms that nonetheless he maintains "the term 'present tense' because it is more expedient than 'the expression of simultaneity with the moment of speaking.'" I would observe, first, that present tense is expressed by a nonverbal sentence without a participle in direct speech (see, for example, [43] and [48] and n. 109 above). Pace Joosten, present tense is a real tense in BH, as are past tense expressed by narrative *wayyiqtol* and future tense expressed by x-*yiqtol* and *wĕqatal* in direct speech. Note that the concept of present tense is different from that of contemporaneity; the latter belongs to aspect and is expressed by a nonverbal clause with circumstantial function. Second, when present in a nonverbal sentence, the participle adds the aspect of continuity ("cursive present"). The participle has no tense value for itself but assumes that of the dominant finite verb in its environment: future, past, or present (see my "Basic Facts,"

on the sentence level and on the text level.[121] Once a precise and coherent analysis of the sentence structures and syntactical patterns is achieved, the problem of word order is automatically settled. The following outline of word order in BH takes into account the results of the present paper and of previous essays mentioned in the footnotes.

(a) Unmarked or plain predicative sentences, both with and without a finite verb, show the pattern P–S. Both P and S are elements expected in their respective roles, as explained in §3.2 above. The emphasis falls on P, which occupies first place.[122]

(b) Marked predicative sentences, both with and without a finite verb, show the pattern P–S. Both P and S are elements not expected in their respective roles, as explained in §3.2 above. The emphasis falls on the nonverbal element or the particular term that occurs in first position. This element is promoted to the role of P, while the finite verb or the universal term is demoted to the role of S.[123]

(c) Marked nonpredicative sentences, both with and without a finite verb, show the same word order as (b). The difference is that no emphasis falls on the element that occupies first place. On the one hand, the nonverbal element or the particular term that heads the sentence is not promoted to the role of P

---

examples 16d, 18e, 22e, and §8). Third, contrary to the main thesis by Joosten in the paper under consideration, word order in the nonverbal sentence with or without a participle is not a question of aspect but of syntactical function as results from the evidence presented in this paper.

121. Until one establishes the syntactical function(s) of the alternative word orders VSO/OVS, statistics do not help, and real progress is hardly possible. See, among recent treatments, K. Jongeling, "On the VSO Character of Classical Hebrew," in *Studies in Hebrew and Aramaic Syntax Presented to Professor J. Hoftijzer on the Occasion of His Sixty-Fifth Birthday* (ed. K. Jongeling, H. L. Murre-van den Berg, and L. van Rompay; Leiden: Brill, 1991) 103–11; and L. J. de Regt, "Word Order in Different Clause Types in Deuteronomy 1–30," *Studies in Hebrew and Aramaic Syntax Presented to Professor J. Hoftijzer*, 152–72. Instead of VSO/SVO, one should speak of syntactical predicate/subject. As for the object, it is an optional satellite (§1.1) unless it occurs sentence-initially.

122. In earlier essays of mine, an unmarked sentence having a finite verb in first position is called a "verbal sentence" while a marked sentence having a finite verb in second position is called a "complex (or compound) noun sentence"; see, e.g., my *Syntax*, 163–67, §§6. The terminology "unmarked/marked sentence" has the advantage of being applicable to sentences without a finite verb as well. Thus, both sentence-types can be described by means of the same pattern, and the coherence of the BH tense system becomes clearer. See my considerations in "Basic Facts," §8. The terms "unmarked/marked sentence" correspond to the "relaxed/excited speech" of V. Mathesius (see Garvin, "Czechoslovakia," 502) and to the "ruhige/erregte rede" of H. Ewald, *Ausführliches Lehrbuch der Hebräischen Sprache des Alten Bundes* (8th ed.; Göttingen: Dieterich, 1870) §306.

123. Examples of the marked predicative sentence with a finite verb include Gen 1:27, Exod 5:17, Judg 1:1–2, 2 Sam 24:17, and Job 32:2–3, which I have analyzed in "Essential Hebrew Syntax," 111–25, esp. p. 115; idem, "Finite Verb," 435.

but plays its role of grammatical subject, object, complement, or adverb, according to its nature. On the other hand, the finite verb or the universal term plays its role of grammatical predicate. However, the whole sentence is syntactically dependent in the sense of needing to rely on another sentence having a finite verb or a universal term in first position; in other words, this kind of sentence cannot stand alone in the text. Circumstantial sentences with a finite verb are x-*qatal* and x-*yiqtol*; they need to rely on a preceding or a following *wayyiqtol*.[124] Marked nonpredicative sentences without a finite verb are either circumstantial or presentative.[125]

---

124. Examples of a "compound nominal sentence" depending on a preceding *wayyiqtol* (i.e., way*yiqtol* → *waw*-x-*qatal*, namely a tense shift from a main-line verb form expressing foreground information to a secondary-line verb form expressing background information) include Gen 4:2b–5a; Exod 18:25–26; Judg 1:25; and 1 Sam 16:22, 26:3, which I have discussed in "Essential Hebrew Syntax," examples 1–4; idem, "Finite Verb," 435–36. Examples of a "compound nominal sentence" depending on a following *wayyiqtol* (that is, *waw*-x-*qatal* → *wayyiqtol*, namely a tense shift from a secondary-line verb form expressing "antecedent information" or the setting of a story to a main-line verb form marking the beginning of the narrative) include Gen 2:5–7, 16:1–2, and 29:16–18, which I have discussed in "Essential Hebrew Syntax," examples 5–7; idem, "Finite Verb," 438–39.

125. In Moabite we find comparable constructions, that is, a presentative sentence with personal pronoun + finite verb (with no emphasis on the personal pronoun) (for example, *ʾnk.mšʿ* 'I am Mesha', *KAI* no. 181 line 1) and a marked construction with personal pronoun + finite verb (with emphasis on the personal pronoun) (for example, *ʾnk.bnty.qrḥh* 'It is I that built Qerihoh', line 21). A marked construction noun + finite verb (with no emphasis on the noun) indicating syntactical dependence is also attested. Consult my paper "The Stele of Mesha and the Bible," esp. §6.

# Semantic and Pragmatic Approaches

❖ ❖ ❖

# Relative Definiteness and the Verbless Clause

## Kirk E. Lowery

*Westminster Theological Seminary, Philadelphia*

## 1. Background

This essay has its roots in a previous study read before the Fourth International Colloquium of the *Association Internationale Bible et Informatique* in 1994.[1] That study was an attempt to present a set of tags of both formal and semantic variables that could be assigned values in a straightforward and systematic way, using rules that could be thought of as "algorithmic." There I argued that a set of purely formal tags—although easier to define and establish rules for encoding—were inadequate.

For the past twenty years, biblical scholars have been toying with the notions of discourse grammar because of its explanatory potential to solve both exegetical and linguistic questions of the Hebrew Bible and its language.[2] It is no surprise that the syntax of Biblical Hebrew has been undergoing considerable reevaluation in recent years, paralleling this interest in Biblical Hebrew

---

1. K. E. Lowery, "The Role of Semantics in the Adequacy of Syntactic Models of Biblical Hebrew," in *Bible and Computer—Desk and Discipline: The Impact of Computers on Biblical Studies* (Proceedings of the AIBI 4th International Colloquium; Travaux de Linguistique Quantitative 57; Paris: Honoré Champion, 1995) 101–28.

2. *Discourse grammar* is a specific theoretical perspective (among the more general theories of text), and the primary theoretician behind it is R. E. Longacre, *The Grammar of Discourse* (New York: Plenum, 1983). For a discussion of how discourse theories relate to Biblical Hebrew, see my "Theoretical Foundations of Hebrew Discourse Grammar," in *Discourse Analysis of Biblical Literature: What It Is and What It Offers* (ed. W. R. Bodine; SBLSS 27; Atlanta: Scholars Press, 1995) 103–30, as well as the other essays in that volume. Another collection representing some of the latest thinking about theory and application is R. D. Bergen (ed.), *Biblical Hebrew and Discourse Linguistics* (Dallas: Summer Institute of Linguistics, 1994).

discourse structure.[3] Just as morphological forms are often made up of combinations or sets of phonemes (that is, from the lower level of the language), so it turns out that discourse concepts such as episodes, participants and their roles, foreground, and background (or mainline and off mainline clauses) are often defined in terms of sets of features in the next lower level of language—syntax.[4]

Discourse analysis is a relatively new and rapidly developing field. There is a multiplicity of theories, proposed discourse notions, and their concomitant linguistic signs. In such an environment, there is a great need, not only for rapid testing and validation of these hypotheses, but also for accuracy in linguistic description. In order to confirm hypotheses, a significant sample of text is needed for validation, both from the standpoint of statistical sampling and from the very nature of discourse analysis itself. The unit of study is not a single sentence or part of a clause but a group of sentences, bodies of text that are related to one another in some way. Such a large body of text, combined with sets of complex variables, makes the task of linguistic description much more complex than it has been in the past.

Fortunately, information technology provides us with a tool to handle this complexity. What is needed is a database of a morphologic and syntactic description of the Hebrew Bible. Such a database can:

- allow rapid cycles of hypothesis testing and theory modification
- handle the complexity of collating *sets* of linguistic features
- provide data whose features are consistently analyzed.

But such a database also comes with unique problems and constraints. The use of databases for statistical confirmation of linguistic theories assumes that the representation of the text in digital form *accurately* represents reality. This means that a hypothesis must clearly predict results and that the definitions used to encode features are absolutely consistent. Inconsistently coded data will provide inconsistent results, although the codes themselves do not show this. The application of any tagging scheme is actually an interpretation of the text. And any use of the computer to tag the text is a *simulation* of the text and

---

3. Even B. Waltke and M. O'Connor acknowledge the force of this thrust (*An Introduction to Biblical Hebrew Syntax* [Winona Lake, Ind.: Eisenbrauns, 1990] 53–55), although they chose not to use the explanatory power of discourse analysis, being content with classic descriptive syntax.

4. This is even more frequently experienced when attempting to give operational definitions of classic literary concepts in linguistic terms. For one of the more sophisticated attempts to apply this approach to Biblical Hebrew, see N. Winther-Nielsen, *A Functional Discourse Grammar of Joshua: A Computer-Assisted Rhetorical Structure Analysis* (ConBOT 40; Stockholm: Almqvist & Wiksell, 1995) 79–96.

therefore only an approximation of reality. With improper coding techniques, it is possible to prejudice the tagging and read the desired results into the criteria used to encode the text. Worse, it is possible to confirm or disconfirm hypotheses with data that accurately reflects the database—a database that imperfectly models reality.

The elements of a computer-assisted linguistic database are: (1) the text itself, (2) the linguistic feature set used to describe the text, (3) the descriptions and definitions of those features, and (4) the criteria and practices used to encode those features, using their descriptions and definitions. Since the computer is absolutely consistent in its actions, following mindlessly and ruthlessly the algorithms given to it, the best method is to build the database by using programs. This has the advantage of consistent encoding, and all the rules are to be found in one place. The disadvantage is that natural language is inconsistent, multivalued, and generally unruly. Computer programs do not understand natural language easily. Fallible and inconsistent human intervention is required.

Formal linguistic variables are very amenable to computer-assisted analysis. But human beings use not only formal but semantic cues to process the text. Hence, a tagging scheme—since it *simulates* the reality of the text—must also use both formal *and* semantic tags. The semantic tags must have concrete definitions, and these must be applied rigorously, ideally by a computer program. Errors and improvements in our understanding of the text can then be easily applied to the program's algorithm and the text processed once again.

Take, for example, the case of the Hebrew verbal clause. In the tagging scheme cited above,[5] five formal variables are defined: subject, verb, object, satellite (verbal adjunct), and margin (interclause relation). Each of these can be easily defined in terms of morphology combined with word order. Semantic roles for the arguments of the verb are much more difficult. They are the interaction of the lexical meaning of the verb with the lexical meaning of the verbal adjunct. In this case, algorithmic definitions are less applicable—at least, as far as we know up to this point.[6] Nevertheless, regardless of difficulty, I suggest that the semantics of syntax is the only way to solve certain

---

5. Lowery, "The Role of Semantics," 106–7.

6. Not much is being done in this area for Biblical Hebrew syntax. The most recent consistent attempt at this is Winther-Nielsen, *Functional Discourse Grammar*. A general discussion of verbal arguments, syntactic case roles, and their relationships may be found in W. A. Cook, *Case Grammar: Development of the Matrix Model (1970–1978)* (Washington, D.C.: Georgetown University Press, 1979) and more recently, R. D. van Valin, Jr. (ed.), *Advances in Role and Reference Grammar* (Amsterdam Studies in the Theory of Linguistic Science, Series IV—Current Issues in Linguistic Theory; Amsterdam: Benjamins, 1993) 82.

problems, especially those of determining where clauses end and identifying embedded and elliptic clauses.[7]

## 2. Syntactic Tags for Hebrew Verbless Clauses

We come, then, to the question of verbless clauses. In light of the foregoing discussion, the purpose of this study is to:

- establish a set of formal and semantic tags for verbless clauses
- develop concrete criteria for each tag and their analysis
- evaluate the tagging scheme for linguistic adequacy and consistency.

The questions at hand are, simply, (1) in what way should we think about the verbless clause, and (2) how can we represent those thoughts in such a way that can be accurately mirrored in a database? The first question is a basic one of Hebrew syntax. The second has to do with the nature of linguistic reality.

### 2.1. The Grammars' Point of View
I review here briefly the standard understanding of the verbless clause as a point of departure. We want to know if the classic descriptions are adequate for our purposes.

#### 2.1.1. Gesenius-Kautzsch-Cowley
The noun clause has both the subject and the predicate in a nominal form (GKC §140a).[8] Noun clauses with a substantive as a predicate express something "fixed, a state, or a being," in contrast to verbal clauses, which represent an event or action. When the predicate is a participle, actions or events can also be represented, but the participle has a fixed or abiding character (§140e). Arab grammarians defined every independent subject as nominal, even when a finite verb occurs later in the sentence (§140f).

The subject may be a substantive or pronoun (§141a). The predicate may be a substantive, adjective, participle, numeral, pronoun,[9] adverb of time, place, quality, or possessor. When both subject and predicate are substantives, the clause expresses *identity*. When the predicate is an adjective or participle, it is often used with *waw* to express a state contemporaneous with the time of

---

7. Lowery, "The Role of Semantics," 116.

8. Kautzsch, *Gesenius' Hebrew Grammar* (trans. A. E. Cowley; Oxford: Clarendon, 1909) 450–55. The relevant sections for the nominal clause are §§140–41. Use of participles in nominal clauses: §116m–r. Use of negatives: §152a, d, i–m. Use of the relative, §155e. For the reader's convenience, I have cited the section and paragraph numbers in the text.

9. In §126k, it is asserted that substantives that are definite are the subjects rather than the predicates when appearing with a pronoun. Thus he argues that nouns with the definite article are higher in definiteness than a pronoun. Examples are found in Gen 10:12, Exod 9:27, Gen 24:65 (מִי), 1 Kgs 9:13 (מָה).

the action of the main verb (§141b). A substantival predicate has a greater stress than an adjectival or verbal predicate, since it represents something *identical* with the subject (§141c). Sometimes juxtaposition is used to establish the *relationship* between subject and predicate (§141f), but not infrequently the third-person pronoun expressly resumes the subject, or the verb היה is used to specify the time as well as strengthen the subject (§141g).

The "natural" word order is S–P, since the subject is the object of description. The reverse word order is used when the predicate is being emphasized, when it is an interrogative word or when an adjectival predicate is comparative (§141 l–m).

The participle can be used in the noun clause for past, present, or future time (§116n–p). When used as a predicate and emphasized, it precedes subjects that are pronouns or substantives (§116q). Inherently, the negative particle לֹא or the particle of negative existence אַיִן provides emphasis and marks the predicate.

**2.1.2.** Joüon-Muraoka on the Nominal Clause

A basic definition of the clause influences the understanding of the verbless clause.[10] The clause is defined as a subject and predicate. If the predicate is a noun, it is called a "nominal" clause. If the predicate is a verb, then it is a "verbal" clause.[11] Participles and prepositional phrases are included in the definition. The subject can be a prepositional phrase, an infinitive construct, and, rarely, an infinitive absolute. The predicate can also be a noun, substantive, adjective, participle, pronoun, prepositional phrase, adverb, or infinitive construct with לְ, usually with the verb היה.[12]

What are the logical and semantic relationships possible between the subject and predicate? The relationship may be *descriptive*: the predicate describes the entity represented by the subject (equivalent to Andersen's "classifying"). The nominal clause may also *identify* and point out the entity expressed by the subject. If the subject or predicate is the recipient of some special prominence or emphasis, this will influence the word order.[13] Statistically, the more frequent word order is S–P, at about 66%.[14] A pronoun occupies the second slot when no prominence is intended to be given to it.[15]

---

10. Joüon, *A Grammar of Biblical Hebrew* (trans. and rev. by T. Muraoka; 2 vols.; Subsidia Biblica 14/1–2; Rome: Pontifical Biblical Institute, 1991) 564–77 (§154).

11. Ibid., 561. Cf. Otto Jespersen (*The Philosophy of Grammar* [London, 1924] 145–56) and P. H. Matthews (*Syntax* [Cambridge, 1981] 96–113) for general linguistic discussion of the nominal clause.

12. Joüon, *Grammar*, 565.

13. Ibid., 566–67.

14. Ibid., 568.

15. Ibid., 569. But the issue may be that the first element may have a higher level of definiteness. The problem is that if, as he argues, there is an emphatic P–S pattern, and a nonemphatic P–S pattern, then what criterion is used for distinguishing the two?

With the relative אֲשֶׁר we usually find S–P as the word order, and the participle is always preceded by a pronoun: Relative + Pronoun + Participle. The demonstrative pronoun זֶה (זֹאת and אֵלֶּה) receives some prominence when it occupies the first slot.[16] An indefinite participle occupies the second slot when the other constituent is *not* a pronoun, and this pattern is viewed as unmarked.[17] The unmarked pattern for participles and pronouns is Participle + Pronoun.[18] When a third element is added to a Participle + Pronoun clause in the first position, the pattern usually is x + Pronoun + Participle. When P is a prepositional phrase, its unmarked position is the second slot.[19] An interrogative clause's normal emphasis is upon the predicate and so the normal word order is P–S, with ellipsis of S quite common. In the reply, the P–S word order is maintained.[20]

**2.1.3.** Waltke and O'Connor[21]

The term used for predicates in nominal clauses is "predicate nominative" (§8.3a). A nominal or verbless clause is composed of a subject and predicate, two nouns juxtaposed to indicate a predication (§8.3c).

Rules governing word order:

1. The first issue is the relative definiteness of S and P. If the predicate is definite, then it *identifies* (complete overlap of S and P) a definite subject. If it is indefinite, it *classifies* (partial overlap of S and P) a definite subject. Identifying clauses usually have the order S–P, while the classifying clause has the reverse, P–S. (§8.4a)[22]

2. The usual order is S–P for identification clauses, but suffixed nouns in the predicate usually—but not always—take precedence: Predicate + Suffix + Subject (§8.4.1a). Nominal clauses can also take three parts, through the use of a pleonastic personal or demonstrative pronoun,

---

16. Ibid., 569–70.

17. Ibid., 570. How is this to be distinguished from a simple *adjectival* use of the participle?

18. Ibid., 571. Note the parallel with the unmarked pattern of V–S in verbal clauses! We should probably distinguish between "verbal" and "nominal" uses of the participles, especially when the participle is used to express continuous action or present time.

19. Ibid., 572.

20. Ibid., 572.

21. Waltke and O'Connor, *Introduction to Biblical Hebrew Syntax*. The relevant sections are §8.3c, §8.4; also "Predicate" §4.5; "Modification Functions of the Noun" §9.1a; "Apposition" §12; "Uses of the Adjective" §14.3.1–2; "Hiphil Stem, Form and Meaning" §27.1a–d; "Fientive and Stative Verbs" §22.2.1–2; "Waw + Prefix, After Circumstantial Phrases and Clauses" §33.2.4; "Waw + Prefix, After Nominal Clauses" §33.3.4; "Infinitive Absolute, Other Nominal Uses" §35.3.3; "Infinitive Construct, With the Preposition לְ" §36.2.3a–b.

22. Ibid., 130. They essentially accept Andersen's view of the verbless clause.

S–pleoPro–P; for example, Gen 36:8: עֵשָׂו הוּא אֱדוֹם 'Esau, he is Edom' (§8.4.1b).[23] When the subject is a member of a *class* referred to by the predicate, the usual order is P–S. However, suffixed nouns appear in the initial position (S–P) if the subject is an infinitive or if the clause is declarative and the predicate is used in "an essentially verbal way."[24]

### 2.1.4. Is Word Order the Diagnostic Criterion?

It would seem that the standard grammars' grouping of clauses into identifying and classifying clauses is primarily based upon word order. Since there seem to be only two constituents to most verbless clauses (subjects and predicates), there are only two possible word-order patterns. If we associate one pattern (formal variables) with one type (semantic variables), then we have a clear way to make decisions on tagging. However, in each case, exceptions are listed for reversal of word order. The problem with these "exceptions" is that they are indistinguishable from their counterpart, since there are only two possible types of word order, S–P or P–S.[25] Each grammar adds additional criteria: GKC notes interrogative words or comparative adjectival predicates that can disturb the "normal" S–P word order, and the negative particle is always followed by the predicate. Joüon-Muraoka speak of reconstructing the "question" to which the verbless clause is an "answer." Depending on how that question is construed, the determination is made.[26] Waltke and O'Connor, in keeping with their descriptive style, offer definiteness as the primary distinction between verbless clause-types but do not associate definiteness with either the predicate or the subject. Either one can be definite, so the identification must be on other, unspecified, grounds.

It is disturbing that the grammars confidently distinguish between identifying and classifying clauses with opposite word order and yet offer no distinctive criterion for that determination. A subjective element—no matter how accurate—remains as the final arbiter of linguistic description of the verbless clause. Is it possible to discover and define that intuition? The work of Francis Andersen offers a possibility.

---

23. Alternatively, this pattern could be understood as a form of emphasis, so that the subject is the pronoun הוּא 'he', the predicate remains אֱדוֹם 'Edom', and עֵשָׂו 'Esau' is some sort of emphasis or "focus" (ibid., 131).

24. Ibid., 133.

25. I omit, for the sake of simplicity, the problem of the use of the recapitulating pronoun. My own view is that the "pleonastic" pronoun is really the subject, and the pronoun's referent is actually a left-dislocated form of focus.

26. This also raises the very uncomfortable question of ambiguity: could a verbless clause be *both* identifying *and* classifying? Certain examples cited by Joüon-Muraoka seem to be so. See their discussion of the problem (ibid., 567).

**2.2.** Francis Andersen's Theory

> Explanations of exceptions to the supposed rule S–P are often given in terms of concepts like *emphasis* or *importance*, which have no empirical status.[27]

With this criticism, Andersen turns to more modern linguistic methods to find a better solution to the problem of word order and taxonomy of the verbless clause. Using the syntactic model of *tagmemics*, Andersen takes on the terminology of his forebears and speaks of two types of verbless clauses, a clause that identifies the subject and one that classifies the subject.[28] Of course, the next problem is identifying which is subject and which is predicate. He defines the subject as the constituent that continues the topic of discourse in the preceding text, citing the pronoun as an example.

> The referential use of a pronoun or of the article often serves as a clue to S. The matching rule that P is indefinite in relationship to S is of some use; but these tests fail when both core constituents are definite.[29]

These tests fail when both core constituents are indefinite as well.

> By distinguishing between proper nouns, definite nouns, suffixed nouns, and indefinite nouns, the question of the grammatical function of definiteness is raised. . . . The results given below indicate that definiteness is the key to understanding the structures of verbless clauses in Hebrew.[30]

There is a correlation between word order and definiteness. When the predicate is definite, the word order tends to be S–P. When the predicate is indefinite, the word order is reversed. Further, Andersen uses this correlation to define his verbless clause types: when S and P are definite, the predicate supplies the *identity* of the subject, the normal word order being S–P. When P is indefinite and S is definite, then the predicate supplies the *class* of the subject, the normal word order being P–S.[31] It is important to note that the underlying assumption here is that definiteness is a discrete value, that is, either present or absent.

---

27. F. I. Andersen, *The Hebrew Verbless Clause in the Pentateuch* (Journal of Biblical Literature Monograph Series 14; New York and Nashville: Abingdon, 1970) 18.

28. Ibid., 19.

29. Ibid., 21. Ideally, we want to be able to identify the subject and predicate by formal means within a clause independent of its context. But ambiguity in language is often only resolved by recourse to the next higher level of language. In this case, a syntactic ambiguity for subject or predicate can be resolved at a higher level, that of discourse or text, just as nouns that are ambiguous in morphology as to their state (absolute or construct) are only resolvable at the syntactic level.

30. Ibid., 22.

31. Ibid., 32.

Andersen, therefore, distinguishes between identification and classification clauses on the basis of the feature of definiteness. He does not define subject and predicate using this feature. Rather, he uses a semantic definition that is much less defined—"new" (predicate) and "old" (subject) information.[32] To his credit, he recognizes the problem as a "vexed" one but one that is essential to the question of the nature of verbless clauses, since the syntactic features of subject, predicate, and word order are precisely those that we wish to fix, ideally in terms of morphology.

J. Hoftijzer[33] observed that Andersen does not use formal criteria exclusively but only as "clues," to which must be added nonformal (intuitive) criteria based upon logic and semantics that sometimes even contradict the formal criteria.

> The two core tagmemes of the nominal clause cannot be mutually distinguished by the formal character of the classes of morphemes and morpheme groups that belong to them. Moreover the decision whether one has to do with a definite or indefinite noun, a decision of importance for the recognition of subject and predicate in individual cases, can in a number of cases only be made on nonformal grounds.[34]

While natural languages do use both formal and semantic elements to organize information structures, a methodology for discovering those structures cannot afford this level of inconsistency. A combination of both formal and semantic features will probably be necessary to determine subjects and predicates, but they must be consistently applied by the researcher so that the limits of the adequacy of those models can be known.

## 3. Variables of the Verbless Clause

The foregoing review leaves us with several impressions. First, there is a consensus that the "function" of verbless clauses can be generally grouped into clauses in which the predicate *identifies* the subject and clauses in which the predicate *classifies* the subject. Second, definiteness plays a major role in distinguishing between subject and predicate and is semantically linked to the function type.[35] Third, the important issue of expected ("normal") word order versus unexpected word order is dependent upon the definition of subject and predicate. Since no one is suggesting that S and P should be defined on the

---

32. Ibid., 21. Nevertheless, he later declares that subjects are generally more definite than predicates. Cf. pp. 40–41.

33. J. Hoftijzer, "The Nominal Clause Reconsidered," *VT* 23 (1973) 450.

34. Ibid., 451.

35. For example, it is hard to conceive of an instance in which a predicate is more specific than a subject when the predicate either classifies or identifies the subject.

basis of their position in the clause, we must look to other language features for their definition.

An independent definition and determination of S and P is needed to resolve our questions. In a normal verbal clause, the verb itself provides a great deal of the semantic ordering of the clause, clues that are lacking in a verbless clause. The only distinguishing syntactic features available to us—apparently—are *juxtaposition* and *constituent order*. Are these adequate to the task? Andersen adds definiteness as a semantic category. For example,

(1)  Judg 6:10

אֲנִי יְהוָה אֱלֹהֵיכֶם      I (and not someone else) am *the LORD your God*[36]

Andersen would call this an *identifying* clause where a definite predicate, יְהוָה אֱלֹהֵיכֶם, identifies the subject. Below we have an example of a *classifying* clause, again using Andersen's approach:

(2)  Judg 3:29

וְכָל־אִישׁ חָיִל      And every man is *strong* (and not something else)

An indefinite predicate refers to a general class of which the subject is a member. Thus we ought to conclude that when the predicate is definite, it identifies the subject, and when it is indefinite, it classifies the subject. Yet what do we do with this clause?

(3)  Judg 1:26

הוּא שְׁמָהּ עַד הַיּוֹם הַזֶּה      which [is] *its name (Luz)* until today

The predicate is definite because it is a suffixed noun, and the subject is also definite as a personal pronoun. Since it is a definite predicate, it should function as an identifying clause. But the clause also is saying that the name of the city is Luz and not something else, which would imply that the clause's function is a classifying one. So which is it, and how can we decide?

What distinguishes between S and P? How does the recipient track the relationship between components? Can we make a rule for determining what is S and what is P? If we can compose a rule without recourse to word order or to the ideas of *classifying* and *identifying*, then we will be in a position to describe clause function in terms of S and P and can also make meaningful observations about the role of word order.

---

36. All examples are taken from the book of Judges. Translations given here are very literal and slanted to illustrate the point at hand. The predicate is italicized in the translation of each example.

**3.1.** The Semantic Component

Example (1) illustrates our problem. What is the difference between these two?

אֲנִי יְהוָה אֱלֹהֵיכֶם

יְהוָה אֱלֹהֵיכֶם אֲנִי

There is no change in subject. Both S and P are definite. Andersen would say that we can track the subject because it is more highly presupposed. The pronoun אֲנִי 'I' requires the reader to know more about it than יְהוָה אֱלֹהֵיכֶם 'the LORD your God'.

The key insight resolving our difficulty is this: tracking highly presupposed information in text vis-à-vis "new" information is handled in verbless clauses by the semantic feature of definiteness. A necessary corollary to this proposition is that because presupposed information and new information are relative to each other, definiteness is also relative. The subject is more presupposed relative to the predicate. Hence, it is *relatively more* definite as compared to the predicate. Definiteness is not a discrete variable but a continuous one.

Returning to example (1) above, we see that the independent personal pronoun אֲנִי is the subject because it is more highly presupposed than the nominal phrase יְהוָה אֱלֹהֵיכֶם. In example (2), the nominal phrase כָּל־אִישׁ is relatively more definite than the adjective חָיִל. Again, the independent personal pronoun הוּא is more definite than the suffixed noun שְׁמָה in example (3). It also explains how we know when S and P exchange positions in the clause.

How is definiteness tracked? The answer is, apparently, via morphology. Although some kinds of definiteness have been associated with specific forms such as the definite article or specific categories such as pronouns and "definite" articles, this conception requires us to reconsider all nominal forms and their definiteness relative to one another.

**3.2.** Relative Definiteness

The very term *relative* implies ordering. Definiteness is a feature that has to do with how precisely known an entity is. It is a combination of lexical and morphological features. For example, a proper noun is more precisely known than a common noun or even more than a common noun with a pronominal suffix—this illustrates the logic involved.

Although Andersen does not apply or even explain his reasoning, he does propose[37] an ordering of nominal constructions in terms of morphology and even observes that definiteness is relative.[38] Even so, he still uses definiteness

---

37. Andersen, *Hebrew Verbless Clause*, 30, 109 (see table 1 below, p. 265).

38. "The predicate is usually less definite semantically than the subject, even when both are formally definite" (ibid., 41).

as a discrete variable in the evaluation of his evidence.[39] What is needed is a consistent evaluation of relative definiteness and a validation of the relative ordering of morphological features in terms of definiteness in order to be able consistently to apply and use the rule for the determination of S and P. The consistent application of the rule is crucial for a tagging system of linguistic databases of Biblical Hebrew.

The figure below summarizes Andersen's list of nominal constructions and their relative definiteness. It provides us with a convenient beginning point for systematically evaluating their definiteness.

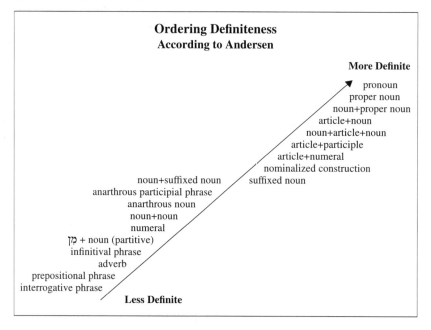

### 4. Validating Relative Definiteness

The goal of this study is to arrive at an *algorithmic* way of determining the S and P of verbless clauses. Algorithms are rules or recipes that are used to make decisions—in this case, about the identity of clause constituents. When we can formulate a simple rule, we can test its adequacy, modify it, and add additional rules to cover a larger number of cases. The point in this process is to encapsulate human intuition into explicit knowledge. The fact that we are

---

39. "When the predicate is indefinite, inversion of the normal sequence from P–S to S–P is a signal along with the use of *w-* that the clause is circumstantial" (ibid., 35).

sometimes unable to complete this process only serves to demonstrate the limits of our understanding.

### 4.1. Method

The next step in this process is determining how we confirm or disconfirm the proposed ordering. We shall use a modified version of the standard linguistic technique of *minimal pairs*. First, we must find an example of a hypothesized higher-order constituent in the subject position paired with a hypothesized lower-order constituent. Next we must show, if possible, that this ordered pair is not exceptional but typical. Finally, either counter-examples must be adequately explained or the hypothesized pairing must be rejected.

The verbless clauses of the book of Judges will be used in this study as representative of a significant sample of Biblical Hebrew. It must be stated here that *any* counter-example from the Hebrew Bible will invalidate the hypothesized pairing, unless a reasonable explanation for the exception can be made. Hence, although the results here will give us a reasonable degree of confidence, they cannot be taken as conclusive without a complete survey of the entire text.

### 4.2. The Test Grid

In surveying the book of Judges for verbless clauses, I chose to include classic verbal nouns (infinitives and participles), both because they are included in Andersen's list and because one of the questions we want to answer is the nature of the verbless clause and its limits. Obvious adjectival uses of the participle were excluded from the study. I included participles and infinitives when there was an actual predication relative to the top level of the surrounding clauses.

I examined each clause and asked the question "Which element is more highly presupposed by the context?" This constituent was marked arbitrarily as S. "New information" or at least less highly known information was marked P. We now have the semantic side of the equation. This information was correlated against Andersen's morphological categories, the formal side. We are now ready for testing our expectations.

We want to know if a particular morphological category is always used as S when it occurs with any other category. This lends itself to a 19 × 19 grid for a total of 361 cells. The X-axis represents constructions that are coded P, while the Y-axis is S, each pair representing a specific hypothesis: is category X higher in relative definiteness than category Y?

This means that in the lower left half of the grid (in the shaded area) are the clauses in which the constituents are coded contrary to expectation (according to Andersen). The upper right half of the grid (the unshaded portion) represents expected results, conforming to the hypothesis. Every theoretically possible

S–P combination of the 19 categories is represented. Naturally, not all combinations occur in Judges, nor would we expect all combinations to occur, from a logical standpoint. The grid shows which combinations occurred and in what frequency.

Table 1 presents a summary of the results. Table 2 (see pp. 271–72) gives a detailed listing of the biblical references for each occurrence.[40] If a reference to a verse occurs more than once, it means more than one verbless clause is found in that verse.

## 5. Results and Discussion

Out of the 323 verbless clauses identified for this study, 47 clauses (15%) did not conform to expectations. As might be expected, the independent pronoun was the most frequent constituent and without exception more highly presupposed.

For the S–P pairings that are attested in Judges, we can generally conclude that (1) there is an ordering to relative definiteness, and that (2) the order approximates Andersen's expectations. Definiteness and these morphological constructs are correlated. Hence, the general algorithmic rule can be used to identify S–P pairings without first examining the semantics of every clause manually. But not in every case.

Can our rule be modified or adjusted to account for the exceptions? Have we missed a consideration in our proposed rule for identifying verbless clause constituents? An examination of the lower left grid-cells may provide an answer. These are cases where the semantics of the clause violates our expected use of that morphological construct. Can we explain why this occurred?

**5.1.** The Highest Level of Definiteness
The tables fail to include one very important category of verbless clause: clauses that only have one constituent present, P.

(4) Judg 9:28

הֲלֹא בֶן־יְרֻבַּעַל    [is he] *not the-son-of Jerubbaal?*[41]

There is no other possible candidate for S here. We must search for the subject earlier in the context. This also accounts for the idiom

---

40. The original raw data and programs used to extract the data and reports are available by request. Contact me at ⟨KirkLowery@xc.org⟩.

41. The translations that follow are very literal, following the Hebrew word order and ignoring English usage of definite articles. Hyphens are used when more than one word translates one word of Hebrew text.

## Table 1. Summary

More "Known" (Subject) → rows; Less "Known" (Predicate) → columns

| More "Known" (Subject) \ Less "Known" (Predicate) | Pronoun | Proper noun | Construct noun + proper noun | Article + noun | Construct noun + article + noun | Article + participle | Article + numeral | Nominalized construction | Suffixed noun | Construct noun + suffixed noun | Anarthrous participial phrase | Anarthrous noun | Construct noun + anarthrous noun | Anarthrous numeral | Partitive (*min* + noun) | Infinitival phrase | Adverb | Prepositional phrase | Interrogative |
|---|---|---|---|---|---|---|---|---|---|---|---|---|---|---|---|---|---|---|---|
| Pronoun | | 7 | 5 | 6 | | | | | 5 | 1 | 38 | 10 | 5 | | 5 | 6 | 2 | 43 | 1 |
| Proper noun | | | 1 | | | | | | 1 | 1 | 12 | 4 | | | | 2 | | 9 | 3 |
| Construct noun + proper noun | 2 | | | | | | | | | | 2 | | | | 1 | 2 | 1 | 5 | |
| Article + noun | | | | | 1 | | | | | | 7 | 2 | 1 | | 1 | 1 | | 3 | 3 |
| Construct noun + article + noun | 2 | 1 | | | | | | | | | 1 | 1 | | | | | | | |
| Article + participle | | | | | | | | | | | 2 | | | | | | | | |
| Article + numeral | | | | | | | | | | | | | | | | | | | |
| Nominalized construction | | | | | | | | | | | | | | | | | | | |
| Suffixed noun | 3 | 1 | 1 | | | | | | | | 8 | 3 | 1 | | | | 2 | 7 | 2 |
| Construct noun + suffixed noun | | | | | | | | | | | | | | | | | | 1 | |
| Anarthrous participial phrase | | | | | | | | | | | | 1 | | | | 1 | | | 1 |
| Anarthrous noun | | | | | | | | | 1 | | 6 | 13 | | | | 1 | 3 | 10 | |
| Construct noun + anarthrous noun | | | | | | | | | | | 5 | 2 | 1 | | | | | 9 | |
| Anarthrous numeral | | | | | | | | | | | | | | | | | | 1 | 1 |
| Partitive (*min* + noun) | | | | | | | | | | | | | | | | | | | |
| Infinitival phrase | | | | | | | | | | | | | | | | | | 1 | |
| Adverb | | 1 | | | | | | | | | | | 1 | | | | | | 1 |
| Prepositional phrase | | | | | | | | | | | | 2 | | | | | | 2 | 5 |
| Interrogative | | | | | | | | | | | | 2 | | | | | | 1 | |

(5)  Judg 1:14

וַיֹּאמֶר־לָהּ כָּלֵב מַה־לָּךְ    and-he-said to-her Caleb, "*What* [is it] *to-you?*"

At first glance, מַה is the subject. But actually Caleb already knows there is something his daughter wants. He is asking for the thing's *identity.*

Commonly termed *ellipsis,* the absence of any S at all reveals just how highly presupposed S is in the speaker's mind: the speaker has no doubt at all that the listener can easily identify the subject of the predication—so easily, in fact, that the constituent can be safely omitted.[42] We must add, then, a new category to Andersen's list: the Elided Subject.

**5.2.** The Constituent Functions as a Pronoun

There is a class of unexpected results that are explained by the fact that, although the word is not formally a pronoun, it nevertheless "refers" to a previous antecedent and is therefore more highly presupposed.

(6)  Judg 20:27

וְשָׁם אֲרוֹן בְּרִית הָאֱלֹהִים          and-there [was] *ark-of covenant of*
                בַּיָּמִים הָהֵם                         *God in those days*

In order to identify where the ark was located, we must go to the previous verse where we learn that the Israelites had gone to Bethel. The word שָׁם is more known and has a referential function, linking the identity of Bethel to this later clause—just like any pronoun would. Even though שָׁם is usually classified as an adverb and consequently is lower in definiteness than its companion construct chain, nevertheless, it is more highly known.

(7)  Judg 19:16

וְאַנְשֵׁי הַמָּקוֹם בְּנֵי יְמִינִי          and-men-of the-place [were]
                                                        *Benjaminites*

A Proper Noun would seem to be much higher than a construct phrase, until we note that הַמָּקוֹם is referring to Gibeah, mentioned in the previous clause.

(8)  Judg 1:23

וְשֵׁם־הָעִיר לְפָנִים לוּז          and-name-of the-city *previously*
                                                    [was] *Luz*

This is a parallel case to the one just noted, with הָעִיר having the referential function.

It would seem, then, that we need to expand the definition of *pronoun* to include words with syntactic referential functions. It might be that Construct Noun + Article + Noun has a higher relative definiteness than our hypothesis allows, but we have too few examples (3 expected, 3 unexpected) for certainty.

**5.3.** Relative Definiteness between Persons

We have a very interesting and clear example of a case where the person of the suffix determines which is more highly presupposed.

---

42. The other occurrences of subject ellipsis are found in 4:20; 6:13, 15; 8:15; 12:5; 13:8, 11; 14:15; 15:13; 16:2; 17:2; 18:9, 19.

(9)  Judg 8:18

כָּמוֹךָ כְמוֹהֶם    as-you *so-they*

There is no difference between S and P except for the fact that one preposition is inflected in the second-person singular and the other is in the third-person plural. We can hypothesize that the first person is highest in relative definiteness and third person is lowest; second person is intermediate between them.

Could this be the explanation for the coding of a suffixed noun higher than an Article + Noun?

(10)  Judg 6:15

הִנֵּה אַלְפִּי הַדַּל בִּמְנַשֶּׁה    Look! My-clan [is] *the-least in-Manasseh*

It seems that the first-person suffix elevates the relative definiteness of the entire constituent higher than הַדַּל. Could it be that a First-Person Suffixed Noun should also be added?

(11)  Judg 18:6

נֹכַח יְהוָה דַּרְכְּכֶם    *approval-of the-Lord* [characterizes] *your-journey*

Here S is a Second-Person Suffixed Noun that we would expect to be P instead.

(12)  Judg 16:4

וּשְׁמָהּ דְּלִילָה    and-her-name [was] *Delilah*

Again, contrary to our expectations, the Third-Person Suffixed Noun is higher than a proper noun.

Additional study is needed, but it seems that the morphological category of *person* can be further distinguished according to the number of that person. It raises a similar question in relation to independent and demonstrative pronouns. Are they also to be distinguished in relative definiteness? A broader sample may reveal cases that will allow us to answer this question.

**5.4.**  Finer Distinctions within Categories

Apparently we need finer distinctions within our morphological categories.

(13)  Judg 20:16

כָּל־זֶה קֹלֵעַ בָּאֶבֶן אֶל־הַשַּׂעֲרָה    all of these [were] *slingers of stones at a single hair*

Our hypothesis tells us to expect a participial phrase to be higher in definiteness than a construct pair. The use of the demonstrative pronoun, however, changes the strength of presupposed information in the clause and is evaluated as S here. Here is a parallel case with אֵלֶּה:

(14) Judg 20:25

כָּל־אֵלֶּה שֹׁלְפֵי חָרֶב     all-of these [were] *drawers-of sword*

A special case occurs among participles:

(15) Judg 21:18

לֵאמֹר אָרוּר נֹתֵן אִשָּׁה לְבִנְיָמִן     saying, "*cursed* [is] giver-of a-woman to-a-Benjamite"

Here the participle is *Qal* passive and is lower in definiteness relative to the Construct Participle + Noun that follows it. This may be a special case because of the lexical nature of the passive participle.

### 5.5. Interrogatives

For the most part, interrogatives behave as expected. Since they are at the bottom of the scale, we would expect interrogatives always to occur as P. However, there are three cases where they do not.

(16) Judg 14:18

מַה־מָּתוֹק מִדְּבַשׁ     What [is] *sweeter than-honey?*
וּמֶה עַז מֵאֲרִי     and-what [is] *stronger than-a-lion?*

In English there is no question that a comparative is lower than an interrogative pronoun. But it is possible to understand these two clauses slightly differently[43] from the traditional way of translating the comparative in Hebrew:

> *What* is sweetness, *if not honey?*
> *What* is strength, *if not a lion?*

This alternate translation preserves the sense of the nouns מָתוֹק and עַז as subjects, since there is no inflection for the comparative and superlative. The translation also more clearly illustrates the syntax of these clauses: a predicate (מַה), a subject (מָתוֹק and עַז), and a prepositional phrase modifying the predicate. If we understand the clauses in this fashion, the interrogatives are clearly P, and conform to our hypothesis. These examples reinforce the suspicion that verbless clauses strengthen the "nominality" of their constituents.

### 5.6. Reevaluation of Morphology

There are words that, when coded according to the usual understanding of their morphology, give results counter to our expectations. But when we consider more carefully their actual linguistic status, we are able to resolve the problem.

---

43. These clauses occur in poetic parallelism, which warns us that our rule for relative definiteness may need to be applied differently in poetic contexts.

(17) Judg 6:24

עַד הַיּוֹם הַזֶּה עוֹדֶנּוּ בְּעָפְרָת    until the-day this still-it [is] *in-*
אֲבִי הָעֶזְרִי    *Ophrah-of Abiezrites*

The reason this clause does not conform to our hypothesis is that עוֹדֶנּוּ is in-terpreted as an inflected form of עוֹד. However, if we understand the suffix as being an enclitic for the pronoun הוּא, the syntax of the clause conforms to the hypothesis. In this case, then, we have a subject (the suffix נוּ֗-) and a complex predicate with three elements: a local and two temporal adverbials.[44]

(18) Judg 19:1

וּמֶלֶךְ אֵין בְּיִשְׂרָאֵל    and-a-king [was] *an-absence in-Israel*

The word אַיִן is often found in the construct form אֵין, even when there is no true *nomen rectum* following, as is the case here. It is tempting to think of אַיִן as a "particle of nonexistence," translated as 'there is not'. Verbless clauses remind us forcefully of the original nominal status of this word:

(19) Judg 12:3

כִּי־אֵינְךָ מוֹשִׁיעַ    that your-lack [was] *a rescuer*

It sounds strange to our ears, yet it is hard to understand how anything but a nominal could take a pronominal suffix. The use of the second-person suffix may also be heightening its definiteness.

We have a precise parallel in the case of יֵשׁ 'existence':

(20) Judg 18:14

כִּי יֵשׁ בַּבָּתִּים הָאֵלֶּה אֵפוֹד    that an-existence [is] *in-the-*
וּתְרָפִים וּפֶסֶל וּמַסֵּכָה    *houses these ephod and-teraphim and-carved-image and-cast-idol?*

and in the case of a pronominal suffix,

(21) Judg 6:36

אִם־יֶשְׁךָ מוֹשִׁיעַ בְּיָדִי    if your-existence [is] *a rescuer*
אֶת־יִשְׂרָאֵל    *by-my-hand [of-]Israel*

Koehler and Baumgartner (*HALAT*, 423) classify the pronominal suffix of יֵשׁ as the subject of the following participle, מוֹשִׁיעַ. But this is only true of the underlying predication, "if you are going to rescue Israel by my hand." The surface structure says the pronoun is not an *agent* of an action but a *possessor* of a condition. The suffixed noun is higher here than the Anarthrous Participial Phrase, and so our hypothesis is confirmed for this case.

---

44. I am indebted to Vincent DeCaen for suggesting this solution.

Again, we have an illustration of verbless clauses tending to emphasize the original nominal nature of their constituents, a usage to which they return even if they have developed other syntactic usage in other types of clauses.

**5.7.** Participles

There is still one category of unexpected results left: that of participles. A typical example is

(22) Judg 14:5

וְהִנֵּה כְּפִיר אֲרָיוֹת שֹׁאֵג    and-behold young-lion-of lions
לִקְרָאתוֹ    *was-roaring against-him*

This is the ordinary way Hebrew expresses continuous action. It is logical that this completely sidesteps our algorithm. If, by definition, the participle is the predicate, then it does not matter what its definiteness is relative to the subject. It may even be an irrelevant and inapplicable question in this context. So it is not surprising that when the subject's definiteness drops below that of the participle, it will violate our rule.

## 6. Conclusion

The results of this study are sufficient to support the idea that the concept of *relative definiteness* is operative in Biblical Hebrew and that it correlates to an ordered set of morphological categories and constructs. Because verbless clauses lack the morphological and syntactic cues that verbal clauses provide, the nominal feature of definiteness is used to distinguish between subject and predicate. With this approach, the entire question of the use of word order in verbless clauses can now be studied with confidence that our definitions of subject and predicate (and therefore the order in which they appear) are not confused or circular. We also have a means by which clauses can be tagged algorithmically for a first approximation with a reasonable degree of accuracy. However, definiteness is not the only criterion that must be used. Lexical and pragmatic criteria (for example, frozen forms, special expressions) also need to be taken into consideration.

## Table 2. Detailed Listing of Verbless Clauses in Judges

| More "Known" (Subject) \ Less "Known" (Predicate) | Pronoun | Proper noun | Construct noun + proper noun | Article + noun | Construct noun + article + noun | Article + participle | Article + numeral | Nominalized construction | Suffixed noun | Construct noun + suffixed noun | Anarthrous participial phrase | Anarthrous noun | Construct noun + anarthrous noun | Anarthrous numeral | Partitive (*min* + noun) | Infinitival phrase | Adverb | Prepositional phrase | Interrogative |
|---|---|---|---|---|---|---|---|---|---|---|---|---|---|---|---|---|---|---|---|
| Pronoun | | 6:10<br>6:31<br>8:24<br>12:5<br>17:7<br>17:9<br>19:10 | 6:22<br>12:4<br>13:16<br>13:21<br>16:17 | 3:1<br>4:14<br>6:15<br>13:11<br>20:9<br>21:11 | | | | | 1:26<br>2:12<br>9:2<br>9:3<br>9:18 | 8:19 | 2:22<br>3:20<br>3:24<br>4:2<br>4:4<br>4:5<br>4:9<br>4:21<br>4:22<br>6:10<br>6:17<br>6:37<br>8:4<br>8:5<br>8:5<br>9:15<br>9:31<br>9:33<br>9:36<br>10:1<br>11:9<br>11:27<br>13:9<br>14:3<br>14:4<br>15:3<br>17:9<br>18:3<br>18:5<br>18:7<br>18:9<br>18:18<br>19:16<br>19:18<br>19:18<br>19:22<br>20:32<br>20:42 | 7:10<br>7:14<br>9:38<br>11:25<br>13:3<br>18:7<br>18:10<br>18:26<br>18:28<br>21:19 | 11:1<br>11:2<br>20:17<br>20:44<br>20:46 | | 13:6<br>14:4<br>18:16<br>19:12<br>19:18 | 3:27<br>6:18<br>6:18<br>8:3<br>11:16<br>14:11 | 11:34<br>13:18 | 1:16<br>3:19<br>3:20<br>3:27<br>4:11<br>4:13<br>6:11<br>6:11<br>6:21<br>6:25<br>6:30<br>7:1<br>7:2<br>7:12<br>7:18<br>7:19<br>8:4<br>8:5<br>8:21<br>8:26<br>8:26<br>9:6<br>9:32<br>9:44<br>9:48<br>9:48<br>10:4<br>10:8<br>10:8<br>11:26<br>15:19<br>15:19<br>16:3<br>16:30<br>18:3<br>18:10<br>18:28<br>18:28<br>19:11<br>19:14<br>20:13<br>21:12<br>21:13 | 18:8 |
| Proper noun | | | 11:18 | | | | | | 9:28 | 4:2 | 3:3<br>4:11<br>4:22<br>4:22<br>6:11<br>7:12<br>9:31<br>9:45<br>13:19<br>13:20<br>14:4<br>20:28 | 3:17<br>6:13<br>13:19<br>15:11 | | | | 7:15<br>8:7 | | 1:22<br>6:3<br>6:12<br>8:10<br>16:9<br>16:12<br>16:14<br>16:20<br>20:18 | 9:28<br>9:28<br>9:38 |
| Construct noun + proper noun | | 1:10<br>1:11 | | | | | | | | | 18:1<br>20:33 | | | | 8:2 | 2:4<br>18:31 | 12:2 | 1:36<br>3:20<br>8:6<br>8:15<br>21:19 | |

## Table 2.  Detailed Listing of Verbless Clauses in Judges (cont.)

**Less "Known" (Predicate)**

| More "Known" (Subject) | Pronoun | Proper noun | Construct noun + proper noun | Article + noun | Construct noun + article + noun | Article + participle | Article + numeral | Nominalized construction | Suffixed noun | Construct noun + suffixed noun | Anarthrous participial phrase | Anarthrous noun | Construct noun + anarthrous noun | Anarthrous numeral | Partitive (*min* + noun) | Infinitival phrase | Adverb | Prepositional phrase | Interrogative |
|---|---|---|---|---|---|---|---|---|---|---|---|---|---|---|---|---|---|---|---|
| Article + noun | | | | 19:9 | | | | | | | | 9:43<br>16:9<br>16:12<br>16:26<br>16:29<br>18:17<br>19:27 | 7:2<br>7:4 | 17:5 | | 19:16 | 7:19 | 4:22<br>17:2<br>20:34 | 8:18<br>10:18<br>20:12 |
| Construct noun + article + noun | | 1:23<br>18:29 | 19:16 | | | | | | | | | 3:24 | 20:46 | | | | | | |
| Article + participle | | | | | | | | | | | | 8:10<br>16:27 | | | | | | | |
| Article + numeral | | | | | | | | | | | | | | | | | | | |
| Nominalized construction | | | | | | | | | | | | | | | | | | | |
| Suffixed noun | | 13:2<br>16:4<br>17:1 | 18:6 | 6:15 | | | | | | | | 3:25<br>3:25<br>6:36<br>8:10<br>11:34<br>12:3<br>13:2<br>17:2 | 3:16<br>8:20<br>16:15 | 13:6 | 15:2<br>16:25 | | | 8:21<br>16:5<br>16:6<br>16:15<br>19:3<br>19:10<br>19:27 | 9:38<br>13:17 |
| Construct noun + suffixed noun | | | | | | | | | | | | | | | | | | 19:20 | |
| Anarthrous participial phrase | | | | | | | | | | | | 19:28 | | | | 13:19 | | | 6:13 |
| Anarthrous noun | | | | | | | | | | 21:24 | 7:13<br>9:36<br>9:37<br>9:37<br>18:16<br>19:1 | 4:20<br>14:3<br>14:6<br>17:6<br>18:1<br>18:14<br>18:28<br>19:1<br>19:15<br>19:18<br>19:19<br>19:19<br>21:9 | | | | 9:2<br>9:2<br>18:19 | 20:16 | 4:14<br>4:17<br>6:23<br>6:37<br>7:12<br>7:20<br>10:4<br>11:7<br>11:34<br>19:20 | |
| Construct noun + anarthrous noun | | | | | | | | | | | 7:13<br>14:5<br>19:16<br>20:16<br>21:18 | 18:7<br>19:19 | 20:25 | | | | | 1:19<br>3:16<br>3:19<br>4:3<br>6:5<br>8:24<br>14:8<br>19:10<br>21:17 | |
| Anarthrous numeral | | | | | | | | | | | | | | | | | | 8:18 | 21:8 |
| Partitive (*min* + noun) | | | | | | | | | | | | | | | | | | | |
| Infinitival phrase | | | | | | | | | | | | | | | | | | 7:2 | |
| Adverb | | | 16:27 | | | | | | | | | | 20:27 | | | | | | 9:2 |
| Prepositional phrase | | | | | | | | | | | | 18:7<br>18:28 | | | | | | 6:24<br>8:18 | 11:12<br>18:3<br>18:23<br>18:24<br>18:24 |
| Interrogative | | | | | | | | | | | | 14:18<br>14:18 | | | | | | 1:14 | |

# Macrosyntactic Functions of Nominal Clauses Referring to Participants

LÉNART J. DE REGT

*Free University, Amsterdam*

## 1. Introduction

In Schneider's grammar of Biblical Hebrew, §44.2 is devoted to the functions of nominal clauses in various BH text-types. In narrative, nominal clauses describe situations, give other background information, and occur particularly at the beginning of a story. In other text-types, for example, in dialogue and prophecy, nominal clauses are more frequent and, though they still do not report events, they are not limited to giving background.[1] In texts of an expository nature, of which Exod 37:18–21, 27:9–19, and 38:9–20 are typical, the verbless clause is even the main-line clause-type.[2] The present article explores the functions of nominal clauses in different types of corpuses in more detail. One may object that such clauses simply occur in places where that is "logical." But this "does not negate the possibility of macro-syntactic significance"; they might have occurred elsewhere.[3]

The examples in this article are limited to those that refer to participants and are without verbs, whether finite or infinite. Nominal clauses are indeed clauses without any verbal morpheme.[4] However, with Groß I exclude active

---

1. Wolfgang Schneider, *Grammatik des biblischen Hebräisch* (6th ed.; Munich: Claudius, 1985) 161–63, §§44.2.1.2 and 44.2.2.

2. David A. Dawson, *Text-Linguistics and Biblical Hebrew* (JSOTSup 177; Sheffield: Sheffield Academic Press, 1994) 144, 150–52, 213; following Robert E. Longacre, *Joseph: A Story of Divine Providence—A Text Theoretical and Textlinguistic Analysis of Genesis 37 and 39–48* (Winona Lake, Ind.: Eisenbrauns, 1989) 111–17.

3. Dawson, *Text-Linguistics,* 141 n. 40.

4. See Wolfgang Richter, *Grundlagen einer althebräischen Grammatik, III: Der Satz (Satztheorie)* (ATSAT 13; St. Ottilien: EOS, 1980) 12; Rüdiger Bartelmus, *HYH: Bedeutung*

and passive participial clauses from this category.[5] When marking predication, participles still belong to the verbal system.[6]

Nominal clauses that mention a participant's age are one indication that nominal clauses contribute to giving background information in narrative. Some examples are Gen 7:6 (וְנֹחַ בֶּן־שֵׁשׁ מֵאוֹת שָׁנָה 'and Noah was 600 years old'), 12:4, 16:16, 17:24–25, 21:5. Such clauses assign to events of the context a place in time and are thus background information that is not of great importance in the course of the story.[7]

There is a contrast between these verbless clauses and clauses that also specify someone's age but start with וַיְהִי at the same time. Some examples are Gen 5:32 (וַיְהִי־נֹחַ בֶּן־חֲמֵשׁ מֵאוֹת שָׁנָה 'and Noah was 500 years old'), 17:1, 25:20, 26:34. Here the author seems to have put the information in the foreground of the story.[8] But the verbless clause in Zech 4:6 without וַיְהִי (זֶה דְּבַר־ יְהוָה אֶל־זְרֻבָּבֶל לֵאמֹר 'This is the word of the LORD to Zerubbabel . . .') is an introduction to the prophetic message rather than an event.[9] This is not to say that nominal clauses are only there to give background information. On the contrary, their text-structuring function suggests that they can give foreground information as well.

Nominal clauses can occur at the start of something: a participant in the story may be or may just have been introduced, or a paragraph may begin. In such instances one may ask how the paragraph is continued after the nominal clause. What are the verb forms in the main clauses that follow? It turns out that the next main clause may contain a *qatal* or *wayyiqtol* form, for example.

---

*und Funktion eines hebräischen "Allerweltswortes"*—Zugleich ein Beitrag zur Frage des *hebräischen Tempussystems* (ATSAT 17; St. Ottilien: EOS, 1982) 93; O. E. Ravn, "Babylonian Permansive and Status Indeterminatus," *ArOr* 17/2 = *Symbolae F. Hrozný* 2 (1949) 300–306, esp. p. 306; F. R. Kraus, *Nominalsätze in altbabylonischen Briefen und der Stativ* (Mededelingen van de Koninklijke Nederlandse Academie van Wetenschappen, Afd. Letterkunde, Nieuwe Reeks 47/2; Amsterdam: Noord-Holland Uitgevers Maatschappij, 1984) 49/69; A. H. Gardiner, "Non-verbal Sentences," *Egyptian Grammar* (3d ed.; London: Oxford University Press, 1969) §28.

5. Walter Groß, "Syntaktische Erscheinungen am Anfang althebräischer Erzählungen: Hintergrund und Vordergrund," in *Congress Volume: Vienna, 1980* (ed. J. A. Emerton; VTSup 32; Leiden: Brill, 1981) 131–45, esp. p. 135 n. 14.

6. J. Hoftijzer, "A Preliminary Remark on the Study of the Verbal System in Classical Hebrew," *Semitic Studies in Honor of Wolf Leslau on the Occasion of His Eighty-Fifth Birthday, November 14th, 1991* (2 vols.; ed. A. S. Kaye; Wiesbaden: Harrassowitz, 1991) 1.645–51, esp. p. 650; Janet W. Dyk, *Participles in Context: A Computer-Assisted Study of Old Testament Hebrew* (Applicatio 12; Amsterdam: Free University Press, 1994) 51; L. J. de Regt, *A Parametric Model for Syntactic Studies of a Textual Corpus, Demonstrated on the Hebrew of Deuteronomy 1–30* (SSN 24; Assen: Van Gorcum, 1988) 13–16.

7. Bartelmus, *HYH: Bedeutung und Funktion*, 121.

8. Ibid., 122.

9. Ibid., 151.

When one looks at the first two main clauses that follow the nominal clause, frequently the first one has a *qatal* form and the second one a *wayyiqtol* form. This suggests not only that *qatal* clauses as well as nominal clauses are used as initial forms in the introduction of a paragraph but that after the nominal clause in initial position, a main clause with a *qatal* form quite often marks the transition from the nominal clause to the chronologically-determined *wayyiqtol* chain of events in the foreground (→ *qatal*→ *wayyiqtol* or even → *qatal* → *qatal* → *wayyiqtol*; such notations will be given below for examples of nominal clauses that appear at the beginning of a paragraph).

Let us now look into the functions of nominal clauses in the texts of Genesis, Judges, Joshua, and Deuteronomy, on the one hand (§§2.1–4); and Ruth, Esther, Ezra, and Nehemiah, on the other (§§3.1–2). After a very brief section on the nominal clause in poetry (§4), §§5.1–2 are devoted to the way names of participants are introduced in nominal clauses in BH.

## 2. Nominal Clauses in Early Biblical Prose

### 2.1. Genesis
Almost every major section of Genesis is introduced with the nominal clause תֹּ(וֹ)לְדֹ(וֹ)ת אֵלֶּה(וְ) '(And) these are the generations of . . .':

> 'These are the begettings of heaven and earth' (Gen 2:4)
> Noah (6:9 → *qatal* → *qatal* → *wayyiqtol*)
> Noah's sons (10:1 → *wayyiqtol*)
> Shem (11:10) / Terah (11:27 → *qatal* → *qatal* → *wayyiqtol*)
> Ishmael (25:12) / Isaac (25:19 → *qatal* → *wayyiqtol*)
> Esau (36:1 → *qatal* → *wayyiqtol*, 9)
> Jacob (37:2 → *qatal* → . . . → *wayyiqtol*).
> זֶה סֵפֶר תּוֹלְדֹת אָדָם 'This is the book of the generations of Adam' (5:1 → *qatal* → *qatal* → *wayyiqtol*).

The formula mentions the progenitor rather than the progeny and serves as a superscription to the account that follows. By analogy, this applies to the formula in 2:4a as well: 2:4a is not the end of the preceding creation account but the heading of the account that follows.[10]

Apart from the *toledot* formula, nominal clauses referring to participants occur particularly in specific contexts—for instance, when a participant is or has just been introduced:

---

10. Brevard S. Childs, *Introduction to the Old Testament as Scripture* (London: SCM, 1979) 145, 149; Ellen J. van Wolde, "The Text as an Eloquent Guide: Rhetorical, Linguistic and Literary Features in Genesis 1," in *Literary Structure and Rhetorical Strategies in the Hebrew Bible* (ed. L. J. de Regt, J. de Waard, and J. P. Fokkelman; Assen: Van Gorcum / Winona Lake, Ind.: Eisenbrauns, 1996) 134–51, esp. p. 136.

וְאָדָם אַיִן 'and there was no man' (2:5)
Adah, Zillah (4:19 → *wayyiqtol*)
Jubal (4:21 → *qatal* → *qatal*)
Naamah (4:22 → *wayyiqtol*)
Peleg (10:25 → *qatal*)
Joktan (10:25 → *qatal* → . . . → *wayyiqtol*)
Sarai, Milcah (11:29 → *wayyiqtol*)
וְלָהּ שִׁפְחָה מִצְרִית וּשְׁמָהּ הָגָר 'and she had an Egyptian maid whose name
   was Hagar' (16:1 → *wayyiqtol*)
Laban (24:29 → *wayyiqtol*)
Keturah (25:1 → *wayyiqtol*)
Leah, Rachel (29:16 . . . → *qatal* → *wayyiqtol*)
Hirah (38:1 → *wayyiqtol*)
Shua (38:2 → *wayyiqtol*)
Tamar (38:6 → *wayyiqtol*)
וְשָׁם אִתָּנוּ נַעַר עִבְרִי 'and there was with us a Hebrew youth' (41:12,
   Joseph, as introduced by the chief cupbearer).

These and other examples will be discussed in §5.1 on participant introduction in nominal clauses. Protagonists are often introduced as a pair.[11]

Nominal clauses occur when, while relevant to the narrative at large or at a
certain point, a statement concerning a participant stands outside of the chronological chain of events. Most of these instances conclude a narrative section.

הֵמָּה הַגִּבֹּרִים 'They are the heroes' (6:4)
וְחָם הוּא אֲבִי כְנָעַן 'Ham was the father of Canaan' (9:18)
וְהַכְּנַעֲנִי אָז בָּאָרֶץ 'The Canaanites were then in the land' (12:6)
וְאַנְשֵׁי סְדֹם רָעִים 'Now the men of Sodom were wicked' (13:13)
וְאַבְרָם בֶּן־שְׁמֹנִים שָׁנָה וְשֵׁשׁ שָׁנִים 'and Abram was 86 years old' (16:16;
   likewise 21:5)
הוּא אֲבִי־מוֹאָב 'He is the father of Moab' (19:37; likewise 38)
וְיִצְחָק בֶּן־שִׁשִּׁים שָׁנָה 'and Isaac was 60 years old' (25:26)
וְאֵין אִישׁ מֵאַנְשֵׁי הַבַּיִת שָׁם בַּבָּיִת 'and none of the men of the house was
   there in the house' (39:11).[12]

Sometimes the age of a patriarch is mentioned at a paragraph's beginning
rather than at the end (7:6 → *qatal* → *wayyiqtol*, 11:10 → *wayyiqtol*, 12:4
→ *wayyiqtol*, 41:46 → *wayyiqtol*).

Nominal clauses referring to participants occur when (a section on) genealogical information is brought to a close:

---

11. Francis I. Andersen, *The Sentence in Biblical Hebrew* (Janua Linguarum Series
Practica 231; The Hague: Mouton, 1974) 32–33.

12. Gen 39:11 is mentioned by Longacre (*Joseph*, 80).

אֵלֶּה בְּנֵי 'These (. . .) are the sons of . . .' (9:19; 10:20, 29, 31; 25:16; 35:26; 36:5, 19; 46:15, 18, 22, 25)

אֵלֶּא מִשְׁפְּחֹת בְּנֵי־נֹחַ 'These are the families of the sons of Noah' (10:32)

כָּל־אֵלֶּה בְּנֵי קְטוּרָה 'All these were the sons of Keturah' (25:4)

כָּל־נֶפֶשׁ 'All (the) persons . . . were thirty-three' (46:15; cf. 46:27)

כָּל־אֵלֶּה שִׁבְטֵי יִשְׂרָאֵל שְׁנֵים עָשָׂר 'All these tribes of Israel: twelve' (49:28).

They are to be found elsewhere in genealogical lists:

בְּנֵי '(And) the sons of . . .' (10:2–4, 6–7, 22–23; 25:4; 35:23–26; 46:9–14, 16–17, 19, 21, 23–24)

וְאֵלֶּה שְׁמוֹת בְּנֵי 'These are the names of the sons of . . .' (25:13, 36:10, 46:8; similarly 36:40).

They occur at the start of direct speech:

זֹאת הַפַּעַם עֶצֶם מֵעֲצָמַי וּבָשָׂר מִבְּשָׂרִי 'This one at last is bone of my bones and flesh of my flesh' (2:23)

אַיֶּכָּה 'Where are you?' (3:9)

אֵי הֶבֶל אָחִיךָ 'Where is Abel your brother?' (4:9)

הֵן עַם אֶחָד וְשָׂפָה אַחַת לְכֻלָּם 'Behold, they are all one people and one language' (11:6)

אֲחֹתִי הִוא 'She is my sister' (20:2, 26:7)

אֲנִי יהוה 'I am the LORD' (15:7, 28:13)

חֲמָסִי עָלֶיךָ 'The wrong done me be on you' (16:5 → *qatal* → *wayyiqtol*)

הִנֵּה שִׁפְחָתֵךְ בְּיָדֵךְ 'Behold, your maid is in your hands' (16:6)

אֲנִי־אֵל שַׁדַּי 'I am El Shaddai' (17:1)

אַיֵּה שָׂרָה אִשְׁתֶּךָ 'Where is Sarah your wife?' (18:9)

אַיֵּה הָאֲנָשִׁים 'Where are the men?' (19:5)

עֹד מִי־לְךָ פֹה 'Whom else have you here?' (19:12)

אָבִינוּ זָקֵן וְאִישׁ אֵין בָּאָרֶץ 'Our father is old and there is not a man on earth' (19:31)

מַה־לָּךְ הָגָר 'What troubles you, Hagar?' (21:17)

אֱלֹהִים עִמְּךָ 'God is with you' (21:22)

הִנֵּנִי 'Here I am' (22:1, 7, 11; 27:1, 18; 46:2)

גֵּר־וְתוֹשָׁב אָנֹכִי עִמָּכֶם 'I am a stranger and a sojourner among you' (23:4)

בַּת־מִי אַתְּ 'Whose daughter are you?' (24:23, 47)

עֶבֶד אַבְרָהָם אָנֹכִי 'I am Abraham's servant' (24:34 → *qatal* → *wayyiqtol*)

מִי־הָאִישׁ הַלָּזֶה . . . הוּא אֲדֹנִי 'Who is that man? . . . It is my master' (24:65)

אַךְ הִנֵּה אִשְׁתְּךָ הִוא 'Behold, she is your wife' (26:9)

לָנוּ הַמָּיִם 'The water is ours' (26:20)

אָנֹכִי אֱלֹהֵי אַבְרָהָם אָבִיךָ 'I am the God of Abraham your father' (26:24)

מִי־אַתָּה 'Who are you?' (27:32)

הֵן עֵשָׂו אָחִי אִישׁ שָׂעִר וְאָנֹכִי אִישׁ חָלָק 'Look, my brother Esau is a hairy man and I am smooth-skinned' (27:11)

אֲנִי בִּנְךָ בְכֹרְךָ עֵשָׂו אָנֹכִי עֵשָׂו בְּכֹרֶךָ (27:19) 'I am Esau (. . .) your firstborn' → qatal → imperatives; 27:32)

אַתָּה זֶה בְּנִי עֵשָׂו 'Are you really my son Esau?' (27:24)

אָכֵן יֵשׁ יְהוָה בַּמָּקוֹם הַזֶּה 'Surely the LORD is in this place' (28:16)

אַחַי מֵאַיִן אַתֶּם . . . מֵחָרָן אֲנָחְנוּ 'My brothers, where are you from? . . . We are from Haran' (29:4)

אַךְ עַצְמִי וּבְשָׂרִי אָתָּה 'Surely you are my bone and my flesh' (29:14)

הֲכִי־אָחִי אַתָּה 'Because you are my brother . . .?' (29:15)

הֲתַחַת אֱלֹהִים אָנֹכִי 'Am I in the place of God?' (30:2)

הִנֵּה אֲמָתִי בִלְהָה 'Here is my maid Bilhah' (30:3)

הַעוֹד לָנוּ חֵלֶק וְנַחֲלָה בְּבֵית אָבִינוּ 'Is there any portion or inheritance left to us in our father's house?' (31:14 → qatal → wayyiqtol)

הַבָּנוֹת בְּנֹתַי וְהַבָּנִים בָּנַי 'The daughters are my daughters and the children are my children' (31:43)

מַחֲנֵה אֱלֹהִים זֶה 'This is God's camp' (32:3)

מִי־אֵלֶּה לָּךְ 'Who are these with you?' (33:5)

הָאֲנָשִׁים הָאֵלֶּה שְׁלֵמִים הֵם אִתָּנוּ 'These men are friendly with us' (34:21)

שִׁמְךָ יַעֲקֹב 'Your name is Jacob' (35:10)

הַיֶּלֶד אֵינֶנּוּ 'The boy is not there' (37:30)

אַיֵּה הַקְּדֵשָׁה 'Where is the prostitute?' (38:21)

הֲלוֹא לֵאלֹהִים פִּתְרֹנִים 'Do not interpretations belong to God?' (40:8)

אַף־אֲנִי בַּחֲלוֹמִי 'I also was in my dream' (40:16)

אֲנִי פַרְעֹה 'I am Pharaoh' (41:44)

מְרַגְּלִים אַתֶּם 'You are spies' (42:9, 14)

שְׁנֵים עָשָׂר עֲבָדֶיךָ 'Your servants are twelve' (42:13)

אֲבָל אֲשֵׁמִים אֲנַחְנוּ עַל־אָחִינוּ 'Alas, we are guilty concerning our brother' (42:21)

(הֲ)שָׁלוֹם (ל) . . . 'Peace to . . .(?)' (43:23, 27–28)

הֲזֶה אֲחִיכֶם הַקָּטֹן 'Is this your youngest brother?' (43:29)

אֲנִי יוֹסֵף 'I am Joseph' (45:3–4)

אָנֹכִי הָאֵל 'I am God . . .' (46:3)

מִי־אֵלֶּה 'Who are these?' (48:8)

בָּנַי הֵם 'They are my sons' (48:9)

הִנֶּנּוּ לְךָ לַעֲבָדִים 'Here we are, servants to you' (50:18).

The other examples in this category occur at the beginning of (further) embedded direct speech:

אִשְׁתּוֹ זֹאת 'This is his wife' (12:12)

אֲחֹתִי הִוא 'She is my sister' (12:19, 20:5, 26:9)

אָחִי הוּא 'He is my brother' (20:5, 13)

בַּת־מִי אַתְּ 'Whose daughter are you?' (24:47)

הִנֵּנִי 'Here I am' (31:11)

כֵּנִים אֲנַחְנוּ 'We are honest men' (42:31 → *qatal* → 32 → *wayyiqtol*)

הֲיֵשׁ־לָכֶם אָב אוֹ־אָח 'Have you a father or a brother?' (44:19)

יֶשׁ־לָנוּ אָב זָקֵן וְיֶלֶד זְקֻנִים קָטָן 'We have an old father and a young child of his old age' (44:20).

In five instances where direct speech begins, *qatal* clauses come between the nominal clause and the chain of main clauses that follows.

In the above categories, most third-person participants are referred to in full, not with pronominal forms. This accords with the observation that, in Biblical Hebrew in general, participants tend to be referred to by their names at the beginning of a paragraph[13] and that, in genealogies, names are naturally specific.

Nominal clauses referring to participants frequently occur as a כִּי clause of motivation:

כִּי־עֵירֹם אָנֹכִי 'because I am naked' (3:10)

כִּי־עָפָר אַתָּה 'for dust you are' (3:19)

כִּי יֵצֶר לֵב הָאָדָם רַע מִנְּעֻרָיו 'for the imagination of man's heart is evil from his youth' (8:21)

כִּי־אֲנָשִׁים אַחִים אֲנָחְנוּ 'for we are brothers' (13:8)

כִּי־נָבִיא הוּא 'for he is a prophet' (20:7)

כִּי עָיֵף אָנֹכִי 'because I am faint' (25:30)

כִּי־אִתְּךָ אָנֹכִי 'for I am with you' (26:24)

כִּי־בֶן־זְקֻנִים הוּא לוֹ 'because he was a son of old age to him' (37:3 narrator)

כִּי־אָחִינוּ בְשָׂרֵנוּ הוּא 'for he is our own brother' (37:27)

כִּי כָמוֹךָ כְּפַרְעֹה 'for you are like Pharaoh' (44:18)

כִּי־טוּב כָּל־אֶרֶץ מִצְרַיִם לָכֶם הוּא 'for the best of all the land of Egypt is yours' (45:20)

כִּי־תוֹעֲבַת מִצְרַיִם כָּל־רֹעֵה צֹאן 'for every shepherd is an abomination to the Egyptians' (46:34)

כִּי מְנַשֶּׁה הַבְּכוֹר 'for Manasseh was the firstborn' (48:14 narrator)

כִּי הֲתַחַת אֱלֹהִים אָנִי 'for am I in the place of God?' (50:19). Gen 29:15 at the beginning of direct speech (see above) should be mentioned here as well.

Some of the clauses of motivation do not start with כִּי:

---

13. L. J. de Regt, "Participant Reference in Some Biblical Hebrew Texts," *JEOL* 32 (1991–92) 150–72, esp. p. 156.

בְּשַׁגַּם הוּא בָשָׂר 'for he is flesh' (6:3)

אָנֹכִי מָגֵן לָךְ 'I am your shield' (15:1)

וּבֶן־מֶשֶׁק בֵּיתִי הוּא דַּמֶּשֶׂק אֱלִיעֶזֶר 'and the heir . . . is Eliezer' (15:2)

אוּלַי יֵשׁ חֲמִשִּׁים צַדִּיקִם בְּתוֹךְ הָעִיר 'Perhaps there are fifty righteous within the city' (18:24)

וְגַם־אָמְנָה אֲחֹתִי בַת־אָבִי הִוא 'and besides, she is in truth my sister' (20:12)

נְשִׂיא אֱלֹהִים אַתָּה בְּתוֹכֵנוּ 'you are a mighty prince among us' (23:6)

אֵין זֶה כִּי אִם־בֵּית אֱלֹהִים 'this is none other than the house of God' (28:17)

מִקְנֵהֶם . . . הֲלוֹא לָנוּ הֵם 'Their cattle . . ., are they not ours?' (34:23)

וַאֲנִי מְתֵי מִסְפָּר 'and I am small in number' (34:30)

בַּאֲשֶׁר אַתְּ־אִשְׁתּוֹ 'since you are his wife' (39:9)

יוֹסֵף אֵינֶנּוּ וְשִׁמְעוֹן אֵינֶנּוּ 'Joseph is no more and Simeon is no more' (42:36). Gen 19:31; 27:11; 31:14, 43; 34:21; 40:8; and 42:21 at the beginning of direct speech (see above) should be mentioned here as well.

Some כִּי clauses are object clauses of a verb of perception:

כִּי טוֹב הָעֵץ 'that the tree was good' (3:6)

כִּי עֵירֻמִּם הֵם 'that they were naked' (3:7)

כִּי עֵירֹם אָתָּה 'that you are naked' (3:11)

כִּי טֹבֹת הֵנָּה 'that they were beautiful' (6:2)

כִּי רַבָּה רָעַת הָאָדָם בָּאָרֶץ 'that man's wickedness on earth was great' (6:5)

כִּי אִשָּׁה יְפַת־מַרְאֶה אָתְּ 'that you are a beautiful woman' (12:11)

כִּי־יָפָה הִוא מְאֹד 'that she was very beautiful' (12:14)

כִּי אִשְׁתְּךָ הִוא 'that she is your wife' (12:18)

כִּי אֲחִי אָבִיהָ הוּא 'that he was her father's brother' (29:12)

כִּי כַלָּתוֹ הִוא 'that she was his daughter-in-law' (38:16)

כִּי יְהוָה אִתּוֹ 'that the LORD was with him' (39:3)

כִּי לֹא מְרַגְּלִים אַתֶּם 'that you are not spies' (42:34)

הַעוֹד לָכֶם אָח 'that you had another brother' (43:6)

כִּי־אֵין הַנַּעַר 'that the boy is not with us' (44:31).

What is perceived can also occur as a main clause:

וְהִנָּם זֹעֲפִים 'and behold, they were distraught' (40:6).

There is a striking, repetitive concentration of similar nominal clauses in the dialogues of the parallel chapters 12, 20, and 26, and particularly in the exciting chapters 42 (beginning at v. 6) and 44 (beginning at v. 7). Nominal clauses can mark a climactic point in the text:

וּלְשָׂרָה בֵן וְהִנֵּה־בֵן לְשָׂרָה 'and Sarah (. . .) shall have a son' (18:10, 14, with opposite word order, both ending direct speech)

הַקֹּל קוֹל יַעֲקֹב וְהַיָּדַיִם יְדֵי עֵשָׂו 'The voice is Jacob's voice, but the hands are the hands of Esau (27:22, starting direct speech)

וְהִנֵּה־הִיא לֵאָה 'and behold, it was Leah' (29:25).

To sum up their macrosyntactic function, nominal clauses in Genesis are frequently used to initiate direct speech or a paragraph or major section, or to introduce a participant (normally a minor, but significant one). Much less frequently, they mark the end of a genealogical section.

**2.2.** Judges

In Judges, nominal clauses are much less frequent. In the narrator's text, nominal clauses referring to participants occur particularly when the participant is or has just been introduced:

Manoah and his wife (13:2 → *qatal* → *wayyiqtol*)
Delilah (16:4 → *wayyiqtol*)
Micah (17:1 → *wayyiqtol*)
young Levite (17:7 → *qatal* [or participle] → *wayyiqtol*)
וְהָאִישׁ מֵהַר אֶפְרַיִם 'and the man was from the hill country of Ephraim' (19:16 → *qatal* [or participle] . . . → *wayyiqtol*).

Compare §5.1 on participant introduction in nominal clauses.

They occur when, while relevant to the narrative at a certain point, a statement concerning a participant stands outside of the chronological chain of events:

וְעֶגְלוֹן אִישׁ בָּרִיא מְאֹד 'Now Eglon was a very stout man' (3:17)

כִּי שָׁלוֹם בֵּין יָבִין . . . וּבֵין בֵּית חֶבֶר 'for there was peace between Jabin . . . and the house of Heber' (4:17)

הוּא גִדְעוֹן 'that is Gideon' (7:1)

וְזֶבַח וְצַלְמֻנָּע בַּקַּרְקֹר וּמַחֲנֵיהֶם עִמָּם 'Now Zebah and Zalmunna were at Karkor and their army was with them' (8:10)

וְרַק הִיא יְחִידָה אֵין־לוֹ מִמֶּנּוּ בֵּן אוֹ־בַת 'and she was an only child; he had no son or daughter beside her' (11:34 P–S)

וְשָׁמָּה כֹּל סַרְנֵי פְלִשְׁתִּים 'and all the kings of the Philistines were there' (16:27)

וּפִילַגְשׁוֹ עִמּוֹ 'and his concubine was with him' (19:10)

וְאַנְשֵׁי הַמָּקוֹם בְּנֵי יְמִינִי 'and the people of that place were Benjaminites' (19:16)

וְהִנֵּה אֵין־שָׁם אִישׁ מִיּוֹשְׁבֵי יָבֵשׁ גִּלְעָד 'and there was not one of the inhabitants of Jabesh-Gilead' (21:9)

בַּיָּמִים הָהֵם אֵין מֶלֶךְ בְּיִשְׂרָאֵל 'In those days there was no king in Israel' (17:6, 18:1, 21:25).

They occur when a paragraph comes to an end:

וְהִנֵּה אֲדֹנֵיהֶם נֹפֵל אַרְצָה מֵת 'and there their master lying dead on the floor' (3:25)

וְהִנֵּה סִיסְרָא נֹפֵל מֵת וְהַיָּתֵד בְּרַקָּתוֹ 'and there Sisera lying dead and the pin in his temple' (4:22, assuming the participles are used attributively in these two examples)

(אֶת־)כָּל־אֵלֶּה אַנְשֵׁי־חָיִל 'all these were men of valor' (20:44, 46).[14]

Of the above examples, 17:6 and 21:25 are to be mentioned here as well; 18:1 is the start of the paragraph rather than the end. These three instances do not start with וֹ; they are not closely linked with what precedes, but they facilitate the transition from the judges to the kings in the final redaction of the histori- cal books.[15]

Nominal clauses occur at the beginning of direct speech:

דְּבַר־אֱלֹהִים לִי אֵלֶיךָ 'I have a word from God for you' (3:20)

יְהוָה עִמְּךָ גִּבּוֹר הֶחָיִל 'The LORD is with you, valiant warrior!' (6:12)

רַב הָעָם 'The people are too many' (7:2 P–S)

עוֹד הָעָם רָב 'The people are still too many' (7:4)

הֲכַף זֶבַח וְצַלְמֻנָּע עַתָּה בְּיָדֶךָ 'Is the palm of Zebah and Zalmunna already in your hand?' (8:6)

הִנֵּה זֶבַח וְצַלְמֻנָּע 'Here are Zebah and Zalmunna' (8:15 P–S)

אַחַי בְּנֵי־אִמִּי הֵם 'They were my brothers, the sons of my mother' (8:19 P–S → *qatal*)

אָחִינוּ הוּא 'He is our brother' (9:3 P–S)

מִי־אֲבִימֶלֶךְ וּמִי־שְׁכֶם 'Who is Abimelech and who are we of Shechem?' (NRSV 9:28 P–S)

מַה־לִּי וָלָךְ 'What have you against me?' (11:12)

פְּלִיטֵי אֶפְרַיִם אַתֶּם גִּלְעָד 'You Gileadites are renegades from Ephraim' (12:4 P–S)

הַאֶפְרָתִי אַתָּה 'Are you an Ephraimite?' (12:5 P–S)

הַאַתָּה הָאִישׁ 'Are you the man?' (13:11)

מָה אַתֶּם 'What have you found? (18:8 P–S)

מַה־לְּךָ 'What is the matter with you?' (18:23).

The other examples in this category occur at the beginning of embedded direct speech:

הֲיֵשׁ־פֹּה אִישׁ 'Is anyone here?' (4:20 P–S)

הֲכַף זֶבַח וְצַלְמֻנָּע עַתָּה בְּיָדֶךָ 'Is the palm of Zebah and Zalmunna already in your hand?' (8:15)

---

14. Rudolf Meyer classifies these two constructions in 20:44, 46 as nominal clauses (*Hebräische Grammatik, III: Satzlehre* [Berlin: de Gruyter, 1972] §90, 2f; §105, 1b).

15. Bartelmus, *HYH: Bedeutung und Funktion*, 165.

מַה־טּוֹב לָכֶם 'Which is better for you?' (9:2)
מִי אֲבִימֶלֶךְ 'Who is Abimelech?' (9:38)
מַה־לָּךְ 'What is the matter with you?' (18:24).

Less frequently they constitute a כִּי clause of motivation:

כִּי תְּשַׁע מֵאוֹת רֶכֶב־בַּרְזֶל לוֹ 'for he had 900 iron chariots' (4:3 → *qatal*)
כִּי־עֲיֵפִים 'for they are tired' (8:5 P–S)
כִּי עוֹדֶנּוּ נָעַר 'because he was still a boy' (8:20)
כִּי אֲחִיכֶם הוּא 'because he is your brother' (9:18 P–S)
כִּי בֶן־אִשָּׁה אַחֶרֶת אָתָּה 'for you are the son of another woman' (11:2 P–S)
כִּי־נְזִיר אֱלֹהִים אֲנִי 'for I have been a nazirite to God' (16:17 P–S). The
earlier instances in 4:17 ('for there was peace . . .') can be mentioned
here as well.

Most third-person participants are referred to with noun phrases, not with
pronominal forms.

A predicate follows the subject in all instances, except for 11:34 and, where
indicated, for some of the direct speech and motivation examples. This over-
laps with the observation, partly based on nominal clauses with a prepositional
phrase in Judges, that "in a straight nominal clause indicating the existence of
a certain person . . . the normal sequence is Nid-prep. [that is, indeterminate
noun plus prepositional phrase]."[16]

### 2.3. Joshua

Unlike Judges, Joshua does not contain purely narrative material. Nevertheless, it has few nominal clauses. In the narrator's text, a nominal clause can
further describe a participant who has just been introduced. But this occurs
only once: after being introduced, Rahab is named: וּשְׁמָהּ רָחָב 'and her name
was Rahab' (2:1).

More importantly, nominal clauses referring to participants occur in other
contexts, for instance as a כִּי clause of motivation:

כִּי בֵיתָהּ בְּקִיר הַחוֹמָה 'for her house was on a city wall' (2:15)[17]
כִּי־הוּא בְּכוֹר יוֹסֵף 'for he was the firstborn of Joseph' (17:1).

Some of the clauses of motivation do not start with כִּי:

---

16. Takamitsu Muraoka, "The Biblical Hebrew Nominal Clause with a Prepositional
Phrase," *Studies in Hebrew and Aramaic Syntax Presented to Professor J. Hoftijzer on the
Occasion of His Sixty-Fifth Birthday* (ed. K. Jongeling, H. L. Murre-van den Berg, and
L. van Rompay; Leiden: Brill, 1991) 143–51, esp. p. 150.

17. Nicolai Winther-Nielsen refers to this example as a "verbless reason clause" (*A
Functional Discourse Grammar of Joshua: A Computer-Assisted Rhetorical Structure
Analysis* [ConBOT 40; Stockholm: Almqvist & Wiksell, 1995] 137).

אִשֵּׁי יְהוָה ... הוּא נַחֲלָתוֹ 'the fire offerings of the LORD ... are his [Levi's] inheritance' (13:14)

יְהוָה ... הוּא נַחֲלָתָם 'the LORD ... , he is their inheritance' (13:33).

They occur when, while relevant to the narrative at a certain point, a statement concerning a participant stands outside of the chronological chain of events:

וְהַגַּי בֵּינוֹ וּבֵין־הָעָי 'and there was a ravine between him and Ai' (8:11).

Nominal clauses are so infrequent in narrator's text that they do not have a discourse-structuring function. It is only when areas are conquered and divided among the tribes that nominal clauses introduce or end a paragraph. The following nominal clauses are paragraph introductions:

וְאֵלֶּה מַלְכֵי הָאָרֶץ 'And these are the kings of the land' (12:1, 7 → *qatal* [in a subordinate clause] → *wayyiqtol*)

זֹאת נַחֲלַת מַטֵּה בְנֵי־יְהוּדָה 'This is the inheritance of the tribe of the Judahites' (15:20 → *wayyiqtol*).

Likewise in, for example, Exod 37:1, 6, 10, verbless clauses mark initial boundaries of pericopes.[18] "List summaries"[19] end a paragraph:

זֹאת נַחֲלַת 'This is the inheritance of the Reubenites / Gadites / tribe of the Ephraimites / tribe of Simeon / Zebulon / ...' (Josh 13:23, 28; 16:8; 19:8, 16, 23, 31, 39).

Outside of the narrator's text, in dialogue nominal clauses are more frequent. They occur relatively often at the beginning of direct speech:

נַפְשֵׁנוּ תַחְתֵּיכֶם 'Our life for yours' (2:14)

נְקִיִּם אֲנַחְנוּ 'We will be guiltless' (2:17)

כְּדִבְרֵיכֶם כֶּן־הוּא 'According to your words, so be it' (2:21)

הֲלָנוּ אַתָּה אִם־לְצָרֵינוּ 'Are you for us or for our adversaries?' (5:13)

לֹא כִּי אֲנִי שַׂר־צְבָא־יְהוָה 'No, I am captain of the LORD's host' (5:14 → *qatal*)

מַה־לָּךְ 'What to you?' (15:18)

עַם־רַב אַתָּה וְכֹחַ גָּדוֹל לָךְ 'A numerous people you are and great power you have' (17:17)

עֵדִים אַתֶּם בָּכֶם 'You are witnesses (P–S) against yourselves' (24:22).

The other examples in this category occur at the beginning of (further) embedded direct speech:

---

18. Dawson, *Text-Linguistics*, 142–43.

19. Winther-Nielsen, *Joshua*, 290 n. 82.

מָה הָאֲבָנִים הָאֵלֶּה לָכֶם 'What are these stones to you?' (4:6)

מַה־לָּכֶם וְלַיהוָה 'What have you to do with the Lord?' (22:24 → *qatal*)

אֵין־לָכֶם חֵלֶק בַּיהוָה 'You have no portion in the Lord' (22:27; the
preceding three instances initiate children's embedded direct speech)

עֲבָדֶיךָ אֲנַחְנוּ 'We are your servants' (9:11, beginning of the Gibeonites'
further embedded direct speech)

רְחוֹקִים אֲנַחְנוּ מִכֶּם מְאֹד 'We are very far from you' (9:22, beginning of the
Gibeonites' embedded direct speech)

מָה־הַמַּעַל הַזֶּה 'What is this treachery?' (22:16, beginning of Israelites'
embedded direct speech).

Less frequently, nominal clauses outside of narrator's text constitute a כִּי
clause of motivation:

כִּי מְעַט הֵמָּה 'for they are few' (7:3)

כִּי אֵין־חֵלֶק לַלְוִיִּם בְּקִרְבְּכֶם כִּי־כְהֻנַּת יְהוָה נַחֲלָתוֹ 'for the Levites have no
portion . . . (P–S), for the priesthood . . . is their heritage' (18:7;
compare 13:14, 33 above)

כִּי יְהוָה אֱלֹהֵיכֶם הוּא הַנִּלְחָם לָכֶם 'for the Lord your God, he is the one
who fought for you' (23:3, 10)

כִּי־הוּא אֱלֹהֵינוּ 'for he is our God' (24:18)

כִּי־אֱלֹהִים קְדֹשִׁים הוּא אֵל־קַנּוֹא הוּא 'for he is a holy God, he is a jealous
God' (24:19).

A nominal clause may also describe motivation without כִּי: וַאֲנִי עַם־רָב 'since
I am a numerous people' (17:14). Motivational clauses (without כִּי) figure
strongly toward the end of Caleb's plea in 14:6–12:

וְעַתָּה הִנֵּה אָנֹכִי הַיּוֹם בֶּן־חָמֵשׁ וּשְׁמוֹנִים שָׁנָה עוֹדֶנִּי הַיּוֹם חָזָק . . . כְּכֹחִי אָז וּכְכֹחִי
עַתָּה 'and now, behold, I am today 85 years old. I am still strong today
. . . my power now is like my power then' (14:10–11).

Some כִּי clauses are object clauses of a form of ידע—for example, 3:10 and
22:31 (הַיּוֹם יָדַעְנוּ כִּי־בְתוֹכֵנוּ יְהוָה 'Now we know that the Lord is in our midst').
The nominal clause thus frequently functions at the beginning of a paragraph or direct speech and at the end of a paragraph. This is borne out by the
fact that such clauses rarely occur in a central place in the paragraph. This
only happens in the direct speech of 2:19 (דָּמוֹ . . . דָּמוֹ בְרֹאשׁוֹ וַאֲנַחְנוּ נְקִיִּם
בְרֹאשֵׁנוּ 'his blood shall be on his own head but we are innocent . . . his blood
shall be on our head') and 9:25 (וְעַתָּה הִנְנוּ בְיָדֶךָ 'and now, behold, we are in
your hand'). In the narrator's text, on the other hand, statements that are relevant to the narrative but stand outside of the chronological chain of events occur in the middle of a paragraph more frequently. Such statements occur in
Joshua only in 8:11 but appear more often in Genesis and Judges (see above).

The interruptive force of nominal clauses thus seems to be weaker in dialogue than in narration.[20]

Most third-person participants are referred to with noun phrases, not with pronominal forms.

### 2.4. Deuteronomy

Going further away from narrative, in Deuteronomy nominal clauses referring to participants often initiate direct speech. Except for 9:29 and 31:2, these begin embedded direct speech:

רַב־לָכֶם 'Enough for you' (1:6, 2:3, 3:26, beginning of God's direct speech, P–S)

עַם גָּדוֹל וָרָם מִמֶּנּוּ 'The people are greater and taller than we' (1:28 . . . → qatal, beginning of the spies' direct speech)

עֵינֶיךָ 'It is your eyes' (3:21, beginning of Moses' direct speech to Joshua)

רַק עַם־חָכָם וְנָבוֹן הַגּוֹי הַגָּדוֹל הַזֶּה 'Surely that great nation is a people wise and discerning' (4:6, beginning of peoples' direct speech)

אָנֹכִי יְהוָה אֱלֹהֶיךָ 'I am the LORD your God' (5:6)

רַבִּים הַגּוֹיִם הָאֵלֶּה מִמֶּנִּי 'These nations are greater than I' (7:17, beginning of an Israelite's direct speech, P–S)

וְהֵם עַמְּךָ 'They are your people' (9:29, restart of Moses' own direct speech following the embedded direct speech in the preceding verse and the only syndetic instance of the beginning of direct speech in the present study)

מִי־הָאִישׁ 'What man?' (20:5, 8, beginning of the officers' direct speech)

אֲרַמִּי אֹבֵד אָבִי 'a wandering Aramean was my father' (26:5 → wayyiqtol, beginning of an Israelite's direct speech, P–S)

בֶּן־מֵאָה וְעֶשְׂרִים שָׁנָה אָנֹכִי הַיּוֹם 'I am 120 years old today' (31:2 P–S).

Nominal clauses, though not necessarily with participants or at the beginning of direct speech, start some major sections or new paragraphs in the book:

'This is / These are the law / testimonies / commandment / statutes / words / blessing' (4:44–45, 6:1, 12:1, 28:69, 33:1)

מָה הָעֵדֹת וְהַחֻקִּים וְהַמִּשְׁפָּטִים 'What are these testimonies?' (6:20, beginning of a son's direct speech)

בָּנִים אַתֶּם לַיהוָה אֱלֹהֵיכֶם 'You are sons of the LORD your God' (14:1 P–S)

וְזֶה דְּבַר הָרֹצֵחַ 'Now this is the provision for the manslayer' (19:4).

---

20. Mats Eskhult, "The Old Testament and Text Linguistics," *Orientalia Suecana* 43–44 (1994–95) 93–103, esp. p. 102.

Dawson calls these "topical 'paragraph headings'" when he discusses וְזֹאת תּוֹרַת 'And this is the law of' in Leviticus 6–7.[21]

Nominal clauses are to be found when a paragraph comes to an end or when an evaluation is made:

וְהִנְּכֶם הַיּוֹם כְּכוֹכְבֵי הַשָּׁמַיִם 'and behold, today you are as the stars in the sky' (1:10)

זֶה אַרְבָּעִים שָׁנָה יְהוָה אֱלֹהֶיךָ עִמָּךְ 'These forty years the LORD your God has been with you' (2:7 → *qatal* → *wayyiqtol*)

הַנִּסְתָּרֹת לַיהוָה אֱלֹהֵינוּ וְהַנִּגְלֹת לָנוּ וּלְבָנֵינוּ עַד־עוֹלָם 'The secret things are for the LORD our God; the things that are revealed are for us and for our children forever' (29:28).

They often appear as a כִּי clause of motivation:

כִּי הִוא חָכְמַתְכֶם 'for that is your wisdom' (4:6)

כִּי מִי־גוֹי גָּדוֹל 'for what great nation?' (4:7–8)

כִּי מִי כָל־בָּשָׂר 'for who of all flesh?' (5:26)

כִּי עַם קָדוֹשׁ אַתָּה לַיהוָה אֱלֹהֶיךָ 'for a holy people are you to the LORD your God' (7:6 P–S)

כִּי־אַתֶּם הַמְעַט מִכָּל־הָעַמִּים 'indeed, you are the smallest of peoples' (7:7)

כִּי עַם־קְשֵׁה־עֹרֶף אָתָּה 'for you are a stubborn people' (9:6 P–S)

כִּי עֵינֵיכֶם 'for it is your eyes' (11:7)

כִּי אֵין לוֹ חֵלֶק וְנַחֲלָה אִתְּכֶם 'for he has no portion or inheritance with you' (12:12; compare also 14:27, 29 P–S)

כִּי עַם קָדוֹשׁ אַתָּה לַיהוָה אֱלֹהֶיךָ 'for you are a people holy to the LORD your God' (14:2, 21 P–S)

כִּי־טוֹב לוֹ עִמָּךְ 'for he is well off with you' (15:16)

כִּי־הוּא רֵאשִׁית אֹנוֹ 'since he is the beginning of his strength' (21:17)

כִּי אָחִיךָ הוּא 'for he is your brother' (23:8 P–S)

כִּי עָנִי הוּא 'for he is poor' (24:15 P–S).

Many of such clauses refer to God:

כִּי הַמִּשְׁפָּט לֵאלֹהִים הוּא 'for the judgment is God's' (1:17 P–S)

כִּי אֵינֶנִּי בְּקִרְבְּכֶם 'for I am not in your midst' (1:42)

כִּי יְהוָה אֱלֹהֵיכֶם הוּא הַנִּלְחָם לָכֶם 'for the LORD your God, he is the one who fights for you' (3:22)

כִּי יְהוָה . . . . אֵשׁ אֹכְלָה הוּא 'for the LORD . . . , a devouring fire is he' (4:24 P–S)

כִּי אֵל רַחוּם יְהוָה 'for the LORD . . . is a merciful god' (4:31 P–S)

כִּי אָנֹכִי . . . אֵל קַנָּא 'for I . . . am a jealous god' (5:9)

---

21. Dawson, *Text-Linguistics*, 136.

כִּי אֵל קַנָּא יְהוָה ... בְּקִרְבֶּךָ 'for a jealous god is the Lord ... in your midst' (6:15 P–S)

כִּי־יְהוָה ... בְּקִרְבֶּךָ 'for the Lord ... is in your midst' (7:21)

כִּי תוֹעֲבַת יְהוָה אֱלֹהֶיךָ הוּא 'for an abomination is it to the Lord your God' (7:25, 17:1; compare also 22:5, 23:19, 24:4, 25:16 P–S). Compare also 10:17; 20:1; 21:23 (P–S); 31:6, 8 (without כִּי); and 31:17 (with עַל כִּי).

Some of the clauses of motivation do not start with כִּי:

אֲשֶׁר מִי־אֵל 'for what god?' (3:24)

וְיוֹם הַשְּׁבִיעִי שַׁבָּת לַיהוָה אֱלֹהֶיךָ 'and the seventh day is a sabbath to the Lord your God' (5:14)

יְהוָה הוּא נַחֲלָתוֹ 'the Lord is his/their inheritance' (10:9, 18:2)

וְאֵין מוֹשִׁיעַ לָהּ 'and no one to save her' (22:27)

פֶּן־יֵשׁ בָּכֶם אִישׁ אוֹ־אִשָּׁה 'lest there be among you a man or woman' (29:17 P–S).

Some כִּי clauses are object clauses of a form of ידע and, as in Joshua, most of them refer to God:

כִּי־מִקְנֶה רַב לָכֶם 'that you have many cattle' (3:19)

כִּי יְהוָה הוּא הָאֱלֹהִים 'that the Lord (. . .), he is God . . .' (4:35, 39; 7:9; compare 9:3)

כִּי אֲנִי יְהוָה אֱלֹהֵיכֶם 'that I am the Lord your God' (29:5).

After a verb of perception, such clauses should express simultaneity.[22]

Again, these occurrences in Deuteronomy show that in most instances participants in third person are referred to with noun phrases, not with pronominal forms. Third-person pronominal references to participants are only found in some motivation clauses. The examples of the first three functional categories mentioned above show the macrosyntactic importance of nominal clauses in the book. Since Deuteronomy is not a narrative book, the category of relevant nominal clauses outside of the main line does not apply here. But an evaluation like the one in 29:28 comes quite close to it.

When one looks at the various categories in the present section, the predicate precedes the subject only in a minority of instances. This accords with Williams's observations on nonverbal clauses: "The normal word order is subject + predicate +. . . . The predicate may precede for emphasis . . . thus frequently when the subject is a personal pronoun, . . . when the predicate is an adjective. . . ."[23] The predicate–subject pattern may be "typical of . . . sub-

---

22. Bartelmus, *HYH: Bedeutung und Funktion*, 161.

23. Ronald J. Williams, *Hebrew Syntax: An Outline* (Toronto: University of Toronto Press, 1967) 98.

ordinate clauses preceded by the particle כִּי,"[24] although it is not the most frequent one for those clauses, either. Of all the nominal clauses in Deuteronomy
1–30, almost two-thirds (40) of all S–P instances are a main clause, but this is
only true of one-third (21) of the P–S instances.[25]

## 3. Nominal Clauses in Late Biblical Prose

### 3.1. Esther and Ruth

Nominal clauses are not at all frequent in the narrator's text of Esther. They
occur in specific contexts in the narrator's text—for example, when participants are or have just been introduced and need further description:

הוּא אֲחַשְׁוֵרוֹשׁ הַמֹּלֵךְ 'This is Ahasuerus who reigned' (1:1)

וּשְׁמוֹ מָרְדֳּכַי 'and his name was Mordecai' (2:5)

הִיא אֶסְתֵּר . . . וְהַנַּעֲרָה יְפַת־תֹּאַר וְטוֹבַת מַרְאֶה 'that is, Esther . . . and the
girl was fair and beautiful' (2:7).

They occur when, while standing outside of the chain of events, they are
relevant to the narrative at large or at a certain point:

וְהַקָּרֹב אֵלָיו כַּרְשְׁנָא . . . שִׁבְעַת שָׂרֵי פָּרַס וּמָדַי 'Those closest to him were
Carshena . . . the seven nobles of Persia and Media' (1:14)

וּבְכָל־מְדִינָה . . . אֵבֶל גָּדוֹל לַיְּהוּדִים 'And in every province . . . there was
great mourning among the Jews' (4:3).

As indicated by the punctuation in the NJPSV, 4:3 interrupts Mordecai's
mourning and Esther's reaction to it. The participant introductions should be
mentioned in this category as well.

Nominal clauses occur when, incidentally, they mark the end of a section:

וּבְכָל־מְדִינָה . . . שִׂמְחָה וְשָׂשׂוֹן לַיְּהוּדִים 'And in every province . . . there
was joy and gladness for the Jews' (8:17).

The above examples are the only macrosyntactically relevant instances of
nominal clauses in the narrator's text in Esther.

Nominal clauses appear as a כִּי clause of motivation:

כִּי־טוֹבַת מַרְאֶה הִיא 'for she was fair to behold' (1:11)

כִּי־כֵן דְּבַר הַמֶּלֶךְ 'for this was the king's procedure' (1:13)

---

24. Tamar Zewi, "The Nominal Sentence in Biblical Hebrew," in *Semitic and Cushitic
Studies* (ed. G. Goldenberg and S. Raz; Wiesbaden: Harrassowitz, 1994) 145–67, esp. p. 154.

25. L. J. de Regt, "Word Order in Different Clause Types in Deuteronomy 1–30," *Studies in Hebrew and Aramaic Syntax Presented to Professor J. Hoftijzer on the Occasion of
His Sixty-Fifth Birthday* (ed. K. Jongeling, H. L. Murre-van den Berg, and L. v''an Rompay; Leiden: Brill, 1991) 152–72, esp. pp. 163–64.

כִּי אֵין לָהּ אָב וָאֵם 'for she had neither father nor mother' (2:7)

כִּי־גָדוֹל מָרְדֳּכַי בְּבֵית הַמֶּלֶךְ 'for Mordecai was powerful in the king's house' (9:4).

They also appear as an object clause:

אֲשֶׁר־הוּא יְהוּדִי 'that he was a Jew' (3:4).

And in direct speech:

אֲשֶׁר . . . אַחַת דָּתוֹ 'that . . . there is but one law for him' (4:11).

Nominal clauses referring to participants are more important in direct speech than in the narrator's text. They frequently begin direct speech:

יֶשְׁנוֹ עַם־אֶחָד . . . וְלַמֶּלֶךְ אֵין־שֹׁוֶה 'There is a certain people . . . and it is not in the king's interest' (3:8, introduction of the Jews as participants in Haman's speech)

מַה־לָּךְ אֶסְתֵּר הַמַּלְכָּה וּמַה־בַּקָּשָׁתֵךְ 'What troubles you, Queen Esther? And what is your request?' (5:3)

אִם־עַל־הַמֶּלֶךְ טוֹב 'If it is pleasing to the king' (5:4)

מַה־שְּׁאֵלָתֵךְ . . . וּמַה־בַּקָּשָׁתֵךְ 'What is your wish? . . . And what is your request?' (5:6, 7:2)

מִי בֶחָצֵר 'Who is in the court?' (6:4)

אִם מִזֶּרַע הַיְּהוּדִים מָרְדֳּכַי 'If Mordecai is of the Jewish people' (6:13)

מִי הוּא זֶה וְאֵי־זֶה הוּא 'Who is he and where is he?' (7:5)

אִישׁ צַר וְאוֹיֵב הָמָן הָרָע הַזֶּה 'The adversary and enemy is this wicked Haman' (7:6).

The frequent phrase (וְ)אִם־עַל־הַמֶּלֶךְ טוֹב 'If to the king it is pleasing' (3:9, 5:8, 8:5, and 9:13) forms the introduction to the actual request. It starts direct speech in 8:5 and 9:13.

In one instance, a nominal clause marks the end of direct speech:

וּמַה־שְּׁאֵלָתֵךְ . . . וּמַה־בַּקָּשָׁתֵךְ עוֹד 'What is your wish? . . . And what else is your request?' (9:12).

In the narrator's text of Ruth, nominal clauses are also infrequent. They play their part in the (delayed) identification of the participants Elimelech (1:2), Ruth (1:4), and Boaz (2:1, 19). These instances will be discussed in §§5.1–2. Nominal clauses have no other structuring function. Again, they are more important in direct speech, which they frequently begin:

הֲזֹאת נָעֳמִי 'Is this Naomi?' (1:19)

יְהוָה עִמָּכֶם 'The LORD be with you' (2:4)

לְמִי הַנַּעֲרָה הַזֹּאת 'Whose girl is that?' (2:5)

נַעֲרָה מוֹאֲבִיָּה הִיא 'She is the Moabite girl' (2:6)

שֵׁם הָאִישׁ . . . בֹּעַז 'The name of the man . . . is Boaz' (2:19)

קָרוֹב לָנוּ הָאִישׁ 'The man is a relative of ours' (2:20)

מִי־אָתְּ . . . אָנֹכִי רוּת אֲמָתֶךָ 'Who are you? . . . I am Ruth, your servant' (3:9)

מִי־אַתְּ בִּתִּי 'How is it with you, daughter?' (3:16)

עֵדִים '(We are) witnesses' (4:11).

As in Joshua, nominal clauses are rarely found within direct speech. There are only two, crucial, instances in a single verse:

עַמֵּךְ עַמִּי וֵאלֹהַיִךְ אֱלֹהָי 'Your people are my people, and your God is my God' (1:16).

### 3.2. Ezra and Nehemiah

In this corpus, nominal clauses occur particularly in lists and in direct speech. Sometimes, lists are introduced and finished with nominal clauses, for example, the parallel lists of Ezra 2 // Nehemiah 7:

וְאֵלֶּה בְּנֵי הַמְּדִינָה 'These are the people of the province' (Ezra 2:1 // Neh 7:6)

כָּל־הַנְּתִינִים וּבְנֵי עַבְדֵי שְׁלֹמֹה שְׁלֹשׁ מֵאוֹת תִּשְׁעִים וּשְׁנָיִם 'The total of the temple servants and the sons of Solomon's servants was 392' (Ezra 2:58 // Neh 7:60)

כָּל־הַקָּהָל כְּאֶחָד אַרְבַּע רִבּוֹא אַלְפַּיִם שְׁלֹשׁ־מֵאוֹת שִׁשִּׁים 'The whole community together was 42,360' (Ezra 2:64 // Neh 7:66)

וְאֵלֶּה רָאשֵׁי אֲבֹתֵיהֶם וְהִתְיַחְשָׂם 'These are the heads of their clans and their genealogy . . .' (Ezra 8:1)

וְעַל הַחֲתוּמִים 'On the sealed document are . . .' (Neh 10:2)

וְאֵלֶּה רָאשֵׁי הַמְּדִינָה 'These are the heads of the province . . .' (Neh 11:3)

וְאֵלֶּה הַכֹּהֲנִים וְהַלְוִיִּם . . . אֵלֶּה רָאשֵׁי הַכֹּהֲנִים וַאֲחֵיהֶם בִּימֵי יֵשׁוּעַ 'These are the priests and the Levites. . . . These were the heads of the priests and their brothers in the days of Jeshua' (Neh 12:1 and 12:7).

Outside of lists and direct-speech passages, there are very few examples of nominal clauses, and these do not appear to have a macrosyntactic function. The only examples in the narrator's text (including those instances where the narrator is Ezra or Nehemiah) are the following:

כֻּלָּם טְהוֹרִים 'They were all pure' (Ezra 6:20)

הוּא־סֹפֵר מָהִיר בְּתוֹרַת מֹשֶׁה 'and he was a scribe skilled in the law of Moses' (Ezra 7:6, at the end of the introduction of Ezra as participant)

כִּי־רַבִּים בִּיהוּדָה בַּעֲלֵי שְׁבוּעָה לוֹ כִּי־חָתָן הוּא לִשְׁכַנְיָה 'For many in Judah were bound by oath to him, because he was the son-in-law of Shecanaiah' (Neh 6:18 → *qatal*)

מֵרַבִּים . . . כִּי־הוּא כְּאִישׁ אֱמֶת 'for he was a more faithful man . . . than many' (Neh 7:2)

וְהָעָם מְעַט בְּתוֹכָהּ 'but the people within it were few' (Neh 7:4)

וְהָעָם עַל־עָמְדָם 'while the people stood in their places' (Neh 8:7)

כִּי־מִצְוַת הַמֶּלֶךְ עֲלֵיהֶם 'For there was a royal order concerning them' (Neh 11:23)

כִּי שִׂמְחַת יְהוּדָה עַל־הַכֹּהֲנִים וְעַל־הַלְוִיִּם 'for the people of Judah rejoiced over the priests and the Levites' (Neh 12:44)

כִּי־בִימֵי דָוִיד וְאָסָף מִקֶּדֶם רָאשׁ הַמְשֹׁרְרִים 'For in the days of David and Asaph of old there were chiefs of the singers' (Neh 12:46).

Except for Ezra 7:6; Neh 7:4, 8:7, these instances are all clauses of motivation. More importantly, direct speech in Ezra begins with a nominal clause in five cases (including the Aramaic sections):

מַן־אִנּוּן שְׁמָהָת גֻּבְרַיָּא 'What are the names of the men?' (Ezra 5:4)

לְדָרְיָוֶשׁ מַלְכָּא שְׁלָמָא כֹלָּא 'To King Darius all peace!' (5:7)

אֲנַחְנָא הִמּוֹ עַבְדוֹהִי 'We are the servants' (5:11)

יַד־אֱלֹהֵינוּ עַל־כָּל־מְבַקְשָׁיו לְטוֹבָה 'The hand of God is gracious to all who seek him' (8:22)

אַתֶּם קֹדֶשׁ לַיהוָה 'You are holy to the LORD' (8:28).

Elsewhere in direct speech, that is, in Ezra's prayer (particularly at the end), a few nominal clauses occur:

מִימֵי אֲבֹתֵינוּ אֲנַחְנוּ בְּאַשְׁמָה גְדֹלָה 'From the days of our fathers we have been deep in guilt' (Ezra 9:7, → qatal→ qatal)

כִּי־עֲבָדִים אֲנַחְנוּ 'for we are slaves' (9:9, clause of motivation → qatal → wayyiqtol)

יְהוָה . . . צַדִּיק אַתָּה . . . הִנְנוּ לְפָנֶיךָ בְּאַשְׁמָתֵינוּ 'O LORD . . . you are just. . . . Here we are before you in our guilt' (9:15, at the end of the prayer).

The situation is similar in direct speech in Nehemiah. The following nominal clauses open (embedded) direct speech:

הַנִּשְׁאָרִים . . . בְּרָעָה גְדֹלָה וּבְחֶרְפָּה 'The survivors . . . are in great trouble and shame' (Neh 1:3)

הַמְּלָאכָה הַרְבֵּה וּרְחָבָה 'The work is great and widely spread' (4:13)

בָּנֵינוּ וּבְנֹתֵינוּ אֲנַחְנוּ רַבִּים 'Our sons and daughters are many' (5:2)

מֶלֶךְ בִּיהוּדָה 'There is a king in Judah!' (6:7)

הַיּוֹם קָדֹשׁ־הוּא לַיהוָה אֱלֹהֵיכֶם 'This day is holy to the LORD your God' (8:9)

זֶה אֱלֹהֶיךָ 'This is your God' (9:18).

Direct speech in Nehemiah contains a few clauses that can be considered motivational:

וְהֵם עֲבָדֶיךָ וְעַמֶּךָ 'They are your servants and your people' (1:10)

וְעַתָּה כִּבְשַׂר אַחֵינוּ בְּשָׂרֵנוּ כִּבְנֵיהֶם בָּנֵינוּ 'Now our flesh is as the flesh of our brothers; our children are as their children' (5:5)

כִּי־קָדוֹשׁ הַיּוֹם לַאֲדֹנֵינוּ 'for the day is holy to our Lord' (8:10, and similarly v. 11)

כִּי צַדִּיק אָתָּה 'for you are righteous' (9:8, and similarly v. 31).

As in Ezra, nominal clauses are of some importance in prayer. Of the motivational clauses, 1:10 and 9:8, 31 are part of a prayer. The other nominal clauses in the prayer of Nehemiah 9 are:

וְאַתָּה צַדִּיק 'But you are just' (9:33)

הִנֵּה אֲנַחְנוּ הַיּוֹם עֲבָדִים . . . הִנֵּה אֲנַחְנוּ עֲבָדִים עָלֶיהָ 'Here we are, slaves today. . . . Here we are, slaves on it' (9:36)

וּבְצָרָה גְדוֹלָה אֲנָחְנוּ 'and we are in great distress' (9:37, ending this prayer).

Thus, nominal clauses in this corpus have a macrosyntactic function only in lists and in direct speech.

## 4. Nominal Clauses in Poetry

It turns out that nominal clauses contribute to the structuring of texts in prose. In poetry, the text-structuring function of verbless clauses may well be similar. In Psalm 102, for instance, vv. 12 and 28 both consist of a verbless clause (יָמַי כְּצֵל נָטוּי 'My days are like a lengthening shadow' and וְאַתָּה־הוּא 'but You are the same'), which is followed by a complex nominal clause (*zusammengesetzte Nominalsatz*), and in both verses a section is being ended.[26] Schneider's remark that nominal clauses are typical for hymnic psalms is relevant at this point.[27]

Nominal clauses mark the beginning of sections in Genesis 49 in vv. 3, 5, 14, 21, 22: בֵּן פֹּרָת יוֹסֵף 'Joseph is a fruitful bough' (49:22 P–S).

## 5. Nominal Clauses and Participant Reference

### 5.1. Introduction of Participants and Their Names
Frequently, a verbless clause introduces a participant at the same time that it gives him or her a name. Not unexpectedly, this occurs in genealogies, for example, Gen 4:21–22 (Jubal, Naamah) and Num 26:59 (Jochebed). Here one

---

26. Franz Sedlmeier, "Zusammengesetzte Nominalsätze und ihre Leistung für Psalm cii," *VT* 45 (1995) 239–50, esp. p. 248.

27. Schneider, *Grammatik*, 163, §44.2.2.3.

can also think of examples in genealogical and other kinds of lists where the persons concerned are referred to for the first time. Many instances have already been mentioned, but the following are of interest as well:

אֵלֶּה שְׁמוֹת הָאֲנָשִׁים אֲשֶׁר (וְ) 'These are the names of the men who . . .' (Num 1:5, 34:17)

אֵלֶּה שְׁמוֹת בְּנֵי (וְ) 'These are the names of the sons of . . .' (Num 3:2, 18)

וְאֵלֶּה שְׁמוֹתָם 'And these were their names . . .' (Num 13:4; this passage, containing a list of the twelve spies, is finished with another nominal clause in v. 16), Saul's daughters, his wife Ahinoam, and Abner (1 Sam 14:49–50), and the sons of David (2 Sam 5:14).

Another example is clauses that mention the mother of an individual, usually a king, for example, Lev 24:11 (Shelomith), 1 Kgs 14:21, 31 (Naamah, Rehoboam's mother), 2 Kgs 24:18 // Jer 52:1 (Hamutal, Zedekiah's mother): וְשֵׁם אִמּוֹ חֲמִיטַל 'and the name of his mother was Hamutal'. In Ruth 2:19, Ruth introduces Boaz when speaking to Naomi:

שֵׁם הָאִישׁ . . . בֹּעַז 'The name of the man . . . is Boaz'.

But in quite a number of cases a participant is given a name only after he or she has been introduced in the preceding clause. This first clause refers to the participant only in terms of class membership.[28] Examples are Hirah and Shua (Gen 38:1–2), the three eldest sons of Jesse (1 Sam 17:13), and Jarha (1 Chr 2:34). This kind of introduction delays the identification of the participant until the following clause, which is frequently verbless. Again, it occurs in genealogies, for example, Adah and Zillah (Gen 4:19), Peleg and Joktan (Gen 10:25 // 1 Chr 1:19), Reumah (Gen 22:24), and the daughters of Zelophehad (Num 26:33, Josh 17:3; compare also Num 27:1). It may occur when someone is related in some way to the major participant, for example, in Gen 11:29 (Abram's wife Sarai, Milcah), 25:1 (Keturah, Abraham's wife); Exod 18:3 (Gershom, son of Moses); Judg 13:2 (Manoah, Samson's father), 16:4 (Delilah); and 1 Sam 8:2 (Joel and Abijah, Samuel's sons).

Most of the participants introduced in this way are minor participants. But, although their part is not necessarily large, such minor participants may have a significant impact on events.[29] In such cases they belong to the limited cast of major participants, like Jonadab in 2 Samuel 13:

וּלְאַמְנוֹן רֵעַ וּשְׁמוֹ יוֹנָדָב 'And Amnon had a friend and his name was Jonadab . . .' (2 Sam 13:3).

---

28. Andersen, *Sentence*, 31.

29. E. J. Revell, *The Designation of the Individual: Expressive Usage in Biblical Narrative* (Contributions to Biblical Exegesis and Theology 14; Kampen: Kok Pharos, 1996) 73.

Other minor participants that play a short but significant role and are introduced in the same way are, for example, Hagar (Gen 16:1), Tamar (38:6); Shiphrah and Puah (Exod 1:15); Eldad and Medad (Num 11:26); Rahab (Josh 2:1); Micah (Judg 17:1); and Hannah and Peninnah (1 Sam 1:2). Revell mentions examples from Judges, Samuel, and Kings, such as Doeg (1 Sam 21:8).[30]

This device of naming the participant in a verbless clause that follows occurs only incidentally when the character introduced will become a major participant later in the narrative: Laban (Gen 24:29), Leah and Rachel (29:16); Saul (1 Sam 9:2), Goliath (17:4, 23); Job (Job 1:1); Ruth (Ruth 1:4); and Mordecai (Esth 2:5).

It is a usual pattern that the name of a participant is mentioned in the clause following the clause in which he or she is introduced. But the name-giving clause that follows is not always verbless. When a participant is given a name in a clause with קָרָא שֵׁם 'call his/her name . . .', the reason for the name is often stated as well—for example, in Exod 2:22 (Gershom, son of Moses) and Hos 1:4, 6, 9 (Jezreel, Lo-Ruhamah, and Lo-Ammi). Characters named in such a clause are major participants slightly more often—for example, Noah (Gen 5:29), Esau and Jacob (25:25–26); and Samson (Judg 13:24).

### 5.2. Delayed Participant Reference

In the above examples, the identification was only delayed until the clause following the clause in which the participant was introduced. But some passages show an unusual pattern in that the full identification of the participant is delayed further than one clause.[31] This is how more suspense is achieved. Apart from 2 Sam 4:4 (delayed identification of Mephibosheth), these examples concern (at least temporarily) major participants. In Genesis 31, Jacob tells his wives that the angel of God spoke to him in a dream (vv. 11–13). The angel of God does not identify himself to Jacob until v. 13: אָנֹכִי הָאֵל בֵּית־אֵל 'I am the God of Bethel'. In Ruth 1, Elimelech is only given a name in v. 2. Other examples are Zimri and Cozbi (Num 25:14–15), Boaz (Ruth 2:1), and Nabal (1 Sam 25:3, 25). It is interesting that the story about Nabal begins largely with a string of nominal clauses (v. 2),[32] the first of which introduces Nabal without naming him.

In Ezekiel 23, it is the prophet's illustrative narrative itself (vv. 1–21) in which delayed identification occurs: both Oholah and Oholibah are introduced in v. 2, but they are only identified by name in v. 4.

---

30. Ibid., 73.
31. De Regt, "Participant Reference," 166.
32. Groß, "Syntaktische Erscheinungen," 136–37.

## 6. Summary

Schneider's brief description as to how nominal clauses function in a text is largely borne out by the data investigated in the present article. Nominal clauses are found at the beginning of a paragraph but occur especially for the purpose of introducing minor participants and beginning direct speech (partly, but not only, as questions and answers). When they provide background information, they stand outside of the chronological chain of events. In Judges, they occur less often than in Deuteronomy and Joshua and certainly less often than in Genesis. In Genesis, and to a lesser extent in Deuteronomy, nominal clauses start the major sections of the book.

In Esther, Ruth, Ezra, and Nehemiah, nominal clauses are macrosyntactically important in direct speech, mostly by initiating it. In the narrator's text, they do not function macrosyntactically in Ezra and Nehemiah, only marginally in Esther and, for identification of participants, in Ruth.

A nominal clause at the beginning of a paragraph occurs before a *qatal* clause when that clause marks a transition to a chain of events in the paragraph.

When the identification of a participant in a nominal clause is delayed for more than one clause for the sake of suspense, this participant is likely to be a major one.

# Thematic Continuity and the Conditioning of Word Order in Verbless Clauses

E. J. REVELL

*University of Toronto*

## 1. Introduction

In this paper I explore the implications of the choice of a particular form of clause for use in a particular context rather than attempt to establish an essential meaning that a particular form of clause must carry in any context. The corpus studied is formed by the verbless clauses (including those with participial predicate) in the books of Judges, Samuel, and Kings. The study is restricted to clauses in declarative form. Interrogative clauses are not included, and there is no question of modal clauses. The vast majority of the verbless clauses are coordinate (introduced by the conjunction *waw*), asyndeton (with no introductory particle), or כי clauses (introduced by the particle כי).[1] This study is restricted to members of these groups. Description of relative position is here based on the head of the structure. In a clause with the structure adverbial–head A–head B, where the adverbial modifies head B, head A is said to be "in first position," with the adverbial "preposed." In a clause showing "leftward dislocation," with constituents nominal–pronoun–head B, where the pronoun is co-referent with the nominal, the pronoun is said to be head A, in first position. The nominal is "extraposed."[2] This permits the treatment of all verbless clauses together. The study begins with a survey of

---

1. In this study, the designation "כי clause" refers to clauses that present either something known (or perceived) about a theme in the previous context, as in example (10), or some explanatory circumstance related to a theme, as in (11). Other functions of כי are not represented.

2. A structure of this sort is used to draw attention to a theme that is new, has not been mentioned recently, or is unexpectedly replacing another. In a few cases, the co-referent item is a pronoun in an adverbial constitutent, as in Judg 17:5 and 1 Kgs 7:30, or is a nominal, as in 1 Sam 14:49.

clauses in which one constituent is a third-person pronoun, since relationship to the context is most easily evaluated in these.

## 2. One Constituent of the Clause Is a Third-Person Pronoun

### 2.1. The Pronoun Stands in First Position (Pro1)

Coordinate clauses showing Pro1 order are most commonly used to add some detail, some "circumstance," to the information supplied in the preceding clause:

(1) Judg 3:20

[וְאֵהוּד בָּא אֵלָיו] וְהוּא־יֹשֵׁב
בַּעֲלִיַּת הַמְּקֵרָה אֲשֶׁר־לוֹ לְבַדּוֹ

[Ehud came to him,] and he (was) sitting in the cool upstairs room which he had, alone.

Asyndeton clauses showing Pro1 order are used in a similar way; they add detail to the information previously presented:

(2) 1 Kgs 3:27

[תְּנוּ־לָהּ אֶת־הַיָּלוּד הַחַי וְהָמֵת
לֹא תְמִיתֻהוּ] הִיא אִמּוֹ:

[Give her the living child, and on no account kill him.] She (is) his mother.

An asyndeton clause of this type is sometimes used at the beginning of a new unit of text as the first of a pair presenting synchronous events:

(3) Judg 18:3

הֵמָּה עִם־בֵּית מִיכָה [וְהֵמָּה
הִכִּירוּ אֶת־קוֹל הַנַּעַר הַלֵּוִי]

They (were) at Micah's house, [and they recognized the voice of the Levite lad.]

A coordinate clause is occasionally used as the first of a synchronous pair of this type, as in 1 Kgs 1:22 (cf. 1 Kgs 1:42) and 2 Kgs 2:23.

The corpus includes 95 examples of these standard forms of Pro1 order (A1).[3]

### 2.2. Less-Common Uses

The order Pro1 is typical where some component of the nonpronominal constituent other than its head begins the clause:

---

3. The letter *A* followed by a number refers to a section of the appendix (pp. 316–19) of this paper. "The corpus" should include all verbless clauses of the type studied in Judges, Samuel, and Kings. However, collection of the examples was manual and inclusion or exclusion may occasionally be arbitrary and idiosyncratic, so the figures given are best taken as approximations.

(4) 2 Kgs 17:34

עַד הַיּוֹם הַזֶּה הֵם עֹשִׂים     Until today they (are) following
כַּמִּשְׁפָּטִים הָרִאשֹׁנִים     the original customs.

Other examples occur in Judg 6:24, 1 Sam 17:5, 2 Kgs 17:40, and, in כי clauses presenting explanation, in Judg 14:4; 2 Sam 9:13; and 2 Kgs 12:16, 22:7.

Pro1 order is also typical where the referent of the pronoun is presented as an extraposed nominal:

(5) 1 Sam 17:14

וְדָוִד הוּא הַקָּטָן     And David—he (was) the youngest.

The corpus includes 16 examples (A2).

Apart from cases in which the clause has a preposed component or an extraposed nominal, as in (4) and (5), Pro1 order occurs in a clause beginning a speech only in 2 Sam 9:4:

(6) 2 Sam 9:4

[וַיֹּאמֶר צִיבָא אֶל־הַמֶּלֶךְ]     [Ziba said to the king] "Look, he
הִנֵּה־הוּא בֵּית מָכִיר בֶּן־עַמִּיאֵל     (is) at the house of Machir
בְּלוֹ דְבָר:     b. Ammiel in Lo-davar."[4]

The usual order in such clauses is Pro2; see (9).

Pro1 order occurs in a few examples in which the clause is introduced by כי:

(7) 1 Kgs 2:22

כִּי הוּא אָחִי הַגָּדוֹל מִמֶּנִּי     For he (is) my elder brother.

Other examples occur in 1 Kgs 3:4, 5:4, 9:22, 21:2. The usual order in such clauses is Pro2; see (10), (11).

Pro1 order also occurs in a clause coordinate with one introduced by כי:

(8) 1 Sam 17:33

[לֹא תוּכַל לָלֶכֶת אֶל־הַפְּלִשְׁתִּי     [You cannot go against this
הַזֶּה . . . כִּי־נַעַר אַתָּה] וְהוּא     Philistine . . . for a lad you (are)],
אִישׁ מִלְחָמָה מִנְּעֻרָיו:     and he (has been) a warrior from his youth.

Compare (12), (13).

**2.3.** The Pronoun Stands in Second Position (Pro2)

Pro2 order is typical in asyndeton clauses that begin a speech:

---

4. The speaker responds to a question by the king. Possibly the order represents formal usage.

(9) 1 Sam 19:14

[וַיִּשְׁלַח שָׁאוּל מַלְאָכִים לָקַחַת   [Saul sent messengers to get David,
אֶת־דָּוִד וַתֹּאמֶר] חֹלֶה הוּא:   and she (Michal) said,] "He (is) ill."

The corpus includes 11 examples (A3).

Pro2 order is also usual in clauses introduced by כי. Examples occur in Judg 18:26 (10) and 8:24 (11):

(10) Judg 18:26

[וַיֵּלְכוּ בְנֵי־דָן לְדַרְכָּם וַיַּרְא   [The b. Dan went on their way, and
מִיכָה] כִּי־חֲזָקִים הֵמָּה מִמֶּנּוּ   Micah realized] that they (were)
                                        stronger than he. . . .

(11) Judg 8:24

[נִזְמֵי זָהָב לָהֶם] כִּי יִשְׁמְעֵאלִים   [They had gold rings,] because
הֵם:   they (were) Ishmaelites.

The corpus includes 33 examples of a כי clause with Pro2 order (A4).

**2.4.** Less-Common Uses

Pro2 order may also occur in a clause coordinate with one for which that order is characteristic, for example, after introductory כי:

(12) 2 Sam 17:8

[אַתָּה יָדַעְתָּ . . . אֶת־אֲנָשָׁיו   [You know his men, that heroic
כִּי גִבֹּרִים הֵמָּה] וּמָרֵי נֶפֶשׁ הֵמָּה   (are) they] and embittered (are)
                                        they.

This occurs where כי is not involved:

(13) Judg 18:7

[וַיִּרְאוּ אֶת־הָעָם אֲשֶׁר־בְּקִרְבָּהּ   [They saw the people who were in
יוֹשֶׁבֶת־לָבֶטַח . . . שֹׁקֵט   it living securely . . . quiet, secure
וּבֹטֵחַ . . .] וּרְחֹקִים הֵמָּה   . . .] and distant (were) they from
מִצִּדֹנִים   the Sidonians. . . .

The phrases preceding the clause in question are, like the nominal constituent of the clause, descriptive.[5] Like them, the clause presents a fact perceived about the referent of the pronominal constituent, information more often presented by a clause introduced by כי.

---

5. The first of the excised passages represented by the dots is an adverbial phrase modifying the preceding nominal phrase; the second contains two nominal phrases that are obscure in meaning but used syntactically (as far as one can tell) parallel with the others. The phrases, of course, represent perceptions about "the people," such as are more commonly presented in clauses introduced by כי, as in (10).

Pro2 order also occurs after a speech-initial asyndeton clause, in a coordinate clause in 1 Kgs 20:28, and in a parallel asyndeton clause in 1 Sam 20:26, where the pronouns in the two clauses have different referents.

Pro2 order occasionally occurs where Pro1 is expected under the general description:

(14)  1 Kgs 11:14

| | |
|---|---|
| [וַיָּקֶם יְהֹוָה . . . אֶת הֲדַד | [Yahweh raised up . . . Hadad the |
| הָאֲדֹמִי] מִזֶּרַע הַמֶּלֶךְ הוּא | Edomite.] From the royal family he |
| בֶּאֱדוֹם: | (was), in Edom. |

There is a similar example in narrative in 1 Kgs 7:14 and one in speech in 2 Sam 13:20.

Pro2 order occurs after an extraposed nominal in 2 Kgs 7:9:

(15)  2 Kgs 7:9

| | |
|---|---|
| הַיּוֹם הַזֶּה יוֹם־בְּשֹׂרָה הוּא | This day a day of tidings it (is). |

Another example occurs in 2 Sam 21:2 and two in 1 Kgs 20:3.

**2.5.** Summary

In a clause of which one constituent is a third-person pronoun, this pronominal constituent most commonly stands in first position. Where this is the case, the relationship of a coordinate or asyndeton clause to what precedes is much like that of an אֲשֶׁר clause: it presents some item of information about the referent of the pronoun.[6] The situation is the same where the clause is first in a synchronous pair (see [3]). A pair of clauses of this sort effects a transition from one phase of the action to the next. The pair initiates a new phase of the action, but the pronoun links the pair with the referent in the preceding context. The initial position of the pronoun gives prominence to this link.

Where a third-person pronominal constituent is used in the first clause of a speech, the speech commonly responds to speech by another, in which the theme represented by the pronoun is also mentioned. In some cases, the speech to which response is made is not given in the text (as in [9]), and the speech may respond to an action or event, rather than to another speech, as in 1 Sam 20:26 and 2 Kgs 9:36. Nevertheless, the fact that a pronoun is used shows that its referent is clearly established as theme in the mind of the

---

6. In the corpus, a two-part verbless clause is introduced by אֲשֶׁר in some 55 cases. A third-person pronoun forms (the head of) one constituent in 13 of these. Clearly, coordinate verbless clauses with a third-person pronominal constituent must carry a good deal of the load for which an ordinary relative clause might have been used. A participle with the definite article is similarly often used as a modifier where a relative clause might be used, as one is in 1 Kgs 5:13.

speaker, and (at least in the speaker's view) also in the mind of the addressee. It seems reasonable to argue that the relationship is so clearly established in such cases that it is not necessary to draw attention to it by placing the pronoun in initial position. This can be used to give prominence to the new information presented in the other constituent of the clause.

The use of כִּי to introduce a clause shows, in the examples available, that (unlike coordinate or asyndeton clauses) the clause stands in a specific relationship to what precedes. Consequently, the new information can be given the prominence of first position; there is no need to place the pronoun first to draw attention to the relationship. In fact, where the clause presents something perceived or known about the referent of the pronoun, the relationship is so clearly marked that the pronoun is superfluous and is sometimes not used. Compare כִּי־טוֹב ('Good [was it]', Gen 1:4), with כִּי־טוֹב הוּא ('Good [was] it', Exod 2:2).[7] In the other cases in which Pro2 order also occurs, the relationship of the clause to what precedes is not in doubt, being marked either by the introductory particle or by the situational context in which the clause is used. As with speech-initial clauses, the referent of the pronoun in these other types may not be represented in the preceding text but is clearly established as thematic in the context, as in 2 Kgs 18:36.

## 3. One Constituent of the Clause Is a Third-Person Pronoun with a Prefixed Preposition

The pronoun bound to the preposition represents a theme in the preceding text, as do pronouns elsewhere. The same theme may or may not be continued in what follows. Clauses in this group are mostly coordinate, with a few asyndeton examples used in the same way. The examples introduced by כִּי are noted below. The clauses occur within narrative or speech; none appears to begin a new section.

### 3.1. Typical Usage

Where the adverbial constituent (the preposition with pronoun) stands in first position (PPro1), the nominal constituent usually represents a nonhuman entity:

---

7. A third-person pronoun is occasionally not used in a כִּי clause that presents an explanation but only (as far as I am aware) in poetry, as in Ps 106:1. Similarly, the most common type of אֲשֶׁר clause is composed of אֲשֶׁר and an adverbial; the inclusion of a third-person pronoun (as in Judg 19:12; 1 Kgs 8:41, 9:20) is rare and so marked. Failure to use a pronoun (like failure to use a direct object with a verb that usually takes one) can of course be described in terms of grammatical or lexical difference but shows only that the speaker or writer considers the text to be intelligible without it.

(16) 1 Sam 10:5

[. . . וּפָגַעְתָּ חֶבֶל נְבִיאִים]     [You will meet a band of prophets
וְלִפְנֵיהֶם נֵבֶל וְתֹף וְחָלִיל וְכִנּוֹר     . . . ,] and before them (will be)
musical instruments.

The corpus includes 14 examples (A5).

The referent of the nominal is also nonhuman in Judg 17:5, where PPro1
order is used following an extraposed nominal representing the referent of the
pronoun.

Where the adverbial constituent stands in second position (PPro2), the
nominal constituent usually represents participants, either an individual (God
or human), or a group. The corpus includes 26 examples (A6), as in:

(17) 1 Kgs 18:7

[וַיְהִי עֹבַדְיָהוּ בַּדֶּרֶךְ] וְהִנֵּה     [Obadiah was on the road,] and here
אֵלִיָּהוּ לִקְרָאתוֹ     (came) Elijah to meet him.

Usage typical for both PPro1 and PPro 2 occurs in Judg 19:10:

(18) Judg 19:10

וְעִמּוֹ [. . . וַיָּקָם וַיֵּלֶךְ וַיָּבֹא]     [He rose, set out, and came . . .] and
צֶמֶד חֲמוֹרִים חֲבוּשִׁים     with him (was) a pair of saddled
וּפִילַגְשׁוֹ עִמּוֹ:     donkeys, and his concubine (was)
with him.[8]

**3.2.** Less-Common Examples with Initial Adverbial (PPro1)

Where the order PPro1 is used, the nominal constituent can typically be
seen as representing an attribute of the referent of the pronoun, as in (16). This
is usually a reasonable view in the few cases in which the referent of the nominal is human, as with family members:

(19) 1 Sam 17:12

[וְדָוִד בֶּן־אִישׁ . . . וּשְׁמוֹ יִשַׁי]     [David was son of a man . . . whose
וְלוֹ שְׁמֹנָה בָנִים     name was Jesse,] and to him (were)
eight sons.

---

8. The value of the expected PPro2 order in the second of these clauses is not neutral
(cf. the similar situation in the contrasting pair in [8]). The information in the two clauses
could have been combined, as in the passage where the donkeys are first mentioned, in Judg
19:3, וַיֵּלֶךְ . . . וְנַעֲרוֹ עִמּוֹ וְצֶמֶד חֲמֹרִים 'He went . . . and his lad (was) with him, and a pair of
donkeys'. The use of a separate clause to present the concubine, the use of PPro2 order, contrasting with the preceding clause, and the presentation of nonhuman before human, so that
the mention of the concubine ends the unit, are all unusual features. They draw attention to
this clause and thus alert the reader to the fact that the concubine will play a significant part
in what follows.

Other examples occur in Judg 11:34 and 1 Sam 1:2. When a nominal in second position in a clause of this sort designates a group of supporters, they play no part in the context. The 3,000 chosen men with Saul in 1 Sam 26:2 do not participate in any conflict; they simply enhance the narrator's picture of David's danger.[9] The 20 men with Joab in 2 Sam 3:20 indicate his status (and the extent of David's hospitality). The 50 men in 2 Kgs 15:25 have a similar function: the fight is over before they are mentioned.[10] In 2 Sam 23:9, 23:11, the clauses 'after him (was) PN' (in a list) represent a different situation. The list context shows that the nominal represents the topic of the section introduced in this way. PPro1 order can be used to give prominence to thematic continuity.

PPro1 order is also used in three cases in which the initial adverbial is preceded by הנה(ו). This particle usually stands before a nominal, as in the example with PPro2 order in (17) (see also [6], [32]). In 2 Sam 15:32, where the clause has content very similar to (17), PPro1 order is used, also preceded by והנה.

(20) 2 Sam 15:32

[. . . וַיְהִי דָוִד בָּא עַד־הָרֹאשׁ]     [David came to the peak . . . ,] and
וְהִנֵּה לִקְרָאתוֹ חוּשַׁי הָאַרְכִּי . . .     here (came) Hushai the Archite to
meet him. . . .

It is reasonable to suggest that the use of הנה before an adverbial is marked and draws attention to the unusual position of the nominal, which is thus highlighted. This explanation would also be fitting in 1 Kgs 19:13 (cf. 1 Kgs 19:9). The same argument can be applied in 1 Kgs 19:6:

(21) 1 Kgs 19:6

[וַיַּבֵּט] וְהִנֵּה מְרַאֲשֹׁתָיו עֻגַת     [He looked,] and here at his head-
רְצָפִים וְצַפַּחַת מָיִם     place (was) a bannock and a flask
of water.

PPro1 order is expected in this case because the nominal designates inanimate objects, but it is reasonable to suggest that the marked usage is intended to highlight their unexpected and significant appearance.[11]

---

9. Other features of the context seem to serve the same purpose; see E. J. Revell, *The Designation of the Individual: Expressive Usage in Biblical Narrative* (Biblical Exegesis and Theology 14; Kampen: Kok Pharos, 1996) §§13.3.5, 16.3.5. However, PPro2 order is used in 1 Sam 17:41, where the nominal represents Goliath's shield-bearer, whose only function in the narrative appears to be to enhance the picture of Goliath as a menace to David. The description of the characteristics of the nominals that appear in either order can only give rise to generalizations. The choice of first position for one or other constituent depends on the communicative intention of the narrator.

10. In fact, it is not wholly clear which of the protagonists they are supporting.

11. The corpus does not include any כי clauses of this type that present what is perceived.

**3.3.** Less-Common Examples with Initial Nominal (PPro2)

Where PPro2 order is used, the individual or group designated by the nominal constituent can be understood to play an important part in the following events, although it may be implied, not described, as for example when Yahweh is named in Judg 1:22; 1 Sam 16:18, 18:14; and 2 Sam 5:10. PPro2 order is used in the six clauses of this type that are introduced by כִּי. In the examples in Judg 1:19 and 4:3, the initial nominal, '(900) chariots of iron', can be considered to represent a group of supporters and therefore typical for this order. In the other cases, the referent of the nominal is inanimate; thus PPro1 order would be expected, as in 1 Sam 13:6:

(22) 1 Sam 13:6

[וְאִישׁ יִשְׂרָאֵל רָאוּ] כִּי צַר־לוֹ     [The men of Israel saw] that trouble (had come) to them.

Other examples occur in Judg 8:24 and 1 Kgs 18:27 (twice). The use of PPro2 order recalls the common use of Pro2 order in clauses introduced by כִּי.

PPro2 order is also used in Judg 18:28 in a clause coordinate with a clause introduced by כִּי (which has Pro2 order) and in Judg 18:7, in a similar situation (see [13]). In these cases, the relationship of the clause to what precedes is clear from the context, so there is no need to place the pronoun in first position to draw attention to it.

PPro2 order is characteristic of passages describing structures or objects for the same reason, as in 1 Kgs 7:28:

(23) 1 Kgs 7:28

[וְזֶה מַעֲשֵׂה הַמְּכוֹנָה]     [This (was) the structure of the
מִסְגְּרֹת לָהֶם     bases:] borders (were belonging)
to them.

Other examples occur in 1 Kgs 7:25, 7:35; 2 Kgs 25:17; and also in 1 Kgs 7:30, where the pronoun is co-referent with an extraposed nominal representing the referent of the pronoun.

PPro2 order is also used to give prominence to a nominal in a contrast or comparison with what precedes (Judg 10:4, 1 Sam 25:25). PPro2 order is probably similarly intended to draw attention to the referent of the nominal in 1 Kgs 19:19:

(24) 1 Kgs 19:19

[וַיֵּלֶךְ מִשָּׁם וַיִּמְצָא אֶת־אֱלִישָׁע     [He left there and met Elisha b.
בֶּן־שָׁפָט וְהוּא חֹרֵשׁ] שְׁנֵים־     Shaphat, and he (was) ploughing;]
עָשָׂר צְמָדִים לְפָנָיו     twelve yoke (were) before him.

Another example occurs in 1 Sam 19:16.

## 4. Analysis

It seems clear from the above description that the order of the constituents of a verbless clause is not determined either by their composition in terms of word class or by the particle used to introduce the clause. The explanations offered typically have a semantic basis. A variety of explanatory categories has been suggested. Since meaning is involved, it has proved difficult to set up a uniformly satisfactory categorization.[12] The terms used here are defined below.

### 4.1. Topic–Comment and Subject–Predicate

The term *topic* is used here to refer to one of the two constituents of a verbless clause, the other being called the *comment*.[13] This pair of terms is, I believe, a suitable translation of the Arabic *mubtada'* and *ḫabar* recommended by Michel for reference to the two parts of a verbless clause.[14] The terms *subject* and *predicate*, which Michel rejects, are generally seen as referring to the grammatical relationship of the parts.[15] The *topic* of a clause is also usually its subject; this is not necessarily the case, but I have not noted any examples of verbless clauses in which the two are clearly distinct.

### 4.2. Focus

It is generally agreed that the constituent in first position in a clause has greater prominence than the other. The topic is often placed in this position. This is sometimes seen as the default situation. From this point of view, comment-initial order is seen as "marked"; a comment used in this position is said to be in "focus." However, in some cases (as in situations in which Pro2

---

12. See the problems with "subject" and "predicate" described by Diethelm Michel in "Probleme des Nominalsatzes im biblischen Hebräisch," *ZAH* 7 (1994) 217. The discussion on pp. 220–22 shows that the terminology he prefers is also not free from problems. Because of such difficulties, in the description above I have used objective terms, and this is continued as far as is possible.

13. I use "topic" as defined by David Crystal, in *A Dictionary of Linguistics and Phonetics* (Oxford: Blackwell, 1980; 3d ed., 1991) 354. This term is sometimes used to refer to an item represented in several successive clauses. See Talmy Givón, "Topic Continuity in Discourse: An Introduction," in *Topic Continuity in Discourse: A Quantitative Cross-Language Study* (ed. T. Givón; Amsterdam: Benjamins, 1983) 1-41. The term "theme" is used here. "Topic" may also be used, by means of the term "topicalization," to refer to the initial component of a clause, as in Barry L. Bandstra, "Word Order and Emphasis in Biblical Hebrew Narrative: Observations on Genesis 22 from a Discourse Perspective," *Linguistics and Biblical Hebrew* (ed. Walter R. Bodine; Winona Lake, Ind.: Eisenbrauns, 1992) 120. Here the constituent is said to be "in first position."

14. Michel, "Probleme des Nominalsatzes im biblischen Hebräisch," 217.

15. See Crystal, *Dictionary of Linguistics* (pp. 273, 333), although in origin, "subject" and "predicate" no doubt also referred to semantic rather than to grammatical structure.

order is typical), comment-initial order seems to result from rule-governed variation, so that it is unmarked. If so, the comment in such cases is accorded the prominence typical of first position, nothing more. "Focus" should refer to the deliberate placing of an item in first position in contrast to the expected usage. In most cases where the term "focus" might be used with a looser definition,[16] the clause either appears to belong to a "rule-governed" category or is an example of a type that shows no clear default order. To avoid confusion, the nontechnical term *highlighted* is generally used here in place of "focus."

### 4.3. Definiteness and Referentiality

Definiteness, long recognized as important for the understanding of verbless clauses, is categorized in various grades. The main basis of the gradation is often specificity of reference, but it appears that a more important aspect of definiteness for the present topic is "referentiality," understood as the degree to which a constituent is co-referent with some item in the context.[17] Referentiality also must be graded. The reference may be "internal": reference to the immediately preceding narrative, or to an item mentioned earlier in the speaker's speech or in the speech of another, to which he is responding. The speaker, addressee, others involved with them, and the immediate physical context of the speech would also be included. The less-important "external" reference is to other information shared by narrator and reader or by speaker and addressee. The relevance of referentiality is also affected by other criteria, such as the proximity of the referent in the preceding context, its categorization as "human" or "other," its degree of specificity, and the directness of the reference in terms of the function of the pronoun that carries it as head or modifier in the constituent. Siewierska includes these factors in the semantic or pragmatic categories conditioning word order.[18]

### 4.4. The Conditioning of Word Order

Where a pronoun acts as a constituent of a verbless clause, Pro1 order is by far the most common over all. Such a pronoun typically represents a theme represented by a noun in the previous context. In the vast majority of cases, if not in all, it also represents both topic and subject in the clause in which it stands. This status is not affected where the clause stands first in a speech or is

---

16. Revell, *Designation of the Individual*, 379 n. 18.

17. The graded list in Francis I. Andersen, *The Hebrew Verbless Clause in the Pentateuch* (JBL Monograph Series 14; New York and Nashville: Abingdon, 1970) 109 (table 1) is mainly based on specificity of reference. The importance of previous reference in the speech is noted in Takamitsu Muraoka, *Emphatic Words and Structures in Biblical Hebrew* (Jerusalem: Magnes, 1985) 8.

18. Anna Siewierska, *Word Order Rules* (London: Croom Helm, 1988) 263.

introduced by כי, situations in which Pro2 order is characteristic. However, the relation of the clause to what precedes is clear in these situations, which is not the case with typical coordinate clauses or asyndeton clauses that do not begin a speech. Clear indication of relationship is also characteristic of the other situations in which Pro2 order is found. The only content of a pronoun representing the topic is referentiality. Clearly, it was desirable to place an item with high referentiality in first position and so to give prominence to the maintenance of thematic continuity (cohesion). Where this continuity is adequately maintained by the use of introductory כ or by some other feature of the context, the prominence of initial position can be accorded to the new information presented in the other constituent (the comment, or predicate). The situation just outlined can be considered to represent the unmarked situation and its rule-governed variations. The few examples of exceptional order result from the deliberate highlighting of the item placed in first position: these items are "in focus" (see [6], [7], [8], [14], [15]).

The topic stands first in the majority of verbless clauses (nearly 70% of some 1260 clauses in the corpus). The placing of the topic in first position was clearly desirable. The constituent representing the topic is often also the one with the higher referentiality, as in the examples in which one constituent is a pronoun described in the last paragraph. In this case the two priorities, the claims of higher referentiality and of topic status on first position, do not conflict. An item that carries both features typically stands in first position. Where one constituent is a pronoun bound to a preposition, it has the higher referentiality, but it does not represent the topic, so each constituent has a claim on first position. The choice between the two priorities appears to be determined by the function of the nominal in the narrative. Where the nominal has an important function (usually where it represents a divine or a human participant), it takes first position. The order is PPro2. Where the narrative function of the nominal is of little significance (usually where its referent does not represent such a participant), the constituent containing the pronoun is placed in first position. This PPro1 order gives prominence to the pronoun and so maintains thematic continuity, as does Pro1 order. It appears that the use of introductory כי or other features of the context that usually correlate with Pro2 order also correlate with PPro2 order in situations in which PPro1 order is expected under the general description. The same order (Pro2 or PPro2) is also used in a clause coordinate with a clause of this sort. The evidence is limited, but this fact appears to support the view that כי affects word order simply because it establishes the relationship of the clause it introduces to what precedes, so that there is no need to place a pronoun in first position for this purpose.

## 5. One Constituent of the Clause Is Nominal, One Is an Adverb or a Nominal with a Prefixed Preposition

A third-person pronoun is simply the least specific of the range of structures available for the designation of any particular entity. The use of a more specific designation in place of a pronoun does not entail change in structure. Where one constituent of the clause is a noun phrase and the other an adverb or a preposition followed by a noun phrase, the pattern described above is generally followed. In a coordinate clause or an asyndeton clause that does not begin a speech, an adverbial constituent standing in first position typically has a higher degree of referentiality than does the nominal:

> (25) 2 Sam 3:7
>
> וּלְשָׁאוּל פִּלֶגֶשׁ [וּשְׁמָהּ רִצְפָּה]     And (belonging) to Saul (was) a concubine, [and her name (was) Rizpah].

The corpus includes 48 examples (A7).

The nominal in second position appears to have a higher degree of referentiality only in Judg 18:6:[19]

> (26) Judg 18:6
>
> [וַיֹּאמֶר לָהֶם הַכֹּהֵן לְכוּ     [The priest said to them, "Go in
> לְשָׁלוֹם] נֹכַח יְהוָה דַּרְכְּכֶם     peace.] Before Yahweh (is) your
> אֲשֶׁר תֵּלְכוּ־בָהּ׃     journey on which you are going."

Where the nominal constituent precedes the adverbial in a coordinate clause or an asyndeton clause that does not begin a speech, the nominal is often the more highly referential:

> (27) 2 Kgs 9:20
>
> וְהַמִּנְהָג כְּמִנְהַג יֵהוּא בֶן־נִמְשִׁי     The driving (is) like the driving of Jehu b. Nimshi.[20]

In some cases, neither constituent is clearly higher in referentiality:

> (28) 2 Kgs 7:1
>
> [כֹּה אָמַר יְהוָה] כָּעֵת מָחָר     [Thus has Yahweh said,] "At this
> סְאָה־סֹלֶת בְּשֶׁקֶל וְסָאתַיִם     time tomorrow, a measure of wheat
> שְׂעֹרִים בְּשֶׁקֶל בְּשַׁעַר שֹׁמְרוֹן׃     (will be) worth a shekel, and two measures of barley (will be) worth a shekel at the gate of Samaria."

---

19. The referentiality of the two constituents appears equal in 1 Sam 16:6, where the adverbial is also 'before Yahweh'.

20. The 'driving' is an internal reference, but the personal name, which makes the nominal in the adverbial definite, is an external one.

The initial nominal sometimes has a lower degree of referentiality than the adverbial:

(29) Judg 14:6

| וּמְאוּמָה אֵין [. . . וַיְשַׁסְּעֵהוּ] | [He tore it (the lion) apart . . .] and |
| בְּיָדוֹ | nothing (was) in his hand. |

The corpus includes 124 examples of coordinate and asyndeton clauses of this sort (A8).

Where the clause is introduced by כִּי, the adverbial typically has higher referentiality.[21] Nevertheless, it usually stands in second position:

(30) 2 Sam 11:16

| הַמָּקוֹם אֲשֶׁר יָדַע] כִּי | [. . . the place of which he knew] |
| אַנְשֵׁי־חַיִל שָׁם: | that men of valor (were) there. |

The corpus includes 13 examples (A9).

Where the adverbial stands first in a clause introduced by כִּי, it is reasonable to argue that it is highlighted:

(31) 1 Sam 22:22

| יָדַעְתִּי בַּיּוֹם הַהוּא] כִּי־שָׁם | [I knew on that day] that there (was) |
| דּוֹאֵג [ק] הָאֲדֹמִי | Doeg the Edomite. |

Other examples occur in Judg 8:21, 18:14; 1 Sam 2:8, 7:17, 14:6, 17:47, 24:12.[22]

A less referential nominal constituent may also be used in first position in asyndeton clauses that stand first in a speech:

(32) 1 Sam 9:6

| הִנֵּה־נָא אִישׁ־ [וַיֹּאמֶר לוֹ] | [He said to him,] "Note, please, a |
| אֱלֹהִים בָּעִיר הַזֹּאת | man of God (lives) in this city. . . ." |

There are four such examples, five where the initial nominal clearly has higher referentiality (though not necessarily greater specificity), and two in which there is no clear difference. The references to these in A8 are underlined.

---

21. In some cases, as with בְּקִרְבּוֹ in 1 Kgs 3:28, the adverbial constituent could be classed as a preposition followed by a nominal phrase, 'in his middle', or a compound preposition followed by a pronoun, 'within him'. The former is chosen here, but the classification is not relevant to the argument.

22. In 1 Sam 17:47, such highlighting is given added impact by the repetition of Yahweh where a pronoun would suffice: לֹא בְּחֶרֶב וּבַחֲנִית יְהוֹשִׁיעַ יְהוָה כִּי לַיהוָה הַמִּלְחָמָה 'Not by sword and spear does Yahweh liberate, because (belonging) to Yahweh (is) battle' (the definite article used in the Hebrew is generic, not anaphoric). On the function of this sort of repetition of names, see Revell, *Designation of the Individual*, §4.4.

An initial nominal often has lower referentiality in asyndeton or coordinate clauses in passages of extended description:

(33) 1 Sam 17:4–5

| | |
|---|---|
| [וַיֵּצֵא אִישׁ־הַבֵּנַיִם . . . . גָּלְיָת] | [A champion came out. . . . Goliath |
| שְׁמוֹ . . . גָּבְהוֹ שֵׁשׁ אַמּוֹת . . .] | (was) his name. . . . His height |
| וְכוֹבַע נְחֹשֶׁת עַל־רֹאשׁוֹ | (was) six cubits. . . .] A brass |
| | helmet (was) on his head. |

Other examples occur in 1 Kgs 6:24–25; 7:17, 42; 10:19.

The relative frequency of the use, in these two situations, of an initial nominal with lower referentiality also corresponds with the patterns shown by clauses with a PPro constituent.

Nothing suggests that these examples should not be interpreted in the same way as those with a pronominal constituent. The nominal constituent represents the topic. In a coordinate clause or an asyndeton clause that is not speech-initial, there is a strong tendency to place the adverbial in first position where it has the higher degree of referentiality, just as is true where an adverbial is composed of a pronoun bound to a preposition. However, a nominal standing in second position in these clauses quite often does represent a human participant who has an important role in the following narrative (as in [25]; also 2 Sam 4:4; 9:2, 12; 13:1; etc.), unlike the situation where the adverbial is a preposition followed by a pronoun (see §3.1). This supports the idea that the adverbial is placed in first position mainly to give prominence to an item important for thematic continuity. As has been shown, this continuity can be maintained through features of the context, as speech-initial position, or presence in a passage of description, or by syntactic features such as the use of כִּי. Where this is the case, there is no need to accord first position to the constituent with higher referentiality. Accordingly, in situations of this sort, an adverbial with higher referentiality is placed in second position much more often, just as occurs in such situations where the adverbial is a preposition with pronoun. However, a topic nominal stands in first position much more frequently than does a topic pronoun in such situations. A pronoun carries only referentiality, whereas a nominal carries additional information. An initial particle or a contextual situation that makes it unnecessary to give prominence to referentiality has no relevance for this additional information, which may require the prominence usually accorded to the topic.

## 6. Both Constituents Are Nominal

### 6.1. One Constituent Is Headed by a Participle or Adjective

In the majority of clauses composed of two noun phrases, one is substantival (the topic), and the other (the comment) is headed by a participle or adjective. The topic regularly stands in first position in coordinate clauses (over 95% of some 180 clauses). The proportion is similar in asyndeton clauses that do not begin a speech. Topic–comment order is also used where a component of the comment is preposed, as in the כי clauses in 1 Kgs 20:22; 2 Kgs 2:3, 5; 6:9. Where a participle or adjective heading the comment takes first position, any modifiers typically follow the topic in any clause.[23] However, a modifier with high referentiality usually precedes the topic:

(34) 1 Kgs 19:7

[וַיֹּאמֶר קוּם־אֱכֹל] כִּי רַב מִמְּךָ      [He said, "Rise. Eat], for too great

הַדָּרֶךְ:      for you (is) the way."

Other examples occur in Judg 15:11, 20:34; 1 Sam 3:13, 29:6; 2 Sam 14:32.[24] There is an exception in 2 Sam 19:43:

(35) 2 Sam 19:43

[וַיַּעַן כָּל־אִישׁ יְהוּדָה עַל־אִישׁ      [All the men of Judah answered the

יִשְׂרָאֵל] כִּי־קָרוֹב הַמֶּלֶךְ אֵלַי      men of Israel,] "For closely-related

(is) the king to me."[25]

Comment-initial order is used more freely in asyndeton clauses that begin a speech (19 of 39 examples) and in clauses introduced by כי (13 of 27 examples). This bears out the comment made above. A topic pronoun carries only referentiality. A topic nominal carries other information in addition, which increases the desirability of using it in first position. Most speech-initial asyndeton clauses of this sort with initial comment are used to present a blessing or curse, to express approval or disapproval, or to present a comparison. That is, the head of the comment is to be considered highlighted. The 20 examples in the corpus are listed in A10.[26]

Some idea of the value of the contrasting orders can be gained through comparison of similar passages. Comment-initial order occurs in 1 Sam 9:10:

(36) 1 Sam 9:10

[וַיֹּאמֶר שָׁאוּל לְנַעֲרוֹ] טוֹב      [Saul said to his lad,] "Good (is)

דְּבָרְךָ [לְכָה נֵלֵכָה]      your word. [Come on. Let us go]."

---

23. In 1 Kgs 11:28, the nominal object follows the initial participle immediately because the words function substantivally.

24. Highly referential items are similarly placed before the topic in PPro1 clauses in Judg 11:34 (מִמֶּנּוּ) and 2 Sam 14:30 (שָׁם). Compare the position of בַּחֲצֵרוֹ in 2 Sam 17:18.

25. This example shows that the length of the component, though possibly a conditioning factor, does not determine the choice of position. In 2 Sam 19:43, the marked order can be seen as drawing attention both to the nominal (representing the person over whom speaker and addressee are arguing) and to the pronoun in the adverbial.

26. The content is similar where a comment-first pattern is used in other asyndeton clauses (1 Sam 26:16, 2 Sam 14:32) or in coordinate clauses (1 Sam 25:33, 29:6; 2 Sam 18:3, 22:47).

Topic-first order occurs in similar wording in 2 Sam 15:3:

(37) 2 Sam 15:3

| | |
|---|---|
| [וַיֹּאמֶר אֵלָיו אַבְשָׁלוֹם רְאֵה] | [Absalom said to him, "Look,] your |
| דְּבָרֶךָ טוֹבִים וּנְכֹחִים [וְשֹׁמֵעַ | words (are) good and right, [but |
| אֵין־לְךָ מֵאֵת הַמֶּלֶךְ:] | there (will be) no listener for you from near the king]." (The government will not listen to you.) |

The comment-initial pattern gives prominence to the adjective; the statement indicates approval, encouraging the intended action. The topic-initial pattern gives the adjective no prominence; the statement accepts the argument but discourages the intended action. The corpus includes 20 topic-initial clauses of this sort (A11).

The value of the contrasting orders in clauses introduced by כִּי can similarly be illustrated by comparison. Comment-initial order occurs in 2 Kgs 12:11:

(38) 2 Kgs 12:11

| | |
|---|---|
| [וַיְהִי כִּרְאוֹתָם] כִּי־רַב הַכֶּסֶף | [When they saw] that much (was) |
| בָּאָרוֹן . . . | the silver in the chest. . . . |

The same adjective heads the comment where topic-initial order is used in 1 Sam 12:17:

(39) 1 Sam 12:17

| | |
|---|---|
| [וּדְעוּ וּרְאוּ] כִּי־רָעַתְכֶם רַבָּה | [Know and see] that your wicked- |
| אֲשֶׁר עֲשִׂיתֶם בְּעֵינֵי יְהוָה . . . | ness (is) much which you have done in the eyes of Yahweh. . . . |

The collection of money in a chest is the theme of the context preceding the first example, but the initial adjective 'much' represents the perception that triggered further action and so deserves prominence. In 1 Sam 12:17, the adjective is not given prominence; the unmarked topic-initial order states a fact of which no consequences are represented. The 27 כִּי clauses of this sort in the corpus are listed in A12.

**6.2.** Both Constituents Are Substantival

Where neither constituent is headed by a participle or adjective, it is still often clear that one (the comment) provides information about the other (the topic). Many clauses of this sort present a number, weight, measure, age, or name. The nominal designating the item to which this information relates, which represents the topic, is also the more highly referential constituent. There is no conflict of priorities, and this nominal typically stands in first position:

(40) 1 Sam 17:5

וְשִׁרְיוֹן קַשְׂקַשִּׂים הוּא לָבוּשׁ]    [Scale-armor he (was) wearing,]
וּמִשְׁקַל הַשִּׁרְיוֹן חֲמֵשֶׁת־אֲלָפִים    and the weight of the armour (was)
שְׁקָלִים נְחֹשֶׁת:    5,000 shekels of bronze.

Other examples occur in Judg 8:10; 1 Sam 11:8, 17:7; 2 Sam 12:30, 24:9;
1 Kgs 2:11, 7:32, 11:42, 14:20, 18:22; 2 Kgs 10:36, 25:17. Similarly, in a
clause that gives the name of a character, the constituent identifying the character named, which represents the topic and is also the more highly referential, stands first, just as it does where a pronoun is used for this purpose:[27]

(41) Judg 17:1

וַיְהִי־אִישׁ מֵהַר־אֶפְרָיִם]    [There was a man from Mount
וּשְׁמוֹ מִיכָיְהוּ:    Ephraim] and his name (was)
                         Micaiah.

Where the clause is asyndeton, this topic-initial order is often reversed.
This occurs with statements of length or height in the description of the
Temple and its furnishings, already noted as passages in which unusual word
order is characteristic.[28] A clause giving the age of the king in this form typically follows (immediately or closely) a statement that he became king:

(42) 2 Sam 5:3-4

וַיִּמְשְׁחוּ אֶת־דָּוִד לְמֶלֶךְ עַל־]    [They anointed David as king over
יִשְׂרָאֵל: [ בֶּן־שְׁלֹשִׁים שָׁנָה    Israel.] Thirty years old (was)
דָּוִד בְּמָלְכוֹ . . .    David when he became king. . . .

The corpus includes 14 examples (A13).

A naming clause showing this order stands in quasi-appositional relationship immediately or soon after a character has been introduced but not named:

(43) 2 Sam 20:21

אִישׁ מֵהַר אֶפְרַיִם] שֶׁבַע    [A man from Mount Ephraim]
בֶּן־בִּכְרִי שְׁמוֹ . . .    Sheba b. Bichri (was) his name.

(See also [33].) The name is presumably highlighted in such cases. The choice
of this form of presentation may indicate that the name was expected to be

---

27. Other examples of naming clauses of this sort are quoted in (19), (25). In all, there
are 57 in the corpus. Where several characters are named together, the nominal identifying
the individual named is placed first in 1 Sam 1:2, 14:49, and (following ויהי) in 1 Sam 8:2,
2 Sam 3:2. An exception occurs in 1 Sam 17:13. Here, the word "name" is used only in the
introduction to the list, not in the clauses forming it as well, as is the case in 1 Sam 14:49, a
fact possibly related to the difference in order.

28. 1 Kgs 6:3, 10, 23, 24; 7:2, 6, 15, 23, 27, 38. The clause in 2 Kgs 25:17 occurs in the
description of some of those furnishings taken as booty

well known to the reader or to the addressee.[29] Compare the topic-initial order used where the narrator's concern is simply to provide information:

(44) 1 Sam 1:2

[וְלוֹ שְׁתֵּי נָשִׁים] שֵׁם אַחַת חַנָּה    [He had two wives.] The name of
[וְשֵׁם הַשֵּׁנִית פְּנִנָּה]    one (was) Hannah, [and the name of
    the second (was) Peninah].

In a few asyndeton clauses, the topic is placed first, and the age or measurement follows, as in the default order. Where this occurs, the presentation of age or measurement is unexpected. The context gives the reader no reason to expect a statement of Goliath's height in 1 Sam 17:4 (33). The statement concerning the height of a cherub in 1 Kgs 6:26 follows what could easily be taken as the end of the description of the size of the cherubim. Topic-initial order is used in a statement of age in 1 Kgs 22:42:

(45) 1 Kgs 22:42

יְהוֹשָׁפָט בֶּן־שְׁלֹשִׁים וְחָמֵשׁ    Jehoshaphat (was) thirty-five years
שָׁנָה בְּמָלְכוֹ    old when he became king.

Jehoshaphat is the first of the two kings mentioned in the statement of synchronic date given in the preceding verse. Such age-statements typically refer to the second. The topic is no doubt given prominence to obviate confusion.

## 7. Conclusion

Michel sees the difference between the two types of naming clauses as syntactic: coordinate clauses are 'dependent' (*hypotaktisch*); asyndeton are 'non-dependent' (*unabhängig*).[30] This is clearly true in terms of the use of the conjunction, but this fact in itself does not determine word order.[31] Beyond that, there appears to be no significant difference in the situations in which the two types of clauses are used in 2 Sam 16:5 and 1 Sam 17:23 (relating to the subject of a clause with a participial predicate introduced by והנה) or in Judg 16:4 and 1 Sam 17:4 (relating to a nominal in the preceding narrative clause). If clauses other than this naming type are included, the list can easily be extended.

---

29. Other cases occur in 1 Sam 17:23, 25:25; 2 Sam 20:21; and 1 Kgs 13:2. The name is also placed first in Judg 18:29 to highlight a contrast also marked by ואולם (cf. Gen 28:19). Like כי, this particle shows specifically how what follows relates to what precedes.
30. Michel, "Probleme des Nominalsatzes im biblischen Hebräisch," 222-23.
31. See Alviero Niccacci in "Simple Nominal Clause (SNC) or Verbless Clause in Biblical Hebrew Prose," *ZAH* 6 (1993) 222 (on his examples 19 and 20).

The above discussion suggests that word order is to a large extent conditioned by the desirability, for purposes of communication, of giving the prominence afforded by first position to the constituent representing the topic of the clause and also to the constituent that has the higher referentiality and therefore is best suited to maintaining thematic continuity. Where one constituent carries both features, it is typically placed first. Under certain conditions, this order is reversed. These conditions can to a large extent be described in terms of syntax. In a small proportion of cases, however, the initial constituent is "in focus." It is given first position in contrast to the common pattern according to the particular communicative purposes of the narrator or speaker.

Where topic status and higher referentiality are carried by different constituents, either may be placed in first position. The topic is more commonly found in this position but not so often as to justify calling this the default order. The choice of order seems to be conditioned by the content of the context rather than by its grammatical structure. No doubt further study will make possible a more comprehensive and more objective description of the conditioning of word order in such clauses than has been attempted above. No doubt also further study of verbless clauses from different viewpoints will increase our knowledge of the implications of word order in any given situation. Since semantic and pragmatic factors are involved, however, a comprehensive and also wholly objective description is scarcely to be expected from our distant vantage point.

## APPENDIX

**A1.** Pro1 clauses, standard examples

   1a. Coordinate clauses

      Judg 3:20, 25, 27; 4:2, 5, 21; 9:31; 10:1; 11:1, 34; 13:9, 18; 17:7 (2×); 18:28; 19:16

      1 Sam 1:10; 9:22; 10:5; 16:12; 17:5, 23; 19:9; 21:6; 23:1; 25:17, 36; 28:14

      2 Sam 4:5, 7; 11:4; 13:8; 15:30; 17:2, 10; 21:16; 23:18; 24:13

      1 Kgs 1:6, 22, 25; 10:25; 11:29; 14:5; 16:9; 19:19 (2×); 20:12

      2 Kgs 2:12, 18, 23; 4:5; 5:18; 6:30; 14:21; 17:26, 34; 22:14

   1b. Asyndeton clauses

      Judg 1:26; 7:1; 19:10

      1 Sam 4:8; 8:8

      2 Sam 5:7; 18:14

      1 Kgs 1:45; 3:3, 27; 6:1, 17, 38; 8:1, 2

      2 Kgs 7:13 (2x), 15:12; 17:34; 18:9; 25:8

1c. "Synchronous pairs"
    Judg 18:3; 19:11, 22
    1 Sam 9:11, 14, 27
    2 Sam 13:30; 20:8
    1 Kgs 1:42; 14:17
    2 Kgs 2:11; 4:5; 6:33; 8:5; 13:21; 19:37

**A2.** Pro1 clauses with an extraposed constituent
    Judg 4:4
    1 Sam 11:7; 13:7; 17:14; 21:10
    2 Sam 23:18
    1 Kgs 8:60; 14:19; 18:24, 39 (2×)
    2 Kgs 15:11, 15, 26, 31; 17:41

**A3.** Pro2 asyndeton clauses beginning a speech
    Judg 3:24; 8:19; 9:3; 20:32, 39
    1 Sam 19:14; 20:26
    1 Kgs 13:26; 22:32
    2 Kgs 1:8; 9:36

**A4.** Pro2 כי clauses
    Judg 6:22; 8:5, 24; 9:18; 13:16, 21; 14:4; 18:26, 28
    1 Sam 12:21; 15:29; 20:31, 33; 22:17; 24:7; 25:25; 28:14
    2 Sam 13:2; 17:8; 19:33
    1 Kgs 8:51; 11:28; 14:5; 18:27; 20:31, 41
    2 Kgs 4:9; 5:7; 8:27, 29; 9:34; 18:36; 19:18

**A5.** PPro1 clauses: The referent of the nominal is nonhuman
    Judg 3:16; 6:5; 11:34; 19:10
    1 Sam 10:5; 18:8; 25:2, 36
    2 Sam 13:18; 14:30; 16:1; 17:18; 20:8; 23:18

**A6.** PPro2 clauses: The referent of the nominal is a participant
    Judg 1:22; 4:14; 8:10; 13:9; 19:3, 10
    1 Sam 10:10; 14:13; 16:18; 17:41; 18:14; 20:35
    2 Sam 5:10; 10:8, 16; 16:1, 15; 19:18 (2×)
    1 Kgs 11:29; 18:7; 19:9; 20:1
    2 Kgs 8:21; 23:2; 25:25

**A7.** Clauses with initial nonpronominal adverbial
    Judg 6:37; 7:12, 20; 16:27 (2×); 18:6; 20:16; 21:9
    1 Sam 1:2 (2×), 3; 14:4; 16:6; 20:18; 27:11; 28:24
    2 Sam 3:7; 4:4; 9:2, 10, 12; 12:3; 13:1, 3; 16:23; 17:3; 23:21
    1 Kgs 4:7; 6:20, 26; 7:22, 29 (3×), 35 (2×); 8:9; 19:11 (3×), 12 (3×); 20:40
    2 Kgs 3:11; 10:1; 18:21

**A8.** Clauses with a nonpronominal adverbial in second position

8a. The nominal has higher referentiality
Judg 1:36; 4:22; 8:10; 13:6; 16:15, 29 (2×); 19:16, 27; <u>20:18</u>[32]
1 Sam 4:12; 14:2; 17:7; 18:10; <u>19:19</u>; 23:15, 24, 26; <u>24:2</u>; 25:2; <u>28:7</u>
2 Sam 2:16; 16:2 (3×), 23; 20:23 (2×), 24; 21:16, 19; 24:22
1 Kgs <u>2:39</u>; 4:4, 5, 6 (2×); 5:28; 6:27; 7:18, 32; 10:28
2 Kgs 5:3; 9:20

8b. The nominal has lower referentiality
Judg 7:16; 14:6, 8; 19:19 (2×); <u>21:17</u>
1 Sam 2:13; <u>9:6</u>; 17:5, 6 (2×), 57
2 Sam 1:2; 15:32; <u>18:29</u>; 22:10
1 Kgs 3:18; 5:28; 6:18; 6:24, 25; 7:2, 6 (2×), 17 (2×), 20, 24, 30 (2×),
31, 32 (2×), 33, 34, 38, 42; 10:19 (3×); 12:16; 22:48
2 Kgs <u>4:40</u>; 11:14; 25:4, 17

8c. There is no clear difference in level of referentiality
Judg 17:6; 18:1; 19:1; 21:19, 25
1 Sam 7:17; 17:40; 18:25; 19:9, 16; <u>20:5</u>; 25:2
2 Sam 8:16; 15:16, 17; 23:2; 24:22
1 Kgs 3:18; 6:3, 8; 7:28, 32 (2×), 34, 38; 11:29
2 Kgs 4:38; 6:30; 7:1 (2×), 4, 7, 10; <u>10:24</u>

**A9.** כי clauses composed of a nominal constituent followed by an adverbial
Judg 4:17
1 Sam 6:4; 9:12; 17:46; 18:28; 21:10; 22:17
2 Sam 11:16; 14:1
1 Kgs 3:28; 10:22
2 Kgs 5:8, 15

**A10.** Speech-initial clauses with initial constituent headed by a participle or
adjective
Blessing or curse (ארור or ברוך)
Judg 17:2; 21:18
1 Sam 14:24, 28; 25:39
2 Sam 18:28
1 Kgs 1:48; 5:21; 8:15; 8:56
Approval or disapproval
1 Sam 9:10
2 Sam 17:7
1 Kgs 2:38, 42; 18:24

---

32. References to asyndeton clauses that begin a speech are underlined.

Comparison (adjective plus מִן)
    Judg 7:2
    2 Sam 17:14
    1 Kgs 12:28
Other:
    1 Sam 19:2
and (where the speech is introduced by כִּי)
    2 Sam 19:43

**A11.** Speech-initial clauses with a constituent headed by a participle or adjective in second position
    1 Sam 14:11, 33; 16:15; 23:1; 24:10; 28:14
    2 Sam 11:11; 12:22; 15:3; 18:26; 19:2, 9; 20:21
    1 Kgs 1:51; 13:2; 14:5; 18:44
    2 Kgs 2:19; 6:1; 20:17

**A12.** כִּי clauses with one constituent headed by a participle or adjective

The head of the comment stands first in
    Judg 15:11; 20:34
    1 Sam 2:24; 3:13, 20; 23:10; 30:6
    2 Sam 13:15; 17:10; 24:14
    1 Kgs 19:7
    2 Kgs 6:16; 12:11; 22:13
The topic stands first in
    1 Sam 3:8; 12:17; 19:4; 26:12
    2 Sam 12:19
    1 Kgs 8:7, 64; 21:15
    2 Kgs 4:27
and with a component of the comment preposed
    1 Kgs 20:22
    2 Kgs 2:3, 5; 6:9

**A13.** Asyndeton clauses giving age showing comment-initial order

The clause closely follows a statement of accession in
    2 Sam 2:10; 5:4
    1 Kgs 14:21
    2 Kgs 8:26; 16:2; 21:1, 19; 22:1; 23:31, 36; 24:8, 18. Cf. the similar, formally verbal, clauses in 2 Kgs 8:17; 14:2; 15:2, 33; 18:2.
The clause in 1 Sam 13:1 is separated from the statement that Saul was made king (1 Sam 11:15) by Samuel's sermon on the establishment of a king in chapter twelve. 2 Kgs 12:1 follows the detailed description of the installation of the king in chap. 11.

# The Verbless Clause and
# Its Textual Function

ELLEN VAN WOLDE

*Tilburg Faculty of Theology*
*The Netherlands*

## 1. Introduction

What is the function of a verbless clause in a text in the Hebrew Bible? To answer this question one might look for an explanation in the Hebrew language system or for a description of the individual forms in particular contexts. In my opinion, an integrated approach is necessary. The study presented here is based on the linguistic concepts of markedness/unmarkedness and grounding/saliency, in order to discuss the interaction among the Biblical Hebrew language system, the verbless clause in its textual context, and the reader's mental representation. Its goal is to clarify the function of the Biblical Hebrew verbless clause in a text.

## 2. Linguistic Concepts

### 2.1. The Concept of Markedness
"Markedness" is a concept introduced and applied by Nikolai Trubetzkoy to explain important features of phonology. He defines the terms "marked" and "unmarked" as a binary opposition in which two phonemes are identical except that one contains a mark that the other lacks (for example, "open" versus "closed").[1] Influenced by these ideas, Roman Jakobson developed a

---

1. He distinguished also two other phonemic oppositions: the gradual oppositions (for example, /i/ ~ /e/ ~ /æ/) and the equipollent oppositions, in which each member has a mark that the others lack (for example, /p/ ~ /t/ ~ /k/; Trubetzkoy 1931).

theory of morphological markedness.[2] He started from binary oppositions and added to it the notion of asymmetry, so that the unmarked term is not on a par with the marked term. Such an opposition is privative—the marked member implies the presence of a feature, but the unmarked member does not imply its logical opposite. In morphology, "marked" means the necessary presence of an element, while "unmarked" means the element may or may not be present; it is simply not specified. Therefore, unmarkedness does not necessarily imply negation.[3] Jakobson's concept of "markedness" has been generally accepted in linguistics, especially in morphology and syntax; in this paper I elaborate on his view.

Clause forms in general and the verbless clause in particular can be analyzed in their mutually exclusive and inclusive relationships on the basis of this Jakobsonian concept of "markedness." It postulates a set of distinctive features which can be placed in an asymmetric markedness relationship; in this relationship the linguistic sign that is marked for a certain (semantic) feature, makes a specific claim for the presence of that feature.[4] The linguistic sign that is unmarked is neutral with regard to that semantic feature: it may indicate either its presence or its absence and does not make any specific claim for that feature.[5] This asymmetric relationship between markedness and unmarkedness partly determines the choice of one specific clause-type rather than another. This choice is not determined arbitrarily but is motivated by exclusive and inclusive relationships in the language system.

If in the paradigm (or language system) a collection of choices is offered, specific choices are made in the syntagmatic (or textual) arrangement. One clause-type is more suitable to express a specific kind of message than another. What is suitable, therefore, depends both on the paradigmatically defined collection of possibilities and on the context in which the selected clauses function, as the context is defined in exclusive and inclusive relationships with other clauses. The selection of the marked versus unmarked forms is not random, but is related to the contextual lines in a specific text. The choice of a specific form is therefore also motivated by textual coherence.

The intended communicative function of a text plays an important role as well. The text anticipates the reader's need for coherence and "passion for iconization," and (s)he builds "iconicity" in his or her textual arrangement. The concept of iconicity in language explains the fact that the systematic relationships of language elements (which do not themselves resemble their referents) reflect the experienced relationships of their referents in reality.

---

2. Jakobson 1984.

3. For an extensive study of markedness, see Andrews 1990.

4. See Tobin 1994: esp. 41–45.

5. For example: in Biblical Hebrew the noun form xxx-*im* is marked for plural and for gender, while the noun form xxx-*ayim* is marked for dual, but unmarked for gender.

Jakobson argues that markedness is an iconic principle of language: a simple form reflects a neutral or unmarked function; a compound or complex form reflects a marked function.[6] This idea of (diagrammatic) iconicity, namely that increasing complexity is reflected in increasing markedness in the language, implies for syntax that the choice of a clause-type, for example, a verbless clause, is partly iconic in character and that it assumes the reader's iconizing activity. In verbal clauses, syntactic arrangements are presented in which the sequence of actions refers to analogously experienced sequences in reality. This iconic relationship enables the reader to understand the difference between "she becomes pregnant and marries" and "she marries and becomes pregnant." Textual order reflects (or is understood as reflecting) the order in the experienced world, and that is why a reader is able to interpret the difference between these two sentences. Because of the lack of verb forms, in verbless clauses other means to express differences in markedness have to be used in order to guide the reader's iconization.

### 2.2. The Concept of Grounding

The marking of coherence, or continuity, and of interruption, or discontinuity, is one of the main characteristics of a narrative text. Since the Prague school in the 1930s, the relationship between continuity and discontinuity in a text is described as the relationship between "topic" and "comment," the former referring to "the things we talk about" and the latter to "what we say about the topical things." This distinction is later on also referred to as "given" information (already known material) versus "new" information (added to the given material). From the 1970s onward there has been a fair amount of discussion in linguistic literature about how to relate various syntactic phenomena to this "new–given" distinction. The earliest proposals are those of Harald Weinrich[7] and of William Labov.[8] A later study by Paul Hopper became more influential, and an approach developed that came to be called "foregrounding and backgrounding"; therefore, I will use Hopper's study in the description that follows.[9]

---

6. Jakobson 1963. For an extensive study of the function of iconicity in biblical studies, see van Wolde 1994: 160–85.

7. Weinrich (1964) proposed the category "Reliefgebung," that is, the distinction between *Vordergrund* ('foreground') and *Hintergrund* ('background') as a determinative category of markedness in French and German. His study strongly influenced the Biblical Hebrew text-linguistic studies of Schneider (1974), Talstra (1978, 1982, 1992), and Niccacci (1990). At the moment, a rather odd situation exists. Although Weinrich's book is the cornerstone of European Biblical Hebrew text-linguistic studies, it is not accepted in general linguistics. At the same time, Biblical Hebrew text-linguistic studies neglect recent developments in functional and cognitive linguistics with regard to modern concepts of grounding.

8. Labov 1972.

9. Hopper 1979; Hopper and Thompson 1980.

**2.2.1.** Foreground and Background

In a narrative text, Hopper distinguishes the language of the actual story line from the language of supportive material, which does not itself narrate the main event. The former he calls "foreground," that is, the language that relates events belonging to the skeletal structure of the discourse, and the latter he calls "background," that is, the language of the supportive material. The difference between the clauses in the foreground (the "main line" of events) and the one in the background (the "shunted" events) is to be seen in connection with *sequentiality*. The foreground events succeed one another in the narrative usually in the same order as their succession in the real world (iconicity); the background events are not in sequence to the foreground events but are simultaneous with them. Background events usually amplify or comment on the events of the main narrative and are, therefore, not sequenced with respect to one another. Because the sequentiality constraint is lifted, background clauses may be located at any point along the time axis or indeed may not be located on the time axis at all. Consequently, the relationships between background clauses are often quite loose. Nevertheless, the reader is able to understand their connection because of his or her iconizing abilities. Only foreground clauses are, strictly speaking, being narrated. Background clauses do not themselves narrate, but instead they support, amplify, or comment on the narrative. In a narrative, the author is asserting the occurrence of events. Background, however, does not constitute the assertion of the events in the story line but makes statements that are dependent on the story line event.

Hopper summarizes the characteristics of the foreground clauses as follows: (a) The subject of the verbs is "given" or "topical." This topicality of the subject in the foreground is a natural consequence of the tendency for narratives to be concerned principally with a small number of participants and, hence, to have continuity of topic-subject in the main story line. (b) The time frame of the foreground clauses is measured and unidirectional. It represents a chronological sequencing, without backtracking or glances forward. (c) The verb forms tend to be active and punctual. Foreground clauses denote the discrete, measured events of the narrative and generally refer to events that are dynamic and active. (d) Foregrounding requires fronting of the verb. Because the foreground clauses are the locus of the actions and events, the new part of the narrative clause is focused upon and therefore put in the clause's first position, which is usually the verb form (in VSO languages).

Background clauses, on the other hand, have different characteristics. (a) The subjects of the verbs are relatively new or unexpected, that is, nontopical. Because the information given in the background clauses is new, the subjects are usually indefinite and must be spelled out in full. There is no stability in subject either, but frequent changes of subjects occur. (b) Simultaneity or overlapping of situations is essential for background clauses. The time frame of the narrative framework with sequenced actions is distorted. In the background, access to any point on the time scale can be made. Often a "wandering" up and down the temporal-deictic axis occurs. (c) Because of its static nature, the background contains mostly verbs denoting states, processes, and descriptions. (d) Background requires fronting of the topic focused upon: this could be a subject focus, an instrument focus, or an adverbial focus. In many languages the foreground/background distinction is realized through word order, specialized verb morphology, and sentence particles.

Hopper's (and Hopper and Thompson's) description of foreground and background is followed by many linguists but criticized as well.[10] In the first place, criticism is raised against the terminology. Developed in the beginning as a temporal juncture, the terms and their interpretation suggest that foreground clauses carry the most important material of the story and the backgrounded clauses the less important material. The temporal ordering criterion and the criterion indicating importance need, however, to be sharply distinguished. Temporality might be relevant syntactic marking; importance may not be.[11] Another point of criticism concerns Hopper's elaboration of the background. It is simply not true that the subjects in background clauses are always new or unexpected. Often the subjects are known from the previous context and therefore topical. Additionally, the suggestion that the background presupposes simultaneity with regard to the actions of the foreground disregards occurrences of backgrounded clauses that refer to previous or future events.

**2.2.2.** Grounding in a Functional Approach.

From the mid-1980s onward, syntactic studies of foreground and background have become part of general functional grammar. In this functional perspective, the foreground-background distinction is reframed in cognitive terms as "ground" and "figure," or as "grounding" and "saliency."[12] "Grounding" means that a coherent text is organized in a way that makes information accessible and predictable to a reader. A coherent text tends to maintain the same referent or topic, the same or contiguous time and location, and sequential action. At the same time, new or marked information is focused upon by the procedure of saliency. Therefore the "ground" is the context vis-à-vis which new or salient information is given.

---

10. See, among others: Neubauer (ed.) 1983; Weber 1983; Dry 1983; Reinhart 1984; Chvany 1985; Tomlin 1987; Fleischmann 1990: 168–214.

11. Thompson 1987: esp. 436.

12. Givón 1987.

Texture or textual coherence is determined by the way information is grounded in a narrative text. A grounding procedure consists of two processes. The first one is essentially *anaphoric*, involving grounding of a particular point in the text in relation to the preceding context; or, to be more precise, grounding with regard to what the author can assume about shared knowledge with the reader. The second is a *cataphoric* process, involving clues the author gives the reader at a particular point in the text on how to ground it in relation to the following context. The differentiation between anaphoric and cataphoric orientation in a text is known as the grammar of referential coherence. Anaphoric references, as related to previously given information, very often function as a motivation or explanation of introduced topics (or topic-subjects). In contrast, cataphoric references, which are related to material in the following context, have a wider and less predictable scope of reference. Anaphoric grounding has been studied much more extensively, while cataphoric grounding has been studied in much less detail. Since Talmy Givón is the most influential linguist publishing on the topic of "grounding," his insights will be summarized here.[13]

Cataphoric or "anticipatory" grounding involves the opening of pending connections in yet-to-be completed structures, in anticipation of a text that is in the process of being constructed: incoming text-connections are grounded cataphorically to text-connections that have not yet been processed. Cataphoric grounding is an extensive, grammar-cued phenomenon, involving referential, temporal, and thematic coherence. In the grammar of referential coherence, referent clauses are identified as either those that will be important, topical, and therefore persistent in the subsequent discourse, or those that will be unimportant, nontopical, and therefore nonpersistent. Topical referents are most commonly given special grammatical marking, while nontopical ones are left unmarked: 65% of the newly presented subjects that are marked with an indefinite article recur within the following ten clauses.[14] Thus the *topic persistence* of cataphorically introduced elements is their main characteristic. Other grammatical devices may also be used for the cataphoric grounding of indefinite referents. A common one is restrictive relative clauses in combination with the indefinite article (for example, "A woman who didn't speak English then stepped forward"). In addition to tagging the newly introduced element as an important topic in the subsequent text, the information in the relative clause makes the referent grounded, so that it can now be attached at a relevant location in the mental representation of the incoming text.

In anaphoric or "backward" grounding, on the other hand, an author codes a referent as definite because he/she assumes that it is identifiable or accessible to the reader. By "accessible" is meant that it is represented in and can be

---

13. Givón 1984–91: vol. 2; 1995.
14. See Givón 1995: 348.

retrieved from some preexisting mental structure in the reader's mind. When an author reintroduces a referent in a context, it is grounded by various grammatical devices. Through the first device the text is understood as coherent because of the anaphoric elements referring to the speech situation; grounding is achieved by indicating their relation to the participants in the discourse (the interlocutors "I," "you," "we," or other referents such as "this one," "that one") or by indicating their temporal relations to the time of speaking ("here," "there," "way over there," "now," "then," "long ago," "tomorrow"). Second, references can be anaphorically grounded in permanent generic knowledge. In this case the referents are accessible because they are uniquely identifiable to all members of the relevant speech community (culture, subculture, family). Generic access is, for example, required in "She went into a restaurant and asked the waiter for the menu." The definite referents "the waiter" and "the menu" receive their anaphoric grounding from the antecedent referent "restaurant" in the preceding text, plus generic-lexical knowledge of a restaurant. The third and most important type of anaphoric grounding is textual or episodic grounding in the current text. A textual constituent is introduced earlier in the text and is later on referred to anaphorically.

Givón developed a method to analyze the textual or episodic anaphoric grounding on the basis of the referential distance or anaphoric gap. This heuristic measure (which became generally used in linguistics[15]) records the gap, in number of clauses backward, between the referent's current text-location and its last previous occurrence.[16]

| Construction | Mean referential distance (number of clauses) | Degree of clustering around the mean |
|---|---|---|
| a. Zero anaphora | 1.0 | 100% at mean |
| b. Unstressed pronoun | 1.0 | 95% at mean |
| c. Stressed pronoun | 2.5 | 90% between 2–3 |
| d. Y-movement | 2.5 | 90% between 2–3 |
| e. Definite noun | 7.0 | 25% at 1.0<br>35% scattered 5.0–19.0<br>40% at 20+ |
| f. Definite noun with modifier(s) | 10.0 | 55% scattered 5.0–19.0<br>45% at > 20 |
| g. Left-dislocated definite noun phrase | 15.0 | 60% at > 20<br>(25% at 4–9)<br>(13% at 10–19) |

15. See, among others, Givón (ed.) 1983.
16. The diagram appears in Givón 1995: 353.

Maximal textual continuity is signaled by anaphoric devices such as zero anaphora and unstressed pronouns, which usually occur in consequent clauses
with very small referential distance. These "short-distance" anaphoric devices
activate the reader to attach incoming new information under the continuing
thematic chain-node. The topical referent is, consequently, the node label of
the thematic chain. In addition to zero markedness and unstressed forms,
agented continuous active verbs achieve a maximum of anaphoric continuity.

Examples of "middle-distance" anaphoric devices are, among others, case
markers such as את, the marker of a definite direct object in Biblical Hebrew,
and variations in the default word order. The case markers are part of the
grammar of topic continuity: subjects tend to be the more continuous topics,
while direct objects tend to be less continuous topics. Newly introduced subjects therefore show stronger topic persistence and have, consequently, a
stronger cataphoric function than newly introduced objects. Another grounding device is word order. Every language knows a simple word order ("We
saw John yesterday"), which signals topic continuity, and light variants, such
as left-dislocation ("John, we saw him yesterday"), right-dislocation ("We
saw him yesterday, John") or Y-movement ("As for the trees, God made them
beautiful and attractive"), the latter referring to contrastive topicalization or
object fronting. These "middle distance" anaphoric devices signal the activation of a new referent without terminating the thematic chain.

"Long-distance" anaphoric devices are definite full lexical nouns, definite
noun phrases, nouns defined by demonstratives or deictics, as well as variations in word order, such as dislocated definite noun phrases or preposed
adverbial clauses ("When the time for fighting came . . ."). They signal topic-
switching and a deactivation of the current topic. Their anaphoric topic is reactivated after a long gap of absence, and these devices refer to the opening of
a new thematic chain, in which the reactivated referent is the topic or node
label. These anaphoric devices thus indicate the terminated activation of the
current topical referent by creating a new node label of the thematic chain.

Givón's study of grounding shows how textual coherence is a matter of degree. The grammatical and textual features of definiteness, word form, and
word order create an image of textual coherence in the mind of a reader. Most
coherent texts fall somewhere in the middle between the two extremes of total
redundancy and utter incoherence. In moving across adjacent clauses, one
encounters some recurring and some nonrecurring elements. But neither the
amount of new (= disjointed) information nor the amount of old (= connect-
ing) information is totally unconstrained. The multiple grounding connections
of a clause in a text make it more accessible to the reader, and thus more coherent relative to the text in which it is embedded.

## 3. Biblical Hebrew

**3.1.** Previous Study of the Verbless Clause in Biblical Hebrew

How can these linguistic concepts and approaches clarify the function of verbless clauses in the Hebrew Bible? Usually the verbless clause in the Hebrew Bible is studied through the concepts of "subject" and "predicate," which go back to the Aristotelian distinction between substance or singulars on the one hand and accidental properties or universals on the other.[17] Substances are persons or things of which accidental properties (quantity, quality, relation, action, place, state) can be predicated in propositions. Accidental properties function in clauses as predicates, indicating quantity, quality, relation, action, place, and state. Subjects are usually either proper names, nouns, or pronouns, which identify; they are particular terms denoting the definite and individual substances. Predicates are indefinite, general, or abstract nouns, which do not denote individual substances, but classes or qualities. This Aristotelian distinction, which is more philosophical than linguistic, has been determinative in Biblical Hebrew studies of the verbless clause till the present day: from Albrecht (1887) and Gesenius-Cowley (1910), to Andersen (1970), Jenni (1978), Richter (1980), and Waltke and O'Connor (1990).[18] This is confirmed by their description of the nuclear sequences in a verbless clause: the sequence "predicate–subject" makes them define the clause as "classification," and the sequence "subject–predicate" makes them define the clause as "identification."[19] These Biblical Hebrew studies presuppose logical categories—logical concepts such as individuality, quantifiability, qualifiability, or classifiability. In the Hebrew verbless clause, however, neither the entity nor the connection is clearly logically determined.

Recently, Diethelm Michel pointed out the inadequacy of the terms "subject" and "predicate" for Biblical Hebrew.[20] He clarifies the difference between a philosophical and linguistic study by an example previously provided by Snell.[21] In the two clauses *The hare is in a field* and *In the field is a hare*, from a logical point of view *the/a hare* is the subject, and *is in a/the field* is the predicate. From a linguistic point of view, however, these clauses differ. The first clause starts with the known (and therefore definite) entity *the hare*, of which it is stated that he *is in a field*. The second clause takes *the field* as starting point and relates it to *a hare*. *The hare* and *the field* are the entities focused upon, respectively: in the first clause a statement is made about *the hare*; in

---

17. Cf. A. Niccacci 1993: esp. 216–17.
18. Albrecht 1887, 1888; GKC 454; Andersen 1970; Jenni 1978; Richter 1980; Waltke and M. O'Connor 1990.
19. Cf. Andersen 1970: 45; Jenni 1978: 95; Richter 1980: 87.
20. Michel 1994.
21. Snell 1952. See Michel 1994: 217.

the second clause a statement is made about *the field.*[22] Consequently, one cannot conclude that the "given" or "known" element is always a particular or individual substance (or subject) or that the new element is always a universal class or quality (or predicate). It is not the distinction between "particular" and "universal" but between "given" and "new" that counts. What is "given" and "new" is partly defined by the context. The terms "subject" and "predicate" therefore fail to explain the syntactic features in Biblical Hebrew. Michel proposes to use the Arabic terms *mubtada'* and *ḫabar* instead of the Aristotelian terms: *mubtada'* for what is the starting point or "known" information (comparable to the linguistic term "topic" or "given") and *ḫabar* for the "new" information (comparable to the linguistic term "comment" or "new"). This proposal of Michel's is very much in line with Givón's research. One could therefore consider combining their insights in order to explain and analyze verbless clauses in Biblical Hebrew.

**3.2.** A Functional Approach to the Hebrew Verbless Clause

Biblical Hebrew verbless clauses are marked, because they differ from the default (unmarked) verbal clauses. It is only in terminology that their characteristic is described negatively, since it is based on the absence of a verb form. Their function is, however, a positive one, namely the presentation of *background* information in which a situation, circumstance, or event is depicted that occurs simultaneously with the sequence of actions expressed in the preceding foreground clause. A verbless clause contains two or more constituents, of which one is taken as a starting point and is thus focused upon, and another supplies information on the focused topic. The former can be named the "given" constituent, and the latter can be named the "new" constituent. The "given" element is previously introduced and therefore relatively less definite in form, whereas the "new" element is relatively more definite. Neither classification nor identification is an adequate category to describe these verbless clauses, since they are strictly logically defined. A more accurate heuristic tool is needed that accounts for the contextual aspects of the verbless clause and its constituents. Three analytical steps are proposed here to explain the main features of the verbless clause: the analysis of the word form (including the degree of definiteness), the analysis of the word order in the clause, and the analysis of the textual clause order (including the anaphoric and cataphoric relationships).

The first step, the analysis of the morphological word form in relation to its degree of definiteness, is important for a verbless clause so that the "newness"

---

22. "Snell schlägt (. . .) für den determinierten Ausgangspunkt der Mitteilung die Bezeichnung 'Insbildsetzung' vor: Es handelt sich um eine Größe, die ins Bild setzt, wovon die folgende neue Aussage/Mitteilung gilt" (Michel 1994: 217).

or "givenness" of the clause constituents can be determined. Definiteness is not a discrete variable or a member of a binary opposition in which some terms are definite and others indefinite (as is often supposed[23]) but a continuum: the degree of definiteness may vary. One can develop a scale of definiteness in which proper nouns (person or place-names) are maximally definite. Definite nouns, demonstrative articles, definite numerals, and the case marker את with direct definite noun are considered to be somewhat less but still considerably definite. Another degree in the continuum of definiteness shows independent pronouns, suffixed nouns, indefinite nouns, and indefinite numerals—closer to indefiniteness than the previous groups. Very indefinite indeed are clitic pronouns and zero anaphora.[24] This scale of definiteness surely needs further elaboration, but even at this stage it may clarify how definiteness functions in a clause as a grounding device, creating textual coherence for the reader. The least definite elements are the words that are assumed to be the most easily identified by the reader, since they refer to previously presented elements in the text, to generic knowledge, or to a shared communicative situation. They show an obvious textual continuity and are read in strong anaphoric relationship to the previously provided information. Consequently, minimal definiteness corresponds to maximal continuity, and maximal definiteness corresponds to minimal continuity.

In the second step the sequence of the two constituents in a verbless clause is analyzed. The word order of the relatively more definite or "new" element and the relatively less definite or "given" element to a great extent determines the functioning of the verbless clause. In verbless clauses with a relatively less-definite element in first position and the relatively more-definite element in second position, the starting point is the "given" or less definite element, of which additional information is provided. This verbless clause does not interrupt the topic chain but situates the previously mentioned referent in the speech situation, attaches it to generic knowledge, or grounds it in textual knowledge, thus strengthening topic continuity. In verbless clauses with a new or relatively more definite element in front position and the given (less definite) element in second position, the topic chain is (often) interrupted. The new element is focused upon and asks the reader's attention. The word order necessitates a topic persistence of the newly introduced element in the following context, thus grounding a cataphoric referent.

---

23. Unfortunately Michel, though stimulating in his rethinking of the concepts of "subject" and "predicate," does not rethink the category of definiteness. He still starts from either definite or indefinite elements.

24. Cf. Andersen 1970: 109; Fox 1983: esp. 219; and see the article by K. Lowery in this volume, pp. 251–72.

Particles often influence word order in (verbal and) verbless clauses. On the basis of a study of the verbless clauses in the Torah, Michel states that verbless clauses opening with the particles אשר, הנה, and עוד show the default word order "given–new" ("subject–predicate"), whereas verbless clauses following the particles אם, אולי, אז, and כי show a relatively more marked sequence of a relatively less-definite constituent and a relatively more-definite constituent, that is, the word order "new–given." Interrogative adverbs such as מי, מה, למה, and מדוע and negative adverbs such as לא, בל, בלי, בלתי, and לבלתי indicate the same word order, "new–given." These data seen in the light of my analysis are quite explicable. The first group of verbless clauses opening with אשר, and so on, and having the word order "given–new," actually consists of verbless clauses depending on the preceding clauses. This fact can be seen by the fronting of the known element that the verbless clause has selected to focus upon and for which additional information is provided. The second group opening with interrogatives and the above-mentioned particles mainly contains independent verbless clauses. They start with the introduction of a new aspect, element, or feature, thus creating the word order "new–given."

In the third step the clause order in a text is analyzed. As far as Biblical Hebrew is concerned, research is still in a preliminary stage. To start with some of Givón's insights might be helpful in this respect. The diagram in §2.2.2. shows how specific higher degrees of definiteness are required when there is a longer referential distance between the referent clauses in a text. The choice of word form and its degree of definiteness is thus partly bound to a larger context. Unstressed or clitic pronouns, indefinite nouns, suffixed nouns, and direct objects with case markers require small referential distance, to enable the verbless clause to provide background information. Their minimal definiteness creates maximal continuity based on anaphoric reference. Stressed or independent pronouns, definite participles, definite numerals, and nominalized constructions are more definite and are chosen to function over a longer clausal distance, thus bridging an anaphoric gap of more clauses. Only word forms with this degree of definiteness are still able to create the possibility for a reader to link the offered information backwards to previously mentioned elements, up to ten clauses backwards. At the same time these definite constituents can function cataphorically, while signaling topic switching and topic persistence in the context to come. Thus more definite verbless clause constituents can at the same time bridge the anaphoric gap with the previous context and create a cataphoric reference to the following context. These textual features, distance and definiteness, enable the reader to create a mental representation of textual coherence.

**3.3.** A Heuristic Model of Verbless Clauses in Biblical Hebrew

---

1. Verbless clauses are *marked*; they differ from verbal clauses because they
   a. contain no verbal form
   b. always present *background* or *simultaneous information*
   c. are *a-temporal*; their temporal aspects depend on the context

---

2. Verbless clauses consist of two or more *constituents* which can be
   a. *given* or relatively more definite
   b. *new* or relatively less definite
   To determine degree of definiteness, the following scale is of use:
   > MAXIMAL DEFINITENESS
   > proper noun (person or place-name)
   > definite noun
   > demonstrative article
   > definite numeral
   > case marker את with direct object
   > independent pronoun
   > suffixed noun
   > indefinite noun
   > indefinite numeral
   > clitic pronoun
   > zero anaphora
   > MINIMAL DEFINITENESS

---

3. The word order of the constituents in verbless clauses can be
   a. default, that is, relatively less marked:
      *new–given* or relatively more definite–relatively less definite
   b. relatively more marked:
      *given–new* or relatively less definite–relatively more definite

---

4. Verbless clauses function in textual coherence, which is based on features of distance and definiteness:
   a. features: minimal definiteness, small referential distance (1–2 clauses)
      function: maximal anaphoric continuity
   b. features: more definiteness, longer clausal distance (3–5 clauses)
      function: strong anaphoric relation
   c. features: still more definiteness, maximal clausal distance (5–10 clauses)
      function: reinstalled anaphoric relation, bridging an anaphoric gap,
         installation of a cataphoric relation
   d. features: maximal definiteness, topic switching, less influence of
         clause-distance
      function: minimal anaphoric continuity, maximal cataphoric persistence

5. Verbless clauses are presented by
   a. the narrator in a *narrator's text*:
      the verbless clauses' anaphoric and cataphoric references are related to
      * the speech situation of narrator and implied reader
      * the generic knowledge assumed by the narrator to be accessible to the
        reader
      * the episodic knowledge of the previous narrator's texts and character's texts
   b. a character in a *character's text*:
      the verbless clauses' anaphoric and cataphoric references are related to
      * the speech situation of the speaking character and his/her listeners in the text
      * the generic knowledge assumed by the speaking character to be accessible
        to his/her listeners in the text
      * the knowledge of the previous character's texts assumed by the character
        to be accessible to the listeners; no knowledge of the narrator's text is
        assumed

## Bibliography

Albrecht, C.
   1887–88  Die Wortstellung im hebräischen Nominalsatze. *Zeitschrift für die Alttes-
            tamentliche Wissenschaft* 7: 218–24; *Zeitschrift für die Alttestamentliche
            Wissenschaft* 8: 249–63.
Andersen, F. I.
   1970     *The Hebrew Verbless Clause in the Pentateuch.* Journal of Biblical Litera-
            ture Monograph Series 14. New York and Nashville: Abingdon.
Andrews, E.
   1990     *Markedness Theory: The Union of Asymmetry and Semiosis in Language.*
            Durham, N.C.: Duke University Press.
Chvany, C. V.
   1985     Foregrounding, Saliency, Transitivity. *Essays in Poetics* 10/2: 1–23.
Dry, H. A.
   1983     The Movement of Narrative Time. *Journal of Literary Semantics* 12/2:
            19–53.
Fleischmann, S.
   1990     *Tense and Narrativity: From Medieval Performance to Modern Fiction.*
            Austin, Texas: University of Texas Press.
Fox, A.
   1983     Topic Continuity in Biblical Hebrew. Pp. 215–54 in *Topic Continuity in
            Discourse*, ed. T. Givón. Amsterdam: Benjamins.
Gesenius, W., and Kautzsch, E.
   1910     *Hebrew Grammar.* Trans. A. E. Cowley. Oxford: Oxford University Press.
Givón, T.
   1977     The Drift from VSO to SVO in Biblical Hebrew: The Pragmatics of Tense-
            Aspect. Pp. 181–254 in *Mechanisms for Syntactic Change*, ed. C. Li. Aus-
            tin, Texas: University of Texas Press.

1984–91    *Syntax: A Functional-Typological Introduction.* 2 vols. Amsterdam: Benjamins.

1987    Beyond Foreground and Background. Pp. 175–88 in *Coherence and Grounding in Discourse*, ed. R. S. Tomlin. Amsterdam: Benjamins.

1995    *Functionalism and Grammar.* Amsterdam: Benjamins.

Givón, T. (ed.)

1983    *Topic Continuity in Discourse: Quantified Cross-Language Studies.* Typological Language Studies 3. Amsterdam: Benjamins.

Hopper, P. J.

1979    Aspect and Foregrounding in Discourse. Pp. 213–41 in *Discourse and Syntax*, ed. T. Givón. Vol. 12 in *Syntax and Semantics*. New York: Academic Press.

Hopper, P. J., and Thompson, S. A.

1980    Transitivity in Grammar and Discourse. *Language* 56/2: 251–99.

Jakobson, R.

1963    Implications of Language Universals for Linguistics. Pp. 263–78 in *Universals of Language*, ed. J. H. Greenberg. Cambridge, Massachusetts: MIT Press.

1984    Shifters, Verbal Categories and the Russian Verb. Pp. 130–47 in vol. 2 of *Selected Writings*. The Hague: Mouton. First published, 1957.

Jenni, E.

1981    *Lehrbuch der hebräischen Sprache des Alten Testaments.* 2d ed. Basel: Helbing & Lichtenhahn. First edition, 1978.

Joüon, P.

1991    *A Grammar of Biblical Hebrew.* Trans. and rev. by T. Muraoka. 2 vols. Subsidia Biblica 14/1–2. Rome: Pontifical Biblical Institute.

Labov, W.

1972    The Transformation of Experience in Narrative Syntax. Pp. 354–96 in *Language in the Inner City*, ed. W. Labov. Philadelphia: University of Pennsylvania Press.

Michel, D.

1994    Probleme des Nominalsatzes im biblischen Hebräisch. *Zeitschrift für Althebraistik* 7: 215–24.

Neubauer, F. (ed.)

1983    *Coherence in Natural Language Texts.* Hamburg: Helmut Buske.

Niccacci, A.

1990    *The Syntax of the Verb in Classical Hebrew Prose.* Journal for the Study of the Old Testament Supplement Series 86. Sheffield: Sheffield Academic Press.

1993    Simple Nominal Clause (SNC) or Verbless Clause in Biblical Hebrew Prose. *Zeitschrift für Althebraistik* 6: 216–28.

Reinhart, T.

1984    Principles of Gestalt Perception in the Temporal Organizations of Narrative Texts. *Linguistics* 22: 779–809.

Richter, W.

1980    *Grundlagen einer althebräischen Grammatik, B. Die Beschreibungsebenen III: Der Satz.* Arbeiten zu Text und Sprache im Alten Testament 13. St. Ottilien: EOS.

Schneider, W.
1974    *Grammatik des biblischen Hebräisch.* Munich: Claudius.
Snell, B.
1961    *Der Aufbau der Sprache.* 2d ed. Hamburg: Claassen. First edition, 1952.
Talstra, E.
1978    Text Grammar and Hebrew Bible, I: Elements of a Theory. *Bibliotheca Orientalis* 35: 168–75.
1982    Text Grammar and Hebrew Bible, II: Syntax and Semantics. *Bibliotheca Orientalis* 39: 26–38.
1992    Text Grammar and Biblical Hebrew: The Point of View of Wolfgang Schneider. *Journal of Translation and Text Linguistics* 5: 269–87.
Thompson, S. A.
1987    "Subordination" and Narrative Event Structure. Pp. 435–54 in *Coherence and Grounding in Discourse,* ed. R. S. Tomlin. Amsterdam: Benjamins.
Tobin, Y.
1994    *Invariance, Markedness and Distinctive Feature Analysis: A Contrastive Study of Sign Systems in English and Hebrew.* Current Issues in Linguistic Theory 111. Amsterdam: Benjamins.
Tomlin, R. S.
1987    *Coherence and Grounding in Discourse.* Amsterdam: Benjamins.
Trubetzkoy, N. S.
1931    Die phonologischen Systeme. *Travaux du Cercle Linguistique de Prague* 4: 96–116.
Waltke, B. K., and O'Connor, M.
1990    *An Introduction to Biblical Hebrew Syntax.* Winona Lake, Indiana: Eisenbrauns.
Weber, J.-J.
1983    The Foreground-Background Distinction: A Survey of Its Definitions and Applications. *Language in Literature* 8/1: 1–15.
Weinrich, H.
1964    *Tempus: Besprochene und erzählte Welt.* Stuttgart: Kohlhammer.
Wolde, E. J. van
1994    *Words Become Worlds: Semantic Studies of Genesis 1–11.* Biblical Interpretation Series 6. Leiden: Brill.
Wolde, E. J. van (ed.)
1997    *Narrative Syntax and the Hebrew Bible: Papers of the Tilburg Conference 1996.* Biblical Interpretation Series 29. Leiden: Brill.

# Index of Topics

# Hebrew Terms

# Index of Authors

# Index of Scripture

Scripture is indexed according to Hebrew chapter and verse divisions. Bold page numbers indicate more extensive discussions of a text, usually as an example of a linguistic feature.